W9-BMH-073

The **Rough Guide** to

Puerto Rico

written and researched by

Stephen Keeling

www.roughguides.com

Contents

◄◄ Puerto Rican flag mural ◄ Reserva Marina Tres Palmas beach, near Rincón

Introduction to
Puerto Rico

It's graced by fabulous beaches, year-round sun and numerous opportunities for deep-sea fishing, diving and surfing, but there's far more to Puerto Rico than suntans and snorkelling. Beyond the glitzy veneer of San Juan the coast remains incredibly raw and unspoiled, lined with miles of glittering white sands. Dig deeper and you'll see the influence of the island's rich stew of cultures – African, European and Taíno – in an exuberant array of festivals, tantalizing criollo food, gracious colonial towns, world-class rum and a dynamic musical tradition that gave birth to salsa. The scenery is similar but this is not the West Indies (think baseball not cricket), and despite its links with the US, Puerto Rican identity – like Cuba – remains proudly Latino.

The island boasts an astounding diversity of **landscapes**, from the misty rainforests of El Yunque and the crumbling outcrops of karst country, to reef-encrusted desert islands and the withering dry forests of the southwest. And in several places, impenetrable mangrove swamps cradle one of nature's most mind-boggling spectacles, the glowing waters of **bioluminescent bays**. Rent a car and it's easy to escape the tourist areas, and you can zip between cool mountain forests and sun-bleached beaches in minutes. The island is remarkably safe, and though it can be tough for budget travellers, Puerto Rico compares favourably with other islands in the region.

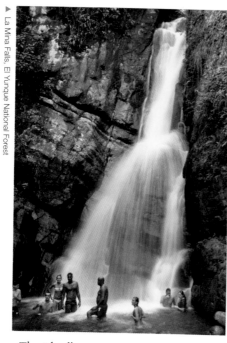

Beaches understandably remain one of the biggest draws here. Thanks in part to a small but vigorous coalition of environmental groups, property development has been confined to small clusters, with low-key resorts such as Rincón successfully holding back the tide of condo and hotel building, at least for now. Occupied by the United States Navy until relatively recently, Vieques and Culebra in particular offer some of the most idyllic coastlines in the Caribbean, the military having ensured that both islands were spared the excesses of tourism.

The island's mountainous interior is just as enticing, a land of torpid Spanish hill towns and gourmet **coffee** plantations. Ranches still raise **Paso Fino horses**, the finest in the Americas, and state forests preserve lush, jungle-covered peaks, fish-filled lakes and gurgling waterfalls. Yet it's the juxtaposition of old and new, rather than a nostalgic throwback frozen in time, that makes Puerto Rico such a beguiling destination. The old Puerto Rico of suntanned *jíbaros* and horsedrawn carts has largely disappeared, and instead you'll find towns where bareback horse riders use mobile phones, and beautifully preserved colonial architecture coexists with modern shopping malls and speeding SUVs.

Despite all this, the perception of Puerto Rico is inextricably shaped by its sometimes bewildering relationship with the US. Not a state, nor independent, Puerto Rico has been a "commonwealth" since 1952, making it especially attractive to Americans looking for a passport- and hassle-free holiday in the sun, but creating the misconception elsewhere that the island is simply an extension of the US in the Caribbean – quite untrue. While it lacks the revolutionary chic of other Latin American nations, Puerto Ricans have created one of the region's most vibrant cultural identities; they may be divided over their political future, but their sense of cultural pride in **Boricua** – the indigenous name for the island and its people – unites them.

5

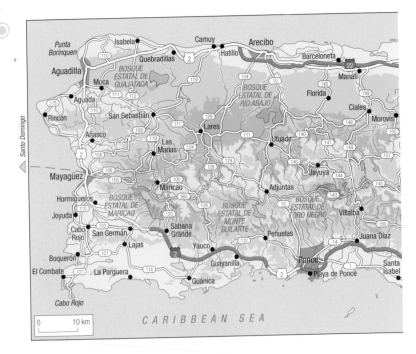

△ Santo Domingo

▶ Coquí frog

Where to go

Most trips to Puerto Rico start in the capital, **San Juan**, one of the largest and most dynamic cities in the Caribbean. Old San Juan is a Spanish colonial gem, its cobbled streets lined with elegant eighteenth-century flower-strewn houses, chapels and grand mansions. Nights out in the capital are especially lively, while the resort zones of Condado and Isla Verde have surprisingly handsome stretches of beach.

Wickedly tempting *kiosco* food is one of the main reasons

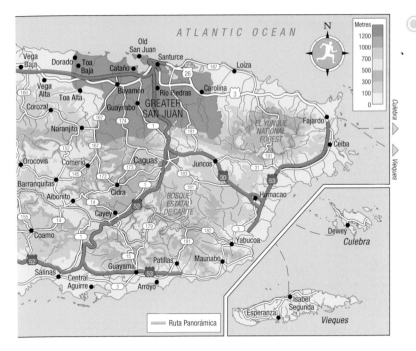

to visit **Luquillo**, the gateway to the **east coast**, while **Fajardo** is the departure point for **La Cordillera**, a haven for snorkelling and swimming. Looming over the whole region, **El Yunque National Forest** is a rainforest of lofty, jungle-covered peaks crisscrossed with hiking trails.

Offshore, the smaller island of **Vieques** is blessed with vast stretches of sugary sand backed with nothing but scrub, palm trees and sea grape. Swimming in the **bioluminescent bay** here is a bewitching experience, boats leaving ghostly clouds of fluorescence in their wake. **Culebra** is much smaller and even more languid, a rocky island ringed with turquoise waters, empty beaches and dazzling cays.

Inland from the **north coast** lies the bizarre, crumbling limestone peaks of **karst country**, containing the **Observatorio de Arecibo**, the **Cavernas del Río Camuy** and the ruined Taíno ball-courts at the **Centro Ceremonial Indígena de Caguana**.

The **Porta del Sol**, or "gateway to the sun", starts at the **northwest coast**, justly regarded as a surfing paradise that peaks at **Rincón**. Divers should check out **Isla Desecheo**, a protected island reserve encircled by brilliant sapphire waters. Back on land, **Mayagüez** is the "sultan of the west", a once-depressed industrial city gradually regaining its former colonial glory. Beyond the city lies a chain of low-key resorts: **Playa Buyé** and **Boquerón** boast gorgeous white sand beaches, before the west coast ends at the weathered cliffs of

US colony or 51st state?

Puerto Rico's political status is a highly emotive issue, and though it looks set to remain a Commonwealth of the US for the immediate future, there's a lot of truth in the old adage, "after two or three drinks every Puerto Rican is pro-independence". Most Puerto Ricans fear that becoming a US state would mean a dilution of their Hispanic identity, but that full independence would lead to economic and political chaos – even a cursory look at the modern history of Cuba, Haiti and the Dominican Republic looks pretty bleak. Although the island has a lot more freedom than the stereotypical colony, liberals and artists generally despair at the US association. Esmeralda Santiago in *Island of Lost Causes* says, "the truth is, we do have a history of struggle for independence, but the opposition has always won. The failure of our best hopes…has caused many Puerto Ricans to simply give up." That may be true: many Puerto Ricans now believe US statehood is inevitable.

Cabo Rojo. On the south coast, **La Parguera** faces a tangled labyrinth of channels and mangrove cays while inland, **San Germán** is crammed with flamboyant mansions and charming Spanish churches. East of here, the southern coastal plain is known as the **Porta Caribe**, or "gateway to the Caribbean". Don't miss **Guilligan's Island**, a mangrove cay spliced by a lagoon of crystal-clear water, and **Ponce**, still proud of its fine mansions, museums and richly stocked **art gallery**. The city's annual carnival, (held one week before Ash Wednesday), features parades, salsa and the unforgettable ghoulish masks known as *vejigantes*. Just to the north, the **Centro Ceremonial Indígena de Tibes** is another rare reminder of Puerto Rico's pre-Columbian past, while the best of the once booming sugar towns are **Guayama** and **Coamo**.

▶ Kiosco in Luquillo

While the coast attracts the most tourists, the spiritual heart of Puerto Rico lies in the mountains, accessed by the winding **Ruta Panorámica** and famous for its **lechoneras**, roadside diners roasting whole pigs over wood or charcoal fires. Other highlights include the massive flower festival at **Aibonito**, the jaw-dropping **Cañón de San Cristóbal**, and the rural town of **Jayuya**, which offers poignant reminders of Puerto Rico's Taíno heritage. At the far end of the route, **Maricao** is the producer of some of the world's finest coffee.

When to go

P uerto Rico has a hot and sunny tropical climate with an average yearly temperature of 26–27°C (80°F), but this can drop well into the teens at higher elevations in January and February. The driest period of the year runs roughly between January and April, but the island doesn't really have distinct dry and wet seasons – showers are possible year-round, though the southwest corner is extremely dry and the north coast gets twice as much rain as the south. Rainfall usually picks up between May and October, and hurricanes are possible anytime between June and November. Major hurricanes are mercifully rare, but can be devastating if they score a direct hit.

◀ Playa Crash Boat, near Aguadilla

The **peak tourist seasons** run roughly from December to April and all of July and August. The winter sees North Americans flock to the island to escape cold weather, with San Juan inundated by cruise-ship visitors, while high summer is the holiday season for Puerto Ricans. Prices are highest and crowds thickest at these times, especially on the coast, and if you intend to visit at Christmas, New Year or Easter, book well in advance. The island has also been a popular **Spring Break** destination in recent years, with thousands of US college students invading the main resorts between February and March ¬ bear this in mind when booking accommodation, especially if you want a tranquil experience.

Average daily temperatures and monthly rainfall

	Jan	Feb	Mar	Apr	May	Jun	Jul	Aug	Sep	Oct	Nov	Dec
San Juan												
Max/min (°F)	82/71	83/71	83/72	85/73	86/75	88/77	87/77	88/77	88/77	88/76	85/74	83/72
Max/min (°C)	28/22	28/22	28/22	29/23	30/24	31/25	31/25	31/25	31/25	31/24	29/23	28/22
Rainfall (mm)	76	51	51	102	127	102	102	127	152	127	152	127
Mayagüez												
Max/min (°F)	86/64	86/64	87/65	88/67	89/69	91/70	91/70	91/70	91/70	90/70	89/68	87/66
Max/min (°C)	30/18	30/18	31/18	31/19	32/21	33/21	33/21	33/21	33/21	32/21	32/20	31/19
Rainfall (mm)	25	76	76	102	178	152	229	229	279	229	127	51

things not to miss

It's not possible to see everything Puerto Rico has to offer in a single trip – and we don't suggest you try. What follows is a selective taste of the island's highlights: spectacular beaches, historic towns and a host of natural wonders. They're arranged in five colour-coded categories with a page reference to take you straight into the guide, where you can find out more.

01 **Diving** Page **183** • The crystalline waters off Puerto Rico contain some of the best-kept secrets in the Caribbean, making it an underwater paradise ideal for diving and snorkelling.

02 Old San Juan

Juan Page **55** • Explore one of the best-preserved colonial centres in the Americas, where the narrow streets are lined with elegant townhouses and a rich choice of enticing restaurants.

03 Paso Fino horses

Page **115** • Ride these friendly horses along the beach or through the jungle and experience their exceptionally smooth gait.

04 Playa Flamenco, Culebra

Page **144** • Nothing beats waking up on this unspoiled expanse of silky white sand, one of the most dazzling beaches in the world.

05 **Observatorio de Arecibo** Page **161** • The world's largest radio telescope is an awe-inspiring sight, with plenty of thought-provoking exhibits on hand to satisfy budding scientists and aspiring astronauts.

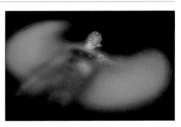

07 **Bioluminescent bay, Vieques** Page **132** • This mind-blowing phenomenon is best experienced during a nocturnal swim, with water glowing in the dark and dripping from your fingers like tiny sparkling gems.

06 **Beach hopping in Vieques** Page **131** • Tour the mesmerizing beaches of Vieques, precious slices of untouched Caribbean wilderness.

08 **Ponce** Page **209** • Puerto Rico's second city is a showcase of ebullient architecture, impressive art and poignant museums, including the lavish home of the Don Q rum empire, Castillo Serallés.

09 **Salsa** Page **78** • Learn to dance, check out a salsa club or just sit back and enjoy the pros on the island that was home to El Cantante, Gran Combo and Ricky Martin.

10 **Piña colada**

Page **75** • This sumptuous blend of rum, pineapple and coconut is served everywhere, from ritzy hotel bars to shacks on the beach.

11 **San Germán**

Page **200** • Soak up the colonial history in this charming old town, with ornate mansions and delicate churches harking back to the boom days of sugar and coffee.

12 Surfing Page **171** • Puerto Rico is hammered by the full force of the Atlantic swells in the winter, its north coast lined with dizzying breaks.

13 Casa Bacardi Page **84** • Learn everything there is to know about the Caribbean's favourite tipple at the "Cathedral of Rum".

14 Coffee Page **258** • Puerto Rican coffee once supplied the Vatican, and today the island's fertile soils and ideal climate are fuelling a resurgence in potent, gourmet brands.

15 Centro Ceremonial Indígena de Tibes Page **221** • These ancient ball-courts offer a unique insight into Pre-Taíno culture.

16 **El Yunque National Forest** Page **93** • Puerto Rico's most enchanting reserve of pristine rainforest, jungle-covered peaks and bubbling cascades is laced with panoramic trails.

18 **La Ruta Panorámica** Page **237** • Explore this winding route along the island's mountainous spine, a world of misty forests, coffee farms and roadside stalls selling roast pork.

17 **El Morro** Page **59** • Even Sir Francis Drake couldn't take this spectacular Spanish fortress, a whopping sledgehammer of stone and cannons that has guarded San Juan Bay for over four hundred years.

Basics

Basics

Getting there

The easiest way to get to Puerto Rico is to fly, though the island is also connected to the Dominican Republic and Virgin Islands by ferry. The island's international gateway is the Aeropuerto Internacional Luis Muñoz Marín in San Juan, with numerous connections to the US and all over the Caribbean, while regional airports at Aguadilla and Ponce are increasingly accepting direct flights from the US mainland and nearby islands.

Visitors from outside North America usually have to fly via the US. To a certain extent, the vast number of Puerto Ricans travelling between the island and the US throughout the year, in addition to a steady stream of business traffic, means that **airfares** remain fairly consistent, though weekend flights always carry a premium. Fares do tend to rise slightly during the **peak holiday season** between November and April, and soar during **Easter** (see p.10) – the biggest holiday of the year for most Puerto Ricans – Christmas and New Year. For US flights it's especially important to book well ahead if you want to benefit from lower prices.

Flights from the US and Canada

Numerous daily **nonstop flights** connect Puerto Rico with cities all over the US, but the cheapest and most frequent depart from "gateway" cities in the south and east, most commonly **Miami** and **New York** (JFK and Newark). San Juan is the Caribbean hub for American Airlines, so it's no surprise that this airline operates the most flights to the island and usually has the most competitively priced **fares**, though all the major US carriers offer services, including Continental and Spirit Airlines, and US Airways. The lowest return tickets to San Juan in high season (excluding holidays), typically average $300 from New York and Miami, $400–500 from Houston/Dallas and $450 from Chicago. If you're prepared to change planes a couple of times, flights from Los Angeles can be as low as $450, but American Airlines flies direct for around $700. Flights to Aguadilla and Ponce are similarly priced. If you're flying off-peak, it's

also worth checking out budget airline JetBlue, which flies nonstop from Orlando and New York's JFK to San Juan, Aguadilla and Ponce – book online and flights can go for as little as $160 return. **Flying times** are relatively short: around 3hr 45min from New York, 2hr 30min from Miami, 4hr 30min from Chicago, and just over 4hr from Dallas and Houston.

There are few direct flights from **Canada**, with Air Canada flying the only nonstop service from Toronto (4hr 35min; Can$1250). Your options increase (and prices fall) greatly if you fly through the US: fares from Montréal and Toronto via US carriers start at around Can$480.

Flights from the UK and Ireland

One of the principal reasons that Puerto Rico attracts just one to two percent of European tourists to the Caribbean is the dearth of charter and **direct flights** between Europe and the island. Things look set to change with British Airways and Virgin Atlantic now operating seasonal direct flights to San Juan via Antigua for around £700–800 (10.5hr). Otherwise, coming from the UK or Ireland you'll need to change planes at least once for cheaper flights, usually in the US. From **London** the cheapest option is usually to fly with American Airlines via New York, but travel websites will also come up with various combinations of British Airways and American carriers via Miami and Washington DC. Prices for return flights in peak season usually start at £550, depending on the strength of the pound. Iberia offers the only nonstop flight to San Juan from Europe, a

Six steps to a better kind of travel

At Rough Guides we are passionately committed to travel. We feel strongly that only through travelling do we truly come to understand the world we live in and the people we share it with – plus tourism has brought a great deal of **benefit** to developing economies around the world over the last few decades. But the extraordinary growth in tourism has also damaged some places irreparably, and of course **climate change** is exacerbated by most forms of transport, especially flying. This means that now more than ever it's important to **travel thoughtfully** and **responsibly**, with respect for the cultures you're visiting – not only to derive the most benefit from your trip but also to preserve the best bits of the planet for everyone to enjoy. At Rough Guides we feel there are six main areas in which you can make a difference:

- Consider what you're contributing to the **local economy**, and how much the services you use do the same, whether it's through employing local workers and guides or sourcing locally grown produce and local services.
- Consider the **environment** on holiday as well as at home. Water is scarce in many developing destinations, and the biodiversity of local flora and fauna can be adversely affected by tourism. Try to patronize businesses that take account of this.
- Travel with a purpose, not just to tick off experiences. Consider **spending longer** in a place, and getting to know it and its people.
- Give thought to how often you **fly**. Try to avoid short hops by air and more harmful night flights.
- Consider **alternatives to flying**, travelling instead by bus, train, boat and even by bike or on foot where possible.
- Make your trips **"climate neutral"** via a reputable carbon offset scheme. All Rough Guide flights are offset, and every year we donate money to a variety of charities devoted to combating the effects of climate change.

---

thrice-weekly service from **Madrid**: from London you can get return tickets on this route from around £520 in peak season.

From **Dublin**, you might save a few euros flying the same routes via London; otherwise it's faster and cheaper to fly with US Airways or Delta via New York – flights cost around €650.

Flights from Australia, New Zealand and South Africa

Getting from **Australia**, **New Zealand** or **South Africa** to Puerto Rico means changing planes at least once somewhere in the US. From **Sydney** flights in high season will set you back at least Aus$1600, usually via Delta with two layovers. The cheapest flights from other Australian cities route through Sydney too. From **Auckland**, Air New Zealand and Qantas fly via Los Angeles to connect with the American Airlines flight

for around NZ$3000. Note that all these flights can entail long layovers in the US.

From **South Africa**, various combinations of airlines will get you to San Juan via layovers in the US or Spain (via Iberia) from R7500 to R12,000.

Flights from the Caribbean

San Juan is one of the largest regional hubs in the **Caribbean**, making it an easy fit into a larger tour of the Antilles, or an excellent base for further exploration. The most frequent flights link San Juan with the **US** and **British Virgin Islands** (typically for $200 return), but there are also direct services from Antigua, St Vincent and Dominica on LIAT, plus several charter airlines fly from the Dominican Republic. Jet Blue also has flights direct to Santo Domingo. American Eagle uses San Juan as a hub and flies all over the Caribbean, while Copa Airlines flies from

Panama City. Smaller airlines also link Vieques with St Croix (see p.24).

Ferries

American Cruise Ferries (☏787/832-4800 or 787/622-4800, ⓦwww.acferries.com) operates a twice-weekly ferry service between **Santo Domingo** in the Dominican Republic and Mayagüez on the west coast of Puerto Rico (Tues & Thurs), a journey that usually takes around twelve hours. Rates start at $169 one-way, plus $96–216 for a cabin. The same ferry runs between Santo Domingo and San Juan on Sundays (13hr). Prices start at $189 one-way, with the additional $96–216 for a cabin berth.

At the time of writing you could also travel between St Thomas and St John in the US Virgin Islands and Fajardo on the east coast of Puerto Rico: boats depart St Thomas at 4pm on Saturdays only. One-way is $70, return is just $90 (see p.111).

Agents and operators

ebookers UK ☏0800/082 3000, Republic of Ireland ☏01/488 3507, ⓦwww.ebookers.com. Low fares on an extensive selection of scheduled flights and package deals.

North South Travel UK ☏01245/608 291, ⓦwww.northsouthtravel.co.uk. Friendly, competitive travel agency, offering discounted fares worldwide. Profits are used to support projects in the developing world, especially the promotion of sustainable tourism.

STA Travel US ☏1-800/781-4040, Canada ☏1-888/427-5639, UK ☏0870/1630 026, Australia ☏1300/733 035, New Zealand ☏0508/782 872, ⓦwww.statravel.com. Worldwide specialists in independent travel; also student IDs, travel insurance, car rental, rail passes and more. Good discounts for students and under-26s.

Trailfinders UK ☏0845/058 5858, Republic of Ireland ☏01/677 7888, Australia ☏1300/780 212, ⓦwww.trailfinders.com. One of the best-informed and most efficient agents for independent travellers.

Specialist tour operators

Acampa ☏787/706-0695, ⓦwww.acampapr .com. San Juan-based adventure tour outfit.

AdvenTours ☏787/530-8311, ⓦwww .adventourspr.com. Features customized private tours that include birdwatching, hiking, camping, visits to coffee plantations and kayaking.

Amazilia Tours ☏506/273-6500, ⓦwww .amaziliatours.com. Bird-watching tours of Puerto Rico.

Classic Golf Tours ☏303/751-7200, ⓦwww .classicgolftours.com. Plans and arranges vacations of Puerto Rico with golf as the focus.

Golden Heron Ecotours ☏787/426-0979, ⓦwww.golden-heron.com. Variety of guided tours including snorkelling trips to La Cordillera and Vieques and hikes to El Yunque, all emphasizing the culture, history and ecology of the island.

Legends of Puerto Rico ☏787/605-9060, ⓦwww.legendsofpr.com. Offers fascinating guided walks and bus tours of Old San Juan and beyond.

Getting around

Puerto Rico is a relatively small island and therefore easy to get around, with one important catch: formal public transport is virtually nonexistent, which means unless you rent a car or motorbike you'll be reliant on the highly localized network of *públicos*. Internal flights connect Ponce and Mayagüez with San Juan, and also Vieques and Culebra – both islands are also connected to the main island by ferry.

By bus (*público*)

No subject seems to elicit more confusion in Puerto Rico than **públicos** (bus services), mostly because the vast majority of Puerto Ricans never take them. *Públicos* operate on set routes, but at the whim of the driver, waiting until the vehicle is full before departing and usually dropping people off along the way. Rates are very cheap – San Juan to Ponce is just $15 – and it's often a great way to meet some of the locals (the system tends to be used predominantly by students and the elderly).

If you intend to travel extensively in Puerto Rico, though, *públicos* are not recommended. Though San Juan is well connected with most of the towns on the island, services between other places are patchy at best, and these days *públicos* tend to operate more like local buses, serving the immediate area. Long-distance trips across the country can mean changing several times, and once you get to your destination, you'll find your options extremely limited without wheels.

If you do end up taking a *público*, speaking Spanish definitely helps (drivers rarely speak English), and you must **plan ahead**. For busy routes, you can simply turn up at the local bus station (usually known as the **Terminal de Carros Públicos**, or just *la terminal*) early in the morning (7am or earlier, Mon–Sat) and pick one up, but at other times and locations you'll need to call ahead, reserve a space and arrange a pick-up time. Some locals differentiate between *lineas* and *públicos*: *lineas* are minibuses that follow fixed routes and timetables (like a normal bus service), while true *públicos* (which can also be taxi-like cars) go only when full, stop a lot and vary departure times. In practice it doesn't make a lot of difference, and there are very few true *lineas* in any case. These days most *públicos* are Ford minibuses with special yellow licence plates marked "*Público*".

By car

Renting a car in Puerto Rico is by far the most efficient and convenient way to get around. You'll find all the major agencies and several local companies (usually cheaper) in San Juan, with a handful of offices scattered around the island. Culebra and Vieques have their own local companies – it's expensive and time-consuming to take rental cars across by ferry. Note that you should arm yourself with a decent map, road atlas or GPS system if travelling the island this way.

Rates for economy-sized cars with unlimited mileage start at $40–50 per day or $250 for seven days, but can escalate dramatically during holidays and the busy July–August period – the longer you rent, the cheaper it gets per day. Basic **insurance** (loss damage waiver, no deductible/excess) can add another $20 per day, but is highly recommended as scrapes and knocks are common (especially in car parks). Most **US insurance policies** should be valid in Puerto Rico, but check before you go.

Renting in Puerto Rico is much like the US and fairly straightforward for most visitors. You must have a credit card and a **driver's licence** valid for up to 120 days (all major countries are accepted). You must be at least 25, although some companies (Budget and most of the local outfits) allow drivers over 21 for an additional charge.

Car rental agencies

Avis ⓦ www.avis.com.
Budget ⓦ www.budget.com.
Charlie Car Rental ⓦ www.charliecars.com.
Hertz ⓦ www.hertz.com.
National ⓦ www.nationalcar.com.
Thrifty ⓦ www.thrifty.com.

Driving in Puerto Rico

Driving conditions vary wildly, but your biggest headache is likely to be the sheer **volume of traffic**. The main highways in San Juan and around much of the densely populated coastline are the most congested – it's best to travel at off-peak times to avoid the worst of it. In contrast, driving in more remote areas and especially in the mountains can be a real delight, and while often winding and narrow, unless it's been raining heavily, these roads are rarely dangerous.

Those used to driving in London, LA or New York shouldn't be too fazed by the mildly frenzied driving displayed on San Juan's crammed highways, and even when driving aggressively, Puerto Ricans rarely lose their cool on the road. Nevertheless, locals do tend to drive far more recklessly than most of their compatriots on the US mainland: speeding, jumping lanes, pulling out without warning and thrashing along the shoulder are all normal practice. Puerto Ricans are also compulsive tailgaters and accidents are common, despite a fairly heavy police presence on the roads and a system of severe fines; Puerto Rico had the highest number of car accident deaths (308) in any US jurisdiction in 2010.

Carjacking was a big problem in Puerto Rico in the early 1990s, but incidents have dropped off dramatically and tourists are rarely affected. The vast majority of crimes occur outside the tourist zones in Greater San Juan (in areas like Río Piedras), late at night, so to be safe, avoid driving in urban areas after midnight and ignore anyone trying to wave you down. It's also a bad idea to pick up hitchers. **Car theft** is a problem in some areas, which is why insurance is crucial, and you should never leave valuables in your vehicle. If you **break down**, call the rental company.

Should you have a minor **accident**, exchange names, addresses and driver's licence details with the other parties if you can, before contacting the rental company. Officially, you are supposed to notify the state police within four hours if the accident has caused damage in excess of $100, but your rental company should be able to advise you.

With driving such an important part of life in Puerto Rico, you are never far from a **petrol station** in the cities, and many open 24 hours. **Fuel** follows US standards, with unleaded the most common option, though it's sold by the litre and is slightly cheaper than on the US mainland.

Roads and rules

The Puerto Rican **road system** is the best in the Caribbean, with freeways (motorways) known as *autopistas* fanning out from San Juan and four-lane highways (dual-carriageways) covering all the major routes. *Autopistas* carry frequent tolls of $0.50–1.25, so bring coins if you can: lanes on the right marked "C" or *cambio* provide change, but the middle lanes are reserved for *cambio exacto* (throw coins in the bucket) and are usually faster. Avoid the *autoexpreso* lanes on the left, which require an electronic pass (you'll be fined if you go through without one).

All roads are given numbers, usually written with the prefix "PR" or "Puerto Rico", as in PR-2. Distances on the island are given in kilometres (1km=0.62 miles) and therefore appear this way in the Guide. Signage is in Spanish, but in a concession to American car makers, **speed limits** are in miles per hour: the **maximum speed limit** on most roads is 55mph, though some sections of highway and *autopista* range from 65–70mph, and you should stick to 30mph in residential areas. Laws against drunk driving and speeding are strictly enforced, and everyone in the car must wear a seatbelt. It is legal to turn right on a red light, after coming to a full stop (except where signs expressly forbid this), and thanks to the threat of **carjacking**, you are permitted to ignore red lights altogether between midnight and 5am. Road rules otherwise follow US norms and cars **drive on the right**. For a glossary of driving terms and road signs in Spanish, see p.287.

By boat

The Puerto Rico Port Authority (☎1-800/981-2005 or 787/863-0705) runs

Addresses and road names

Puerto Rican addresses can be a little confusing, with several systems employed using a combination of English and Spanish. All roads have a number: you'll often see these prefixed by "Carr" or **Carretera** (meaning "highway" or "route") when written down, though you rarely see this on actual road signs, where just the number or the "PR" prefix is more common. Note that a sign reading "INT 3" means that an intersection with PR-3 is coming up, not that you are currently driving on PR-3.

In many places street numbers are not used, and locations are either described (*esquina* means "corner") or given a kilometre reference. A location at PR-3 km 2.1 would be 2.1km from the beginning of PR-3, though in practice it's hard to know where this is or even which end of the road is considered the beginning. In some places useful markers on the roadside show the distance every tenth of a kilometre, but these are becoming rarer. It's always faster to call your destination for directions.

regular **passenger ferries** to Vieques and Culebra from Fajardo, as well as a less frequent vehicle and cargo ferry; see p.110 for details. Reaching other offshore islands, such as Isla de Mona (see p.196), requires the services of a private boat operator.

By air

Domestic flights from San Juan's Aeropuerto Internacional Luis Muñoz Marín to Mayagüez and Ponce are operated by Cape Air for around $75–80 one-way, though fares vary according to what day and time you fly.

More useful for most visitors are the frequent flights from San Juan or Fajardo to the islands of **Culebra** and **Vieques**. Several airlines run these routes, though planes are tiny eight-seaters (neither island can accept jets), so tend to book up fast during holidays. The cheapest flights operate from San Juan's tiny domestic airport, Isla Grande, and cost around $100 return. Cape Air and a few other airlines also fly direct from the international airport, which is more convenient for connections but more expensive ($160–180 return).

Domestic airlines

Air Flamenco ⓦ www.airflamenco.net.
Air Sunshine ⓦ www.airsunshine.com.
Cape Air ⓦ www.flycapeair.com.
Seaborne Airlines ⓦ www.seaborneairlines.com.
Vieques Air Link ⓦ www.vieques-island.com.

Accommodation

Puerto Rico offers travellers a wide range of accommodation, from small, family-run guesthouses to plush luxury resorts, though true budget options are few in number. Finding a room is rarely a problem, though even San Juan can fill up during some holiday weekends. Prices vary considerably, but usually increase dramatically at weekends or public holidays. Rates also tend to be higher during the two peak seasons (early Dec to early May, and July & Aug), while rates between September and November are usually the lowest.

Hotels

Puerto Rican **hotels** run the gamut from simple guesthouses or bed and breakfasts to standard hotels and mega-resorts. For tax purposes, the government divides accommodation into **three classes**: hotels with casinos (mostly in San Juan); standard hotels, guesthouses and motels; and small inns or *paradores* (see opposite). English is usually spoken by someone at even the smallest hotel, and these days almost every place has **air conditioning** and **TV** (though not all have cable with English-language channels). Exceptions tend to be in the mountains, where it's cool enough to use ceiling fans at night, or at hotels where the lack of TV or modern facilities is seen as a plus – perversely, you'll usually pay extra for such designer simplicity.

As there are no true hostels in Puerto Rico, **budget hotels** offer some of the cheapest accommodation on the island, but bargains are hard to find. You'll rarely get a room for less than $50, with only a handful of older, slightly run-down places in the mountains offering these sorts of rates. You'll find more choice above $75, but it's unusual to find good-quality accommodation with all the amenities for less than $100.

Most places describing themselves as guesthouses and bed and breakfasts fall into the **mid-range** category in Puerto Rico, more akin to the smart US version of the genre than the cheaper European variety, and can cost anything from $80 to $250. Standards vary considerably depending on the location and age of the property – price isn't always a good indication of quality, so

Accommodation price codes

The accommodation listed in this book has been assigned one of nine price codes representing the price of the cheapest **double room** in peak season, which for most hotels runs from late November or early December to April. Prices between May and November will often be far lower, though some places hike prices again in July to catch vacationing Puerto Ricans.

❶ $49 and under
❷ $50–74
❸ $75–99
❹ $100–124
❺ $125–149
❻ $150–199
❼ $200–249
❽ $250–299
❾ $300 and over

always check the room before agreeing to pay. In general, smaller family-run places offer the best value, although some business hotels in the cities can be affordable, assuming there are no extra charges (see box, p.26).

You'll find huge **resorts** and a smaller number of posh **boutique hotels** spread across the island, predominantly on the coast. Prices can range from $150 up to $400 and beyond, depending on room type, resort facilities and season, but you'll always get the best deals online. Resorts are the biggest culprits when it comes to extra charges, however (see box, p.26).

Paradores and hotel programmes

The **Paradores Puertorriqueños** programme was established in 1973 by the Puerto Rico Tourism Company, and while being dubbed a *parador* ("country inn") brings a certain amount of cachet to a hotel, the classification has nothing to do with the Spanish system of expensive historic properties. To qualify for official *parador* status in Puerto Rico, hotels must simply maintain quality standards set by the PRTC: minimum requirements include being located outside Greater San Juan and in an area deemed of historic or cultural importance, having fewer than 75 rooms, and being managed by the owner and their family (who are supposed to live on the property). To add to the confusion, some equally atmospheric guesthouses that are not approved use the word *parador* anyway. Prices range from $80–120; for the official list visit ⓦseepuertorico.com/paradores.

The *paradores* programme is similar to the "small hotels of Puerto Rico" scheme (ⓦpuertoricosmallhotels.com) established by

the **Puerto Rico Hotel & Tourism Association** (☎787/758-8001, ⓦwww .prhta.org), which promotes small guest-houses and hotels across the island (some hotels are members of both programmes). If not a member of either programme, hotels and guesthouses can opt to be simply **endorsed** by the PRTC: in return for passing basic requirements (like having parking, smoke detectors, security chains and maid service for all rooms), these hotels appear in official publications and can promote their PRTC approval. Even then, it's difficult to make generalizations: while hotels that fall in any of the three categories above will usually offer decent accommodation, standards vary wildly, and hotels that for whatever reason have opted to remain unaffiliated can be just as good.

Rental apartments and villas

Increasingly popular on the island, **renting apartments** and **villas** is an appealing alternative to staying in hotels, and is becoming relatively easy via reputable broker websites. Properties tend to be in good condition, come with kitchens, living rooms and other facilities, and are often located in some of the most attractive parts of Puerto Rico, particularly Vieques and Culebra. Note, however, that you'll usually need a car to access such properties, and that they tend to be pricey unless you're willing to stay for at least a week or have a large group. Villas that can sleep six people or more are usually a far better deal for groups than hotels. **PR West** (☎787/420-5227 or 826-6748, ⓦwww .prwest.com) is a good place to start, with listings of hundreds of properties all over the

Taxes and charges

One of the only negative aspects of staying in Puerto Rico, and particularly San Juan, is that **taxes and charges** can increase your hotel bill by 25 percent or more. To be fair, this is common practice all over the Caribbean, but it's important to know what's mandatory and what is simply being added to your bill as a disguised **service charge**: ask to speak to the manager if it is not absolutely clear. Most of the larger hotels do spell out the extra charges, such as the notorious **"resort fee"** – to pay for things like use of towels, pool and spa whether you use these or not – but some will simply add a combined figure to your bill. Always demand to know exactly what's being added and why.

As of April 2011, **mandatory government taxes** on hotel occupancy were as follows: hotels with casinos 11 percent; hotels without casinos, guesthouses and motels 9 percent; small inns (*paradores*), bed and breakfasts and short-term apartment or villa rentals 7 percent. Anything in excess of this has been levied by the hotel – there is **no additional sales tax** on hotel occupancy.

island. Prices vary considerably, but you'll get great deals at around $1000 per week in most locations – daily rates, where available, tend to be much more expensive ($200/night).

Campgrounds and cabañas

Camping is possible in Puerto Rico, though with much of the island in private hands you're generally limited to official campgrounds on public beaches and forest reserves (a law was passed in 1995 forbidding camping on public beaches without facilities). The six beach campgrounds are operated by the **Compañía de Parques Nacionales** (☏787/622-5200, ⓦwww.parquesnacionalespr.com), and all come with showers, toilets and barbecue grills. Rates start at $10 per night for a basic pitch. Locations include Playa La Monserrate (Luquillo), Playa Seven Seas (Fajardo), Sun Bay (Vieques), Playa Tres Hermanos (Aguada), Punta Guilarte on the south coast and Playa Cerro Gordo on the north coast. You can just turn up without a reservation at any of these places, but in peak season (especially July & Aug) spaces can fill up fast and it's best to call in advance.

Campsites within Puerto Rico's forest reserves are managed by the **Departamento de Recursos Naturales y Ambientales** (DRNA, ☏787/999-2200, ⓦwww.drna.gobierno.pr), but to stay at any of them you must apply for a permit in advance (15 days ahead for Isla de Mona;

see p.196). You can apply in person, by mail, by fax and online, but the website is in Spanish only. Once you've made a reservation online, you still need to pay at the nearest DRNA office within three working days; if all else fails, take a taxi to the office in San Juan (PR-8838 km 6.3, Sector El Cinco, Río Piedras) and apply in person. Rates are very cheap: $5 per person per night, and campgrounds usually come with basic toilets and showers. Note that many of these sites close in the low season.

You can also camp on **Playa Flamenco** on Culebra, perhaps the most stunning location of all (see p.143 for details), and within **El Yunque** (see p.97). It's important to note that **theft** can be a problem in all these locations, and if you leave anything valuable unattended in your tent it's likely to be stolen, especially on the beaches. You'll rarely encounter more serious problems, but camping alone when no one else is around is not a good idea.

The Compañía de Parques Nacionales also runs a system of **cabañas** on the public beaches at Humacao, Boquerón and Añasco, as well as Monte del Estado. Known as **Centros Vacacionales**, these are far more popular with Puerto Rican families than foreign tourists but a lot more comfortable than camping. Rates range $75–80 for basic *cabañas* to $125 for larger villas, but accommodation is still basic – modern concrete and wood cabins with one or two bedrooms, minimal furniture and facilities – and usually uninspiring compared to the rustic chalets you might find elsewhere in the Caribbean; the locations, however, steps away from the beach, are unbeatable. You can make reservations by phone or on the website (Spanish only); there is a **minimum stay** of two nights and a maximum of four weeks (or seven days during the peak season).

Food and drink

Puerto Rican food is an exuberant blend of Spanish, Taíno, American and African influences, a rich Caribbean melange known as *cocina criolla* (Créole cooking), not unlike Cuban and Dominican cuisine. Traditional food can be exceptionally appetizing, but it can also get monotonous after a while, the repertoire of dishes being fairly similar at most restaurants. To spice things up, seek out the island's surprising number of local specialities, or at the top end, sample some of the region's most creative restaurants, innovators of Nuevo Latino cuisine. When it comes to drinks, Puerto Rico is well entrenched as the Caribbean's leading rum producer and inventor of the *piña colada*, while its once lauded coffee is gradually winning back international acclaim.

Core components in any Puerto Rican meal are **plantains** (*plátanos*), a type of savoury banana that is only eaten cooked: *tostones* are fried plantains usually served as an appetizer or starchy side dish. **Mofongo** is the best-known plantain dish (see box below) and essential eating, at least once. **Rice**, invariably accompanied by **beans** (*arroz con habichuelas*) or *gandules* (pigeon peas), is often served as a meal by itself in cheap canteens, and considered stereotypically Puerto Rican. It's the dish Puerto Ricans feel most nostalgic for overseas and not as bland as it sounds: kidney beans are richly stewed with pork and spices, Spanish-style, before being poured over the rice.

Puerto Rican cuisine has inherited plenty of other **Spanish** legacies. **Adobo** was

---

Mofongo

Stay in Puerto Rico long enough, and you'll come to either love or hate **mofongo**, the celebrated national dish that appears on almost every menu on the island. Made from fried plantains mashed with garlic and olive oil, the origins of *mofongo* are hazy (it's also popular in Cuba and the Dominican Republic), but most experts think it was influenced primarily by the island's African traditions. Puerto Ricans are addicted to the stuff but, because it can be time-consuming and hard to make, tend to eat it in restaurants rather than at home. After an initial taste, most foreign tourists tend to avoid *mofongo*, put off by its heavy, starchy base, but the secret is to know where to go: not all *mofongo* is made equal, and variations differ wildly from place to place. *Mofongo* can be served plain, shaped into balls as a side dish for fried meat, or stuffed (*mofongo relleno*) with pork, chicken or seafood such as shrimp, octopus or lobster. The mashed and fried base can vary, made with savoury green plantains or sweet bananas, while cooks tend to have their own interpretation of how to present the various components: some simply stuff the meat inside while others fill the plantain base like a giant bowl. Vegetarians should check before ordering plain *mofongo*, as traditionally the plantains are also mashed with pork crackling.

originally a Spanish marinade, spreading throughout the colonies where it was adapted to local ingredients. In the Philippines *adobo* became the national dish, while in Puerto Rico the word generally refers to the seasoning of crushed peppercorns, oregano, garlic, salt, olive oil and lime juice rubbed into meats before grilling. Other Spanish traditions include mouthwatering **lechón asado**, or barbecued pig, still a Castilian speciality but with an earthier quality here, inherited from the Taíno.

Another national favourite is **asopao**, a rice stew served with chicken or seafood from a *caldero* (traditional kettle). Like *mofongo*, each restaurant tends to have its own unique interpretation of the dish.

Puerto Ricans love **pork** and **chicken**, with *arroz con pollo* (fried chicken and rice) featuring on just about every menu along with various incarnations of *pechuga* (grilled chicken breast) and *chuletas* (pork chops). Other juicy grilled meats that appear regularly in most restaurants include *churrasco* (skirt steak) and *chuletón* (T-bone steak).

Being an island, it's no surprise that **seafood** and **shellfish** form an important part of the restaurant scene, with prawns, crab, lobster and octopus popping up on most menus along with the ever-present *chiollo* (red snapper) and *dorado* (mahi-mahi).

See the Costs section (p.37) for more guidance on prices for eating out.

Desserts

Everywhere you go in Puerto Rico, meals invariably end with coffee and **flan** (a rich blend of eggs, milk and cream cheese, a bit like a custard tart), usually vanilla-flavoured but occasionally involving tropical fruits such as guava. Restaurants often engage in feverish competition to decide who has the best *flan*, and as with many modest-looking Puerto Rican dishes, the results can be spectacular and bursting with flavour.

Other traditional desserts include *guayaba* (guava) with *queso blanco* or *queso del país* (white cheese), though the guava is usually preserved in syrup and is sickly sweet – best eaten in small doses. **Cakes** feature heavily, and are also available through local bakeries and supermarkets. **Coconut** is a common ingredient in many desserts, and you'll come

across plenty of examples of crispy coconut squares and candied coconut rice. Candied fruits such as *dulce de papaya* are also common sweet treats. Locally made **ice cream** (*helados*) in tangy fruit flavours is incredibly refreshing and can be found in even the smallest towns, sold in cones or tubs for under $2.

Vegetarian food

Vegetarians will not be overly excited by the options in Puerto Rico, though San Juan does have several vegetarian restaurants and diners all over the island are starting to offer vegetarian choices. Though *cocina criolla* isn't particularly vegetarian-friendly, given their links with the US, most Puerto Ricans understand the concept and are fairly sympathetic when it comes to special requests. Remember that even plain *mofongo* or rice and beans often contains pork or pork fat.

Fruit

Puerto Rico's tropical climate is perfect for growing all sorts of luscious, exotic **fruits**, though modernization (and US import practices) has taken its toll and the selection on offer can be remarkably poor compared to other countries in the tropics. Most notably, the range of local fruits stocked in supermarkets is tiny, reflecting the relatively small scale of fruit farming on the island: drive around the hills in the summer and you'll see literally thousands of juicy, ripe **mangoes** that have been left to rot on the ground (it's usually OK to help yourself, but check first if it looks like the tree stands on private land). The best place to buy fresh fruit is at the roadside, where local vendors sell seasonal crops: in addition to mangoes, you'll see huge **avocados** (Feb to April) and **pineapples** (summer). **Guava** and **papaya** are traditional Puerto Rican fruits that have lost popularity in recent decades, but are still used in numerous preserves and jellies (jams). **Bananas** are also still grown on the island.

Adventurous eaters should try Puerto Rico's more unusual fruits: kids love the *caimito* (also known as the star apple, with a vaguely grapelike flavour), *quenepa* (Spanish lime) and *zapote* (a small fruit with a complex taste, blending peach, avocado and vanilla).

Kioscos

Snacking is a Puerto Rican passion, and the island's *cocina en kiosco* provides a highly addictive (if coronary-inducing) plethora of deep-fried delights to savour. Roadside **stalls**, generally known as **kioscos** (also *kioskos*) are some of the best places to try cheap Puerto Rican food: some *kioscos* are collected together in areas on highways (such as those in Luquillo), along the coast (in Piñones) or in the mountains (Guavate), but you'll find individual stalls all over the island and in many town plazas. In larger towns, the **market** (*mercado*) is the best place to seek out no-frills snack stalls, as well as sellers of fresh fruit and coconut juices, while almost every town and village has a local **café** or bar that sells similar fare along with potent cups of coffee and cold beer.

The most common *kiosco* food (*cocina en kiosco*) is **deep-fried fritters**, especially *bacalaítos*, thin and crunchy cod fritters, battered with garlic, oregano and sweet chilli, and *alcapurrias* (mashed yautia root and green plantain, stuffed with ground meat and fried). Other favourites are *rellenos de papa* (ground meat and mashed potato balls), *empanadillas* (turnovers filled with meat, more crispy than the Mexican version) and deep-fried tacos, more like Chinese spring rolls than Mexican-style filled tortillas. See the Language section on p.288 for a complete menu reader.

Drinks

Tap water in Puerto Rico is technically safe to drink, though locals have mixed feelings about it: it's treated so it should be clean, but the amount of chemicals in the water means you that may prefer to use a filter. Note also that after heavy rains some of the supply can get contaminated, so tap water is best avoided at these times. If in doubt, stick to **bottled water**, which is cheap and easily available.

Soft drinks and juices

The full range of **soft drinks** and carton **juices** are available from shops, cafés and supermarkets in Puerto Rico, but far more tempting are natural juices, such as *jugo de china* (orange juice), and *batidas* (fruit shakes), sold from stalls all over the island. **Coconut juice** (*agua de coco*) is also best experienced fresh, from small vendors at local markets or from private sellers and roadside stalls in the country. Other local drinks to watch out for are *parcha* (made from passion fruit) and *tamarindo*, the sour-sweet juice made from tamarind.

On a sweltering day, nothing provides relief like a **piragua**, shaved ice drizzled with syrup and sold for around $1 from brightly decorated carts all over the island. For a real local experience, seek out **maví**, a fermented drink made from tree bark and often described as root beer. Primarily a home-made drink sold at markets and food stalls in towns, or from private houses in the country, you'll have to ask around to find the best supplier.

Coffee

Puerto Rico has produced some of the best **coffee** in the world since the nineteenth century, and the island is beginning to win back international respect for its small gourmet brands. The lush Central Cordillera cradles over ten thousand coffee farms, most selling beans to just two large roasters: **Grupo Jiménez** (which produces Café Rico, Café Yauco Selecto, and the most successful brand, Café Yaucono) and **Garrido & Co** (Café Crema and Café Adjuntas). Collectively they control around ninety percent of the domestic market and often dominate supermarket shelves, but a growing number of smaller cooperatives cultivate, process and sell their own coffee. You can visit many of these mountain *fincas* and buy whole or ground beans directly from them, though drinking coffee in cafés and restaurants is another story: most of these are supplied by the mass producers, and sometimes you'll be drinking coffee that hasn't even been grown on the island. *Café* can be ordered *con leche* (with milk), *negrito con azúcar* (black with sugar) or just *cortao* (with a drop of milk) and *puya* (no sugar). For decaf, ask for *sin cafeína* or just *descafeinado*. **Tea** is available in some places, usually the imported black or herbal varieties you'd expect to find in the US, but Puerto Ricans are not big tea drinkers.

Alcohol

Puerto Rico's favourite drink and one of its biggest exports is **rum** (*ron*), a potent spirit often served with Coke (rum and Coke with a wedge of lemon or lime is called a *Cuba libre*) and various liquors to create all sorts of mind-bending cocktails. Buying rum in supermarkets is much cheaper than in the US and Europe, with decent bottles of the main brands around $10.

Puerto Rico once had hundreds of small, family-owned distilleries, but only two operate today. The largest by far is **Bacardi** (see p.84), which produces its signature Superior brand as well as various fruit- and coconut-laced flavours at its plant in Cataño. The other producer and only home-grown Puerto Rican distiller is Ponce-based **Destilería Serrallés** (see p.218), which produces the **Don Q** brand of rums. **Ron del Barrilito** (see p.58) is now the most respected independent brand on the island, though it has to buy raw product from Bacardi.

Puerto Rico's national cocktail is the **piña colada**, supposedly created in a San Juan hotel in the 1950s (see p.75), and you'll also see **sangría** served in bars and restaurants, particularly on the west coast: the Puerto Rican version is usually a potent rum cocktail mixed with fruit juices.

Puerto Rican **beer** is less appealing, now represented solely by the Medalla brand, produced in Mayagüez by Cervecería India, a light lager that's refreshing enough on a hot day but nothing special. Presidente beer from the Dominican Republic is almost as prevalent. Imported beers tend to follow the traditional US school of light, Budweiser-type brews, and it's hard to find a wider selection of real ales and microbrews, even in San Juan.

Note that the **legal drinking age** in Puerto Rico is 18, but it is strictly forbidden to drink on the streets (the beach is fine).

Festivals and public holidays

One of Puerto Rico's greatest attractions is its range and depth of festivals. Traditional festivals are thoroughly grounded in the island's Spanish heritage, with African and Taíno elements added over the years to create a truly criollo mix. These include the fiestas patronales or fiestas del pueblo observed by each of the 78 municipalities to honour patron saints – the main ones are listed below and in relevant chapters. Public holidays are marked with a (P) and include all US federal holidays, when government-run offices and attractions, as well as banks, will be closed. Shops and other businesses tend to close only on New Year's Day, Three Kings' Day, Good Friday and Easter Sunday, Mothers' and Fathers' Day, Thanksgiving and Christmas Day. However, even if it's not an official holiday, any of the festivals listed here can mean closures and time changes, so plan ahead.

January

Día de Año Nuevo/New Year's Day January 1 (P). Usually celebrated with fireworks displays.
Día de los Tres Reyes (Three Kings' Day) January 6 (P). This is the day children receive gifts (in addition to Christmas Day).
Natalicio de Eugenio María de Hostos Second Monday in January (P). Commemorates the famous independence advocate, born in Mayagüez on January 11, 1839.

Martin Luther King's Birthday Third Monday in January (P). US federal holiday to honour the African-American civil rights leader gunned down in 1968.

February

Carnaval de Ponce Week before Ash Wednesday. This traditional pre-Lenten carnival is one of the most important festivals in Puerto Rico.
Día de los Presidentes (Presidents' Day) Third Monday in February (P). Another US holiday, originally

commemorating George Washington's birthday on February 22, and associated locally with the birth of Luis Muñoz Marín on February 18, 1898.

March

Día de la Abolición de la Esclavitud (Emancipation Day) March 22 (P). Commemorates the abolition of slavery in 1873.

March/April

Viernes Santo (Good Friday) and **Domingo de la Resurrección** (Easter), the first Sunday after the first full moon between March 22 and April 25. Both (P). **Holy Week** (*santa semana*) is the most important Catholic festival and consequently the busiest holiday in Puerto Rico.

April

Natalicio de José de Diego Third Monday in April (P). Celebrates the birth of José de Diego on April 16, 1867, the beloved poet and political leader.

May

Día de las Madres (Mothers' Day) Second Sunday in May (P). Major celebration in Puerto Rico, with restaurants and beaches swamped.
Memorial Day Last Monday in May (P). Federal holiday to commemorate the men and women who have died serving in the US military.

June

Día de los Padres (Fathers' Day) Third Sunday in June (P). Almost as big as Mothers' Day.
Día de San Juan Bautista June 24. John the Baptist is the patron saint of Puerto Rico and the capital, and the biggest festivities take place in San Juan.

July

US Independence Day July 4 (P). Major federal holiday.
Natalicio de Luis Muñoz Rivera Third Monday in July (P). Celebrates the birthday of Luis Muñoz Rivera on July 15, 1859, in Barranquitas.
Día de la Constitución del Estado Libre Asociado (Constitution Day) July 25 (P). Commemorates the signing of the 1952 constitution of Puerto Rico.
Natalicio de José Celso Barbosa July 27 (P). Commemorates the birth of the celebrated doctor and Republican Party founder in 1857.

Fiestas Tradicionales de Santiago Apóstol Last week in July. The most vigorous celebration of St James' Day (July 25) takes place in Loíza (see p.88).

September

Día del Trabajo (Labor Day) first Monday in September (P). US tradition that started in the 1880s as a holiday for workers.

October

Día del Descubrimiento de América (Columbus Day) second Monday in October (P). Commemorates the arrival of Columbus in the New World on October 12, 1492. Celebrated with pride in Puerto Rico, but not in other parts of Latin America, where it's known as Día de la Raza (Day of the People).

November

Día del Veterano (Veteran's Day) November 11 (P). Federal holiday that honours military veterans, held on the anniversary of the armistice that ended World War I.
Día del Descubrimiento de Puerto Rico (Discovery of Puerto Rico Day) November 19 (P). Remembers the "discovery" of the island by Columbus in 1493.
Thanksgiving Fourth Thursday in November (P). US federal holiday to commemorate the Pilgrim Fathers' survival in 1623.

December

Encendido Navideño December 1. Marks the beginning of the Christmas season, with celebrations to light Christmas trees.
Las Mañanitas Ponce, December 12. Major religious procession to honour the patron saint of the city, Nuestra Señora de la Guadalupe.
Navidad Christmas Day, December 25 (P). Puerto Rican Christmas dinner (usually featuring *lechón*, roast pork) is typically served on Christmas Eve, followed by Midnight Mass – presents are exchanged on Christmas Day.
Festival de las Máscaras (Mask Festival) Hatillo, December 26–28. Originally commemorating King Herod's attempt to kill baby Jesus by ordering the murder of all firstborn sons. The men of the town wear florid masks and costumes to collect money (with as many pranks as possible) for local churches or charities.

Sports and outdoor activities

Watersports rule supreme in Puerto Rico, with swimming and surfing the most popular activities. The coral-smothered coastline is home to some of the Caribbean's best diving and snorkelling, while the trade winds that pummel the north and east coast make for some magnificent windsurfing. The island's rugged interior, great for hiking, is a potential gold mine for all types of adventure sports. Specialist operators have started to exploit the densely forested slopes and mountains, with canyoning, caving, kayaking and whitewater rafting all on offer.

Cycling and mountain biking

Given its hilly terrain, it's surprising Puerto Rico hasn't developed more of a **mountain biking** scene, but thanks to the Comisión Mountain Bike de Puerto Rico (Puerto Rican Mountain Bike Commission, an independent biking organization; Ⓦwww.cmtbpr.org) and a handful of hardcore enthusiasts, the sport is starting to take off. **Hacienda Carabalí** (☎787/889-5820, Ⓦwww.haciendacarabali puertorico.com) at PR-992 km 3 is a good place to start, a ranch near El Yunque offering a choice of four trails through the rainforest, helmets and instruction provided ($40/hr). The trails feature exhilarating downhill courses, some technical rock gardens and plenty of jumps and berms. Other easily accessible trails can be found in the **Guánica dry forest** (p.226), **Bosque Estatal de Cambalache** (p.151) and along the more sedate **Cabo Rojo Refuge Bike Trail** (p.200), though in all cases you'll need to bring bikes from elsewhere. Check out Ⓦwww.dirtworld .com or www.singletracks.com for a full listing of tracks or rental outlets, or contact Puerto Rico's **International Mountain Biking Association** (Ⓦwww.imba.com).

Touring the island by bike is a bleak prospect, mainly because of the volume of traffic, though things are better in the mountains and parts of the southwest. **Vieques** and **Culebra** are far nicer and safer areas to explore by bike, with plenty of places willing to rent (see p.137 & p.148).

Diving and snorkelling

For the best **snorkelling**, aim for **Culebra** and **Vieques**, or take a charter out of Fajardo (see p.110) to reach the more secluded cays of **La Cordillera**. Though it's theoretically possible to snorkel almost anywhere along the coast of Puerto Rico, the power of the surf in winter, the pollution and the large number of silt-carrying rivers flowing into the sea year-round make much of it inaccessible or unremarkable – beaches in the Porta del Sol are slightly better, but in general the cays offshore offer the brightest coral and fish life.

Divers should also head for Culebra (p.130), with the other major diving highlights being **La Pared** (the spectacular wall off La Parguera, p.206), **Isla de Mona** (p.196) and **Isla Desecheo** (p.184) on the west coast. Mona is best appreciated by taking a multi-day excursion planned long in advance – the waters here are unbelievably clear and teeming with exotic marine life.

Fishing

Puerto Rico has been a light tackle and deep-sea **fishing** destination for years, especially known for its **tarpon** and **blue marlin**: the north coast is known as "blue marlin alley" thanks to the hordes of migrating fish that pass near its shores, especially in the summer, and the island plays host to an **International Billfish Tournament** (Ⓦwww.sanjuaninternational .com) each year. Fishing is excellent year-round, but winter (Oct–March) is the best time for dolphinfish (*mahi-mahi* or *dorado*), wahoo, white marlin, yellowfin tuna and the occasional sawfish and sailfish. Tarpon and **snook** thrive in the shallower waters of the island's lagoons and bays, and make easier targets from smaller boats.

Charters are available from San Juan and the major resort areas: Culebra, Vieques, Fajardo, Palmas del Mar and all the west coast towns; see relevant chapters for details. You can expect to pay around $500 for a half-day, and up to $900 for full-day excursions.

Golf

Puerto Rico is justly regarded as the **golf capital of the Caribbean**, with 23 highly acclaimed courses designed by international stars Robert Trent Jones Jr, Jack Nicklaus, Gary Player and Arthur Hills, as well as the most successful Puerto Rican player, **Juan "Chi-Chi" Rodríguez**, who won eight titles on the PGA Tour between 1963 and 1979. Most of the courses are concentrated in Dorado or along the east coast, usually as part of luxury resorts such as *Palmas del Mar* (see p.114), which offers one of the toughest courses in the world. Day rates are expensive ($100–160), but considering the standard of the courses, not a bad deal. Renting a set of clubs will set you back at least $60.

Hang gliding and skydiving

Xtreme Divers (☎787/852-5757, ⊛www .xtremedivers.com) is a **skydiving** school based at Humacao regional airport, offering parachute jumps for beginners (with forty seconds of freefall) during the first two weeks of every month: tandem jumps for up to four people are $210 per person. The maximum body weight permissible is 240lb (17 stone or 109kg), and jumpers must be 18 years of age. To try **hang gliding**, contact Team Spirit Hang Gliding (☎787/850-0508, ⊛www.teamspirithang gliding.com), based southwest of El Yunque (see p.100).

Hiking

Contrary to the widely held images of sea and sand, much of Puerto Rico is covered by **tropical wilderness** that offers some of the Caribbean's most scintillating **hiking** possibilities, enhanced by hundreds of tropical birds, scurrying green lizards and a chorus of chirping *coquis* (frogs). The most accessible reserve is **El Yunque National Forest** (see p.93), managed by the US Forest Service and laced with well-maintained trails: highlights include the trek up El Yunque itself and the tougher climb up El Toro.

Elsewhere on the island, the DRNA maintains *reservas forestales* or **forest reserves**, also latticed with trails in varying states of upkeep. **Toro Negro** (see p.247), which sits astride the Central Cordillera, is the most rewarding, close by the island's highest peak, **Cerro de Punta** (1338m), but you'll find the best-maintained trails in the **Bosque Estatal de Guajataca** (p.159) and within the very different landscapes of the **Guánica dry forest** (p.226). One hike that you should attempt only with a guide is the spellbinding traverse of the **Cañon de San Cristóbal** (see p.243).

In all cases elevations are not high, removing the need for serious advance preparation or above-average fitness. Your biggest problems are likely to be rain and cloud cover, and **the lack of signs**: always plan your route in advance, with local maps if possible, and avoid the mountains altogether during heavy rain.

Horseriding

Puerto Rico has long attracted equestrians for the chance to ride its unique Paso Fino **horses** (see p.115), lauded for their imperious, luxuriously smooth walk. Several ranches offer guided trail rides, one of the best being **Rancho Buena Vista** on the east coast (see p.114), which offers excursions from $45 for one hour.

Kayaking

Kayaking is often the best way to experience the raw beauty of the Puerto Rican coastline – the island's **bioluminescent bays** are especially magical by kayak. You can also explore the tangled mangrove lagoons of La Parguera (p.204) and Guánica (p.226), while the pristine waters and cays off Culebra (p.142) are ideal for leisurely paddling.

Sailing

The east coast of Puerto Rico is a **sailing** paradise, with massive marinas such as **Puerto del Rey** (see p.111) and **Villa**

Marina (see p.111) home to charter yachts that ply the waters all the way to the Virgin Islands. You'll also find operators in Culebra, Vieques and in all the major southwestern resorts, but although the south and west coasts are also popular with yacht owners, unless you have your own boat it can be hard to get on the water, and it's unusual to find anywhere in Puerto Rico that rents single- or two-person boats to tourists.

Surfing

Puerto Rico is the Caribbean version of Hawaii, and surfers have been coming here since the 1960s to enjoy some of the hardest and most consistent waves in the Americas. After the World Championships were hosted at **Rincón** in 1968, the island was firmly established on the international **surf** circuit. Rincón (see p.177) is still at the heart of the Puerto Rican surf world, though the beaches around Aguadilla on the **northwest coast** (see p.171) offer just as much action, while the scene in **San Juan** (p.64) is developed and easy to get into. You'll also find plenty of great beaches along the **north coast** (Jobos, p.171), around **Luquillo** (p.104), and off **PR-901** (see p.116) in the east; the calmer, Caribbean south coast doesn't see as many waves. The best time to surf is during the winter (Oct–Feb), when northerly swells slam into Puerto Rico.

Abseiling, canyoning and caving

The overgrown gorges and caves around **Parque de las Cavernas del Río Camuy** (p.162) are prime territory for abseiling, caving and canyoning. More adventures await within the forests of the Central Cordillera and the **Bosque Estatal de Toro Negro** (p.247). Unless you have lots of experience, you're better off working with established companies to make the most of these sites – access is often difficult and conditions can be precarious. See individual chapters for operators.

Windsurfing

Since the **windsurfing** World Cup was held here in 1989, the local scene has grown rapidly, centred on the San Juan beaches of Ocean Park and Isla Verde – the shops here are the best places to get oriented (see p.70). Other hot spots are northwest beaches such as Playa Crash Boat (p.175) and Jobos (see p.171), while beginners are better off at *El Conquistador* (p.107), or the calmer west coast waters around La Parguera (p.204) and Boquerón (p.197). Check out Ⓦwww.windsurfingpr.com before you go.

Spectator sports

The most popular spectator sports in Puerto Rico are American imports: **baseball**, **basketball** and **boxing**. **Cockfighting** and **horseracing** hark back to the island's Spanish roots, and remain important elements of island culture.

Baseball

Puerto Rico's national sport is **baseball**, and the island has produced some of the US mainland's greatest ever stars, including **Roberto Clemente**.

Baseball was introduced to the island with the arrival of the Americans in 1898, and though the sport is played fanatically at school and amateur levels, Puerto Rico's **professional league** has struggled in recent years, with low crowd attendance and reduced income leading to the **cancellation** of the 2007–2008 season (games are played over the winter to avoid overlap with the US Major Leagues). In 2008 the league resumed and currently features five teams: Criollos de Caguas, Gigantes de Carolina, Indios de Mayagüez, Leones de Ponce and Senadores de San Juan. Champions normally take part in the **Caribbean Series** in February to face teams from Venezuela, Mexico and the Dominican Republic.

Games can be an entertaining and cheap way to see some explosive talent close up. **Ballparks** are generally modern, with covered seating and parking (small fee charged). The upper seats are unreserved; the lower *palcos* cost more. **Ticket prices** have varied wildly over the years, depending on the team and importance of the game (sometimes reaching as high as $85), but the cheapest should be around $10.

Basketball

Basketball is played avidly on the island, with the Puerto Rican national squad becoming only the second team in history to defeat the US "Dream Team", at the 2004 Athens Olympics. The national league (Baloncesto Superior Nacional; @www.bsnpr.com) comprises ten teams, with San Juan's Cangrejeros de Santurce playing well-attended games at the Coliseo de Puerto Rico (@www.coliseodepuertorico.com) in Hato Rey (in San Juan), which can be reached via the Tren Urbano. Tickets range from $6 to $25. The Vaqueros de Bayamón and Atléticos de San Germán are the all-time championship leaders (14 each), and the Ponce Leones are also worth checking out.

Boxing

Puerto Rico has an impressive history of championship **boxing**: **Héctor Camacho** (who hails from Bayamón) held several world championship titles in the 1980s and 1990s, while **Félix Trinidad** (from Cupey Alto) was the world welterweight and then middleweight champion between 1993 and 2001. However, it's rare to see major fights on the island, as most of the action takes place on the mainland (screened to massive audiences via cable TV).

Football (soccer)

Football (*fútbol*), or soccer, is slowly catching on in Puerto Rico, with its main professional team, the **Puerto Rico Islanders** (@www.puertoricoislandersfc.com), founded in 2003. The Islanders are a member of the North American Soccer League, and currently play between April and September at Juan Ramón Loubriel Stadium in Bayamón, near Deportivo Tren Urbano station. For tickets, check online agents @www.tcpr.com or www.ticketpop.com.

The domestic Puerto Rico Soccer League or PRSL (@www.prsoccer.org) was established in 2008 and now has nine teams in its first division with big plans to expand.

Cockfighting

Introduced to Puerto Rico in around 1770, **cockfighting** (*peleas de gallos*) was legalized in 1933 and remains the island's most controversial pastime, regularly condemned by animal rights activists all over the world. If you have the stomach, cockfights offer a vivid insight into traditional Puerto Rican culture and can be atmospheric, raucous affairs – for the best introduction check out the **Club Gallístico de Puerto Rico** in Isla Verde (p.65).

Despite regulations limiting time spent in the pit, fights should be strictly avoided by animal lovers: contests are extremely vicious, with beaks used to literally peck the opponent's head into a bloody mess. Fights stop when one of the birds is too exhausted to continue, and watching them stagger around for one last desperate attack can be disturbing. Even worse, fights sometimes end quickly when a rooster makes a strategic or "lucky" hit, cutting nerves to its opponent's brain. When this happens the hapless victim loses all control of its movements, lying frozen on the ground, running around in circles or even cartwheeling around the pit. Nevertheless, supporters defend the sport as a key aspect of Puerto Rican culture.

Horseracing

The only **racecourse** in Puerto Rico is the Hipódromo Camarero, in Canóvanas at PR-3 km 15.3, 22km east of San Juan. The atmosphere can be electric during races, which take place on Monday, Wednesday, Friday, Saturday and Sunday from 3pm, usually wrapping up by 6 or 7pm. The **Clásico del Caribe**, the Caribbean's richest race, is held here every December. **Gambling** on all races is legal and big business on the island.

Culture and etiquette

Puerto Rico is a curious blend of Spanish tradition, dynamic criollo culture and recent Americanization. Most Puerto Ricans are broadly familiar with mainland US culture and behaviour, and you are unlikely to face the cultural misunderstandings that sometimes occur, for example, in rural parts of Mexico or South America.

Vestiges of the island's conservative roots do remain, however, and it pays to maintain a degree of friendly formality when meeting people for the first time – being polite and courteous is always a good idea. When it comes to bars and restaurants (unless on the beach), Puerto Ricans tend to dress up, and men with shirt-tails hanging out are regarded as a bit scruffy. Many restaurants and casinos have **dress codes**, although women tend to be treated more leniently than men. The **Catholic Church** remains very important, so always be respectful when wandering around churches, especially during Mass. Locals are generally tolerant of foreign visitors and will only approach you if you are making lots of noise, but it's best to dress conservatively (no shorts or bare shoulders).

Above all, Puerto Ricans are extremely sociable, family-oriented and friendly people. As a traveller, especially if you stay within the main tourist zones, that last quality may not always be apparent, but attempting to speak a little **Spanish** will go a long way. One of the things that makes Puerto Rico such an easy place to visit is the abundance of English-speakers – in fact, the vast majority of Puerto Ricans can understand basic English, though only those in the tourist zones speak it every day. Nevertheless, language is an important element of Puerto Rican identity, so trying to communicate in Spanish will yield far better results than assuming that a person understands *inglés* – you might end up speaking English anyway, but your efforts will still be appreciated. See p.285 for more on language.

Gay and lesbian travellers

Puerto Rico is something of a trailblazer for **gay rights** in Latin America, making it a burgeoning holiday destination for gay travellers, especially the Condado and Santurce areas of San Juan (see p.76). San Juan's **gay pride** events run for a week in June, with parties, fashion shows and art exhibitions culminating in a parade through Condado attended by thousands: the annual gay pride parade in Boquerón also attracts huge crowds.

Other parts of the island, too, are refreshingly open-minded when it comes to gay travellers. In areas such as El Yunque, Vieques, Fajardo and Boquerón, where many guesthouses are run by liberal US expats and easy-going locals, gay couples are welcome. You can even find a list of gay-friendly hotels at Ⓦpuertoricosmall hotels.com. For more information visit the **Puerto Rico Rainbow Foundation** website (Ⓦwww.orgulloboricua.net) and the directory at Ⓦwww.gaysanjuan.com to get the latest on what's going on. For info on **Vieques**, visit Ⓦwww.gayvieques.net.

Women travellers

Women travelling alone are perfectly safe in Puerto Rico, and although gender roles remain traditional, the island has a strong record of fighting sexual discrimination. In fact, Puerto Rican women often display a degree of self-confidence and independence that many overseas female visitors find liberating. **Machismo** still exists, but it's not as prevalent as in other Latin American nations, and in the cities you'll see plenty of single women out and about – the worst you'll get is the odd catcall or beep of a horn. As always, things are a little more conservative in rural areas, but if anything, locals tend to be overprotective rather than critical of single women travellers. As anywhere, the usual **precautions** apply;

take extra care when out in the evening and, if solo, avoid local bars late at night; take reputable taxis to get around San Juan; and avoid empty streets and deserted beaches if you're on your own.

Smoking

In March 2007 smoking was **banned** in all restaurants, bars and casinos in Puerto Rico. Smoking on terraces or in outdoor bars and in cars carrying children under 13 is also prohibited, making this the Caribbean's most stringent anti-smoking law by far. On-the-spot fines start at $250 for the first offence, rising to $500 and $2000 thereafter.

Tipping

Given Puerto Rico's ties with the US, it's no surprise that **tipping** is an important part of life on the island and often an important source of income, especially for waiting staff in **San Juan** restaurants, where a tip of fifteen to twenty percent is expected – unless you've had unusually bad service, anything less will be received very poorly. In local *cocinas* or bars in smaller towns and villages tips are not so common – never tip in fast-food or self-serve buffet restaurants. Porters generally expect $1 per bag, and maids $1–2 per day in posh hotels (ask the reception at other places, and leave the money in the room when you check out). Taxis get ten to fifteen percent, though this isn't as rigorously adhered to.

Travel essentials

Costs

Prices in Puerto Rico tend to be similar to the US, so for non-US citizens much depends on the exchange rate: while the US dollar remains relatively low, Puerto Rico will stay much more affordable than some of the glamorous resort islands in the eastern Caribbean.

Though it's hard to survive comfortably in San Juan on less than $80 a day, it is possible if you self-cater, take buses everywhere and stay in the cheapest hotels – in theory, you'd find this sort of budget easier outside the city, but without a car (which will add at least $50 per day), your options are extremely limited. You can tour the island with careful planning for $100–150 per day, and in style for over $200. Depending on the season, comfortable mid-range **accommodation** in Puerto Rico can cost anything from $80–$250, but you should be able to snag comfortable two- to three-star rooms from $75–150. **Eating out** can be pricey: dinners at restaurants, especially in the cities, can be very expensive, though you should be able to find something in the $20–30 range. Lunch is much cheaper (under $20) and breakfast should be under $10. You can pick up local snack food for a few dollars at any time, comparable in price (and fat quotient) to US fast food, which is likewise available everywhere. Puerto Rico does apply a **sales tax** (see p.41) and **tipping** in restaurants and at hotels is standard practice (see above).

Admission prices to most museums and tourist sights are usually quite reasonable; government-run venues are typically **free**, while the cost of privately operated attractions rarely tops $10. Discounts are usually given to children, seniors and students. Activities such as **diving** will add another $80–100 per day.

Crime and personal safety

Despite worrying **crime statistics** and highly publicized carjackings, tourists rarely run into trouble in Puerto Rico. On the contrary, most of the island is extremely **safe**, with petty theft (especially off the beaches) an occasional problem and even the mean streets of San Juan posing little danger if you stick to the main tourist zones and exercise common sense. On paper, however, it doesn't look good. Puerto Rico's **homicide rate in 2010** (22.5 per 100,000 people) is much higher than any state on the US mainland outside Washington DC, and robberies and murders rose between 2008 and 2010.

Puerto Rico's main problem is **drugs**: the island has become one of the most important transshipment points to the US mainland for the Colombian cocaine cartels, which typically smuggle the product across from the Dominican Republic. Gun crime is overwhelmingly linked to the drug trade, with police attributing 75 percent of all murders to wars between gangs (the remainder are mostly a result of domestic disputes). Visitors are rarely affected by any of this: crime is concentrated in housing projects well away from tourist zones (which are in any case heavily policed), and if you exercise caution at night you should have no problems. In other areas Puerto Rico has made good progress in stemming petty crime in recent years, and most of the scare stories you might hear relate to the 1990s. For any **emergency**, call ☎911.

Electricity

The **electrical current** in Puerto Rico is 110 volts, exactly the same as the continental US and Canada, and outlets take the same two-prong plugs.

Entry requirements

Puerto Rico is a commonwealth of the US, so **US citizens** do not need a passport to enter the country: all you need is some form of official government-issued picture ID (a current driver's licence is fine).

For everyone else, the passport and visa requirements for entering Puerto Rico are the same as for **entering the US**. Note however, that there is no passport control on flights between the US mainland and Puerto Rico – non-US citizens will have cleared immigration upon arrival in the US. Citizens of 27 countries including Australia,

Ireland, New Zealand and the UK are granted **visa-free entry** (known as visa waivers) to the US for up to ninety days. You will, however, need to obtain **Electronic System for Travel Authorization** (ESTA) online before you fly (at ⓦhttps://esta.cbp .dhs.gov/esta), which involves completing a basic immigration form in advance, on the computer. There is a processing fee of $4, and a further $10 authorization fee once the ESTA has been approved (all paid via credit card online). Once given, authorizations are valid for multiple entries into the US for around two years – it's recommended that you submit an ESTA application as soon as you begin making travel plans (in most cases the ESTA will be granted immediately, but it can sometimes take up to 72hr to get a response).

You'll also need to present a machine-readable passport and a completed visa waiver form (I-94W) to Immigration upon arrival; the latter will be provided by your airline (it's the green one, not the white one). Canadians now require a passport to cross the border, but can travel in the US or Puerto Rico for up to 6 months without a visa. For visa information, visit ⓦwww.travel.state .gov. For **customs** information, visit ⓦwww .cbp.gov. South Africans and other nationalities not eligible for ESTA must apply for a tourist visa at their nearest US embassy.

Health

As one of the Caribbean's most developed destinations, Puerto Rico doesn't present any significant **health** risks for foreign travellers and residents – health care is on a par with the mainland US, and taking the usual precautions will be more than enough to stay healthy. For **emergencies** call ☎911.

Medical facilities in the big cities are of a high standard, although English-language abilities vary among staff, so if you don't speak Spanish you may need the help of someone who does – doctors will almost certainly speak English, however. There are **hospitals** and clinics in most towns: see relevant chapters for details, or call the Departamento de Salud (Health Department; ☎787/766-1616) to find the closest.

Puerto Rico's health system was **privatized** in the 1990s and works in a similar way to the US system: visitors must pay for health care on the spot and claim back the costs from their insurance providers later. Costs vary widely, ranging from $300 upwards for treatment in A&E, to less than $60 to see a local doctor.

There are **pharmacies** (*farmacias*) every-where, and US chain Walgreens (Ⓦwww .walgreens.com) has a major presence, with many stores in the cities open 24 hours.

Health risks

Your biggest health risk in Puerto Rico is likely to be **sunburn** or **dehydration**, though minor stomach upsets are also possible, with **travellers' diarrhoea** the most common ailment. Serious cases may need antibiotics, but most bouts pass within 24 hours after drinking plenty of clean water and avoiding solids. Prevention is key: avoid unpeeled fruits or uncooked vegetables, unpasteurized milk and food that looks as if it's been left out in the sun. If you are prone to stomach upsets, avoid food from street vendors, *kioscos* and raw seafood, and drink bottled or purified water. It's always a good idea to keep up with **hepatitis A**, **typhoid** and **tetanus** shots before you travel, though these diseases are not common in Puerto Rico.

Mosquitoes can be a problem in parts of Puerto Rico, and though there is no malaria, **dengue fever** – a mosquito-borne viral disease whose symptoms are similar to malaria – does occasionally appear. Dengue fever has no cure, but the illness is rarely life-threatening to adults and the flu-like symptoms usually subside after several days of rest; seniors and young children are most at risk.

The only way to prevent dengue fever is to **avoid being bitten** by mosquitoes. The *aedes aegypti* mosquitoes that transmit dengue bite day and night, so you should use insect-avoidance measures at all times. Cover exposed skin with **insect repellent** containing 20–35 percent DEET, wear loose-fitting, long sleeves and trousers, and avoid dark colours. At night, make sure your room is sealed from the outside or has **mosquito nets**. For more information about dengue, visit the Centers for Disease Control and Prevention website at Ⓦwww.cdc.gov.

Insurance

It's important to take out an **insurance policy** before travelling to Puerto Rico, as much to cover against theft as illness and accidental injury. However, it's worth checking whether you are already covered: some all-risks home insurance policies may cover your possessions when overseas, and many private medical schemes include cover when abroad – this is especially true for US visitors. Given the likelihood that you'll find yourself **driving** in Puerto Rico, you should make sure this is covered as well.

Internet

Puerto Rico is geared up for travellers who bring their own **laptop computers**, with plenty of small hotels, restaurants and coffee-shop chains such as Starbucks offering free **wi-fi** connections. Accessing the **internet** can be frustrating otherwise, as internet cafés are rare and only the top hotels tend to have business centres or computer rooms where you can surf the net.

Rough Guides travel insurance

Rough Guides has teamed up with WorldNomads.com to offer great **travel insurance** deals. Policies are available to residents of over 150 countries, with cover for a wide range of **adventure sports**, 24hr emergency assistance, high levels of medical and evacuation cover and a stream of **travel safety information**. Roughguides.com users can take advantage of their policies online 24/7, from anywhere in the world – even if you're already travelling. And since plans often change when you're on the road, you can extend your policy and even claim online. Roughguides.com users who buy travel insurance with WorldNomads.com can also leave a positive footprint and donate to a community development project. For more information go to Ⓦ**www.roughguides.com/shop**.

The best strategy for those without a laptop is to locate the nearest **public library** (*biblioteca pública*), which increasingly offer **free internet** access. The only downside is that most are closed in the evenings, and some impose time limits on computer usage – students are often given priority.

Laundry

Most large hotels in Puerto Rico provide a **laundry service**, but in almost every town you can find *lavanderías* (laundromats) that are far cheaper, typically charging $2 for 8–9kg. You'll also find self-service coin laundries that take quarters, typically requiring $1.50 per load.

Mail

Mail in Puerto Rico is managed by the **US Postal Service**, with post offices, stamps and prices identical to those in the US, and most post office workers speaking at least some English. Service to the mainland is fairly reliable, though posting letters and cards back to Europe can take considerably longer, up to two or three weeks in some cases. You can find post offices in almost every town, usually open Monday to Friday 8am to 4 or 5pm, and some on Saturday mornings.

Money

Puerto Rico's currency is the **US dollar**, usually written $ (but sometimes referred to as the *peso* locally, and made up of 100 cents. Notes come in $1, $5, $10, $20, $50 and $100, while coins comprise 1¢ (penny, *chavo* or *perrita* in Spanish), 5¢ (nickel, *vellon* or *ficha*), 10¢ (dime) and 25¢ (quarter or *peseta*). You might also see $1 coins. For current exchange rates, check ⓦ www.xe.com.

Almost all cities and towns have **ATMs** (*cajeros automaticos*), from which travellers can withdraw funds using bank **debit cards** or **credit cards** – this is by far the most convenient and safe method of obtaining cash for daily expenses. Though some ATMs are only for domestic account-holders, many of them take Visa, MasterCard, Accel, Cirrus, Interlink, Plus and Star. The most common ATMs are those of **Banco Popular**. Banking hours are normally Monday to Friday 9am–4pm, while some

branches open Saturday mornings (all Citibank branches open Mon–Fri 8.30am–5pm, Sat till 12.30pm).

Most **hotels** accept **credit card** payment, with Visa and MasterCard the most widely accepted brands. American Express and Diners Club also are fairly commonly recognized. In the cities, stores may accept debit cards, but in many rural areas they won't.

Other than at the international airports, **moneychangers** are rare in Puerto Rico, and if you need to exchange foreign currency you'll have to do so at Banco Popular, the only one with a foreign exchange department (call ☎787/722-3240 for the nearest branch). **Travellers' cheques** are becoming increasingly outmoded in Puerto Rico and are probably more trouble than they're worth if the island is your only destination. US dollar cheques are the easiest to cash for obvious reasons.

Opening hours

Business hours are usually 8.30am or 9am to 5pm, Monday to Friday. Shops are generally open 9am–6pm, closing later on Friday and often all day on Sunday, especially in rural areas. Government offices open 8.30am–4.30pm: in most towns this means that museums and galleries also open at these times on weekdays, closing Sunday and usually Saturday. Conversely, privately owned attractions, and most of the museums and galleries in San Juan, are open weekends, closing Mondays and sometimes Tuesday. For a list of public holidays and festivals, see p.30.

Phones

If you have a **US mobile phone**, it should work as normal in Puerto Rico: in fact, most companies treat the island as part of their domestic network and you'll be charged accordingly. For visitors from other regions, Claro GSM (ⓦ www.clarotodo.com) offers GSM roaming agreements with overseas companies – check with your provider before you go (you'll need an unlocked 3G or tri-band phone that accepts the 850 and 1900 MHz frequencies). Companies such as InTouch SmartCards (ⓦ intouchsmart cards.com) sell SIM cards to use in Puerto

Calling home from abroad

For the US and Canada, just dial 1 followed by the area code and the number, if you're using a land line; for mobile phones you usually don't need to dial 1 (just start with the area code). For other countries, the international access code is 011. Note that the initial zero is omitted from the area code when dialling numbers in the UK, Ireland, Australia and New Zealand from abroad.

Australia 011 + 61 + area code.
New Zealand 011 + 64 + area code.
Republic of Ireland 011 + 353 + area code.
South Africa 011 + 27 + area code.
UK 011 + 44 + area code.

Rico for $59.99, but it's best to arrange this in advance.

Otherwise you can **rent mobile phones** via Phonerental (US ☎1-800/335-3705, international ☎+1-619-446-6980, ⊛www.phonerentalusa.com) for $1.50 per day. You get charged $1.69 per minute for incoming and $1.89 for all local and national outgoing calls. Triptel (☎877/874-7835, ⊛www.triptel.com) offers a similar service with GSM phones.

Within Puerto Rico, dial ☎411 for **directory information** (call ☎787/555-1212 from overseas). To call Puerto Rico from **overseas**, dial your international access code, then 1 (USA country code), then the Puerto Rico area code (787 or, less commonly, 939), then the phone number. Note that you always dial the prefix, even when calling within the island (though some mobile numbers have different codes).

Tax

Puerto Rico has a 5.5 percent **sales tax** (payable on tours and all food and drink). Municipalities have the option of imposing an additional 1.5 percent. Price tags in shops and entry fees at museums do not include these taxes, so the actual price will be at least 5.5 percent higher. For **hotel taxes**, see p.26.

Time

Puerto Rico is four hours behind GMT throughout the year, which means that in summer (March 11 to Nov 4) it's the same as US Eastern Standard Time (New York City, Miami), as Daylight Saving is not observed, and five hours behind BST (in the winter it's one hour ahead of the US east coast). GMT is five hours ahead of US Eastern Standard Time and ten hours behind Australian Eastern Standard Time. For the exact time when in Puerto Rico, call ☎787/728-9595.

Tourist information, websites and maps

The **Puerto Rico Tourist Company** (⊛seepuertorico.com and www.topuertorico.org) has made a concerted effort in recent years to promote the island internationally, but their focus (and their primary market) remains the US. See below for international offices.

In Puerto Rico itself, the best tourist information centres are in San Juan. The PRTC also operates offices at Aguadilla airport, Ponce, Vieques and Culebra, but **local municipalities** otherwise have the responsibility to promote tourism in their own areas; as a last resort, try visiting the local city hall (alcaldía) on weekdays 8am–4pm. The larger tourist offices should have copies of Qué Pasa! (⊛www.casiano.com/quepasa/default.html), a glossy bimonthly magazine that contains a calendar of events, travel-related feature stories and more listings. Other publications include the annual Places to Go (⊛www.enjoypuertorico.com) and Bienvenidos (the annual magazine of the Hotel & Tourism Association), all available for free at hotels and tourist offices. If you can read Spanish you should also check out the **Instituto de Cultura Puertorriqueña** website (⊛www.icp.gobierno.pr), a fount of information on museums, art centres and historic sites.

Puerto Rico tourist offices overseas

Canada 6-295 Queen St East, Suite 465, Brampton, Ontario ☎416/368-2680.
USA 135 W 50th St, 22/F, New York ☎212/586-6262; 3575 W Cahuenga Blvd, Suite 405, Los Angeles, CA 90068 ☎323/874-5991.

Maps

This guide aside, it's hard to find decent **maps** of Puerto Rico. Metro Data (⊛www .metropr.com) produces *Guía Metro*; $16.95, a handy booklet of maps covering every municipality on the island, usually available in pharmacies and bookstores in San Juan, and *Todo Puerto Rico*, with a bit more detail ($26.95). Serious hikers should order topographic maps from the US Geological Survey (⊛www.usgs.gov), while everyone else should be satisfied with National Geographic's detailed foldout map of El Yunque ($9.95). Rand McNally and International Travel Maps produce reasonable foldout maps of the whole island (around $10).

Travellers with disabilities

Puerto Rico prides itself on being one of the most welcoming islands in the Caribbean for **disabled travellers**, and US wheelchair access laws apply here to public buildings and transport – this means city buses, not private *públicos*. All public beaches, museums and galleries are also subject to the **Americans with Disabilities Act**, though again, in practice smaller places tend to have limited accessibility. Larger **hotels** and resorts will have special rooms for disabled guests, but many of the smaller hotels are not yet compliant. Most car parks have special spaces for the disabled.

Despite this, travelling around the island remains tough for many disabled travellers, with even the narrow, steep and generally crowded streets of **Old San Juan** hard work for wheelchair-users. The easiest option for the latter is to check into a larger hotel with spacious disabled rooms, such as the *Marriott Resort* in Condado (see p.54), and explore the island and city with **Rico Sun Tours** (☎787/722-2080, ⊛www.ricosun tours.com), one of the few companies to operate tour vans with wheelchair lifts at the back.

Three noteworthy highlights are a **wheelchair accessible trail** in El Yunque, the Bacardi Distillery, which is fully accessible and finally, the wonderful **Mar Sin Barreras** (Sea Without Barriers; daily 8.30am–5pm) at the **Balneario de Luquillo** (see p.104). This specially constructed ramp, with equipment and staff to help disabled swimmers access the crystal-clear waters off the beach, is the one attraction that thrills every wheelchair-user who visits the island. Similar facilities are available at the **Balneario de Boquerón** (see p.197). For more information, contact the Ombudsman for Persons with Disabilities (☎787/725-2333, ⊛www.oppi.gobierno.pr).

Travelling with children

Puerto Rican culture is very family-oriented, and **travelling with children** presents few problems. Formula, nappies and medication are all easily available and most restaurants and **hotels** welcome youngsters – exceptions are usually confined to expensive or romantic hotels and are noted in the text. Though it's extremely rare to see nappy-changing facilities, it's perfectly acceptable to do as the locals do and change nappies wherever you can; breast-feeding in public is also fine, though you should try to be as discreet as possible. Unless you're staying in one of the large resorts, finding a babysitter will be difficult, however. In general, **resorts** are the best places to find children's activities, and all of them have excellent pools.

With a profusion of **beaches**, Puerto Rico is a fun destination for families, and older kids will enjoy the **snorkelling** and **swimming**: the ideal place to start surfing is Playa de Jobos on the north coast (see p.171). The Río Camuy caves (see p.162), Arecibo Lighthouse (p.157) and Observatorio de Arecibo (see p.161) make popular day-trips in this part of the island.

In San Juan, the Museo del Niño (see p.62) caters specifically to children, but El Morro (see p.59) is also lots of fun, and you can **fly kites** on the grassy *campo* just outside.

In Mayagüez, the **zoo** (p.190) is worth visiting, while Aguadilla has Las Cascadas Water Park, PR-2 km 126.5 ($15.95, children $13.95) and the Aguadilla Ice Skating Arena (daily; $10–13). If it's just too rainy, most malls have **cinemas** where all the Hollywood blockbusters are shown in English.

Guide

Guide

San Juan and around

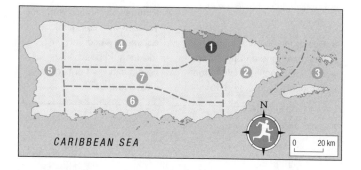

CARIBBEAN SEA

N

0   20 km

CHAPTER 1 # Highlights

* **Old San Juan** Wander the enchanting streets of the old town, crammed with elegant colonial architecture, absorbing museums and the best restaurants on the island. See p.55

* **El Morro** Explore one of the greatest Spanish forts in the New World, a vast bulk of stone guarding San Juan Bay. See p.59

* **Cementerio Santa María Magdalena de Pazzis** This romantic nineteenth-century cemetery is one of the most captivating sights in the city. See p.59

* **Beach life** Swim, surf or lounge around on San Juan's enticing beaches – Isla Verde is the most fun. See p.66

* **Sipping a piña colada** Tropical, glamorous and a symbol of the high life, this celebrated cocktail is said to have been invented in San Juan in the 1950s. See p.75

* **Nuyorican Café** Groove to live salsa or take Latin dance lessons at this small but vibrant club. See p.79

* **Casa Bacardi** The "cathedral of rum" provides an illuminating introduction to the Caribbean's favourite drink. See p.84

* **Piñones** Cycle, surf and stuff yourself with lip-smacking *cocina en kiosco* at this languid beachside community, just outside the city. See p.87

▲ San Juan's Cementerio Santa María Magdalena de Pazzis

San Juan and around

N othing else in the Caribbean quite compares to **SAN JUAN**, the frenetic, party-loving capital of Puerto Rico. With around 1.5 million people, Greater San Juan contains over a third of the island's population. It's also one of the largest urban areas in the region, crisscrossed with highways brimming with SUVs and the proud home of the Caribbean's biggest shopping mall, its only subway system and all the other trappings of a modern American metropolis. Indeed, *sanjuaneros* like to compare their city with Miami, rather than more obvious regional peers like Santo Domingo and Havana. But while San Juan owes much to its links with the US mainland, it's the city's **criollo** roots, a rich stew of cultures and races, which provide the real allure.

The historical heart of the city is **Old San Juan**, a seductive blend of Spanish colonial charm, Caribbean languor and modern chic. Its cobbled streets are laced with brightly painted houses and balconies of vivid tropical blooms, with the odd palm tree squashed in between. Get to grips with the island's turbulent history at **El Morro**, the imposing Spanish fortress that juts into San Juan Bay like a giant stone fist. The old **cemetery** nearby offers a more poignant window into the past, the resting place of many of Puerto Rico's most illustrious citizens, while modest but engaging museums such as the **Museo de Las Américas** provide insights into the island's Taíno and African roots. For a city of this size, San Juan's **beaches** are pretty good too and the well-established **surf scene** has plenty to whet the appetite of serious shredders as well as beginners. The best beach is **Isla Verde**, east of the old town, where smart resorts and boutique hotels face a fine strip of sand and clear, turquoise waters.

If you have the time, it's well worth getting beyond the tourist zones and finding out what makes contemporary San Juan tick. The edgier *barrio* of **Santurce**, behind the beaches, has some of the best clubs in the city, plenty of cheap *comida criolla* and a couple of excellent art galleries, the **Museo de Arte** and **Museo de Arte Contemporáneo**. Further south, **Río Piedras** is a laidback campus district with San Juan's most vibrant market, while rural **Piñones** along the coast is where *sanjuaneros* take weekend escapes to party. The historic town of **Caguas** also makes for an enticing day-trip, with a smattering of less-visited museums and galleries. When it comes to food, the city's **restaurants** are the most innovative in the Caribbean, ranging from rustic local diners to stylish temples of fusion cuisine. San Juan is also one of the best places in the world to experience **salsa** and the distinctively Puerto Rican sound of **reggaetón** – ideally with a rum and Coke or **piña colada** in hand.

Some history

In contrast to other areas of Puerto Rico, Greater San Juan seems to have supported a relatively small number of **Taíno** (p.261) settlements and the modern history of the city begins with the arrival of **Juan Ponce de León** in

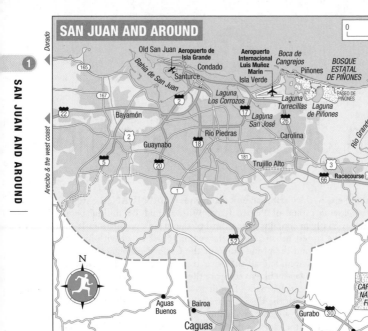

▼ *Ponce*   ▼ *The east coast*

1508. The Spanish conquistador surveyed what today is San Juan Bay and named it Puerto Rico ("Rich Port") before establishing **Caparra** a few miles inland. It didn't take long to realize that laying down roots in such a swampy location was a big mistake. After a prolonged dispute between the settlers and Ponce de León, the colony was moved to today's **Old San Juan** and formally established in 1521. Ponce de León, who never accepted the move, sailed for Florida and died the same year – despite monuments in the city that suggest otherwise, he was not the founder of San Juan. How the name Puerto Rico was switched with "San Juan", the original name of the island, is still a source of debate: the process was probably gradual, but by the mid-eighteenth century the current conventions were firmly established.

As one of the most strategic cities in Spain's vast American empire, San Juan was the constant target of pirates and envious foreign powers. The English attacked in 1595, when **Sir Francis Drake** was rebuffed and again in 1598, when the Earl of Cumberland captured the city for sixty days (see p.264). The Dutch sacked San Juan in 1625, while the British, under **Sir Ralph Abercromby**, were beaten off in 1797 by primarily local militia – a feat that is still the source of immense pride on the island (see p.264).

Despite its capital status, San Juan remained a small city until the twentieth century. Nevertheless, by 1898, when the US took control of the island in the aftermath of the **Spanish–American War** (see p.266), Old San Juan was desperately overcrowded: **Puerta de Tierra** became an overspill area for the city's poor, while **Río Piedras** and **Condado** were absorbed as wealthier suburbs. Under US rule the city was rapidly modernized. **Tourism** developed gradually in the 1920s; boosted by the legalization of **casinos** in 1940, the real boom came in the 1960s, when Condado benefited from the US embargo of Cuba.

After a period of relative decline, the city was given a much-needed face-lift in the mid-1990s and today San Juan receives over a million **cruise-ship passengers** annually, making it one of the busiest cruise ports in the world.

Arrival, orientation and information

The vast majority of visitors to Puerto Rico enter the country through San Juan. Many stagger off cruise ships straight into the old town, but most fly into the modern international airport, further east in Isla Verde.

By air

All international flights and most domestic services arrive at **Aeropuerto Internacional Luis Muñoz Marín**, 14km east of Old San Juan, and just a few minutes' drive from the beach at Isla Verde. The airport hotel (see p.55) is located in concourse D along with a branch of Banco Popular – you'll find **ATMs** all over the airport. The **post office** (Mon–Fri 8am–4pm) is on the lower (arrival) level next to concourse D. The helpful **tourist information centre** (daily 9am–8pm; ☎787/791-1014) is outside concourse C, on the lower level.

Almost every major **car rental** firm operates from the airport, most with 24-hour desks at baggage claim areas. All of them run free shuttle buses from the terminal to their car locations: if the desks are unstaffed, use the courtesy phones to call for a pick-up. See p.22 for a list of rental firms.

Unless your hotel has a shuttle bus or has arranged to pick you up, getting a **taxi** is the most convenient way into the city. Outside the arrival halls, look for the *taxis turísticos* lines. Fares from the airport to the main tourist areas are fixed: Isla Verde is $10, Condado is $15 and Old San Juan is $19. You can also go direct to the ferry terminal in **Fajardo** (for Vieques and Culebra) for a flat rate of $80.

The only useful **city bus** is the C45 (Mon–Sat every 30min, Sun hourly; last bus 5.55pm; $0.75), which stops outside concourse D upper level (departures) before running along Avenida Isla Verde – for anywhere else it's much easier to take a taxi.

A handful of flights from Vieques, Culebra and the US Virgin Islands arrive at **Aeropuerto de Isla Grande**, just across the bay from Puerta de Tierra and 3km from Old San Juan, which has a tiny terminal with a basic café and one ATM. There is no public transport here and though taxis are supposed to meet flights you might end up having to call one – you're better off arranging a pick-up in advance (see taxis p.52). It's just a short ride into Old San Juan or Condado; fares should be around $15.

By bus and by car

Most *públicos* (minibuses and shared taxis) terminate in Río Piedras (see "Moving on" box, p.84) so you'll need to take a taxi or local bus from there to other parts of the city. **Heavy traffic** and **poor signage** in places can make driving around San Juan difficult, though following signs to the airport is relatively straightforward. Try to avoid **rush hour** if you can (Mon–Fri 7–10am & 4–7pm). If you're driving into Old San Juan for the day, aim for a **major car park** such as Paseo Portuario Estacionamiento, on Calle del Recinto Sur (24hr; $2.40/hr). If staying the night, most **hotels** have parking, usually for $10–20 per day.

Orientation

Old San Juan occupies the western end of a narrow island separating San Juan Bay from the Atlantic Ocean and is the historic heart of the city. The eastern half of this island contains **Puerta de Tierra**, connected to the main island by several bridges. From here the beach districts of **Condado**, **Ocean Park** and **Isla Verde** follow the coast towards the east; central **Santurce** lies just inland from Condado. South of Santurce, across the Canal Martin Peña, is **Hato Rey**, with its tower-lined *Milla de Oro* ("Golden Mile") the financial heart of San Juan, while **Río Piedras**, a major transport hub for *públicos*, contains the main campus of the Universidad de Puerto Rico. **Greater San Juan** encompasses several other municipalities: to the east is industrial **Carolina** (the third largest city in Puerto Rico) and suburban **Trujillo Alto**, while **Cataño**, **Bayamón** (the second largest city on the island) and **Guaynabo** lie to the west.

Information

The main **Puerto Rican Tourism Company office** is at c/Tanca 500 (Tues–Sat 8.30am–5.30pm, Sun & Mon 9am–5.30pm; ☎787/722-1709), close to the cruise-ship piers on the south side of Old San Juan. The office is helpful and well stocked with information, including copies of quarterly magazine *¡Qué Pasa!* (ⓦ www.qpsm.com), a great source of listings in English. The city government also operates convenient **San Juan Tourism Information Centres** in Old San Juan, with the main office at c/Tetuán 250 (Mon–Sat 8am–4pm; ☎787/480-2911) and another desk inside the city hall on Plaza de Armas (same hours; ☎787/480-2548).

Getting around

Old San Juan and the beach districts are compact enough for strolling, but Greater San Juan is far too spread out to explore on foot. The cheapest way to get around is to use the **city buses**, which are easy to use and relatively convenient during the day. **Taxis** are relatively expensive, but safer at night and essential for some trips.

Buses

City **buses**, or *guaguas*, are operated by the Autoridad Metropolitana de Autobuses (☎787/977-2200, ⓦ www.dtop.gov.pr) and are cheap, safe and usually air-conditioned. Bus stops are indicated by a "*parada*" sign. Pay as you get on the bus, but make sure you have the correct change

The **Terminal del Viejo San Juan** is under the Covadonga car park on the edge of Old San Juan. First Transit (☎787/622-6161) operates three useful routes from Old San Juan (under contract from the AMA): ME (express to Sagrado Corazón metro station; Mon–Fri 5–8pm); M3 (Mon–Fri 5am–midnight, Sat & Sun 6am–midnight), which also goes to Sagrado Corazón but via Santurce; and M1 (Mon–Fri 5am–11.15pm, every 6min; Sat & Sun 6am–11.15pm, every 12–15min), which runs from Old San Juan to Río Piedras via Santurce and Hato Rey (31–41min). These cost $0.50 per ride.

All other buses cost $0.75 per ride throughout the city. Other useful services are: **B21** (Mon–Fri daytime every 20min; evenings, Sat & Sun every 30min; last departure from San Juan 9pm), from Old San Juan to Condado; and **T5** (Mon–Fri daytime every 8min; evenings & Sat every 15min; Sun every 20min; last departure 9pm), which connects Old San Juan with Isla Verde (via Santurce, not Condado).

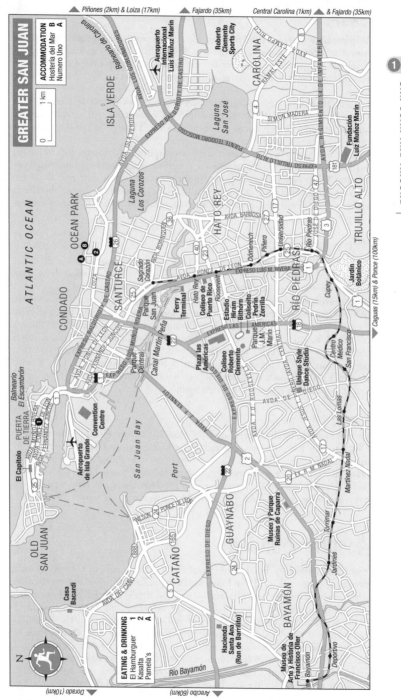

GREATER SAN JUAN

ACCOMMODATION
Hostería del Mar B
Numero Uno A

0 ——— 1 km

ATLANTIC OCEAN

Piñones (2km) & Loíza (17km)
Fajardo (35km)
Central Carolina (1km)
& Fajardo (35km)

Balneario de Carolina
Aeropuerto internacional Luis Muñoz Marín
Roberto Clemente Sports City
CAROLINA
AVDA LOS GOBERNADORES
AVDA ISLA VERDE
ISLA VERDE
EXPRESO BALDORIOTY DE CASTRO
Fundación Luiz Muñoz Marín
SIMON MADERA
AVDA REGIMIENTO 65 DE INFANTERÍA
181
OCEAN PARK
Laguna Los Corozos
Laguna San José
PUENTE TEODORO MOSCOSO
EXPRESO TRUJILLO ALTO
TRUJILLO ALTO
CONDADO
SANTURCE
Sagrado Corazón
HATO REY
AVDA BARBOSA
JOSÉ DE DIEGO
AVDA ROBERTO
AVDA PONCE DE LEON
Hato Rey
EXPRESO LUIS M. RIVERA
Universidad
Río Piedras
RÍO PIEDRAS
Jardín Botánico
Domenech
Piñero
Cupey
Caguas (15km) & Ponce (100km)
Parque San Juan
Ferry Terminal
Coliseo de Puerto Rico
Estadio Hiram Bithorn
Coliseo Pedrín Zorrilla
Parque J.M. Marín
Roosevelt
Canal Martín Peña
EXPRESO LAS AMÉRICAS
Plaza las Américas
Coliseo Roberto Clemente
Unique Style Dance Studio
Centro Médico
San Francisco
Las Lomas
Martínez Nadal
EXPRESO DE DIEGO
AVDA JESÚS T. PIÑERO
AVDA DE DIEGO
El Capitolio
PUERTA DE TIERRA
Balneario El Escambrón
AVDA PONCE DE LEON
AVDA FERNÁNDEZ JUNCOS
Parque Central
Convention Centre
AVDA J.F. KENNEDY
San Juan Bay
Port
Aeropuerto de Isla Grande
OLD SAN JUAN
Casa Bacardi
AVDA DEL CAÑO
CATAÑO
EXPRESO DE DIEGO
GUAYNABO
Museo y Parque Ruinas de Caparra
BAYAMÓN
Hacienda Santa Ana (Ron de Barrilito)
Museo de Arte y Historia de Francisco Oller
Bayamón
Deportivo
Torrimar
Jardines
WILSON
PONCE DE LEON
EXPRESO DE DIEGO
Río Bayamón
Dorado (10km)
Arecibo (60km)

EATING & DRINKING
El Hamburguer 1
Kasalta 2
Pamela's A

N

Taxis

White *taxis turísticos* (cars and minivans) ferry between the airport and the city, and have a monopoly at the taxi ranks in Old San Juan and most hotels along the beaches. Charges are set according to tariff zones (for the airport see p.49), though taxi drivers always seem to charge a little more than the rates issued by the tourist office.

From Old San Juan it's $10 to anywhere in the area or Puerta de Tierra; $15 to Ocean Park, Miramar and Condado; $19 to Isla Verde (taxis will try and charge at least $22); and $14 to Plaza las Américas. Taxis will charge $33 to Bayamón (for other rates see box, p.85).

All other trips go by the meter: the initial charge is $1.75 and then it's $0.10 per 1/19 of a mile thereafter. From 10pm to 6am there is a $1 surcharge and you'll pay an extra $1 for each piece of luggage. In the old town taxis line up near the cruise piers or along Calle del Recinto Sur, at Covadonga; elsewhere, especially late at night, it's best to call cabs in advance, as it can be difficult to hail them on the street (see p.83 for phone numbers).

Tren Urbano

The Caribbean's only metro system, San Juan's **Tren Urbano** opened in 2004. It's super-clean, comfortable and very safe, but – until a long-planned street tram extends the system to Old San Juan – not much use for tourists.

For the foreseeable future the 17.2km system will only cut through the southern half of Greater San Juan from **Bayamón** to **Sagrado Corazón** just north of Hato Rey, via Río Piedras. It makes reaching Bayamón a little more convenient, though it's still a long ride to the nearest station from Old San Juan or Isla Verde. All fares are $0.75, which includes a bus transfer within two hours of leaving your last station. San Juan's subway ticket system is based on New York City's, with machines issuing plastic cards for single or multiple rides – hang on to your card and add value to it if you want to ride again.

Ferries

Ferries operated by Acua Expreso (☏787/758-8012) from Pier 2 on the marina in Old San Juan make the ten-minute trip across the bay to **Cataño** every 15–30 minutes (daily 6am–10pm; $0.50). The commuter service to the northern edge of **Hato Rey** normally runs every thirty minutes (Mon–Thurs 6.30am–6.30pm; Fri–Sun 6.30am–8.30pm; $1), connecting with the Tren Urbano at Hato Rey station, but is sometimes suspended for long periods – check with the tourist office.

Accommodation

You'll find clusters of hotels throughout Greater San Juan, but for visitors only two areas make sense: **Old San Juan**, which has the most historic accommodation and contains the city's best bars, restaurants and sights; and **the beaches**, which have less character but boast a decent range of eating and drinking options in addition to the obvious attractions of surf and sand. **Condado** (the closest to Old San Juan) and **Isla Verde** are more developed resort areas, with **Ocean Park** in between offering a quieter experience without the choice of amenities. By 2012 the newly renovated *Condado Vanderbilt Hotel* (ⓦwww.condadovanderbilthotel .com) at Avda Ashford 1055, a magnificent Spanish Revival villa built in 1919, should be reopened: it's likely to be one of the best hotels in the city.

For longer stays or larger groups, consider **renting apartments** or **villas** via agents such as Caleta Realty (Ⓦwww.caletarealty.com), which has several smart properties in Old San Juan, or PR West (Ⓦwww.prwest.com), which also rents places in Condado and Isla Verde.

Taxes and charges added to the price of a room are outrageously high in San Juan, sometimes increasing the bill by as much as 25 percent: check the **total price** before agreeing to pay. Depending on the size of the hotel, mandatory government taxes range from 7 to 11 percent (see Basics, p.26), and anything in excess of this has been levied as a **service charge**. Some hotels charge a **resort fee** of 10 to 15 percent to pay for things like use of towels, pool and spa.

Old San Juan

Caleta 64 Caleta de San Juan 64
☎787/667-4926, Ⓦwww.caleta64.com. These five luxurious apartment rentals occupy a gorgeous eighteenth-century townhouse. Original fittings and interiors have been enhanced with plasma TVs (with satellite), kitchen, washer/dryer and free wi-fi. The apartments are self-catering but you still get a cleaning service every day. ❻

Chateau Cervantes c/Recinto Sur 329
☎787/724-7722, Ⓦwww.cervantespr.com. Plush boutique hotel with twelve exquisite (but pricey) suites behind the marina. Local style icon Nono Maldonado designed the rooms, which feature a contemporary Puerto Rican theme using natural wood fittings and marble-tiled bathrooms, embellished with LCD TVs, balconies, free wi-fi and modern art. ❼

Da' House Hotel c/San Francisco 312 ☎787/977-1180 or 787/366-5074, Ⓦwww.dahousehotelpr .com. Above the *Nuyorican Café* (the entrance is on Callejón de la Capilla), this atmospheric place features simply decorated rooms with tiled floors, wooden furnishings and large, dazzling paintings from local artists. There's free wi-fi and a rooftop sun deck, but the streets outside can be noisy and there are no TVs. ❹

Gallery Inn c/Norzagaray 204–206
☎787/722-1808, Ⓦwww.thegalleryinn .com. Gorgeous eighteenth-century villa adorned with ornate sculptures created by host Jan D'Esopo, set around a plant-filled patio. The richly decorated rooms come laden with antiques and unusual *trompe l'oeil* walls. Complimentary breakfast is served on the patio and wine and cheese is offered daily from 5.30–6.30pm. Free internet, but no TVs. ❼

Hotel El Convento c/Cristo 100
☎787/723-9020, Ⓦwww.elconvento.com. One of the most stylish hotels in the city, housed within a former seventeenth-century Carmelite monastery. Mahogany beams, antique furniture and Spanish tiled floors add to the historic character of the rooms, which also come with LCD

TVs. The hotel levies a 12 percent "resort fee" in addition to taxes. ❾

Hotel Milano c/Fortaleza 307 ☎787/729-9050, Ⓦwww.hotelmilanopr.com. Popular, reasonably good-value mid-range hotel, though its comfortable but bland modern rooms seem at odds with its attractive nineteenth-century exterior. The best feature is the rooftop restaurant, where complimentary breakfast is served. Internet (free) is available in the restaurant and there's a minimum stay of two nights at the weekend. ❹

Howard Johnson Inn Plaza de Armas, c/San José 202 ☎787/722-9191, Ⓦwww.hojo.com. Historic building, right in the heart of the old town – it's comfortable enough, with basic cable TV and a/c, but the rooms are a little shabby – the cheapest singles have no windows, small beds and small towels and wi-fi (free) only works in the lobby. Bottom line: it's a great deal for this part of town. Singles ❸, doubles ❹

Posada San Francisco c/San Francisco 405 (on Plaza Colón) ☎787/461-2986. Nine budget rooms (with a/c), six with shared bathrooms, in another prime location on the edge of the old town. There's a shared kitchen, free wi-fi, TV lounge, laundry, two balconies and a congenial atmosphere – good place to meet fellow travellers. ❷

San Juan Guest House (aka *Castro Guest House*) c/Tanca 205 ☎787/722-5436. Basic, slightly run-down hostel on two floors, managed by the genial Enrique Castro (he only speaks Spanish). The best double rooms are on the upper floor, facing the road, with brightly painted walls, fridges and balconies ($35–50). The cheapest rooms are $30 with fan (singles pay just $15), while others have a/c; the shared toilets and showers are a bit shabby. Ring the bell or phone to get in. Cash only. ❶

Sheraton Old San Juan c/Brumbaugh 100
☎787/721-5100, Ⓦwww.sheratonoldsanjuan.com. Standard chain hotel, with swish rooms equipped with cable TV and internet (free). If you're into casinos, the hotel has the only one in the old town, but the best amenity here is the rooftop pool and

jacuzzi. If you book online, it's not bad value, though you'll pay the 11 percent "hotel service fee" regardless. ⑦

Puerta de Tierra

Caribe Hilton c/San Geronimo 1 ☎787/721-0303, ⓦwww.hiltoncaribbean.com/sanjuan. Set on its own peninsula with 17 acres of tropical gardens and a private beach, this massive resort dates from 1949 (it's also where the *piña colada* is said to have been invented). It has 900 modern, well-equipped rooms but its vast size means it lacks character. Note the 14 percent "resort fee" and the $15 parking fee. ⑦

Condado

Atlantic Beach Hotel c/Vendig 1 ☎787/721-6900, ⓦwww.atlanticbeachhotel.net. Popular hotel with a beachside location and a lively beach bar, though not so gay-friendly as it once was. The exterior is a little worn, but the rooms are relatively new, stylish and comfortable. Free wi-fi in common areas. ❸

Casa Condado Hotel Avda Condado 60 ☎787/721-5193, ⓦwww.casacondadohotel.com. Great budget boutique, sporting chic rooms with minimalist furnishings, wood floors, plain white walls and free wi-fi, all for a fair price for this part of town. Breakfast is basic and there are no elevators (3 floors), no phones, no hairdryers and no views, though the second-floor terrace is a pleasant place to chill out. ❸

🏃 **La Concha Renaissance Resort** Avda Ashford 1077 ☎787/721-8500, ⓦwww.laconcharesort.com. Reopened in 2007, fusing the building's "Tropical Modernist" 1958 architecture with a chic contemporary look. Its 483 rooms have been refurbished in bright, pastel shades with balconies overlooking the ocean and huge pool. Charges a 13 percent resort fee and parking is $15/day. ⑦

Conrad Condado Plaza Hotel Avda Ashford 999 ☎787/721-1000, ⓦwww.condadoplaza.com. Smart self-contained hotel, with a 24-hour casino on site and a choice of five restaurants (including *Pikayo* see p.73), spa and pool. Rooms feature an elegant, contemporary design, LCD TVs, free wi-fi and balconies. Note that the seafront terrace has no beach and there is a "resort fee" of 14 percent. ❻

Le Consulat Avda Magdalena 1149, ☎787/289-9191, ⓦwww.ascendcollection.com. This cosy modern hotel offers 21 compact but comfy rooms with huge flat-screen cable TV and free wi-fi. Extras include a small pool and tranquil garden where complimentary breakfast is served. ❹

Coral Princess Avda Magdalena 1159 ☎787/977-7700, ⓦwww.coralpr.com. Great little hotel in a quiet residential neighbourhood, a 10min walk from the beach. Rooms are bright and relatively good value; extras include free wi-fi, rooftop lounge and jacuzzi, breakfast and 24hr coffee and juice. On the downside, "taxes" total some 23 percent, most of which are actually service charges. ❺

Holiday Inn Express c/Maringo Ramírez Bages 1 ☎787/724-4160, ⓦwww.hiexpress.com/sanjuanpr. Solid chain option just off the main strip, only a short walk from the beach. Rooms are generic but very comfortable. Pluses include free internet (in-room or in the business centre), a small pool, a jacuzzi and a gym. ❻

Sandy Beach Hotel Avda Condado 4 ☎787/722-8640, ⓦsanjuan-sandybeachhotel.com. Small inn-type place, incongruously located amid the high-rises, but right next to the beach. You get complimentary breakfast and free wi-fi but adequate, nondescript rooms. You're paying a premium for location and it's only worthwhile if you intend to spend lots of time on the beach. ❸

San Juan Marriott Resort & Stellaris Casino Avda Ashford 1309 ☎787/722-7000, ⓦwww.marriott.com. Another monster resort-hotel and casino right on the beach, usually packed with families. Has 511 rooms with snappy, tropical decor and free wi-fi and spray-jet tubs – the best rooms (and the best views) are in the Tower Wing. The restaurant is open 24hr. Add on the extra 12 percent "resort fee". Parking is $16/day. ❾

Ocean Park

At Wind Chimes Inn Avda McLeary 1750 ☎787/727-4153, ⓦwww.atwindchimesinn.com. This whitewashed 1920s Spanish villa is a refuge from the hectic San Juan streets, with bright rooms and terracotta-tiled floors. It's located in a peaceful residential area, a 5- to 10min walk from the beach. With a small pool, jacuzzi and leafy gardens, it's like staying in an exclusive club. Single rooms are a good deal here ($80 in high season). ❹

Hostería del Mar c/Tapia 1 ☎787/727-3302, ⓦwww.hosteriadelmarpr.com. A little gem of a hotel, right on the beach, with a Southeast Asian feel. There's lots of dark wood, rattan and tropical plants throughout, and the excellent *Uvva* restaurant, which looks like a Balinese beach café (though the food is Mediterranean). Rooms are small but cosy, with cable TV. ❺

Numero Uno c/Santa Ana 1 ☎787/726-5010, ⓦwww.numero1guesthouse.com. A former private home built in the 1940s, offering compact but elegant rooms with ceiling fans and a gay-friendly atmosphere. The sleepy location on a pleasant stretch of beach is perfect for lounging, but not ideal for exploring the rest of the city. ⑤

Isla Verde

Best Western San Juan Airport Hotel & Casino Aeropuerto Internacional Luis Muñoz Marín ☎787/791-1700, ⦿www.bestwestern.com. This ultra convenient but pricey airport hotel is literally inside concourse D, with spacious but standard rooms, gym, free internet access and basic breakfast included. ⑤

Coqui Inn c/Mar Mediterraneo 36, Villamar ☎787/726-4330, ⦿coqui-inn.net. Solid budget option, a 10min walk from the beach, offering basic but clean rooms with tiled floors, cable TV and a bathroom. Extras include a pool and free internet access. There's a daily $5.45 "energy charge" per room, but the parking is free. ❸

Hotel Villa del Sol c/Rosa 4 ☎787/791-2600, ⦿www.villadelsolpr.com. Appealing Spanish-villa-style hotel that's a far cheaper alternative to the big resorts nearby. Rooms come with cable TV and have a tropical theme, but some are very shabby – check first before taking one. While the hotel is a few minutes' walk from the beach, its location is marred somewhat by the surrounding high-rise condos and airport noise. ⑤

Ritz Carlton San Juan Hotel Avda of the Governors 6961 ☎787/253-1700, ⦿www .ritzcarlton.com. Self-contained luxury resort, dripping with marble and opulent fittings. The rooms are heavenly, with bright, tropic-inspired interiors. The alluring pool backs onto a gorgeous stretch of beach and there are several high-end places to eat and drink. At least the 14 percent "resort fee" gets you free kayaks, surfboards and use of the spa. Parking is $17/day. ❾

El San Juan Hotel & Casino Avda Isla Verde 6063 ☎787/791-1000, ⦿www.elsanjuanhotel.com. This colossal former haunt of the 1950s Brat Pack injects some glamour to the beachfront, but check your room first; some are way below par considering the price tag. The La Vista and Grande Vista rooms feature bright colours, LCD TVs and hip, contemporary design, but breakfast is overpriced and there's a 14 percent "resort fee". ❾

San Juan Water & Beach Club Hotel c/Tartak 2 ☎787/728-3666, ⦿www.waterbeachclubhotel .com. The city's top boutique hotel is right on the beach, with 84 stylish white rooms equipped with cable TV, CD players and iPod docks. There's a tiny rooftop pool and some of San Juan's best bars and restaurants (see p.77). However, some of the rooms need renovation; parking is $20/day and the hotel adds an additional 12 percent. ⑥

The City

San Juan is a large, sprawling city made up of several diverse *barrios*, but the area of interest for visitors is relatively compact. The obvious place to begin is **Old San Juan**, the city's most enticing district, noted chiefly for its dazzling colonial architecture. This is where the Spanish established their first permanent city on the island in 1521 and their great fortress, known as **El Morro**, is one of its principal highlights. The **Galería Nacional** and **Museo de Las Américas** are the best of numerous museums and galleries here, while a stroll along the outer walls is rewarded with magical views over the bay, especially at sunset.

Beyond the old town, San Juan is all about the **beaches** for most visitors, with condos and hotels lining the sands for 12km between **Puerta de Tierra**, revitalized **Condado** and upmarket **Isla Verde**. Tourists tend to ignore the rest of the city, but you should make time for the two excellent **art galleries** in **Santurce** and the smattering of attractions further south in **Río Piedras**. Both *barrios* have been spruced up in recent years and while remaining a little rough around the edges, offer a more genuine and richer experience of everyday life in the city.

Old San Juan

Thanks to extensive restoration in the 1990s, **OLD SAN JUAN** (*Viejo San Juan*) is a wonderfully preserved slice of eighteenth-century colonial Spain, its narrow streets lined with tempting restaurants and a range of modest but thought-provoking

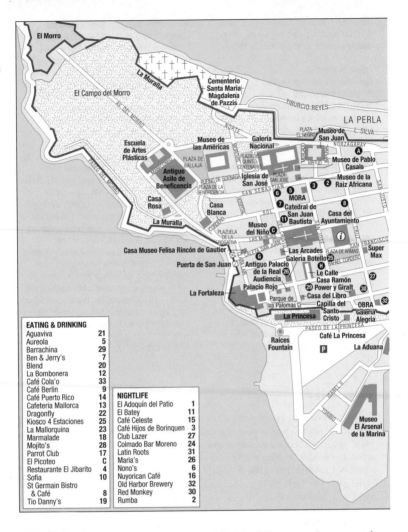

EATING & DRINKING

Aguaviva	21
Aureola	5
Barrachina	29
Ben & Jerry's	7
Blend	20
La Bombonera	12
Café Cola'o	33
Café Berlin	9
Café Puerto Rico	14
Cafeteria Mallorca	13
Dragonfly	22
Kiosco 4 Estaciones	25
La Mallorquina	23
Marmalade	18
Mojito's	28
Parrot Club	17
El Picoteo	C
Restaurante El Jibarito	4
Sofia	10
St Germain Bistro & Café	8
Tio Danny's	19

NIGHTLIFE

El Adoquín del Patio	1
El Batey	11
Café Celeste	15
Café Hijos de Borinquen	3
Club Lazer	27
Colmado Bar Moreno	24
Latin Roots	31
Maria's	26
Nono's	6
Nuyorican Café	16
Old Harbor Brewery	32
Red Monkey	30
Rumba	2

museums. Aimlessly wandering its quiet, cobbled back lanes is enchanting, with salsa music drifting out of half-shuttered windows, blossoms draped over wrought-iron balconies and the tempting aromas of *criollo* cooking wafting through the cracks of wooden doors.

The commercial parts of the old town tend to get overrun by day-trippers from **cruise ships**, but it's easy to avoid the crowds and their presence has beneficial side effects – this is the safest part of the city and English is spoken everywhere.

Despite being fairly steep in parts, the streets of the old town are best appreciated on foot, though there are a couple of **free trolley buses** that trundle between the visitor centre and the main sights (Mon–Fri 7am–7pm, Sat & Sun 9am–7pm, every 15–20min).

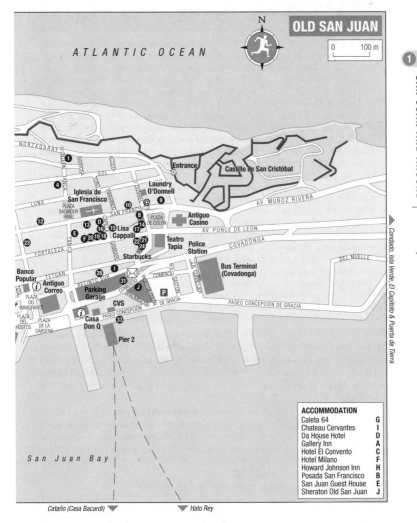

Map labels:
ATLANTIC OCEAN
N
OLD SAN JUAN
0   100 m
NORZAGARAY
Entrance
Castillo de San Cristóbal
AV. MUÑOZ RIVERA
Laundry
O'Donnell
Iglesia de
San Francisco
PLAZA
SALVADOR
BRAU
SAN FRANCISCO
PLAZA
DE COLÓN
Antiguo
Casino
AV. PONCE DE LEÓN
Lisa
Cappalli
Teatro
Tapia
Police
Station
COVADONGA
DEL MUELLE
Starbucks
Banco
Popular
Antiguo
Correo
PLAZA
DEL
INMIGRANTE
PLAZA
DE LA
HOSTOS   DÁRSENA
Parking
Garage
CVS
Casa
Don Q
PASEO CONCEPCIÓN
Pier 2
Bus Terminal
(Covadonga)
COMERCIO
PASEO CONCEPCIÓN DE GRACIA
DE GRACIA
San Juan Bay
Cataño (Casa Bacardi)   Hato Rey

SAN JUAN AND AROUND | The City
Condado, Isla Verde, El Capitolo & Puerta de Tierra

ACCOMMODATION
Caleta 64   G
Chateau Cervantes   I
Da House Hotel   D
Gallery Inn   A
Hotel El Convento   C
Hotel Milano   F
Howard Johnson Inn   H
Posada San Francisco   B
San Juan Guest House   E
Sheraton Old San Juan J

Paseo de La Princesa and around

The **Paseo de La Princesa** forms an elegant promenade along the southern edge of the old town, skirting the base of the imposing **city wall**. It runs west off two adjacent squares: Plaza del Inmigrante, with its simple but poignant contemporary statue commemorating Puerto Rican immigrants, and shady Plaza del Hostos, featuring a sculpture of Eugenio María de Hostos, the nineteenth-century independence activist.

West of Plaza del Hostos the tree-fringed *paseo* becomes a pleasant and traffic-free place to wander, buy snacks (look out for the excellent *maví* sold here, a drink made from fermented tree bark and tasting a bit like cider), or grab a drink at the outdoor *Café La Princesa*. The thin grey building along its final section is **La Princesa**, completed in 1837. A prison until 1960, today it serves as headquarters for the Puerto Rican Tourism Company. At the end of the *paseo* lies a large

Rum capital

As the capital city of the world's leading producer of **rum**, San Juan is the perfect place to get more closely acquainted with the Caribbean's favourite tipple. Top of your list should be **Casa Bacardi**, the "cathedral of rum". Enthusiastic guides and multi-media exhibits introduce every facet of the rum-making process, including special "nosing" barrels of various Bacardi blends – suitably tempted, you get two free cocktails at the end of the tour and a shop selling discounted bottles of its best products. Bacardi's main rival on the island, Don Q, offers free samples at **Casa Don Q** (Mon–Wed 10am–7pm, Fri–Sun 9am–6pm; free), opposite the cruise-ship piers, including the bestselling Cristal, the island's favourite cocktail mixer. The Rums of Puerto Rico association also maintains a small bar at the main visitor centre in Old San Juan (see p.50) where, once again, free rum and knockout *piña coladas* are usually on offer Saturday to Wednesday. Real connoisseurs should enquire here (ask for Ahmed Naveiras) about tours of the **Hacienda Santa Ana** in Bayamón, where the Fernández family still makes the superlative **Ron de Barrilito**. This rich, dark spirit was created in 1880 and is aged in Spanish sherry barrels for a minimum of three years: many consider Barrilito to be the best rum in the world. Private tours are possible, but only through the tourist office. You'll visit the ageing cellars, thick with the burnt, sweet aroma of sugar molasses, the rickety bottling plant and graceful windmill dating from 1827, which today acts as an office adorned with faded photographs and dusty, old bottles of rum. You'll also see "La Doña", or the **Freedom Barrel**, which was laid down in 1942 and will only be opened when Puerto Rico achieves independence – by which time it's likely to have evaporated in the tropical heat.

fountain topped by *Raíces* (1992), an exuberant bronze sculpture by Spaniard Luis Sanguino symbolizing Puerto Rico's diverse cultural roots. From the fountain you can continue walking along the edge of San Juan Bay at the base of the impressively solid city wall, **La Muralla**. Constructed in phases beginning in the seventeenth century, this vast sandstone barrier – which measures 6m thick in places – was finally completed in 1782.

Eventually the walls are breached at the **Puerta de San Juan**, a short stroll north of the fountain. Completed in 1635, this was once the main entrance to the city for officials arriving by boat. You can re-enter the old town here, or continue along the waterside via **Paseo del Morro** as far as the headland beneath El Morro – a much better (and cooler) option at sunset.

Casa Museo Felisa Rincón de Gautier

Once through the city gate, **Caleta de San Juan** leads straight up towards the cathedral, its canopy of tropical trees, vines and flowers make it one of the prettiest streets in the city. The **Casa Museo Felisa Rincón de Gautier** (Mon–Fri 9am–4pm; free; ☎787/723-1897, ⓦwww.museofelisarincon.com) stands on the left-hand corner, the elegant former home of the first woman to become mayor of San Juan. Doña Felisa (1897–1994), as she was also known, is still admired on the island for her support of women's rights and for the modernization of San Juan that she oversaw during her 22 years as mayor (1946–68). Her foundation has maintained the house in superb condition, cramming it with photos, personal effects, awards, period furniture and other memorabilia.

From the museum walk up the street parallel to the city wall and you'll see **Plazuela de La Rogativa** on the left, a tiny plaza overlooking the bay, which features a striking bronze sculpture by Lindsay Daen. The sculpture is a memorial to the defeat of the British fleet in 1797. Legend has it that the hapless Brits mistook a religious procession (*rogativa*) led by the bishop and his female followers as reinforcements and decided to retreat, but there's no evidence that the incident actually took place.

Casa Blanca

Nowhere is more resonant of San Juan's Spanish colonial past than **Casa Blanca** (the White House; Wed–Sun 8.30am–4.20pm; $3; ☎787/725-1454), at the end of Calle San Sebastian. For 250 years the romantic hill-top mansion served as the residence of the descendants of Juan Ponce de León, the first governor of Puerto Rico. The first house was built in 1521 by his son-in-law Juan García Troche but was destroyed by a hurricane two years later and what you see today dates from 1530. San Juan's nascent community of rough-and-ready colonizers grew up around its gleaming white walls, party to all the intrigues, plots and brawls of the early conquistadors.

The compact interior of old brick floors and mahogany beams was being carefully restored in sixteenth-century style at the time of writing; it should be open by the end of 2011.

El Morro

One of the greatest forts in the New World, the Castillo San Felipe del Morro, more commonly known as **El Morro** (daily 9am–6pm; $3 valid for 24hr, under-16s free; $5 with San Cristóbal, valid for 7 days), looms over the Atlantic with virtually impregnable stone walls. It is testimony to Spain's grim determination to defend the island over the centuries and proved an ideal stand-in for the terrifying slave fort in the movie *Amistad* (1997). Today El Morro is a UNESCO World Heritage Site and part of the **San Juan National Historic Site** (⊛www .nps.gov/saju), managed by the US National Park Service.

A short walk from Casa Blanca, the fortress occupies a dramatic spot at the top end of Old San Juan, with six levels of rock-solid defensive positions featuring the distinctive "hornwork" shape, 42m high in places. It dominates the mouth of San Juan Bay, a superb strategic location that made it almost impossible to capture.

Established as a small gun battery in the 1540s, El Morro was constantly expanded and the imposing defences you see today were completed in 1787, thanks in large part to an enterprising Irishman in the pay of Spain, **Thomas O'Daly**. The fort's defensive record is certainly impressive and it was captured only once – by the English in 1598.

You'll enter the fort at the **main plaza**, surrounded by vaulted rooms that once served as officers' quarters, magazines and storerooms. Some of these have been converted into a small **museum** of the site and a **video room** (daily 9am–4pm; English video every 30min). From the main plaza you can clamber over the battlements above and below, taking in the stunning panoramas of the bay and cityscape to the east.

The fort is separated from the rest of the old town by a swathe of green grass, which has no official name but is commonly known as **El Campo**, or just the "*Area Verde*". It's a popular place to **fly kites** – come here on a blustery weekend and the sky is jam-packed with them. To join in, buy one from the stalls nearby.

Cementerio Santa María Magdalena de Pazzis

Wedged between the city walls and the Atlantic on the north side of the *campo*, the **Cementerio Santa María Magdalena de Pazzis** (daily 7am–3pm; free) is one of the most picturesque sights in San Juan, its ornate but tightly packed marble tombs and monuments backed by an immense span of blue stretching far into the horizon. The best views are from the walls above, but to get inside the cemetery walk through the road tunnel at the northeast corner of the *campo*. Although it's

La Perla

La Perla is the ramshackle *barrio* just beyond El Morro and the cemetery, hugging the Atlantic coast below the city walls. It's been one of San Juan's most deprived areas since the eighteenth century, when it became the refuge of city outcasts as well as the poorer families of soldiers stationed at El Morro. It won notoriety in 1966 as the subject of *La Vida*, Oscar Lewis's controversial study of poverty on the island, and in 2006 it was one of the locations for the movie *El Cantante,* the place where salsa legend Héctor Lavoe came to shoot heroin. While it's true that some of La Perla's inhabitants make a living from crime (and drugs are a problem here), they rarely pose a threat to tourists. In fact, locals observe a strict street code – harming outsiders brings unwanted police attention. Having said that, there's little reason to voyeuristically wander the area's narrow streets. You can meet some of the local characters in **La Callejón** (the alley), a cluster of bars at the northern end of c/Tanca, back in the old town above La Perla – it's best if you speak Spanish. Bars such as *El Adoquin del Patio* are usually quite safe and on Friday nights attract a boisterous, friendly crowd with live music and plenty of cheap rum.

located near La Perla (see box above), there are caretakers on duty and it's usually safe to visit here during the day.

The most famous person buried here is **Pedro Albizu Campos**, leader of the Puerto Rican Nationalist Party (see p.268). His marble tomb is marked by two national flags in a corner of the old section. Nearby is the grave of **José de Diego**, topped with a bust of the poet and independence advocate. Look out also for doctor and politician **José Celso Barbosa**, buried in a family tomb in the modern section of the cemetery, on the left side of the main path as you enter and **Gilberto Concepción de Gracia**, founder of the Puerto Rican Independence Party (PIP). Note that the infamous pirate **Roberto Cofresí** (see p.266), who was executed outside El Morro in 1825, was buried somewhere on the *campo* – criminals could not be laid to rest inside the cemetery.

Museo de las Américas and Plaza del Quinto Centenario

One of San Juan's most absorbing museums, the **Museo de las Américas** (Tues–Wed & Sat 10am–4pm, Thurs & Fri 9am–4pm; $3; ☎787/724-5052, Ⓦwww .museolasamericas.org) is a thoughtful collection of art and anthropology relating to Puerto Rico and the Americas as a whole. Facing El Morro on the other side of the *campo*, the museum occupies the second floor of the *Cuartel de Ballajá* (the old Spanish barracks), a grand, three-storey imperial structure built between 1854 and 1864 and arranged around a wide central courtyard.

The museum has four permanent exhibitions. *El indio en América* is a poignant introduction to 22 indigenous American tribes, beginning with the **Taíno** and including others from South and North America. Explanations are in Spanish and English, the well-presented exhibits embellished by bronze statues created by Peru-based artist Felipe Lettersten. *La Herencia Africana* is an enlightening look at the **West African** origins of the region's black population, as well as the horrific **slave trade**; a particular emphasis is placed on Puerto Rico, naturally, and the numerous slave rebellions up to abolition in 1873. Note, however, that there are no English explanations, making this room a bit dull if you don't read Spanish. *Conquista y Colonización* chronicles the history of the island from the arrival of Ponce de León to the US invasion, again in Spanish only. The fourth exhibition, *Las Artes Populares en Las Américas*, is an eclectic collection of traditional folk art from all over the Americas (English labels). Other rooms are used for temporary exhibitions, usually paintings or artwork.

The eastern side of the *Cuartel de Ballajá* borders the **Plaza del Quinto Centenario**, opened in 1992 to commemorate the 500th anniversary of the "discovery" of the New World by Columbus. The centrepiece of the square is a 12m-high monument, designed by Jaime Suarez to look a bit like a totem pole and symbolizing the roots of American history.

Galería Nacional

Puerto Rico has produced many remarkably talented artists over the centuries and the modest **Galería Nacional** (Tues–Sat 9.30am–4.30pm; $3) offers by far the best introduction to their work. The collection is enhanced by its romantic surroundings, the former Convento de los Dominicos, established in 1523 and now a series of beautifully presented galleries. You'll find the entrance on the eastern side of Plaza del Quinto Centenario.

Sala 1 begins with **caste painting** and the **viceregal art** of the eighteenth century, but the real highlights are in Sala 2, dedicated to icons **José Campeche** and **Francisco Oller** (see p.273). Though you won't see their most acclaimed paintings here, there are some great works on display (such as Oller's vivid still life *Cocos*) and it's easy to appreciate the vast gulf that divides the two artistically, in part a reflection of how the art world had been transformed in the nineteenth century. Sala 3 highlights the early twentieth-century **Costumbrista** school, with its idealized view of rural Puerto Rico: **Ramón Frade**'s *El Pan Nuestro* (Our Bread) of 1905 is a memorable depiction of the *jíbaro* (Puerto Rican peasant farmer) and one of the best-known paintings in the gallery. There's also a small exhibition on *santos* carvings here. Sala 4 concludes with modern, abstract work of the 1950s and 1960s, with *La Mixta* (1960), **Fran Cervoni**'s haunting depiction of a meal in a local tavern, one of the highlights.

Iglesia San José

With an appropriately haughty statue of Juan Ponce de León (supposedly made from melted-down cannons captured from the British in 1797), at its centre, the **Plaza de San José** seems a quiet and somewhat forlorn open space most days, ringed by some of the oldest buildings in Puerto Rico. The square is just around the corner from the Galería Nacional, as the old convent adjoins the **Iglesia San José** (second and fourth Sat of each month noon–6pm, first Tues of the month 9am–4pm; free; ☎787/727-7373, ⊛www.iglesiasanjosepr.org) on the plaza's north side. The family church of Ponce de León's descendants and the oldest original church building on the island (construction began in 1523), it has been undergoing a massive (and seemingly never-ending) restoration since 2002 – tours allow you to view ongoing work up close. Painter **José Campeche** is buried inside, along with several of the early Spanish governors.

Museo de Pablo Casals

The eastern side of Plaza de San José is bound by the Casa de los Contrafuertes, one of the oldest houses in San Juan, dating back to the early eighteenth century. Inside is the **Museo de Pablo Casals** (Tues–Sat 9.30am–4.30pm, closed for lunch; $1; ☎787/723-9185), more of a memorial to the great Spanish cellist than a museum, displaying various awards on the first floor and an exhibition of related photography upstairs that tends to change every few months. Casals (1876–1973) moved to Puerto Rico in 1955 after becoming disillusioned with the Franco regime (his mother was from Mayagüez, on the west coast). He established the Puerto Rican Symphony Orchestra in 1957 and **Festival Casals** (tickets $20–40; ☎787/721-7727, ⊛www.festcasalspr.gobierno.pr) – the island's premier classical music festival – in 1956; it still runs from February to March every year.

Museo de La Raíz Africana

Next door to the Casals Museum is the **Museo de La Raíz Africana** (Wed–Sun 8am–1pm; $2; ☎787/724-4294), which has a similar African focus as the slavery exhibit at the Museo de las Américas and is also presented solely in Spanish, but with a slightly stronger, thought-provoking section on the slave trade. Grim displays (note the horrific *collar de hierro*, or "iron necklace") bring home the iniquity of slavery in general and there's a detailed history of the trade in Puerto Rico. On a lighter note, it's also the best place to see the spiky, multicoloured masks used in Loíza's **Fiestas Tradicionales de Santiago Apóstol** (see p.88) and to learn about the *bomba* and *plena* music and dance styles that evolved from African traditions.

Museo de San Juan

Around the corner from Plaza de San José, housed in the former *mercado* building, the **Museo de San Juan** (Tues–Sun 9am–4pm; free) hosts temporary exhibits on aspects of Puerto Rican history, from its early inhabitants to modern San Juan, usually labelled in English. The building itself, constructed in 1855, is a wonderful example of colonial architecture and hosts an organic **Farmers' Market** every Saturday (8am–1pm; Ⓦmercadoagricolanatural.com).

The main entrance is at c/Norzagaray 150 facing the ocean, but you can also use the back entrance at the end of Calle Mercado, off Calle de San Sebastián.

Plaza de Armas

Once the centre of the city and home to a teeming market, **Plaza de Armas** is a far more languorous affair these days, a pleasant, tree-lined square where locals meet to drink *kiosco* coffee and visitors feed the flocks of *tranquilo* pigeons.

To get here from the Museo de San Juan, retrace your steps along Calle Mercado and then head downhill along Calle de San José for three blocks. The northern side of the plaza is taken up by the arcaded facade and twin towers of the **Casa del Ayuntamiento** (City Hall), which was completed in 1799 and still houses local government offices and a visitor information centre. You can get a taster of the historic interior by visiting the **Galería San Juan Bautista** (Tues–Sat 9am–4.30pm; free), which occupies a section of the first floor facing the plaza and showcases local artists.

Catedral de San Juan Bautista

Head west one block along Calle de San Francisco and turn right along Calle del Cristo to reach shady Plazuela de la Monjas, the oldest square in the city and dominated by the **Catedral de San Juan Bautista** (daily 8am–5pm; free; Ⓦwww .catedralsanjuan.com). Puerto Rico's first bishop, Alonso Manso, had the original wooden structure built in 1521, but it was destroyed five years later by a hurricane. The first stone cathedral was completed in 1549, though it's been reconstructed many times since and most of what you see today was part of a major restoration in 1917. Architecturally the cathedral is rather plain, but the interior boasts a few interesting features, notably a marble monument on the left side containing the remains of **Juan Ponce de León**, interred here in 1908 (he had originally been laid to rest in the Iglesia San José). Nearby is a marble tablet marking the tomb of Alonso Manso (buried here in 1539) and a glass case containing relics of San Pío (Saint Pius), an early Christian martyr who was killed in the first century. On the other side of the aisle is a chapel dedicated to Carlos Manuel Rodríguez, the first Puerto Rican to be beatified.

Museo del Niño

Opposite the cathedral, on the other side of the plaza, the **Museo del Niño** (Tues–Thurs 10am–3.30pm, Fri 10am–5pm, Sat & Sun noon–5.30pm; children 1–15 $7, adults $5; ☎787/722-3791, ⓦwww.museodelninopr.org) is a must-see if you're travelling with kids. The three floors are divided into themed areas, with the emphasis on hands-on learning: displays on the culture, geography and ecology of Puerto Rico is the focus on the first floor, while the second floor features giant models of various parts of the body (heart, lungs, eyes and mouth). The third floor contains the **NASA Space Place**, with displays on the space shuttle and solar system, as well as exhibits on caves, hurricanes and water.

La Fortaleza

Described as "half palace, half castle" by US President Theodore Roosevelt, **La Fortaleza** (Mon–Fri 9am–5pm, tours only; free; ☎787/721-7000, ⓦwww .fortaleza.gobierno.pr) is the oldest governor's mansion still in use in the Americas. Since Roosevelt stayed here in 1906 the main building has changed little, its elegant Greek Revival exterior contrasting with the solid stone remnants of the original fortress.

To reach it from the cathedral, head south two blocks along Calle del Cristo and turn right along Calle de la Fortaleza. The only way to visit the grounds is as part of a **guided tour**: get tickets in the yellow-painted former Royal Court of Appeals building, on the south side of the street near the main entrance. There are usually at least two daily tours in English, at 9am and 3pm (more in high season), but only if it's not raining. The thirty-minute tour does not get you inside the main building and if you turn up in beachwear the guides can refuse to take you.

When construction began on La Fortaleza in 1533, the idea was that the building would serve as a fortress to defend the harbour. By the time it was finished in 1540, however, the Spanish had realized that its location was not ideal and El Morro became the focus of subsequent defensive efforts. Initially the home of military commanders, it became the permanent residence of Puerto Rican governors in 1639. Over the years the house has been expanded, notably from 1853 to 1860, when it acquired its current palatial facade, but the core remains the original sixteenth-century fortress.

The enthusiastic guides are a mine of information: you'll be shown the charming inner patio of the original building, site of the governor's offices (second floor) and living quarters (third floor; if the white flag is flying, the governor is in residence), before having a peek in the old dungeon and Saint Catherine's chapel. The tour ends in the pristine half-sunken **Spanish garden** that surrounds the house, with its Mudéjar fountain and wishing well.

Parque de las Palomas and around

Perched at the southern end of Calle del Cristo, **Parque de las Palomas** (daily 7am–6pm; free), a pleasant garden overlooking the walls, is aptly named considering the great flocks of pigeons that congregate here (*palomas* means "doves"). Next to the park at the end of the street, the tiny **Capilla del Santo Cristo de la Salud** (Tues 10.30am–2pm; free), established in 1753, is a much venerated place of worship, with a beautiful altar of silver *repoussé* work, laden with silver and gold ex-votos – offerings left in gratitude for good health granted by the saints worshipped here. The chapel is said to mark the spot where a horse rider was thrown over the walls and miraculously survived. Abandoned by the early twentieth century, it was restored in 1927. Look out for the two oil paintings by José Campeche inside.

Castillo de San Cristóbal

Guarding the eastern side of the old city, the **Castillo de San Cristóbal** (daily 9am–6pm; $3, valid for 24hr, under-16s free, $5 with El Morro, valid for 7 days),

Surfing San Juan

The local **surf** scene in San Juan is well established and with the coast taking an almost constant battering from the Atlantic Ocean, there are plenty of enticing breaks to suit all levels. **La 8 Surf Shop** (Mon–Sat 10am–6pm; ☏787/723-9808, ⓦwww .la8surf.com), at Avda Ponce de León 450 in Puerta de Tierra (near La Ocho), is one of the best in the city, selling, fixing and renting boards ($25/3hr; $50/day), as well as arranging lessons with a couple of pro-surfers. You can also contact the instructors yourself: William "Chino" Sue A Quan (☏787/955-6059; ⓦwww.wowsurfingschool .com) is a good teacher for both beginners and more experienced surfers. Lessons are $50 per person for 1hr 30 min. **Costazul Surf Shop** in Old San Juan at c/San Francisco 264 (daily 9am–7pm) also offers lessons and board rental in addition to surfing gear. In Isla Verde make for **Surf Face**, in La Plazoleta shopping court (Mon–Sat 9am–8pm, Sun 9am–5pm; ☏787/791-6800), for a good selection of surf gear and boards.

The best breaks

Pine Grove: Beginners should make for this fine beach break in **Isla Verde** (in front of the *Ritz*), which has small waves and a sandy bottom.

La Ocho: This break, just west of Escambrón beach in **Puerta de Tierra**, should pose no problems for surfers with slightly more experience. You have to paddle out a bit and there's a rocky bottom, but the water's deep and it's popular with long-boarders.

Piñones (see p.87): Includes **Chatarras**, a hollow, fast reef break, not far from the last line of *kioscos* off PR-187: the swell is not consistent but when it gets up you'll score some excellent tubes. **Playa Aviones** is a more consistent reef break in shallower water suitable for most levels, while **Tocones** is a short beach break with fast waves popular with body-boarders, but watch the **currents** here.

built in stages between 1634 and 1790, is the largest colonial fortress in the Americas. The entrance is near the city walls on Avenida Boulevard del Valle, at the end of Calle del Sol.

In contrast to El Morro, San Cristóbal protected the land approaches to the city and it's a fine example of the principle of "defence-in-depth", where each section of a fort is supported by one or more other parts, making it virtually impregnable. Inside, exhibits outline the history of the fort and particularly the **Fixed Regiment**. Established in 1765, this was one of the first local battalions ever to be raised in the Spanish colonies, and was instrumental in the defeat of the British in 1797.

Puerta de Tierra

To the east of Old San Juan lies **PUERTA DE TIERRA**, a mixture of government offices and low-rent residential neighbourhoods. It also has one of the best-kept secrets in the city: the narrow but sheltered **beach** below El Capitolo, which is just a short walk from the old town. Steps opposite the legislative building lead down to the beach, a thin strip of sand that's rarely busy. At the far eastern end of the district, the **Balneario El Escambrón** (facilities open daily 8.30am–5pm; free) incorporates one of the city's better beaches, with golden sand, a decent restaurant, toilets and plenty of shady palm trees.

El Capitolo

The impressive marble bulk of **El Capitolo** (daily 8.30am–5pm; free) is just a short walk east of Plaza de Colón along Avenida Juan Ponce de León. Constructed between 1925 and 1929, it remains the home of Puerto Rico's legislature and well worth a visit, not least to admire the lavish ornamentation inside and out. The official entrance faces the ocean on Avenida Muñoz Rivera: you should be able to pick up a guide here for a short but animated tour of the building (free), but call ahead to make sure (☎787/724-2030, ext 2472/2518).

Loosely modelled on the US Capitol in Washington, DC, the most impressive section is the rotunda, which contains the original nine articles of the Puerto Rican Constitution in glass display cases. The carved marble panels that ring the walls represent key elements of Puerto Rican political history, beginning with the Taíno and ending with the signing of the 1952 Constitution, while the four giant mosaics in the dome above represent the arrivals of Columbus in 1493 and Juan Ponce de León in 1508, the abolition of slavery in 1873 and autonomy in 1898. The House of Representatives sits on the west side of the rotunda, the Senate to the east – both have public viewing galleries on the third floor where you can watch live sessions (Mon–Fri; call ahead for times).

Condado to Isla Verde

East of Puerta de Tierra, resorts and posh condominiums line the Atlantic almost as far as Piñones, well outside the city limits. Each of the coastal neighbourhoods has its own distinct character, but there's little in the way of traditional sights – the main attraction is undoubtedly the **beach**.

The theme-park atmosphere begins in earnest at **CONDADO**, San Juan's oldest resort neighbourhood, an area gradually recovering some of its former ritz. **Avenida Ashford** is the main strip, running behind the beach from Puerta de Tierra to Ocean Park and lined with fast-food outlets, shops and restaurants. **Playa Condado** proper starts at **Plaza Ventana al Mar**, a small park opposite the junction with Avenida Magdalena. While the sand is thick and golden, it can get dirty and there's not much shade. Loungers can be hired for $4 (per day).

Beyond Avenida José de Diego, the hustle and high-rises of Condado peter out into the quieter residential community of **OCEAN PARK**. The **beach** here is far more attractive than at Condado: it's wider, less busy and backed by a thin line of palm trees, though it also attracts its share of trash – it's still a city beach after all.

Cockfights

Cockfighting is one of the most traditional and controversial pursuits in Puerto Rico, a blood sport which dates back to the Spanish colonial period and is vigorously defended by its chief supporters (see p.35). The main arena for cockfights in San Juan is **Club Gallistico de Puerto Rico**, at Avda Isla Verde 6600 (Tues, Thurs & Fri 4–10pm, Sat 2–10pm). Ringside seats are $40, but the $10.70 seats higher up provide perfectly adequate views. Women are welcome, though in practice you won't see many inside.

After being weighed and given a brief "warm-up", the two combatants are released and the fight begins, accompanied by frenetic shouting around the ring as bets are placed. You'll hear cries of "*azul, azul!*" (blue) for one and "*blanco, blanco!*" (white) for the other, followed by the amount being waged – white or blue ribbons denote which rooster is which. Fights run almost continuously throughout the day and last a maximum of fifteen minutes each, or until one of the roosters can no longer stand (you'll rarely see them die in the ring). It's certainly a unique experience, but be warned: the roosters really do peck the hell out of each other and the arena floor can become bloody – it may be too disturbing for some to watch. The main season is January to May; check in advance at other times.

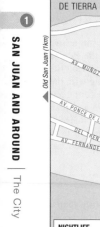

Old San Juan (1km)

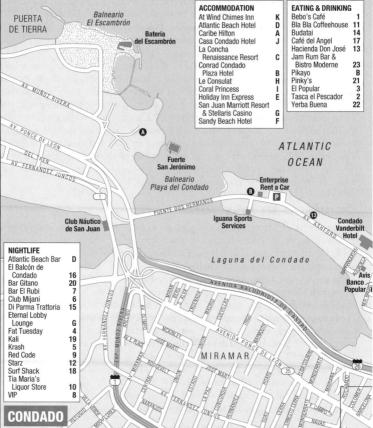

PUERTA DE TIERRA

Balneario El Escambrón

Batería del Escambrón

AV. MUÑOZ RIVERA

AV. PONCE DE LEÓN

DEL TREN

AV. FERNÁNDEZ JUNCOS

ⓐ

Fuerte San Jerónimo

Balneario Playa del Condado

ⓑ

Enterprise Rent a Car

P

Club Náutico de San Juan

PUENTE DOS HERMANOS

Iguana Sports Services

AV. ASHFORD

⑬

Condado Vanderbilt Hotel

Laguna del Condado

ATLANTIC OCEAN

AVENIDA BALDORIOTY DE CASTRO

Avis

Banco Popular

AVENIDA PONCE DE LEÓN

MIRAMAR

25

26

ACCOMMODATION	
At Wind Chimes Inn	K
Atlantic Beach Hotel	D
Caribe Hilton	A
Casa Condado Hotel	J
La Concha Renaissance Resort	C
Conrad Condado Plaza Hotel	B
Le Consulat	H
Coral Princess	I
Holiday Inn Express	E
San Juan Marriott Resort & Stellaris Casino	G
Sandy Beach Hotel	F

EATING & DRINKING	
Bebo's Café	1
Bla Bla Coffeehouse	11
Budatai	14
Café del Angel	17
Hacienda Don José	13
Jam Rum Bar & Bistro Moderne	23
Pikayo	B
Pinky's	21
El Popular	3
Tasca el Pescador	2
Yerba Buena	22

NIGHTLIFE	
Atlantic Beach Bar	D
El Balcón de Condado	16
Bar Gitano	20
Bar El Rubi	7
Club Mijani	6
Di Parma Trattoria	15
Eternal Lobby Lounge	G
Fat Tuesday	4
Kali	19
Krash	5
Red Code	9
Starz	12
Surf Shack	18
Tia Maria's Liquor Store	10
VIP	8

CONDADO

The reef offshore means the water is usually far calmer, making it ideal for **windsurfing** and **swimming** (see p.70); the only downside is that the beach is slightly harder to reach by bus and there are fewer amenities nearby. The beach starts to thin out as it reaches the Punta Las Marías headland.

Lining the coast along Avenida Isla Verde just beyond the headland, **ISLA VERDE** (see map overleaf) is another brash resort of malls, self-contained hotels and international restaurants. While this resembles southern Florida more than Puerto Rico, the palm-fringed **beach** is the best in the city. It's wide with fine sand and gentle waves and the proximity of so many stylish hotels and beach bars creates a party atmosphere at the weekends, attracting a diverse crowd of well-heeled locals, *reggaetón* fans and plenty of cocktail-sipping tourists.

The beach can be accessed via passages between the condos, or Calle Tartak halfway along. Once here, you can hire loungers for $4 (umbrellas for $10). Further east, beyond the *Courtyard* hotel, the beach merges into the **Balneario de Carolina**, the most popular public beach for local families. Though there are

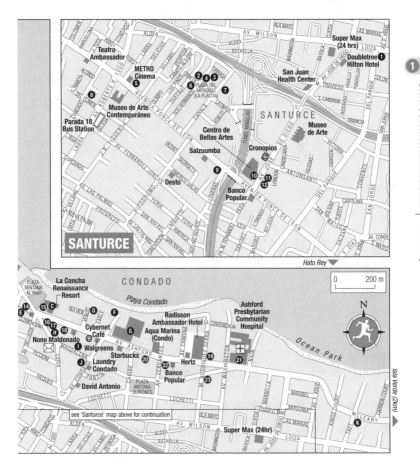

showers here and weekend volleyball tournaments, the beach is otherwise marred by the steel poles sticking into the water (to deter jet skis) and the jets taking off from the airport across the road. From here it's a short bus ride into Piñones (see p.87).

Santurce

The working-class *barrio* of **SANTURCE** lies behind Condado, a gritty neighbourhood that offers a refreshing contrast to the tourist zones on the coast. From the 1920s to the 1950s it was a thriving commercial district, crammed with fine Art Deco buildings. Hard times led to increased crime and the steady migration of its middle class to the suburbs and by the 1980s it had become dilapidated and run-down. In recent years the area has been undergoing much needed regeneration, with a couple of excellent **art museums**, exuberant **nightlife** and plenty of cheap **places to eat** along central Avenida Ponce de León.

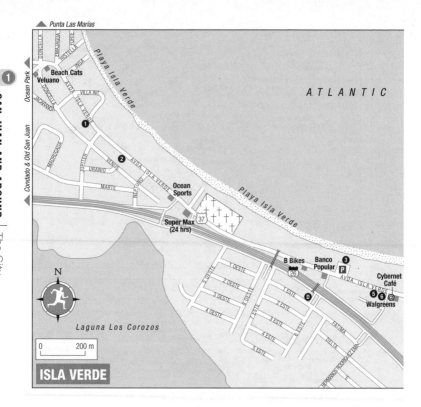

ISLA VERDE

Museo de Arte Contemporáneo and Plaza del Mercado

The **Museo de Arte Contemporáneo** (Tues–Sat 10am–4pm, Sun noon–4pm; free; ☎787/977-4030, ⓦwww.museocontemporaneopr.org), housed in a tastefully restored school building on the corner of Juan Ponce de León and Avenida Roberto Todd, holds temporary exhibitions of bold and experimental post-1940 art from Puerto Rico and elsewhere in the Caribbean. Although the temporary shows sometimes take up every gallery, you may still see pieces from the museum's permanent collection, including the photography of Néstor Millán Alvarez and some of the best abstract work from José Morales. The building – completed in 1918 – is an attraction in itself, its striking red-brick galleries surrounding a bright, glass-covered courtyard.

From the museum it's a short walk south along Juan Ponce de León then left up Calle Dos Hermanos to the **Plaza del Mercado**, where a vibrant indoor **market** (Mon–Sat 5am–5pm, Sun 5am–noon) is surrounded by a collection of fashionable places to eat and drink known as **La Placita** (see p.75). The market contains mostly fruit and vegetable stores and retains a distinctively local character despite the number of tours that come through here.

Museo de Arte

Displaying the finest ensemble of Puerto Rican art on the island, the **Museo de Arte** (Tues & Thurs–Sat 10am–5pm, Wed 10am–8pm, Sun 11am–6pm; $8.56 with tax; ☎787/977-6277, ⓦwww.mapr.org) is housed in another graceful

EATING & DRINKING		NIGHTLIFE		ACCOMMODATION	
Casa Dante	2	El Alambique	4	Best Western	
Lupi's	8	Bed Lounge	5	San Juan Airport Hotel	F
Metropol	10	Café La Plage	3	Coqui Inn	D
Mi Casita	9	Club Brava	B	Hotel Villa del Sol	E
Tangerine	A	Cocobongo	6	Ritz Carlton San Juan	
		Drums	7	Hotel, Spa & Casino	C
		Q Restaurant		El San Juan Hotel & Casino	B
		& Lounge	1	San Juan Water &	
		Wet Bar	A	Beach Club Hotel	A

OCEAN

Punta El Media

Balneario de Carolina

Playa Isla Verde

El San Juan Hotel

Ritz Carlton Hotel

InterContinental San Juan Resort

Charlie Car Rental

Surf Face

Verdanza Hotel

Club Gallistico

Embassy Suites

Aeropuerto Internacional Luis Muñoz Marín

Piñones (2km)

F, Airport entrance, Carolina & the east coast

structure blending Neoclassical styles, built in 1920 and originally serving as a hospital. The gallery is a short walk east of the market, at Avda José de Diego 299. The museum's two main floors are arranged thematically, in roughly chronological order from the seventeenth century to the present day. Start in Gallery 6, in the southern wing on the first floor ("level 3"), which has a modest display of *santos* (carved wooden figures representing the saints), followed by Gallery 7, featuring religious art of the seventeenth and eighteenth centuries. The highlight here is the piercing, anonymous image of the **black Christ**, *El Señor de Esquípulas* (1690–1710), recalling the sacred icon of the same name in Guatemala.

Gallery 8 contains a few devotional paintings from eighteenth-century Rococo master **José Campeche**, while Gallery 10 charts the move from Realism to the more idealized *Costumbrista* school and contains several works by celebrated artists **Miguel Pou** and **Francisco Oller**, including the latter's tropical still-life series. The northern wing houses the Ángel Ramos and Tina Hill collection, thirty paintings that cover the 1940s to 1960s. Highlights include Rafael Tufiño's *La Perla* (1969) and ten paintings by Spanish-born Ángel Botello (1913–1986), who drew much inspiration from the Caribbean (particularly Haiti) and spent most of his career in Puerto Rico.

The second floor ("level 4") contains the museum's substantial collection of **contemporary** painting, sculpture and installation art; the works are organized thematically, but exhibits are often moved around. You can also check out the peaceful sculpture garden on the lower floor ("level 2").

69

Watersports in San Juan

San Juan is not the best place on the island for **diving**, but there are a couple of decent reefs just offshore. **Ocean Sports**, at Avda Ashford 1035 in Condado (☎787/723-8513, ⓦwww.osdivers.com) and Avda Isla Verde 77 in Isla Verde (Mon–Sat 10am–6pm; ☎787/268-2329) offers dives for certified divers from $85. Scuba Dogs (☎787/783-6377, ⓦwww.scubadogs.net) also maintains the artificial **Escambrón Marine Park** near the beach of the same name (p.64), the perfect place for learners.

San Juan has a justifiably good reputation for deep-sea **fishing**: lines go out just twenty minutes offshore, with blue and white marlin the top attractions, but plenty of snapper, dolphinfish, wahoo, sailfish and tuna to aim for as well. The most professional expeditions are arranged by **Mike Benítez' Sport Fishing** (daily 9am–5pm; ☎787/723-2292, ⓦwww.mikebenitezsportfishing.com) and depart from the Club Náutico de San Juan on Avenida Fernández Juncos, at the eastern end of Puerta de Tierra. Charters for a maximum of six people cost $650 for a half-day or $210 per fisherman and $90 per passenger.

For **windsurfing**, head to Punta Las Marías (east of Ocean Park) and the four-mile reef about half a mile out, which is one of the best wave-sailing spots on the island. To get started, visit **Velauno** at c/Loíza 2430 (☎787/728-8716, ⓦwww.velauno.com), close to the top end of Isla Verde and five blocks from the beach. This huge shop is the primary wind- and kite-surfing centre in the city. Beginner lessons cost $110 for two hours, including boards. Nearby is **Beach Cats**, at c/Loíza 2434 (☎787/727-0883, ⓦbeachcatspr.com), another wind- and **kite-surfing** specialist that organizes lessons and rents boards.

Many companies that run **boat trips** from Villa Marina and Puerto del Rey on the east coast offer transport to and from San Juan (see p.110).

Río Piedras

Founded in 1714 and incorporated into San Juan in 1951, **RÍO PIEDRAS** is a low-rise residential *barrio* 12km south of Old San Juan, home to the main campus of the **Universidad de Puerto Rico** (ⓦwww.uprrp.edu) and the city's largest **market**.

The university is worth a visit for the illuminating **Museo de Historia Antropología y Arte** (Mon–Tues & Thurs–Fri 9am–4.30pm, Wed 9am–8.30pm, Sun 11.30am–4.30pm; free; ☎787/763-3939), just inside the main entrance on Avenida Ponce de León (buses stop outside the gate). Though it's small, the galleries here contain a number of very significant artefacts, including some enigmatic **Taíno** finds from around the island. Exhibits from the permanent collection tend to rotate, but highlights include the mystifying stone collars, ritual objects thought to be connected to the ancient ball game (see p.164), and the tiny carved seats known as *duho*. The museum also has an extensive collection of art, including **Francisco Oller**'s masterpiece, *El Velorio* (1893), a richly imagined depiction of a wake in rural nineteenth-century Puerto Rico. Jumping continents, you'll find a rather gruesome pair of Egyptian **mummies** (with mummified cat) incongruously displayed in the reception area. Before moving on, check out the striking **Torre Franklin D. Roosevelt**, clearly visible above the main university buildings, a clock tower constructed in 1937 in Spanish Revival style with an ornate facade and intricately patterned ceiling.

It's a short walk southeast of the university to the **Plaza del Mercado** (Mon–Fri 6am–5pm, Sat 6am–1pm), an indoor market on the edge of the busy commercial centre of Río Piedras. Though it's primarily a collection of fruit and vegetable stalls, you'll come across fascinating *botánicas* selling all sorts of herbal remedies, as

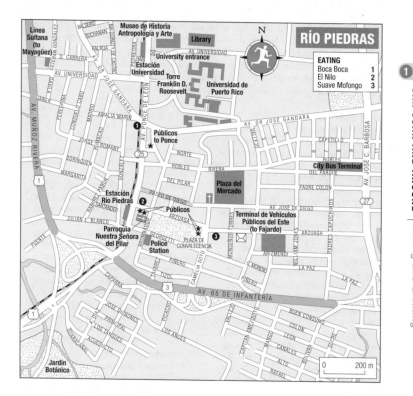

well as a collection of cheap **cigars** at Tabaco Don Bienve ($1.25 *petite*, $3.75 Churchills). The real highlight, however, is the **food court** at the back, where almost every Puerto Rican dish is served up at bargain prices: try *Mrs Batida* for *batidas* and *jugos* and *Doña Alice* for chicken and stews.

Eating and drinking

San Juan has a well-deserved reputation as the **culinary capital** of the Caribbean. The city is packed with restaurants showcasing everything from international haute cuisine and classy Nuevo Latino cooking to American diners and humble canteens serving tasty *cocina criolla*, the perfect introduction to the island's own rich gastronomic traditions.

   Old San Juan offers the most diversity and some of the best restaurants on the island. Meals can be expensive here, but there are plenty of cheap options and the scene is by no means solely tourist-oriented – most of the people eating here will be locals, especially in the mornings. The cheapest places are the stalls along the waterfront, where you can usually pick up fried snacks such as *alcapurrias* and *bacalaítos* (see p.29) for less than $2, or *Kiosko 4 Estaciones* on the northwest side of Plaza de Armas, open 24 hours for pastas, sandwiches (less than $5) and excellent coffee. The most fashionable restaurants in the city are located in Old San Juan's **SoFo** ("South Fortaleza") district, offering superb fusion and international cuisine in equally elaborate premises. For **self-catering** or picnics, stock up at the Super Max supermarket on Plaza de Armas (Mon–Sat 6am–midnight, Sun 9am–9pm).

The beach areas of **Condado** and **Isla Verde** also boast a number of excellent and conveniently located restaurants, while cheaper, no-frills diners can be found in **Santurce**, and there are plenty of fast-food outlets if you get desperate, particularly along the main avenues in Condado and Isla Verde.

Old San Juan

Aguaviva c/Fortaleza 364 ☎787/722-0665, ⓦwww.oofrestaurants.com. Small but stylish SoFo trendsetter with an eclectic menu of international seafood and an azure blue colour scheme. Specialities include fresh oysters ($2.50), *ceviches* ($17), Caribbean coconut shrimp ($16) and sharp, perfectly mixed cocktails ($9–10). Mon–Fri 6pm–midnight, Sat & Sun noon–4pm & 6pm–midnight.

Aureola c/San Sebastián 106 ☎787/722-8635. One of San Juan's fusion cuisine pioneers, showing Spanish, Italian and African influences with a Puerto Rican twist: try the breaded *mahi-mahi* with plantains, or pork stuffed with cranberries and mango. Order mains ($12.95–24.95) or simply share the appetizers, tapas-style. Reservations recommended. Tues–Sun noon–midnight.

Ben & Jerry's c/Cristo 61 ☎787/977-6882. The Vermont ice-cream franchise is a deservedly popular stop in the old town, offering all the usual, addictive flavours in a relaxed environment. Cones and cups come in three sizes ($3.25–5.25) and there are plenty of shakes, brownies and other sweet treats to tempt you. Sun–Thurs 11am–10pm, Fri & Sat 11am–11pm.

Blend c/Fortaleza 309 ☎787/977-7777. This bar, lounge and restaurant features an elegant interior of plush crimson seats and booths and a blend of Mediterranean, Asian and Puerto Rican cuisines: sumptuous soy "guavapple" salmon ($15) and Asian *churrasco* ($17). Live jazz Wed 8pm–midnight and DJs playing upbeat garage at the weekends. Tues–Sat 6pm–2am.

La Bombonera c/San Francisco 259 ☎787/722-0658. Established in 1902, this is one of the city's oldest cafés, with a long bar and waiters dressed in white shirts and red bow ties. The place gets packed at weekends, especially for breakfast, when scrambled eggs or *mallorcas* (toasted pastries filled with bacon, ham or cheese and dusted with icing sugar; $3–5) are served with rich mountain coffee (check out the vintage steamed-milk machine). Daily 7.30am–6pm.

Café Cola'o Pier 2 ☎787/725-4139, ⓦwww .prcafecolao.com. Fine Puerto Rican artisanal coffee from Adjuntas, Ciales and Utuado served right on the harbour. Your order even comes with elaborate designs crafted into the foamy milk on top. You also can buy raw coffee here, whole beans or ground. Mon–Fri 6.30am–6.30pm, Sat & Sun 9am–7pm.

Café Puerto Rico c/O'Donnell 208 ☎787/724-2281, ⓦwww.cafepuertorico.com. This cosy restaurant makes a fine introduction to *cocina criolla*, with rich *asopaos* ($12–25), plenty of seafood and 13 choices of *mofongo*: the national dish is served here as a giant hollowed-out bowl of cassava, plantain or banana, stuffed with codfish, crab, prawn or lobster ($12–24).

Cafeteria Mallorca c/San Francisco 300 ☎787/724-460. Open since 1961, this endearing diner is the less fusty cousin of *La Bombonera*, with uniformed but laidback waiters and an army of loyal regulars enjoying the cheap breakfasts, fluffy *mallorcas* ($2.25–3.50), coffee from $1.35 and solid, great-value meals at lunch (under $10). Eat at one of the small Formica tables or at the bar. Daily 7am–6pm.

Dragonfly c/Fortaleza 364 ☎787/977-3886, ⓦwww.oofrestaurants.com. One of San Juan's most innovative restaurants, fusing Caribbean classics with Asian flavours. Try Peking duck nachos with wasabi sour cream ($21), or marinated *churrasco* with wasabi "dragonflies" (shoestring potatoes) for $25. The ruby-red Chinese dining room was inspired by 1930s Shanghai. No reservations, so be prepared for a wait. Daily 6pm–midnight.

La Mallorquina c/San Justo 207 ☎787/722-3261, ⓦwww.mallorquinapr .com. Founded in 1848, this is the oldest restaurant on the island. It's pricey, but the refined colonial setting, marble floors and antique-filled dining room make this place a must-try. *Asopao* is the speciality here, the soupy rice dish served with chicken or seafood in small "kettles" for $14.95–18.95. Mon–Sat 11.45am–10pm. Closed Sept.

Marmalade c/Fortaleza 317 ☎787/724-3969, ⓦwww.marmaladepr.com. Incredibly creative "Californian-French" cuisine from celebrity chef Peter Schintler. Think miso-blazed black cod ($27.50), braised lamb shank lasagne, with garlic spinach and Persian feta cheese ($27.50), and lots of tempting vegetarian options (black olive papadelle, $16). Mon–Thurs 6pm–midnight, Fri & Sat 6am–2am, Sun 6–10pm.

Mojito's c/Recinto Sur 323 ☎787/725-5691. An ideal spot for a hearty, good-value Puerto Rican lunch – try the *bacalao guisado* (codfish stew) for $9.95 or the ubiquitous *mofongo* ($13.95) served with chunks of fried pork. Close to the marina and extremely popular with local office workers. Despite the name, it's not a great place for a drink. Mon–Sat 11am–10pm.

El Picoteo *El Convento Hotel*, c/Cristo 100 ☎787/723-9202, ⊛www.elconvento.com. This refined Spanish restaurant overlooks the old convent's tranquil courtyard, justly popular for its pricey tapas such as *jamón serrano* ($14) and white anchovies ($11). It also serves the best paella ($28–31) on the island and a playful selection of pizzas for around $16. Tues–Sun noon–midnight.

Parrot Club c/Fortaleza 363 ⊛www.oof restaurants.com. Always busy, the main draw here is the salsa-soaked party atmosphere (Johnny Depp partied here when filming the *Rum Diary* in 2009). Cuban and Mexican classics are given an American slant; try the huge, succulent legs of roast pork or fabulous seared tuna. It's pricey, though (mains $18–28) and the famous house *mojitos* ($8) are a little overrated. No reservations, so come early. Mon–Fri 11.30am–midnight, Sat & Sun 9am–midnight.

Restaurante El Jibarito c/Sol 280 ☎787/725-8375, ⊛www.eljibaritopr.com. Set in a quiet corner of the old town, this recreation of a rustic mountain diner offers a simple wooden interior, daily specials and hearty *comida criolla* such as the oven-baked pork with sweet plantains and plantain *tamales* filled with pork. Most mains are under $10. Daily 10am–9pm.

St Germain Bistro & Café c/Sol 156 ☎787/725-5830, ⊛www.stgermainpr.com. Stylish, clean and bright French restaurant away from the main tourist drag, serving freshly made sandwiches, quiche, salads, *ceviche* and pizzas. Set dinners for two are around $43, while lunches are much less (just $12 or $9 for quiche). No reservations. Tues–Sat 11.30am–3.30pm & 6–10pm; Sun 10am–3pm & 6–10pm.

Tío Danny's c/Fortaleza 313 ☎787/723-0322, ⊛www.tiodannyscafe.com. Welcoming restaurant with a small wooden bar and dining room facing the street. The menu offers a mixture of solid Mexican food ($12–16) and beautifully crafted local classics such as *mofongo* ($18–20), but this is also a popular place for a drink – cocktails are $7, *sangría* is $5 and draft Medalla is $2.50. Tues–Sun 11am–2am.

Puerta de Tierra

El Hamburguer Avda Muñoz Rivera. Since it opened in the 1940s, just up the hill from Escambrón beach, this local barbecue shack has built up a loyal cult following thanks to its flame-grilled burgers, the best in the city. The home-made main event comes in several varieties, the patties roasted over an open fire and served with skinny fries ($2.50–3). Gets jam-packed at weekends. Sun–Thurs 11am–11pm, Fri & Sat 11am–1am.

Condado

Bebo's Café c/Loíza 1600 ☎787/726-1008, ⊛www.beboscafe.com. A neighbourhood institution, this Dominican-owned cafeteria serves hearty portions of *comida criolla* classics such as *mofongo* (from $9.50), but also an incredibly filling *pastelón de amarillos* (fried plantain pie stuffed with meat) for under $10. It's also a good place for Mexican-style breakfasts (under $5). Mains range $7.95–25. Daily 7am–12.30am.

Budatai Avda Ashford 1056 ☎787/725-6919, ⊛www.budatai.com. Creation of US celebrity chef Roberto Treviño, this stylish fusion restaurant blends Asian-inspired dishes with local ingredients and flavours. Expect creative dim sum (seared foie gras with pistachio brioche), sushi, duck fried rice and a mouthwatering Kobe steak. Figure on at least $50/head. Daily 11.30am–midnight.

Café del Angel Avda Ashford 1106 ☎787/643-7594. One of the best bets for reasonably priced Puerto Rican food on the main strip, though it's worthwhile only if you haven't got time to venture further afield. Decent choice of the usual *mofongo*, rice dishes and a large menu of more substantial island favourites (mains from $8.95). Wed–Mon 11am–10pm.

Hacienda Don José Avda Ashford 1025 ☎787/722-5880. Mexican and Puerto Rican standards are served in an open dining room overlooking the ocean at this spot at the western end of Condado. It's a smart choice for an early breakfast (from $6.95), but otherwise it's rather overpriced (*burritos* $15.95, *fajitas* $17.95) – you're paying for the waterside location. Daily 7am–11pm.

Jam Rum Bar & Bistro Moderne Avda Magdalena 1400 ☎787/721-5991. Fashionable Caribbean restaurant from the folks at *Marmalade* (p.72), serving over fifty types of rum and mouthwatering dishes including blue crab cakes, *churrasco* over four-root *mofongo* and incredible beef carpaccio. Mains $24–29. Live music and salsa Thurs–Sat. Sun–Thurs 6–11pm, Fri & Sat 6pm–midnight.

Pikayo *Conrad Condado Plaza Hotel*, Avda Ashford 999 ☎787/721-6194, ⊛www.pikayo.com. Stylish restaurant serving exquisite Caribbean fusion cuisine by award-winning chef Wilo Benet. Be mesmerized by dishes such as halibut with mashed *apio* (celeriac) and sautéed Japanese squid, served in chic dining rooms embellished with modern art. Fixed menus from $49; mains between $30–40. Daily 6–11pm.

Pinky's Avda Ashford 1451 ☎787/727-3347. Perfect for a wholesome brunch before hitting the beach, this bright café is justly popular for its playful, eclectic menu of comfort food such as pork plantains, hummus, vegetarian specials and various wraps from $7.50–11. Tues–Fri 7am–4pm, Sat & Sun 11am–4pm.

Yerba Buena Avda Ashford 1350 ☎787/721-5700. Popular bistro knocking out Caribbean and Cuban classics such as *ropa vieja* (shredded beef) and yam fritters with creole hot sauce, but best known for its authentic *mojitos* and live Cuban music Fri & Sat and the Humberto Ramirez Big Band plays from 8pm on Mondays. Daily 5pm–midnight.

Ocean Park

Kasalta Avda McLeary 1966. This venerable bakery and café has long self-service counters where you can choose various pastries, cakes and local snacks (from $1), though real aficionados come here for the legendary coffee. The *Cubano* sandwiches ($8.95) and Spanish-style *tortilla* (omelette) are excellent ($5.95) and there's good-quality *jamón serrano* from Spain. Daily 6am–10pm.

Pamela's c/Santa Ana 1, *Número Uno Guest House* ☎787/726-5010. This is one of the most appealing (and romantic) places to eat in the city, with an indoor section and tables right on the beach. The menu comprises delectable Caribbean- and Puerto Rican-inspired dishes with a contemporary edge: gems such as jalapeño- and ginger-sautéed shrimp, ($29) and guava rum-glazed double pork chop ($27). Daily noon–10pm.

Isla Verde

Casa Dante Avda Isla Verde 39 ☎787/726-7310. A simple dining room just off the main road, but an excellent place for *comida criolla* and especially the house speciality, *mofongo* – this is the self-styled "*Casa del Mofongo*" after all. The *camarones* (shrimps) and wine list aren't bad either. Tues–Sun 11.30am–1am.

Lupi's Avda Isla Verde 6369 ☎787/253-2198. It's a bit touristy and doubles as a sports bar, but this lively Tex-Mex-style restaurant is an easy option near the big hotels, offering an appetizing array of *fajitas*, *nachos* and *burritos*. Expect live music and a raucous crowd most evenings. Daily 10am–3am.

Metropol Avda Isla Verde, next to *Club Gallistico* ☎787/791-4046, ☜www.metropolpr.com. Local

institution, established in Santurce in 1965, specializing in Cuban and Puerto Rican food. Try the *gallinita relleno* (guinea hen stuffed with a rice-and-black-bean mixture called *congri*) for $13.95, or the *Fiesta Cubana* ($15.95) for a taster of several Cuban favourites (*tamales*, pork, cassava). Daily 11.30am–11.30pm.

Mi Casita La Plazuela shopping court, Avda Isla Verde ☎787/791-1777. A genuinely good-value Puerto Rican café, with ham and egg breakfasts for under $4 and all the *comida criolla* favourites ($7–20), but don't overlook the substantial octopus salad and selection of soups, especially the sublime garlic shrimp. Tends to get swamped with guests from nearby resorts at lunch, looking for a local experience. Daily 7am–10.30pm.

🏃 **Tangerine** *San Juan Water & Beach Club Hotel*, c/Tartak 2 ☎787/728-3666. Best place to splurge in Isla Verde: chic contemporary decor, attentive service and Asian-American fusion cuisine conjured up by award-winning chef Nelson Rosado. Expect delights such as green banana roll of beef, crab tempura or sumptuous Tribal Mongolian ribs (mains $22–30). Tues–Sat 7am–noon & 6.30–11pm.

Santurce

Bla Bla Coffeehouse Avda José de Diego 353, ☎787/724-8321, ☜www.blablacoffeehouse.com. Friendly, modern café, conveniently located in between art museums and perfect for a pre-visit breakfast, coffee break ($1) or light lunch (salads, sandwiches and burgers from $6–8). The refreshing strawberry, papaya and melon *batidas* ($3.50) are superb. Mon–Fri 7.30am–4pm, Sat 8.30am–4pm.

🏃 **El Popular** c/Capitol 205 ☎787/722-4653. One of the best cafés in La Placita, its Spanish-style dining room lined with old photos of the island's political *illuminati*. Service is slow, but the food is fresh and it dishes out some of the best *chicharrones de pollo* (fried chicken) and *olla Española* (Spanish beef stew) on the island. Beers are $1.25 and happy hour is 7–10pm. Tues–Sun 11am–10pm.

🏃 **Tasca el Pescador** c/Dos Hermanos 178 ☎787/721-0995. Another excellent restaurant in La Placita, with an antique wooden bar temptingly laden with all manner of exotic bottles. The Spanish-style menu specializes in fresh fish (try the fabulous salmon in guava sauce; $17.50), but this place is best for lunch or a very early dinner. Tues–Sun 11am–7.30pm.

Río Piedras

Boca Boca c/Amalia Marin 4 ☎787/296-8222. Featuring some exuberant graffiti art, this student café offers free internet access, great coffee, plenty of snacks and cheap Puerto Rican food; cod, roast chicken dishes and *mofongo* from $6.95 and a *menú del día* from $5.95. Mon, Tues & Fri 7am–6pm; Wed & Thurs 7am–midnight, Sat 9am–3pm.

El Nilo Avda Ponce de León 1105 ☎787/759-6630. If the market stalls don't appeal (see p.71), try this down-to-earth cafeteria close to the Tren Urbano station in the heart of Río Piedras. It cooks up the best *comida criolla* in the area and is an old student favourite. Try the sumptuous roast pork sandwiches from $4.95. Mon–Sat 7am–6pm.

Suave Mofongo c/Arzuaga at Camelia Soto ☎787/518-6542. This tiny canteen boasts the best fried treats in Río Piedras, with the full roster of *alcapurrias*, *bacalaítos* and *pasteles* cooked up from early morning for just $1–2 and plastic cup *piña coladas* from $1.30. Mon–Sat 7am–6pm.

Nightlife

Going out in San Juan can be a raucous, all-night affair. Weekends are especially lively and **Calle de San Sebastián** in Old San Juan becomes jam-packed with people out to party. It tends to get busy around 11pm and winds down after 3am, though many **bars and clubs** – especially in the beach districts – keep going well beyond dawn. Lovers of rum, cocktails, salsa and, not least, thumping *reggaetón*, are particularly well catered for; in addition, the **gay scene** is the most sophisticated in the Caribbean. If you want something a little less intense, the large **resorts** offer plenty of activities as well and you can always hit the **casinos** (see p.80).

Bars

Old San Juan has the highest concentration of historic, local cantinas full of character. Many SoFo restaurants double as lounge bars at the weekend, if that's more your thing. In **Condado**, the hotel bars overlooking the beaches are the best places for drinks (see p.54), but there are several pubs inland and **Santurce** is just a short drive or walk away, home to some of the biggest clubs, a thriving gay scene and the lively bar and restaurant area known as **La Placita**, centred on the Plaza del Mercado. Come here on a Thursday or Friday night, when the whole area becomes a wild salsa party. **Isla Verde** nightlife is fairly self-contained but just as animated, with most bars open until dawn, especially on weekends – here also many **restaurants** double as bars and discos (see opposite).

Claiming the piña colada

Synonymous with both tropical languor and the high life, the **piña colada** became Puerto Rico's national drink in 1978, thanks to the widely held view that it was created here over fifty years ago. The official claimant (recognized by the Puerto Rican government) is bartender Ramon "*Monchito*" Marrero, who is said to have created the drink while working in the former *Beachcombers' Bar* of the *Caribe Hilton* in 1954 (their **Piña Colada Club** keeps up the tradition today; Thurs–Sat noon–2am, Sun & Mon noon–midnight). However, if you visit the **Barrachina** restaurant at c/ Fortaleza 104 in Old San Juan (Sun–Tues & Thurs 11am–10pm, Wed 11am–6pm, Fri & Sat 10am–11pm; ⊛www.barrachina.com), a marble plaque on the street claims that Don Ramon Portas Mingot created the drink there in 1963.

The truth is that no one really knows who invented the cocktail – "*piña coladas*" were being made in **Cuba** at the turn of the century, where they literally were just non-alcoholic "strained pineapple". However, some aficionados claim the alcoholic version was mentioned in travel magazines as early as 1922 with reference to Cuba. The latter is definitely the home of the *mojito* and *daiquiri* and perhaps the *piña colada* too – but just don't say that when you're in Puerto Rico.

Old San Juan

El Adoquín del Patio El Callejón, at the top of c/Tanca. This classic Puerto Rican dive bar hosts an eclectic mix of oddballs and party-goers, many of them locals from nearby La Perla. It's open most days at all hours, but most fun late on weekends when the salsa heats up and the rum shots get bigger.

El Batey c/Cristo 101 ☏787/725-1787. This dive bar ("*batey*" is the Taíno word for ball-court), is a San Juan institution, with the walls plastered in graffiti and an eclectic clientele that ranges from cruise-ship tourists to wannabe *reggaetón* gangsters. Incongruously located across from the refined *El Convento*, it tends to get busy in the early hours. Daily 2pm–6am.

Café Celeste Callejón de la Capilla. Aka "*Corozaleño*", this genuine *chinchorro*, or tiny hole-in-the-wall bar with a couple of tables outside, is popular with workmen for breakfast and lunch and open late for cheap drinks in the evenings. Pop in for a quick can of Medalla ($1.50) before hitting the posh restaurants on c/Fortaleza, or *Nuyorican* across the alley. Daily 7am–3am.

Café Hijos de Borinquen c/San José 151 ☏787/723-8126. This classic old town bar opened in 1954 and is the best place to get a sense of the area's Puerto Rican roots and culture, with plenty of faded memorabilia on the walls. Expect it to be empty till 10pm, but overflowing 1–2am. Thurs–Sat from 8pm till late.

Colmado Bar Moreno c/Tetuan 365 ☏787/724-5130. This Dominican liquor store doubles as a 24-hour bar, pumping out salsa and *merengue* at all hours – grab a cheap beer or rum in a plastic cup and sip it inside, or grab some bottles to take away.

Maria's c/Cristo 204 ☏787/721-1678. This small bar has been around for over 40 years and is noted for its quality *piña coladas* and *margaritas* ($6.50). A former haunt of actor Benicio del Toro (his tipple of choice was banana frost cocktails), it's quite touristy these days, but serves a wickedly potent cocktail, *La Norta* (stick to the drinks – the food is poor). Daily 10.30am–3am (4am Fri & Sat).

Nono's c/San Sebastián 100 ☏787/725-7819. Basic cantina-style bar in a colonial building with high wooden ceilings, TVs and pool tables. It's often crammed with expats and boozing tourists on weekend afternoons and late nights on Fri when it plays predominantly rock music. Daily 11am–4am.

Old Harbour Brewery c/Tizol 202 ☏787/721-2100. The only microbrewery in town, just up from the dockside, with beers freshly brewed German-style in the copper-and-steel vats on site. You can order a decent spread of tapas and more substantial meals. The beers, ranging from lagers and hoppy pale ales to robust, creamy stouts, are $5.30. Popular with locals and tourists alike. Daily 11.30am–1am.

Red Monkey c/Cruz 252 ☏787/565-3181. Fun bar that attracts a young and friendly crowd – a good choice if you're travelling solo. Highlights include the infamous "monkey bomb" ($5), home-made burgers ($6) and their zesty mimosa ($4). Tues–Sat from 4pm till late.

Condado

El Balcón de Condado Avda Ashford 1104 ☏787/998-2211. Cheap booze is the main draw here, with $1.75 Medallas and $4.50 shots a real bargain. The bar occupies the second floor, but though it can be lots of fun, there's no view from this "*balcón*".

Gay nightlife

San Juan is generally gay-friendly and most clubs have gay nights. Much of the explicitly gay nightlife in the city once revolved around the gay-oriented hotels and bars in **Condado**, with the **Atlantic Beach Bar** (c/Vendig 1) especially popular on Sunday afternoons (after 4pm). These days, though, you need to head behind the beach to **Santurce** for a more cutting-edge club scene. Grab a drink before (or after) hitting the dancefloor at **Tia Maria's Liquor Store**, Avda José de Diego 326 (☏787/724-4011), a dive bar with a small pool table, which is packed at weekends. You could also try **VIP** (formerly *Junior's Bar*), a gay-friendly local pub at Avda Condado 613 (Thurs–Sun 9pm–late; ☏787/722-5509), recognizable by its rainbow facade. Of the best clubs in the area, **Starz** (☏787/358-0123) at Avda José de Diego 385 (Sat only, 9am–6am), pulls in an overtly gay, extremely fashion-conscious crowd while **Krash** (Wed–Sat from 10pm; ☏787/722-1131, ⓦwww.krashklubpr.com), at Avda Ponce de León 1257, has been around for years, with two levels and a metallic, industrial theme: look out for the rainbow flag and TV screens outside. Check out ⓦwww.orgulloboricua.net (Spanish only) for the latest in gay news, events and nightlife in the city.

Bar Gitano Avda Ashford 1302 ☏ 787/294-5513. Another addition to the Roberto Treviño stable, this old-world Spanish tapas bar is a great place to sip red wine and nibble snacks (from $4). You can also sit and have a full meal here, but the wine list is the real highlight. Mon–Sat 11.30am–noon, Sun 11.30am–10pm.

Di Parma Trattoria Avda Ashford 1901, at Plaza Ventana al Mar ☏ 787/725-5202. This Italian restaurant serves reasonable food (pizza from $10), but is best as a fashionable place to start or end your evening. Sip drinks on the terrace overlooking the park and beach, accompanied by suitably *Café del Mar*-inspired sounds: jazz (Thurs), house (Fri) and Afro-Cuban (Sat) – live music played Sat only. Mon–Thurs 5pm–1am, Fri–Sun 11am–2am.

Kali Avda Ashford 1407 ☏ 787/721-5104, ⒲ www .kalicondado.com. Very hip, dimly lit lounge bar, with minimalist chairs and white sofas, a vaguely Asian theme and stylish clientele. Tues–Sun 6pm–6am.

Surf Shack Avda Ashford 1106 ☏ 787/723-2517. Compact, cosy space managed by Roberto Treviño from *Budatai* down the road, serving the same high quality snacks at a fraction of the price, with cheap beers to wash it down; try the *empanadas*, shark *chicharrones* or juicy burgers.

Isla Verde

El Alambique c/Tartak 102 ☏ 787/253-5860. For a bar that overlooks the beach, without resort prices, try this no-frills place near the *Water Club* hotel. It's located at the base of a high-rise condo, but looks out onto the sand – grab a Medalla beer ($2 on Sat) or *piña colada* in a plastic cup. Hard to believe, but this was a hugely popular club in the 1970s, the beach opposite is still known as "*La Playa del Alambique*".

Bed Lounge Avda Isla Verde 5930 ☏ 939/244-2826. Stylish lounge bar with a posh, club-like atmosphere, real beds to look cool on (which are usually reserved) and a strict dress code (no trainers, no T-shirts and no caps), except on Tuesdays, when there's a studenty dance party 9pm–3am.

Café La Plage Avda Isla Verde 4851 ☏ 787/268-7733. The beachfront restaurant of the *Beach House Hotel* in the middle of Isla Verde is a great place to eat but best for a sundown cocktail or two;

get there early and you can nab one of the private Indonesian beds on the sand.

Drums Isla Verde Mall Suite 104 ☏ 787/253-1443, ⒲ www.drumssanjuan.com. This restaurant/sports bar also morphs into a popular club late nights. Expect anything from the US Superbowl live, to the latest salsa acts and Latin DJs. Wed 11am–1am, Thurs 11am–2am, Fri & Sat 11am–4am, Sun 11.30am–2am.

Cocobongo Avda Isla Verde 5940, corner of c/ Hermanos Rodriquez Ema ☏ 787/727-3422. Not quite as raucous as the legendary Cancún nightspot, but still a top place for drinking and dancing till the early hours, not far from the main resorts. Beer is $2.75 Thurs–Sun 11pm–2am, while at *El Taquito*, underneath, basic and cheap Mexican fare is served 24hr (*tacos* from $1.50). Closed Mon & Tues.

Q Restaurant & Lounge Avda Isla Verde 2480 ☏ 787/728-8663, ⒲ qpuertorico.blogspot.com. Another stylish lounge bar that serves food and turns into a club. Notable for its startling exterior and interior design featuring bold black and white patterns; it's sort of Gothic meets Alice in Wonder-land. Thurs–Sat 10pm till late.

Wet Bar *San Juan Water & Beach Club Hotel*, c/Tartak 2 ☏ 787/728-3666. Seductive rooftop bar and lounge, with an excellent sushi bar and panoramic views of the city and beaches below – it's worth having at least one drink here in the afternoon, just to lounge on the white double beds. High prices give it an exclusive atmosphere: it's $7.50 for beers and $10 for spirits. Latin nights on Thurs from 9pm, club nights Fri & Sat.

Santurce

Bar El Rubi c/Canals 213. This languid bar is a real slice of Caribbean mellow in the heart of the city, serving tapas and cocktails on weekends. Calmer than places around the Plaza del Mercado. Thurs–Sat 7pm–3am.

Fat Tuesday c/Dos Hermanos 180 ☏ 787/723-0121. This New Orleans-theme chain had the audacity to set up right in the heart of La Placita, but the truth is it's a lot of fun. The huge range of infamous frozen daiquiris are excellent (try the 190 Octane), but they also serve the full range of drinks and snack food. Wed–Sat 5.30pm–2am (happy hour till 7.30pm).

Clubs

The major **clubs** in San Juan tend to serve up the usual mix of hip-hop and house variants, but as elsewhere in Latin America, almost all of them splice in (or have nights dedicated to) Latino sounds such as **salsa**. This being Puerto Rico, there's also plenty of **reggaetón** around (see Contexts, p.276).

Club Brava *El San Juan Hotel* Avda Isla Verde 6063, Isla Verde ☎787/602-8222, ⓦwww.bravapr.com. A good place to start, with its two floors, a main room, a more relaxed "ultra lounge" and a glamorous clientele. Dress up and bring ID to get in (over-21s only). College night (Spin) is Thursdays, Ladies' Night is Saturdays (women free before 11pm). Most nights cover is $20 for non Puerto Ricans. Open daily from 10pm.

Club Lazer c/Cruz 251, Old San Juan ☎787/725-7581, ⓦwww.clublazer.com. Three packed floors, with hip-hop and R&B dominating on Fridays, *reggaetón* on Saturdays and a more relaxed Sunday night (free). Cover is usually $15, but women can get in free before midnight. Fri–Sun 10pm–4am.

Eternal Lobby Lounge *The Conrad Condado Plaza* Avda Ashford 999, Condado ☎787/565-7714, ⓦwww.eternalpr.com. Hotel cocktail bar with three sections that morphs into a glamorous club at the weekends, with DJs spinning soulful house and Latin dance Fri & Sat from 10pm in the Fire Bar. The Moon Bar is open daily from 3pm, while the Ice Bar is open Thurs–Sat from 8pm.

Red Code Avda Ponce de León 1420, is the latest club incarnation to grace this corner of Santurce. Late night parties (4am–10am), crazy visuals and light effects, the best sound system in Puerto Rico (drum and bass, electro and techno rule here) and some of the friendliest staff to grace a club – all for $5–10 cover.

Salsa

San Juan is one of the world's great centres of **salsa** and if you love Latin dance you're in for a real treat. **Lessons** are a good way to get warmed up for **clubs** that specialize in salsa beats, but there are also **shows** and **live** performances, many in the resort hotels, where you can watch popular salsa bands and professional dancers do the work. It's also worth checking with the tourist office for upcoming events and salsa **festivals**: the annual **Salsa Congress** (☎787/449-2002, ⓦwww.puertoricosalsacongress.com) is usually held at the Puerto Rico Convention Center every July. You can generally get tickets to watch the main competition for $10, while other performances cost $10–25.

Clubs and live music

El Balcón del Zumbador PR-187 km 5.2, Piñones ☎787/791-9902. It's worth heading out to Piñones for this jumping salsa joint alone, which hosts some fabulous live acts from the salsa and rumba worlds. It's usually open Fri–Sun from 6pm; you'll need to arrange taxis or drive to get here.

Club Mijani c/Dos Hermanos 252, Santurce. This club, catering primarily to a thirty-something crowd, is tucked in among the action in La Placita, absorbing the overspill of salsa-lovers from the restaurants and bars in the plaza from midnight on. Thursday is the main salsa night, while Friday features a variety of Latin sounds. Arrange a taxi pick-up in advance if you want to hang out in this neighbourhood.

El Criollo Expreso Martinez Nadal (PR-20) km 3.2, Guaynabo ☎787/720-0340. Renowned for showcasing the best salsa on the island, the live bands that play here every Wed & Fri (at 8 or 9pm) certainly get the crowds worked up into a dizzying salsa sweat. Cover is usually $5–10, but the real

Salsa lessons

If you're in town for a short time but want to learn to dance salsa, your best bet is to visit *Latin Roots* (see opposite) in Old San Juan. The bar usually offers lessons during the day when cruise ships are in port, but there are always experts around to give advice. The *Picante Lounge* at the *Courtyard Isla Verde Beach Resort* (Avda Boca de Cangrejos 7012, Isla Verde; ☎787/791-0404) offers free lessons Thursday at 8pm, while the *Lobby Lounge* at the *San Juan Marriott Resort* (see above) in Condado serves up nightly Latin live acts and dancing – salsa lessons are also sometimes held (call to check).

For more structured lessons and courses, try **Salzuumba** (☎787/342-6964, ⓦwww.salzuumba.com), in Santurce at Avda Ponce de León 1418. The school is easy to reach by bus and offers ten salsa lessons for $80. It's open Monday to Friday 6–9pm and Saturday 10am–4pm.

downside is the location: it's a long drive or taxi ride from the main tourist zones.

Latin Roots Galeria Paseo Portuario Suite H/I, c/ Comercio 104, Old San Juan ☎787/977-1887, ⓦwww.thelatinroots.com. The newest Latin club is conveniently located in the old town behind the *Sheraton*. Expect live music and dancing every night, though it tends to get more action at the weekends or when lots of ships are in port. Daily 11am–2am.

🏃 **Nuyorican Café** c/San Francisco 312 (entrance on Callejón de la Capilla; no sign), Old San Juan ☎787/977-1180, ⓦwww.nuyorican cafepr.com. If you only visit one salsa club in San Juan, make it this one. Small, intimate and extremely energetic, it's crammed most nights with loyal devotees enjoying the live salsa (Wed, Fri & Sat), Latin dance (Sun), and a fusion of everything (Thurs), from samba to Spanish-guitar music. Tues–Sun 8pm–3am, live music from 10pm. Entry is free.

Rumba c/San Sebastián 152, Old San Juan ☎787/725-4407. Slightly bigger than *Nuyorican* and just as popular, pulling in a mixed crowd of locals, expats and heavy-drinking tourists. It has live salsa most weekends from 10.30pm, but unlike *Nuyorican Café* relies on DJs spinning Latin sounds at other times: it's more of a traditional club where people come to drink and meet as much as dance. Fri & Sat 11pm–6am.

Entertainment

San Juan is one of the most important **cultural centres** in the Caribbean, with a hectic programme of concerts, shows and festivals year-round. **Casinos** play a big part in the city's tourist industry, while **cinemas** show all the US blockbusters as well as Spanish-language films.

Performing arts

Everything from classical music and theatre, to folk music, hip-hop concerts and cutting-edge performance art takes place in San Juan on a weekly basis. To get an idea of what's happening, check the local newspapers or ask at the tourist office. You can also check the websites of the two primary ticket vendors: **Ticket Center** (☎787/724-8321, ⓦwww.tcpr.com), and **Ticketpop** (☎787/294-0001, ⓦwww.ticketpop.com), which has an office opposite the Centro de Bellas Artes in Santurce (Banco Popular Bldg, Avda Ponce de León 1500).

There are numerous concert and performance **venues** in San Juan, but the one with the most character is **Teatro Tapia** on the south side of Plaza Colón in the old town. The **Centro de Bellas Artes**, on Avenida Ponce de León in Santurce, is a lavish, modern arts centre with three theatres and home of the Puerto Rico Symphony Orchestra (ⓦwww.sinfonicapr.gobierno.pr).

Bigger concerts take place at the **Coliseo de Puerto Rico** (☎787/294-0001, ⓦwww.coliseodepuertorico.com), 500 c/Arterial B, Hato Rey (near Hato Rey metro station), everything from Enrique Iglesias and Selena Gomez to Kiss and Maroon 5.

For a complete change of pace from salsa, rum and *reggaetón*, visit the **Poet's Passage** in Old San Juan (daily 10am–6pm; ☎787/721-0564), on Plaza de Armas (next to *Starbucks*). This art, poetry and craft store is owned by local poet Lady Lee Andrews and is host to mellow open-mic **poetry readings** every Tuesday night at 7pm.

Cinemas

Caribbean Cinemas (☎787/727-7137, ⓦwww.caribbeancinemas.com) operates several movie theatres in Greater San Juan. The closest to Old San Juan and Condado is the **Fine Arts Cinema** (☎787/721-4288) at Avda Ponce de León 654, which shows independent or alternative films, and the **Metro** (☎787/722-0465) at no. 1255 in Santurce, featuring all the Hollywood blockbusters. Head to the screens at **Plaza las Américas Shopping Center**, Avenida Roosevelt (T 787/767-4775), for a larger selection of US and international choices. Tickets are usually around $7–8 and films are generally screened in English.

Casinos

All the major hotels and resorts in San Juan have **casinos**, with flashing lights and vast swathes of Las Vegas-style slot machines. Note that many places don't offer much more than this, however, and only the fancier hotels provide the full range of card games, roulette and the like. Top of the list is the 24-hour **Ritz-Carlton Casino** (T 787/253-1700), inside the hotel in Isla Verde, with elegant 1940s decor, the largest floor in Puerto Rico and all the major games on offer. The **El San Juan Hotel & Casino** (daily 10am–4am; T 787/791-1000, W www.elsanjuanhotel .com) down the road comes a close second: this cavernous and opulent wood-panelled palace has the highest number of slot machines (336) and gaming tables (27) in the city, where you can indulge in craps, roulette and Caribbean stud poker till the early hours. Cocktail service is available throughout the casino.

In Old San Juan make for the **Sheraton Old San Juan Hotel Casino** on the waterfront (c/Brumbaugh 100; daily 8am–4am; T 787/721-5100, W www .sheratonoldsanjuan.com), a welcoming place with similarly endless rows of slot machines and plenty of table games. Most casinos have a dress code for men (don't wear shorts).

Festivals

The most festive period to be in San Juan is over the **Christmas** holidays, when you'll hear **live music** everywhere: it's the best time to catch *cuatro* players and performances of *aguinaldos*, a type of Christmas folk music unique to the island, but based on traditional Spanish carols. *Aguinaldos* are performed by groups of singers known as *parrandas*, going from house to house much like carol singers in Europe or North America. On **New Year's Eve** half the city descends on the *campo* in front of El Morro to watch the sun rise amid a real party atmosphere – bring a blanket and plenty to drink. On January 6 crowds gather in Old San Juan for **Three Kings Day**, featuring concerts and the governor handing out presents to children, while the official end to the exhaustive holiday season is marked by the **Fiestas de la Calle San Sebastián** (Jan 18–21), with processions, craft stalls and around 70,000 people crammed into Old San Juan.

One of the city's biggest religious festivals – the **Fiestas Patronales de San Juan Bautista** – honours its patron saint St John the Baptist, with dancing, feasts, bonfires, parades and more. At midnight on June 23 (the day before St John's Day itself), half the city can be found on the beaches, where revellers march backwards into the Atlantic three or seven times, to ward off bad luck and evil spirits. For a list of festivals see Basics on p.30.

Shopping

San Juan is a decent place to pick up general souvenirs, but it also attracts serious collectors looking for contemporary Puerto Rican art. The best streets for browsing in **Old San Juan** are **Calle del Cristo** and **Calle de La Fortaleza**, while for a more conventional experience, **Plaza Las Américas**

(Ⓦ www.plazalasamericas.com), on the western edge of Hato Rey, is the largest mall in the Caribbean, with JC Penney, Macy's and Sears department stores, as well as all the other major US chains.

Antiques, arts and crafts

The narrow streets of **Old San Juan** offer the best opportunities for browsing for **crafts and antiques**. You'll find everything from high-quality gifts, prints and carvings, particularly *santos*, to colourful *vejigante* masks and the usual line-up of tacky T-shirts and souvenirs. Unless stated otherwise, shops tend to open daily from 10am to 6pm.

Butterfly People c/Cruz 257 Ⓦ www.butterfly people.com. This unique shop sells mounted tropical butterflies from all over the world (gathered by humane means, not hunted), and displayed in stunning ensembles that range $40 to $1000 and more. Open 11am–6pm, closed Fri.

Le Calle c/Fortaleza 105. Enticing alley jam-packed with stores selling carnival masks, paintings and all sorts of gifts, as well as the *Café El Punto* at the back, great for a quick coffee or snack.

El Galpón c/Cristo 154. Small place selling primarily Panama hats ($60–65), fine cigars (*cigarellos* from $1.99), high-quality festival masks and *santos*.

Mi Pequeño San Juan at c/Cristo 107, Ⓦ www.mipequenosanjuan.com. This shop sells the hand-painted miniatures of San Juan's colonial buildings local poet Lady Lee and her

French painter husband Nicolas Thomassin. Daily 10am–6pm.

Ole c/Fortaleza 105. Next to the entrance of *La Calle* and specializing in Panama hats (from $75), as well as traditional string puppets and Puerto Rican posters.

Puerto Rican Arts & Crafts c/Fortaleza 204 Ⓦ www.puertoricanart-crafts.com. This spacious two-storey store is the most comprehensive repository of local arts and crafts in town, selling everything from hammocks, carvings and cookery books to paintings and festival masks. Mon–Sat 10am–6pm, Sun 11am–5pm.

Spicy Caribee c/Cristo 154 Ⓦ www.spicycaribbee .com. The owner of this store hails from St Lucia and offers a taste of the West Indies through her home-made sauces (try the Banana Ketchup; $10) and seasonings ($7.50 per bottle), as well as locally sourced Puerto Rican vanilla.

Art galleries

In recent years San Juan's **contemporary art** scene has really taken off, with a strong base of talented local artists and growing international interest. Many of the cutting-edge galleries are in **Santurce**, but there are plenty of showrooms in **Old San Juan**. For any galleries in the former, it's important to call in advance, as opening times tend to be irregular.

Old San Juan

Galería Botello c/Cristo 208 ☎787/723-9987, Ⓦ www.botello.com. This spacious, well-restored former home of Galician artist Ángel Botello is now one of the best galleries in Old San Juan, with work from the Spanish-born painter and local, modern artists on display: Jorge Zeno, Myrna Báez, Nora Rodríguez Vallés and others. Mon–Sat 10am–6pm.

OBRA Galería Alegría c/Cruz 301 ☎787/723-3206, Ⓦ www.obragaleria.com. An extremely plush gallery dedicated to high-quality Puerto Rican art, including the work of Domingo Garcia, Nick Quijano, Félix Rodríguez Báez and Paris-based Ricardo Ramírez. You'll occasionally see gems from Francisco Oller here also. Tues–Sat 11am–6pm.

Santurce

Desto c/Américo Salas 1400 ☎787/633-3381. Experimental collective founded in 2005 and run by the three artists Raquel Quijano, Jason Mena and Omar Obdulio Peña Forty. Call ahead to see what's being shown.

Espacio 1414 Avda Fernández Juncos 1414 ☎787/725-3899. Housed in a former tyre warehouse, this is one of the most fashionable and avant-garde galleries in the city, though it only opens for special events or viewings arranged in advance. Featured artists include Jennifer Allora and Guillermo Calzadilla.

Books and music

Borders Plaza Las Américas, Avda Roosevelt 525, Hato Rey ☎787/777-0916. This megastore has by far the best selection of books in English and Spanish, with plenty on Puerto Rico: check the history and Latin American studies sections for a decent selection (including local fiction). Mon–Thurs 9am–10pm, Fri & Sat 9am–11pm, Sun 11am–7pm.

La Gran Discoteca Plaza Las Américas ☎787/282-0003. This CD shop stocks a wide selection of both salsa and *reggaetón*, as well as Latin pop, rock and international music.

Librería Cronopios Avda José de Diego 314, Santurce. Quiet, cosy bookshop with a small selection of English titles, including some by Puerto Rican authors and books on various aspects of the island, including its history. Also sells local CDs, snacks, drinks and has free internet.

Librería la Tertulia c/Recinto Sur 305, Old San Juan ⓦ www.tertulia.com. Thoughtful selection of books in Spanish and English, including plenty on Puerto Rico. The main store is in Río Piedras at Avda Ponce de León 1002. Mon–Sat 9am–10pm, Sun 10am–8pm.

Fashion

Young Puerto Rican designers are making quite a name for themselves and San Juan is the best place to get a taster of the latest trends. For more information check out ⓦ www.sanjuanfashion.com, or attend **San Juan Fashion Week**, which usually runs twice a year, in March and September.

David Antonio Avda Condado 69. Flashy eponymous boutique of a top local designer, with an eclectic range of stylish clothes for men and women. Antonio is best known for his loosely cut tunics and "Neoclassical" designs. Tues–Sat 10am–6pm.

Lisa Cappalli c/O'Donnell 206 ☎787/289-6565, ⓦ www.lisacappalli.net. The boutique of one of the island's top female designers, noted for her chic,

diaphanous couture. It's facing Plaza Colón in Old San Juan. Tues–Wed noon–7pm, Thurs–Sat noon–9pm, Sun noon–5pm.

Nono Maldonado 2/F Avda Ashford 1112, Condado ☎787/721-0456. Boutique offering elegant clothes for men and women, designed by the former fashion editor of NYC-based *Esquire* magazine and doyen of the local fashion scene. Daily 10am–6pm.

Listings

Airlines Air Canada ☎877/321-0173; Air Flamenco ☎787/724-6464; Air Sunshine ☎787/791-8900; American Airlines ☎800/981-4757; Cape Air ☎787/253-1121; Continental Airlines ☎800/231-0856; Copa Airlines ☎787/722-6999; Delta Airlines ☎800/221-1212; JetBlue Airways ☎800/538-2583; Liat ☎787/791-1030; Northwest Airlines ☎787/253-1505;

Seaborne Airlines ☎877/772-1005; Spirit Airlines ☎800/756-7117; United Airlines ☎800/426-5561; US Airways ☎800/622-1015; Vieques Air Link ☎787/722-3736.

Banks Finding banks and ATMs is easy in San Juan. To change money try Banco Popular at c/Tetuán 206 in Old San Juan (it also has two ATMs on the Plaza de Armas), or at Avda Ashford 1060 in Condado.

The big smoke

Puerto Rican cigars may not be as prized as their Cuban counterparts, but they're almost as good. **Don Collins** (ⓦ www.don-collins.com) is part of the Puerto Rico Tobacco Corporation, with a shop at c/Cristo 59 that sells some wonderful varieties, though like everything else here, they're not cheap. The *Puros Indios* are dipped in rum ($17.26 each) and taste sensational, while the *Lonsdale CF* are cured in vanilla ($10.52). You can buy a selection box of their whole range from $29.99 for four and even tour the **factory** in Bayamón if you contact them in advance. You can also check out Cigar Lounge/Cigar House at c/Fortaleza 277 or El Galpón (see p.81), which both stock a good selection of Puerto Rican and Dominican cigars.

Bicycle rental B Bikes at Avda Isla Verde 4770 (☎787/727-1233) sells and repairs bikes, while Hot Dog Cycling at Avda Isla Verde 5916 (☎787/701-0776, ⓦwww.hotdogcycling.com) rents mountain bikes for $30/day and arranges guided tours.

Car rental Numerous companies rent cars in San Juan. The best deals are usually at Budget (daily 24hr; ☎787/791-0600, ⓦwww.budget.com) at the airport; and Charlie Car Rental at Avda Isla Verde km 0.7, Isla Verde (daily 24hr; ☎787/728-2418, ⓦwww.charliecarrentalpr.com) and Avda Ashford 890, Condado (daily 8am–5pm; ☎787/721-6525). Note that Charlie Car will pick you up from the airport for free, but the cars are all at the Isla Verde office. Avis is at the airport (☎787/253-5925) and in Condado, at Avda Ashford 1052 (☎787/721-4499, ⓦwww.avis.com); Hertz has 24hr desks at the airport (☎787/791-0840), in Condado at Avda Ashford 1365 (daily 7am–5.30pm; ☎787/725-2027) and at the *Marriott*, *Caribe Hilton* and *Sheraton* hotels (daily 7am–noon & 1–4pm); National (☎787/791-1805, ⓦwww.nationalcar.com) and Thrifty (☎787/253-2525, ⓦwww.thrifty.com) are both at the airport. Local outfit Allied (☎787/726-7350, ⓦwww.aaacarrentalpr.com), in Isla Verde at Avda Isla Verde 5910, also offers good deals.

Consulates Canada, Avda Ponce de León 268, Hato Rey (☎787/294-1205); UK "Virtual Consulate" (☎787/750-2400). For other countries contact your embassy in Washington DC, such as: Australia (☎202/797-3000), Ireland (☎202/462-3939), New Zealand (☎202/328-4800) and South Africa (☎202/232-4400).

Emergencies Dial ☎911.

Hospitals and clinics The most convenient hospital is Ashford Presbyterian Community Hospital at Avda Ashford 1451 in Condado (☎787/721-2160, ⓦwww.presbypr.com), with a large emergency room and outpatient clinics.

Internet Old San Juan is packed with wi-fi hotspots where you can use the internet for free, if you have a laptop (check the free zone on Paseo Princesa or *Starbucks* on c/Tetuan); otherwise, try the Seafarer's House at c/O'Donnell 161 (Mon–Fri 10am–6pm, Sat

11am–4pm, Sun 10am–9pm; $0.09/min). This is a seaman's foundation and sailors get priority, but the computer terminals are open to the public. In Condado, try the Cybernet Café at Avda Ashford 1128 (Mon–Sat 9am–10pm, Sun 11am–10pm; $3/20min). In Isla Verde, try Cybernet Café at Avda Isla Verde 5575 (Mon–Sat 10am–10pm; $3/20min).

Laundry In Old San Juan try the bargain Laundromat O'Donnell, c/O'Donnell 155 (daily 8am–6pm; ☎939/262-6656), which charges just $2 for washing and $2 for drying per load (drop-off). In Condado try Laundry Condado at Avda Condado 69 (Mon–Fri 7am–7pm, Sat 7am–5pm; $2.50 per pound, minimum 4 pounds; ☎787/723-1441).

Pharmacies Walgreens (ⓦwww.walgreens.com) has big stores at Plaza de Armas (corner of c/Cruz and c/San Francisco) in Old San Juan (daily 8am–10pm), Avda Ashford 1130 in Condado (24hr) and Avda Isla Verde 5984 (24hr); CVS is also in Old San Juan at c/Marina (daily 7am–midnight).

Police ☎787/343-2020.

Post office Old San Juan Branch, Paseo de Colón 100 (Mon–Fri 8am–4pm, Sat 8am–noon); in Condado, Avda Magdalena 1108 (Mon–Fri 8.30am–4pm, Sat 8.30am–noon).

Taxis Atlantic City Taxi ☎787/268-5050; Metro Taxi ☎787/725-2870; Rochdale Taxi Cabs ☎787/721-1900.

Tours La Rumba (☎787/375-5211, ⓦwww.larumbacruises.com) organizes party cruises around San Juan Bay, Fri–Sun evenings ($14), while Captain Duck Tours (☎787/447-0077, ⓦrideducktours.com) offers 80–90min spins around the city and harbour in an amphibious bus ($26). Tours usually run Thurs–Mon 11am and 1pm from outside the bus station in Old San Juan, but call to confirm. Several companies offer tours further afield, but while these are certainly hassle free, they tend to be expensive. Legends of Puerto Rico (☎787/605-9060, ⓦwww.legendsofpr.com) offers excellent thematic tours of San Juan on foot (from $35) and the island (from $75). Flavors of San Juan (☎787/964-2447; ⓦsanjuanfoodtours.com) runs two-hour walking tours of Old San Juan (from $60), sampling local food, tapas and *sangría* along the way.

Around San Juan

Greater San Juan is a vast, often bewildering mix of residential areas and modern commercial development, but there's plenty to see before moving on. Just across the bay is the **Casa Bacardi Visitor Center**, one of the great shrines to rum-making. **Bayamón** and **Caparra** offer small but important historical attractions, while the bike trails and celebrated *kioscos* of **Piñones** are great fun on weekends. Further south, **Caguas** is a prosperous colonial town with a rich history.

Moving on from San Juan

By air

Vieques Air-Link operates four to five daily flights to **Vieques** from Aeropuerto Isla Grande and two from Aeropuerto Internacional Luis Muñoz Marín, while Cape Air and Air Sunshine operate an additional four to six flights daily from the latter. Seaborne Airlines offers shuttle flights to Vieques from both San Juan airports. Vieques Air-Link also operates two flights daily from Aeropuerto Isla Grande to **Culebra.** From Aeropuerto Internacional Luis Muñoz Marín, Cape Air operates daily flights to **Mayagüez** and **Ponce**. There are no domestic flights to **Aguadilla**.

Air Sunshine connects Aeropuerto Internacional Luis Muñoz Marín with St Thomas in the **US Virgin Islands** and Tortola in the **British Virgin Islands**; Cape Air also flies to Tortola and St Thomas and St Croix in the US Virgin Islands. Seaborne Airlines offers shuttle flights to St Thomas and St Croix from both San Juan airports.

Heading to either airport, it's usually easiest to get your hotel to call a **taxi**, though you can catch **bus C45** from Isla Verde to the international airport. See p.82 for airline contact details.

By car

Most people touring the island leave San Juan by car. Heading **east** to El Yunque or Fajardo is straightforward on PR-66 and PR-3 (this road is the worst on the island for traffic – try to leave early). The lengthy Teodoro Moscoso Bridge ($3) cuts right across Laguna San Juan from Isla Verde and the airport, to Río Piedras and all routes **south** – PR-52 is the main *autopista* to Caguas and Ponce. There are several tolls along the way ($1–1.75; around $5 total to Ponce), but you'll save lots of time taking this road. Heading **west** from the airport you'll need to cut across the city to PR-22 via Avenida De Diego or Kennedy. This *autopista* goes all the way to Arecibo, with four tolls on the way ($3.75 total).

By ferry

American Cruise Ferries was expected to begin a once a week service to Santo Domingo in the Dominican Republic in 2011 (12hr; from $189 one-way) – check details with the tourist office.

Casa Bacardi Visitor Center

Visit the slick **Casa Bacardi Visitor Center** (Mon–Sat 8.30am–5.30pm, last tour 4.15pm, Sun 10am–5pm, last tour 3.45pm; free; ☏787/788-8400, Ⓦ www.casa bacardi.org) inside the "cathedral of rum", the vast Bacardi distillery across San Juan Bay in Cataño and you'll enter another world – Cuba, to be precise. It's a series of fun and illuminating interactive exhibits that emphasize Bacardi's Cuban roots and involve not just watching and listening, but sniffing the products on display. **Guided tours** depart every 15 to 30 minutes and last around 45 minutes.

Established in Santiago de Cuba by Catalan expat Don Facundo Bacardí Massó in 1862, the Bacardi empire now dominates the global rum market, supplying 75 percent of rum sold in the US alone. The Puerto Rican plant was established in Old San Juan in 1936 and moved to this location – when it received its "cathedral" sobriquet from then-governor Luis Muñoz Marín – in 1958. The move here proved timely, as Castro seized the Bacardi assets in Cuba shortly afterwards, precipitating exile in 1960 – the family remain vehement opponents of what they term a "totalitarian" regime.

Today Bacardi is a true multinational organization, headquartered in tax-free Bermuda, and with massive operations in the Bahamas, Mexico and Puerto Rico – the last outpost has the capacity to produce 100,000 gallons of rum every 24 hours and is the biggest taxpayer on the island.

By taxi

Taxi *turísticos* will drive long distance, though their fixed-rates are expensive and, unless you have a group or can't drive yourself, not really worth it; examples include Aguadilla ($140), Caguas ($55), Dorado ($60), Guánica ($155), Luquillo ($72), Mayagüez ($160), Ponce ($125), Rincón ($155) and San Germán ($160). The exception is the run to the **Fajardo ferry terminal** (around 1–2hr depending on traffic), which is $80 and saves a lot of hassle if you're heading straight to Culebra or Vieques by ferry.

By bus

With a few exceptions, the main *líneas* and *público* terminals for San Juan are all in **Río Piedras**, so you'll need to take a city bus or taxi to there from other parts of the city (see Basics, p.21, for general information on *públicos*). Taxi-type *públicos* operated by Choferes Unidos de Ponce (☎787/764-0540) depart for **Ponce** ($20 or $50 for the whole car) from Calle 2, just off Avenida Gandara near c/Saldana, though this service can be erratic: Mondays and Fridays seem to be busiest, but call ahead to confirm. Minibuses to Ponce also run from the Plaza de Convalecencia for $40 return.

Minibus services to **Fajardo** ($5) run fairly frequently and depart the Terminal de Vehiculos Públicos del Este (☎787/250-0717) on c/Arzuaga near c/Vallejo, though not all of them go to the ferry port, so check before you go.

Línea Sultana (☎787/765-9377) on c/Esteban Gonzalez (at Avda Universidad) runs buses every two hours to **Mayagüez** (daily 7.30–4.30pm; $15). The driver will drop you off on the road along the way and anywhere in Mayagüez beyond the terminal for an extra charge (up to $30).

For other locations head to Plaza de Convalecencia, close to **Río Piedras Tren Urbano station**: on the north side there are frequent buses ($1.15) and *públicos* ($1) to **Caguas** (☎787/744-8833), and far fewer services operated by Línea Arecibeña (☎787/751-6178) to **Arecibo** ($10), as well as Choferes Unidos de Aguadilla (☎787/751-7622) and Blue Line (☎787/250-0717) to **Aguadilla** ($15).

Equipped with a hand-held audio guide and accompanied by enthusiastic docents, you'll pass through seven different zones introducing both the history of the company and the rum-making process. Special barrels allow you to "nose" the effects of wood barrelling, ageing and finishing, as well as the various Bacardi brands on offer: sweetly scented apple and melon flavours and the rich, addictive aroma of coconut-laced rum – *piña colada* in a bottle. Mercifully, there are two **free drinks** waiting for you at the end of the tour (and as many soft drinks as you like).

Note, however, that you don't get to visit the actual distillery – for security reasons the real rum-making facilities have been off-limits since 9/11 and are likely to remain that way for the immediate future.

To get to the Visitor Center, take the ferry from Pier 2 in Old San Juan (every 20min; 10min; $0.50) and catch bus C37 on the other side (every 30min; 5min; $0.75). You can also flag down *públicos* for $1. Either will drop you at the main gate from where it's a five-minute walk to the visitor centre. Note that in high season, particularly early in the week, up to 1500 visitors come here each day: arrive early. A **taxi** direct from Old San Juan will be at least $28 one-way.

Bayamón

Well off the tourist trail, 15km from Old San Juan, **BAYAMÓN** is the second largest municipality in Puerto Rico after the capital and though it's usually regarded as part of Greater San Juan, it tries hard to maintain a distinct identity. Established in 1772, today Bayamón is noted as the home of the best rum in Puerto Rico, **Ron de Barrilito** (see p.58), the celebrated fried pork snack **chicharrón** and, more recently, pop superstar **Ricky Martin**.

Due largely to the enterprising **Ramón Luis Rivera** (mayor 1976–2000), central Bayamón is an attractive area of colonial architecture containing several small but engaging museums; times can vary, but all of them should be **open** Monday to Friday 8am to noon and 1 to 4pm, with **free admission**.

Chief among them is the **Museo de Arte y Historia de Francisco Oller**, which commemorates Bayamón's best-known son, born here in 1833 (see p.273). The museum occupies the former city hall built on the central Plaza de Recreo in 1907 and holds a handful of portraits by Oller and a collection of sculptures by Tomás Batista, as well as temporary exhibits by local contemporary artists. Highlights include Oller's earliest surviving painting, a portrait of his grandfather from 1847 (copied from a José Campeche original), and Batista's image of Agüeybaná, "El Bravo", (paramount *cacique*, or ruler of the island in 1508). Behind the museum, on Calle de Degetau, the **Museo de Archivo Histórico** contains a fairly dry collection of old photos and scale models of the city on the first floor and a shrine-like exhibition dedicated to Ramón Luis Rivera upstairs. One of the city's more offbeat museums can be found a little further along Calle de Degetau at no. 18, the **Museo de Muñecas** with its collection of around 1240 Puerto Rican and international **dolls**, including some slightly disturbing creations with human teeth and fixed grins.

Two blocks east, at c/Barbosa 16, the charming wooden *criollo* home and birthplace of José Celso Barbosa (1857–1921) has been preserved as the **Museo de Barbosa**. Barbosa was a medical pioneer and father of the "Statehood for Puerto Rico" movement (see p.267), but while the modest displays inside are a stimulating introduction to his life and work, everything is written in Spanish only.

Practicalities

The fastest way to reach Bayamón is to take a **bus** to Estación Sagrado Corazón (ME and M3 from Old San Juan or C10 and B21 from Condado) and transfer to the Tren Urbano. The bus station and the Tren Urbano terminal in Bayamón are close to each other, three blocks northeast of Plaza de Recreo. **Taxis** from Old San Juan or the beaches will be around $33.

The best place **to eat** near Plaza de Recreo is *Cafeteria La Mia* (Tues–Sat 7am–5pm; ⊤787/787-4433), a cosy place on Calle Maceo just off the square, where you can get hearty *cubano* sandwiches, *chuletas*, or burgers for under $5. Coffee, cinnamon rolls and *kanelles* (sponge cakes) are available for less than $2 at *Kanelle* (Mon–Fri 7am–3.30pm; ⊤787/740-5154), c/Barbosa 43, one block away.

Caparra

In 1508, Juan Ponce de León hacked his way into the swampy jungles south of San Juan Bay to establish Caparra, the first settlement on the island, today preserved as the **Museo y Parque Histórico Ruinas de Caparra** (Mon–Fri 8am–noon & 1–4.30pm; free; ⊤787/781-4795). The ruins are extremely modest, but if you're interested in the history of Puerto Rico (and indeed, the whole Caribbean), this spot has special significance: it contains some of the oldest Spanish remains in the New World. When the settlement was moved to Old San Juan in 1521, Caparra was dismantled and its location lost – it wasn't until 1935 that these remains were uncovered. The foundation stones on display follow the outline of the large mansion-cum-fortress built to house Ponce de León and his government and were moved here from their original location under the adjacent highway.

There's a small **museum** on site, with English-speakers on hand to translate the Spanish explanations if required. Artefacts found here, such as the large wine jars and pretty Moorish tiles, are displayed along with Spanish armaments of the time.

Caparra is wedged between condos in a posh part of Guaynabo on PR-2 (km 6.4), halfway between Bayamón and Hato Rey. **Getting here** is a pain without a car: several buses stop outside the ruins but none run from the main tourist areas, which means you'll have to change at least once. M2 runs past Caparra on its way to Bayamón from Hato Rey and Sagrado Corazón, where there are several connecting buses to Old San Juan and Condado. **Taxis** will charge around $25–30 from Old San Juan.

Fundación Luis Muñoz Marín

Revered by most (but by no means all) *puertorriqueñas* as the man who created modern Puerto Rico, former governor Luiz Muñoz Marín's home has been preserved as the **Fundación Luis Muñoz Marín** (Guided tours only Mon–Fri 10am & 2pm, Sat & Sun 10.30am & 1pm; $6, free on Tues; ℡787/755-7979, ⓦwww.flmm.org) in Trujillo Alto, southeast of San Juan. The house is just off Expreso Trujillo Alto (PR-181), on PR-877 at km 0.4. **Entrance is by guided tour only**, but you must call in advance to reserve a space. Muñoz Marín was the island's first elected governor (see p.268) and spent much of his retirement here in the 1970s; after his death in 1980, his wife, Inés María Mendoza, lived in the house for another ten years. Today the beautifully maintained property offers subtle insights into the life and routine of the influential leader, beginning with an introductory video in the main residence. His office and library are also preserved much as he left them and the garage contains his favourite vintage car. The adjacent Sala Luis Muñoz Marín is crammed with memorabilia, documents, photos, and the like, charting his illustrious career.

Taxis from Old San Juan and the beaches should be around $31; it's best to negotiate a return fare, as taking the bus involves a long wait and changing in Río Piedras.

Piñones

Just 2km beyond central Isla Verde, **PIÑONES** is an entirely different world, a languid, low-rent community of shacks, houses and a couple of thousand tenants scattered along the coast and PR-187. At the weekends the whole area comes alive with salsa and *sanjuaneros* looking to connect with their traditional roots, drink beer and enjoy the *cocina en kiosco*. In addition, the beaches here are excellent for **surfing**, especially in winter (see p.64).

Bus C45 runs into Piñones from Río Piedras via Isla Verde Monday to Saturday: from elsewhere take a bus to Isla Verde and change outside the cockfighting arena. Taxis are impossible to find at the weekends, so you need to arrange transport in advance. Get off the bus as soon as you cross the bridge into **Boca de Cangrejos**, the first part of Piñones at km 4.3, crammed with cheap restaurants and head to **La Paseodora** information centre (daily 9am–6pm), just off the road on the right.

Piñones is home to the descendants of freed African slaves as well as more recent immigrants from the Dominican Republic, making for a vibrant cultural mix. La Paseodora, run by the **Corporación Piñones Se Integra** (COPI; ℡787/253-9707, ⓦwww.copipr.com), acts as a focus for activities to celebrate this heritage and also manages the area's ecological attractions. To explore the latter, **rent a bicycle** here (daily 9am–5pm; $5/hr; photo ID required) and follow the **Paseo Piñones** bike trail.

Paseo Piñones

The well-marked **Paseo Piñones** bike trail cuts through several contrasting environments, from the ramshackle villages and scrubby vegetation that hug the coast, to the **Bosque Estatal de Piñones**, a reserve of thick mangrove swamps around the Laguna de Piñones, and finally to some pristine, palm-lined beaches. The trail is around 9km long (one-way). It can be completed in two hours, but it's best to take the whole morning and stop along the way.

From La Paseodora, the first section snakes around the headland in Boca de Cangrejos and follows the coast to the **Torre Maldonado** (1.8km) on the promontory of the same name (an excellent lookout point). Beyond here there are two rows of *kioscos*, in front of a small lagoon ideal for paddling. The *kioscos* are only open weekends, selling delicious *alcapurrias* and *bacalaítos* (see p.29) fried over wood fires, for around $1.50. From here the trail crosses the road and splits: the left-hand fork takes a shorter route along the coast while the trail on the right slices 2km through dramatically different terrain, a vast forest of twisted mangroves shading hordes of crabs and other tiny mud-dwelling creatures, before rejoining the short cut near PR-187. The route runs along the south side of the road for another 1.8km before heading into the dunes: grab a snack where it crosses the road at *Las Dos Palma*, a popular *kiosco* (weekends only). The final stretch is 1.2km along the coast to the "Fin de Paseo", where you'll find **Playa Tres Palmitas**, a fabulous beach that's never crowded.

Eating and drinking

In addition to the weekend *kioscos* that line PR-187, Piñones is home to some rustic open-air restaurants and trendy beach bars that do business all week. Most can be found in Boca de Cangrejos, or along the main beach on the other side of the headland. Salsa fans should make for *El Balcón del Zumbador* (see p.78), which hosts outstanding live salsa bands most weekends.

St James, Yoruba-style

The town of **Loíza**, 30km from Old San Juan and a short drive east of Piñones, is best known for its **Fiestas Tradicionales de Santiago Apóstol**, the ten-day carnival held every July to honour St James (his feast day is July 25). What makes the festival so special is the town's rich **African heritage**: the religious ceremonies are enhanced with *bomba* music and dancers and with multicoloured spiky **vejigante masks** made from coconut shells.

Like Piñones, Loíza became a refuge for runaway and freed slaves in the seventeenth century, most of them Yoruba people from West Africa, and the festival is the result of a gradual blending of Spanish and African cultures over the years. Santiago (St James) is the **patron saint of Spain**, where he became known as Matamoros ("Moor-slayer") in the Middle Ages for his supposed help in defeating the Moors, and in the sixteenth century Spanish colonists brought his cult to Puerto Rico (the festival masks symbolize the "heathen" Moors). African slaves began to pray to Santiago for help in fending off pirates and enemy attacks, and gradually St James became associated with Yoruba deities such as **Ogun**, the spirit of iron and war. Ironically, St James evolved into a symbol of resistance *against* the Spanish ruling classes, the festival a potent act of defiance against the oppression levelled at slaves and their descendants. Following an influx of Irish settlers in the nineteenth century, the Church made **St Patrick** the town's patron saint, but that only served to make the worship of Santiago more intense.

Most of the festival action takes place in Plaza de Recreo, Loíza's main square: call the local tourist office (☏787/876-3570) for details. The town gets jam-packed at festival time, so you'll need to get there early, preferably with your own car (or via bus C45 from Isla Verde, Mon–Fri, last departure from Loíza 6.30pm). You can purchase masks from **Artesanías Castor Ayala** at PR-187 km 6.6 (daily 9am–6pm), just outside the town, throughout the year.

El Farol Boca de Cangrejos, PR-187 km 4.3. Opposite La Paseodora, this big local favourite is the self-proclaimed "El Palacio de las Frituras" (Palace of Fritters). People line up here for delicious *bacalaítos*, *alcapurrias*, *pionono* (plantains stuffed with ground beef) and *relleno de papa* (stuffed potato).

El Pulpo Loco PR-187 km 4.5. A beach bar and no-frills restaurant, just a short ride or walk along the road from La Paseodora; located in the second collection of places to eat near the main beach. The *arroz juegos* (crab rice) is excellent and there's thumping salsa at weekends.

Reef Bar & Grill Boca de Cangrejos, PR-187 km 4.3. The highlight here is the spectacular view over the ocean and San Juan coastline, shaded by pine trees at the end of the Punta de Cangrejos. There's a pool table, lots of music and happy hour at 6–7pm weekdays – the appetizing *comida criolla*

classics on the menu are also worth a try. A short walk from La Paseodora. Closed Mon & Tues.

Soleil Beach Club PR-187 km 4.6 ☎787/253-1033, ⊛www.soleilbeachclub.com. This two-storey wooden house just off the beach is the most fashionable bar and restaurant in Piñones (it also rents rooms), with plenty of seafood (mains $15–25) and live music at the weekends. It's especially congenial for a relaxed beer or two on Sun afternoon, when the Piñones party scene is at its peak. Sun–Thurs 11am–10pm, Fri & Sat 11am–2am.

La Terrazza Boca de Cangrejos, PR-187 km 4.3. Opposite *Reef*, the speciality at this large, open-air diner is the *carne al pincho*, pork, beef and chicken kebabs barbecued on the street in front. Backs onto adjacent *Puerta del Mar*, with its highly rated *mofongo* and has pool tables for additional amusement.

Caguas

Formally established in 1775 near the site of a far older Taíno village, the thriving community of **CAGUAS** is the fastest growing metropolitan area in Puerto Rico and currently its fifth largest city. The historic core is a compact, attractive area easily explored on foot, surrounded by a great swathe of suburbs and strip malls. Parking is easy and it's only 29km and 25 minutes' drive from San Juan, making the city a tempting day-trip or first stop on the routes south or east. It's also one of the few places served by regular *públicos*, so you won't need a car to get here.

Arrival and information

Arriving by **car**, there are several places to park on the edge of the historic centre – the best is Estacionamiento Lincoln Center Plaza (Mon–Fri 6am–7pm, Sat 7am–8pm; $1.50 first hr, $0.75 thereafter) at the end of PR-1, on the north side of town.

By **público** you'll be dropped at the Terminal Francisco Pereira, two blocks northeast of central Plaza Palmer. The **tourist office** (daily 9am–5pm; ☎787/653-8833 ext 2908, ⊛gotocaguas.com) on the northwest corner of Plaza Palmer, has only basic information on the city but helpful English-speaking staff.

All the **museums** in Caguas open Tuesday to Saturday 9am to noon and 1 to 5pm, and are free. With the exception of the art gallery, you'll need to **read Spanish** to get the most out of them, though you might find helpful English-speaking guides on hand willing to show you around.

The City

At the centre of Caguas is the tree-filled **Plaza Palmer**, one of the largest squares on the island and more like an elegant Mexican *parque* than the cramped plazas of Old San Juan. The **flower clock** at the eastern end was added in 1966 and lined with the faces of the twelve most illustrious *cagüeños*, including José Gautier Benítez (1848–1880), Puerto Rico's finest Romantic poet.

Opposite is the twin-towered **Catedral Dulce Nombre de Jesús** (daily 6am–7pm), most of the structure dating from the 1930s and not especially interesting, though it does contain the tomb of Carlos Manuel **"Charlie" Rodríguez**, the first Puerto Rican to be beatified (see box, p.90). On the other side of the plaza, the Casa Alcadía (town hall) was built in 1887 and contains the **Museo de Caguas**, the city history museum (☎787/744-8833). The exhibits are well presented and particularly enlightening when it comes to the area's Taíno

St Charlie

Born in Caguas in 1918, few would have believed **Carlos Manuel Rodríguez Santiago** was destined to become the island's **first Catholic saint**. Known as "Chali" (which later became Anglicized as "Charlie"), he was an earnest but initially shy boy who struggled with ill health from an early age, seeking solace in scripture and the rituals of the Church. He became a Catholic lay minister at university in the 1940s, preaching all over the island and especially active in the **revival of traditional Catholic customs** such as the Easter vigil. Tragically, this burgeoning Church career was cut short in 1963 when Rodríguez died of intestinal cancer. Regarded as a deeply spiritual man, what grabbed the Vatican's attention was a **miracle**: in 1981, a local woman (and former friend) claimed to have fully recovered from cancer after praying to Charlie. Brought to the attention of the Pope in 1992, the miracle was deemed genuine and the normally tortuously long process of canonization was initiated. Pope John Paul II beatified Rodríguez in April 2001 and he's well on the way to becoming a fully fledged saint, though the Vatican must confirm one more miracle before that can happen – until then he's known as the "Blessed". Not only the first Puerto Rican to be beatified, Charlie was the first layperson in US history and only the second in the western hemisphere to receive that honour.

history, with artefacts such as pottery, shells and beads on display from a nearby archeological site. The Spanish room relates how Ponce de León made contact with the local Taíno in 1510 and covers the tragic 1511 rebellion.

The **Museo Casa del Trovador**, one block north at c/Tapia 18, is another historic property that contains a compact but unique exhibition on local folk singers and troubadours, charting the important role Caguas has played in the development of Puerto Rican folk music.

One block west of here, on the corner of calles Ruíz Belvis and Padial, the modest **Museo de Arte** contains three spacious exhibition rooms housing mostly local, contemporary art: the abstract work of Caguas-born painters Carlos Osorio (1927–1984) and Orlando Vallejo (b. 1955) is well represented and you can admire *Las Tradiciones Puertorriquenas*, the vivid seven-panel mural by Alfonso Arana (1927–2005).

Walk one block south and you'll find the **Museo del Tabaco** at calles Padial and Betances, testament to the area's central role in the Puerto Rican **tobacco industry**, especially between 1890 and 1930. In addition to exhibits and information panels, the museum contains a replica of an old tobacco factory, where ageing but dextrous workers demonstrate how to roll cigars by hand. Today there are only a handful of tobacco factories in the area.

Back towards the bus station, **Casa Rosada** at c/Alejandro Ramírez 14 was the former home of Charlie Rodríguez and local writer Abelardo Díaz Alfaro (1916–1999), beautifully restored and housing a small exhibition on both men.

Eating and drinking

Eating options in Caguas include cheap local restaurants in the centre, fast-food outlets around Plaza Palmer and Puerto Rican snack stalls in the square most days. You'll find a handful of modern and international restaurants on the main highways outside the centre. Cheap snacks and cakes (under $5) can be found at *Asturiana* c/Goyco 58 (open 24hr), a no-frills bakery with heaps of character, open since 1932. *Marcelo*, at PR-1 and Avenida José Mercado (☎787/743-8801; closed Sun) is the top place to eat in the centre of Caguas, just on the edge of the old town, facing the monument to Taíno women. It's nothing special inside but the menu of Cuban and local *comida criolla* is first-rate. Try the house specialities *jamón de pollo* (smoked chicken) and smoked pork loin and paella (mains from $12).

El Yunque and the east coast

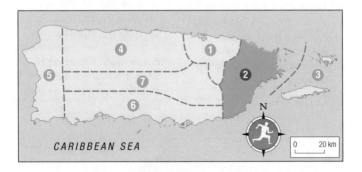

CARIBBEAN SEA

N

0   20 km

CHAPTER 2 # Highlights

✳ **El Yunque National Forest**
Climb the jungle-smothered slopes of El Yunque or bathe in the seductively cool waters at Mina Falls. See p.93

✳ **Balneario de Luquillo** Splash, swim or simply lounge on one of the most dazzling beaches on the island, backed by picture-perfect coconut palms. See p.104

✳ **Luquillo kioscos** Gorge on the best of Puerto Rico's *cocina en kiosco* at these sixty celebrated snack stalls just outside Luquillo. See p.104

✳ **Laguna Grande** Kayak at night across this mesmerizing bioluminescent bay, part of the remarkably unspoiled Reserva Natural Cabezas de San Juan. See p.108

✳ **La Cordillera** This string of alluring cays east of Fajardo is a desert island fantasy, with powder-fine sands ringed with banks of coral and a rich panoply of marine life. See p.108

✳ **Monkey Island** Take an entertaining boat ride around the world's oldest monkey reserve and snorkel above a shipwreck teeming with tropical fish. See p.113

✳ **Rancho Buena Vista** Ride one of Puerto Rico's beloved Paso Fino horses along wild, deserted beaches. See p.114

✳ **Coastal Highway PR-901** Drive this winding road along the rugged southeast corner of the island, with intoxicating ocean views, a handsome Spanish lighthouse and tempting stretches of empty beach. See p.116

▲ View of El Yunque National Forest from Yokahu Tower

2

El Yunque and the east coast

Eastern **Puerto Rico** is a microcosm of the whole island, at times brash, modern and touristy, but also rural, remote and achingly beautiful. Being so close to San Juan, the coastline is sprinkled with luxury resorts, condos and exclusive marinas, while in between you'll find long stretches of primitive beach, festooned with nothing more than the flotsam blown up by the trade winds. Looming over the whole region, the densely forested hills of the **Sierra de Luquillo** were the last parts of Puerto Rico to be settled by the Spanish, thanks to indomitable Taíno resistance and the wet, hurricane-prone climate. In the nineteenth century the area did succumb to sugar and coffee plantations like the rest of the island, but they did not prosper, leaving nature to reclaim much of the land.

The most captivating evidence of this turnaround is **El Yunque National Forest**, a protected reserve of mist-draped mountains and bubbling cascades. The forest receives over one million visitors each year, but you can escape the crowds by **hiking** one of its peaceful and well-maintained **trails**. You'll need at least two days to do it justice. **Luquillo** is the highlight of the northeast coast, a low-key resort town best known for its spectacular beach and legendary snack food, while **Fajardo**, the gateway to Vieques and Culebra, is all about boats. **La Cordillera**, just offshore, encapsulates most dreams about the Caribbean: uninhabited islands with sugary white sand, piles of multicoloured coral, fish and the odd turtle. Nearby, the **Reserva Natural Cabezas de San Juan** is another protected area of untrammelled mangrove swamp and dry forest, also containing **Laguna Grande**, one of Puerto Rico's spellbinding bioluminescent bays.

The east coast proper offers a real contrast, a blend of sleepy villages and a wilder, cliff-backed shoreline laced with secluded beaches. **Playa Naguabo**, noted for its seafood, is also the best embarkation point for **Monkey Island**, while the sprawling condo development of **Palmas del Mar** contains one of the best **horse ranches** on the island. Finally, **highway PR-901** snakes along the vertiginous southeast coastline, a twisting route lined with scenic viewpoints.

El Yunque National Forest

Sacred to the Taíno long before the Spanish conquest, **El Yunque National Forest** dominates eastern Puerto Rico like a protective wall, absorbing most of the rain hurled into the island by the trade winds. Part of the US National Forest

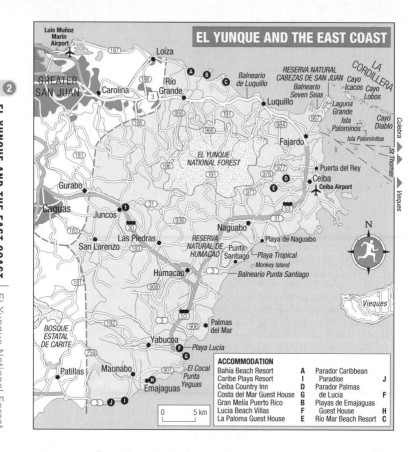

EL YUNQUE AND THE EAST COAST

ACCOMMODATION

Bahía Beach Resort	A	Parador Caribbean	
Caribe Playa Resort	I	Paradise	J
Ceiba Country Inn	D	Parador Palmas	
Costa del Mar Guest House	G	de Lucia	
Gran Melia Puerto Rico	B	Playas de Emajaguas	
Lucia Beach Villas	F	Guest House	H
La Paloma Guest House	E	Río Mar Beach Resort	C

system, its well-paved roads, enlightening visitor centre and network of clearly marked trails make it the most accessible reserve in the Caribbean.

You can **drive** right into the heart of the forest, but to really appreciate the area you need to go **hiking**. The Forest Service maintains thirteen trails ranging from easy, concrete paths to more challenging dirt tracks, but even the trek up to the peak of **El Yunque** itself (the name refers to both the reserve and the mountain) is manageable for anyone of moderate fitness and well worth the effort for the momentous views from the top. Less taxing highlights include a series of plunging **waterfalls** and natural **swimming pools**, perfect for cooling down in the summer and a smattering of whimsical structures created by the Civilian Conservation Corps in the 1930s.

Most tourists visit El Yunque on day-trips, which is a shame – you'll get a lot more out of the place by staying at one of the enticing **guesthouses** nearby. Half the visitors to the forest are Puerto Ricans, who typically come in the hot summer months of July and August when the northern section is often bursting with traffic. More foreigners tend to visit in the winter and early spring, making mid-April to mid-June and September through to October the quietest periods, but it's relatively easy to escape the crowds at any time. The average temperature of the forest is 73°F (21°C), but in winter, the highest peaks can be 20 degrees cooler than the coast (53°F, 12°C). And be prepared for **rain**: El Yunque is a rainforest after all, with an average deluge of 605 billion litres each year.

Some history

The Taíno regarded El Yunque as a sacred mountain, the place where Yokahú or **Yukiyú**, their chief god, made his home (*yuké* meant "white lands" in Taíno, referring to the clouds). For seventy years after the Spanish conquest the **Sierra de Luquillo** was a base for resistance against the invaders, but over the following three centuries, farming gradually made headway and large areas of the lower slopes were converted to fruit or coffee plantations.

Much of what you see in the forest today – cabins, towers and even highway PR-191 – was constructed by the Civilian Conservation Corps between 1935 and 1943. Around 2400 Puerto Ricans were enrolled in this US public works programme, with most of it completed by back-breaking manual labour.

Highway PR-191, which had linked the northern and southern sections of the forest, was seriously damaged by four major **landslides** between 1970 and 1979, and the mid-section was closed permanently in 1972. In 1976, El Yunque became a **UN Biosphere Reserve** and several attempts to rebuild the road (notably in 1993) were thwarted, in part by the opposition of local environmental groups – virtually everyone now agrees that the road is simply not practical to maintain. Despite the inconvenience to visitors, **hurricanes** are regarded as part of the natural cycle, allowing the forest to regenerate. By absorbing the full impact of these storms, many locals believe that El Yunque actually protects Puerto Rico from greater catastrophe: in the Taíno tradition, Yukiyú always fought with Juracán (the god of hurricanes) to save his people.

Arrival and orientation

El Yunque National Forest (pronounced "El Junkay") covers 28,000 acres, but most visitors focus on **El Yunque Recreation Area** in the northern half of the reserve, 43km east of San Juan and accessible from PR-191. With more time, it's worth exploring the quieter southern section of the forest, in the area known as **Cubuy**, but in both cases you'll need a car as public transport is nonexistent. The usual route to the forest from San Juan is along traffic-clogged PR-3 (45min to 1hr): the turning onto PR-955 is clearly marked and this connects with PR-191 in the village of Mameyes, just off the highway. For Cubuy, stay on PR-3 till it becomes the PR-53 *autopista* and take exit 22 west (right) along PR-31, then head north on PR-191. Note that if you are approaching from the south on PR-53, you'll have to take exit 20 and double back to exit 22.

Entry to the forest is **free**. The steel gate across PR-191 at La Coca Falls (km 8.1) opens 7.30am–6pm daily, and most of the reserve lies above this point. Most information offices, sights and food stalls get going after 9am. English and Spanish are used equally in the park.

Information

There are two principal information centres for El Yunque, both on the northern section of PR-191: **El Portal** (see p.98) and the much smaller **Palo Colorado Visitor Center** (daily 9.30am–5pm), further along the road at km 11.8. To **camp** in the park you'll need to apply for a permit (free) by filling in a form available at any of these offices, though rangers prefer campers to use the Palo Colorado site. Permits are usually issued on the spot (or at least the same day), as long as you submit a completed form by 4pm and provide ID (driver's licence and passport is best).

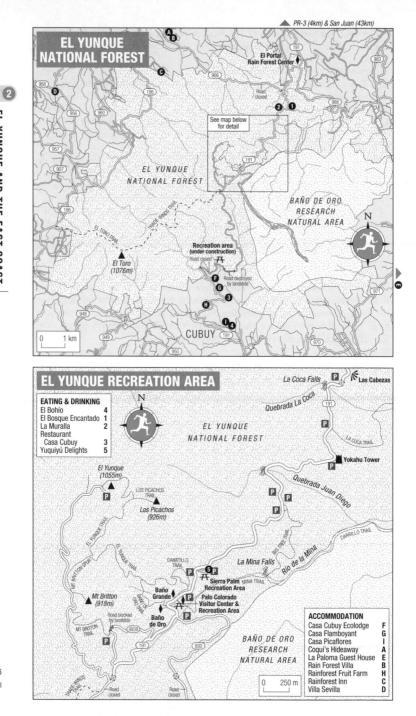

▲ PR-3 (4km) & San Juan (43km)

EL YUNQUE NATIONAL FOREST

El Portal Rain Forest Center

Road closed

EL YUNQUE NATIONAL FOREST

BAÑO DE ORO RESEARCH NATURAL AREA

See map below for detail

TRADE WINDS TRAIL

EL TORO TRAIL

El Toro (1076m)

Recreation area (under construction)
Road closed
Road destroyed by landslide

CUBUY

0   1 km

N

EL YUNQUE RECREATION AREA

EATING & DRINKING
El Bohío   4
El Bosque Encantado   1
La Muralla
  Restaurant
  Casa Cubuy   3
Yuquiyú Delights   5

N

La Coca Falls   Las Cabezas

Quebrada La Coca

EL YUNQUE NATIONAL FOREST

LA COCA TRAIL

Yokahu Tower

Quebrada Juan Diego

El Yunque (1055m)

LOS PICACHOS TRAIL

Los Picachos (926m)

EL YUNQUE TRAIL

MT BRITTON SPUR

CAIMITILLO TRAIL

BIG TREE TRAIL

CARRILLO TRAIL

La Mina Falls

Río de la Mina

MINA TRAIL

Sierra Palm Recreation Area

Baño Grande

Palo Colorado Visitor Center & Recreation Area

Baño de Oro

Mt Britton (918m)

Road blocked by landslide

MT BRITTON TRAIL

BAÑO DE ORO RESEARCH NATURAL AREA

TRADE WINDS TRAIL

Road closed   Road closed

0   250 m

ACCOMMODATION
Casa Cubuy Ecolodge   F
Casa Flamboyant   G
Casa Picaflores   I
Coqui's Hideaway   A
La Paloma Guest House   E
Rain Forest Villa   B
Rainforest Fruit Farm   H
Rainforest Inn   C
Villa Sevilla   D

El Yunque birdlife

Most day-trippers visit only the busiest sections of the reserve and leave El Yunque seeing very little **wildlife**, yet the forest is home to over thirty species of amphibian and reptile, eleven types of bat (the only native mammal) and 68 species of **bird** – it's the last that get naturalists most excited. Early morning (before 10am) and late afternoon (after 4pm) are the best times to hear and see them.

El Yunque's thick, primeval forest is a precious ecosystem of 240 tree species and four distinct zones: 70 percent of the reserve is smothered in *tabonuco* forest, while higher up is Palo Colorado forest, sierra palm forest and at the very top, cloud or dwarf forest, dense vegetation that rarely tops 3m. Tucked within this greenery is the **Puerto Rican green parrot** or *Cotorra Puertorriqueña*, the most celebrated and endangered inhabitant of the forest. When the Spanish arrived in 1508, it was estimated that one million parrots lived on the island: after years of hunting, deforestation and devastating hurricanes, there are thought to be around 50 in the wild, all here in El Yunque (up from a record low of 13 in 1975), thanks to a rehabilitation programme founded in 1968. As you can imagine, you need the eyes of a hawk and lots of luck to spot one. The parrot has a distinctive bright green colour with a red forehead and is usually around 12in long. Nesting season runs from February through to June.

You should have more luck with the **Puerto Rican tody** (*san pedrito*), a small bird with bright green feathers, lemony white breast and scarlet throat, and the **bananaquit** (*ciquita*), a tiny warbler with a black-and-white striped head and yellow breast. You might also hear the "cow cow, kuk krrk" of the **Puerto Rican lizard cuckoo** (*pájaro bobo mayor*), which feasts on lizards and has a long striped tail. You'll find plenty of information on other bird species in the forest visitor centres.

The official El Yunque **website** maintained by the USDA Forest Service at Ⓦ www.fs.fed.us/r8/caribbean is a useful resource, especially for checking current weather and fire conditions.

Accommodation

Several **guesthouses** and **rental villas** in or around El Yunque offer a more intimate experience of the rainforest than the average day-trip provides. Stay on the **north side** of the forest and you'll be closer to the main sights, but the southern slopes of **Cubuy** are just as inviting and much quieter.

Although most of El Yunque Recreation Area is off-limits to campers (including El Yunque peak and PR-191 between La Coca Falls and the gate at km 13), in theory you can **camp** anywhere else provided you have a **permit** (see p.95), though rangers prefer the area just beyond the gate at km 13, as steep slopes and wet weather make finding other suitable sites difficult. There are no officially designated campgrounds and no facilities, so bring everything with you. You can also camp at *Rainforest Fruit Farm* (see p.98).

North side

Coqui's Hideaway PR-966 km 3.6, ☏787/396-4470, Ⓦ www.coquishideaway.com. Set in a secluded nine-acre estate, this modern bungalow has three cosy bedrooms and gorgeous ocean views. Rooms (all with a/c) are simply but thoughtfully decorated with different colour schemes, artwork and vivid wall hangings. It also boasts a pool, kitchen, washer/dryer, satellite TV and wi-fi. ⑥

Rainforest Inn PR-186, ☏1-800/672-4992 or 787/378-6190, Ⓦ www.rainforestinn .com. Real gem of a B&B, with two plush and very unique suites beautifully finished with exposed brick, pine and cedar, in a gorgeous five-acre estate at the edge of the forest. Each unit contains two bedrooms and a kitchen. There's wi-fi but no TV, a/c or radio. Get directions on booking (3-night minimum). ⑤

Rain Forest Villa PR-966, ☎787/809-4172, ⒲www.rainforestvillas.com. Rent this appealing one-bedroom guesthouse, with bath and kitchen on the terrace outside and fabulous views. No TV but free wi-fi and fresh fruit to pick. No children under eight and there's a minimum two-night stay. ⑤

Villa Sevilla PR-956 km 7.9, ☎787/887-5889, ⒲www.villasevilla.net. This inviting rental property comprises four separate units: a large three-bedroom wooden chalet sitting above the garden like a giant treehouse, with enough space for six (5-night minimum; ⑦); a rustic two-bedroom clapboard cottage, decorated in tropical bamboo style (4-night minimum; ⑥); a two-bedroom garden apartment (3-night minimum; ⑤); and the more modern and spacious one-bedroom garden apartment (⑤). It's perfect for families and has a pool on site.

South side and Cubuy

Casa Cubuy Ecolodge PR-191 km 22.4, ☎787/874-6221, ⒲www.casacubuy.com. This wonderful hillside property lies just within the forest boundary at an elevation of 460m. Rooms are simple but comfortable with private bathrooms: no TV or a/c (they have free wi-fi), but it's cool enough with a fan and the views across the Cubuy valley are mesmerizing. Breakfast (9am) is included, while hearty dinners can be booked in advance (6.30pm; $18.50). ④

Casa Flamboyant PR-191 (just before *Casa Cubuy*), ☎787/874-6074, ⒲www.rainforestsafari .com/flamboy.html. This pretty pink B&B offers magnificent views from three stylish rooms and one suite overlooking the Cubuy valley. Each room has slightly different decor, though an elegant nineteenth-century theme dominates overall – ask for the Ginger Room, which has wood furnishings, antiques and a comfy double bed that looks out onto a private terrace. ⑦

Casa Picaflores off PR-191 at km 25.9, ☎787/874-3802, ⒲www.casapicaflores.com. This enticing rental villa is set in a five-acre former fruit farm with three bedrooms, two bathrooms and a shared kitchen. You get satellite TV, DVD, free wi-fi, laundry and whirlpool, but much of the appeal comes from the simple but elegant rooms, all with tiled floors, and the incredible variety of exotic fruits grown on site. ⑨

La Paloma Guest House PR-975 km 8, ☎787/885-4040. This simple family-run guesthouse is halfway between El Yunque and Fajardo, but tends to be favoured by those exploring the former. The biggest draw here is the price – it's one of the few budget guesthouses, with adequate rooms and fridge, pool, a/c and satellite TV thrown in. Cash only. ②

Rainforest Fruit Farm PR-191 km 24.2, ☎787/874-2138 6–9pm only, or ☎787/414-9596, ⒲www.rainforestfruitfarm.com. The only budget option in Cubuy, this no-frills, no electricity wooden cabin, perched 90m above the parking area on the road, is owned by local guide Robin Phillips. You get a double bed, sheets, blankets, hammocks, outdoor toilet and barbecue grill (bring the charcoal, food and flashlight). You can also pick fruit at the Phillips' farm. It's basic but a rare bargain: $40 for the first two nights and $30 thereafter (for 2 people; $10 per extra person). You can camp for $15 per couple ($7 extra person). Cash only. ①

North side: El Yunque Recreation Area

It's a good idea to start your visit at the El Portal Rain Forest Center near the northern entrance of the forest, before heading to the trailheads in the **El Yunque Recreation Area**. All the sights listed below can be reached via PR-191, which cuts into the heart of the forest from PR-3 – note, however, that you cannot drive across El Yunque to Cubuy on this route.

El Portal Rain Forest Center

Surrounded by flourishing *tabonuco* forest in what was once a coffee plantation, **El Portal Rain Forest Center** (daily 9am–5pm; $4; ☎787/888-1880) provides the best introduction to El Yunque, with its soaring white roof sheltering several thought-provoking exhibits. This is the first point of interest inside the forest boundary on PR-191, 4km south of PR-3, and also contains a small café, gift shop and information desk, with a fifteen-minute introductory video narrated by actor Jimmy Smits (whose mother is Puerto Rican) and screened continuously throughout the day.

The exhibition rooms are laid out as a series of open pavilions, each furnished with interactive displays; the first floor provides a basic introduction to the forest while the upper level galleries focus on "Understanding the Forest", "Managing the Future" and "Connections" – the last showing how the rainforest impacts on our daily lives and how materials from the forest are used to produce commonly used household items.

La Coca Falls and around

The first major attraction on PR-191 beyond El Portal, **La Coca Falls** tumbles over a 25m cliff right by the road, a wispy veil of water that folds into the rocks like delicate silk thread. You can glimpse the falls from your car window, but for a more leisurely look, dump your vehicle in one of the car parks either side. You'll find them on PR-191 at around the 8km mark, at an elevation of 460m and just beyond the steel gate (which closes at 6pm; see p.95). Kids like to paddle in the rock pools here.

Another 400m beyond the falls, at km 8.5, is the start of **La Coca Trail** (2.9km), named after the area's former banana plantation owned by Spanish settler Juan Diego de La Coca. The trailhead has space for just four cars, otherwise you'll have to walk up from the falls. The main appeal of this trail is the relative ease with which you become immersed in the forest: few people hike here and the sounds of the road soon melt away. It's steep and rocky in parts and involves crossing two streams via a series of boulders and stones.

Yokahu Tower

Providing stupendous views of the forest, the north coast and, on a clear day, the peak of El Yunque itself, **Yokahu Tower** at km 8.8 is a popular stop along PR-191, with a car park and gift shop at its base. Named after Yokahú, the Taíno's chief deity, the castle-like observation tower was constructed in 1963 to mimic the style of the sham medieval turret built on Mount Britton (see p.101). It's 21m tall, with 98 steps leading to the top for a total elevation of 480m above sea level.

La Mina Falls

Thousands of Puerto Ricans throng into El Yunque in the summer, their towels and swimsuits a sign most of them are heading for just one place. **La Mina Falls** is a relatively modest 10m waterfall on the Río de la Mina, but it's surrounded by pools of cool mountain water and thick swathes of sierra palm deep inside the forest, perfect for a refreshing dip or a meditative afternoon of lounging on the rocks – you can also swim underneath the waterfall. In July it seems half of San Juan is here, but at other times, especially weekdays, you should have it to yourself. Reaching the falls involves a short, energetic walk; the most popular route is the **Big Tree Trail** (1.12km), which starts at km 10.2 with its own small car park and is marked by interpretative panels along the way. The trail snakes through *tabonuco* forest and up and down several flights of steps before ending in around 35 minutes at the small footbridge in front of the falls. **La Mina Trail** (1.12km) starts at the Palo Colorado Information Center (see below) and follows the river downhill like a concrete ribbon, through a *Jurassic Park*-like landscape of giant palms, rustic barbecue pavilions and *palo colorado* forest – the only steep section is the steps down to the falls at the end, where it connects with the Big Tree Trail. You can make a loop by hiking both trails, but this would include a 1.8km stretch along the road – appealing only if traffic is light. Along the section of PR-191 between the two trailheads you'll pass the **Sierra Palm Recreation Area** (km 11.3), which has a small snack stall but nothing to see.

Palo Colorado Recreation Area

Serious hikers should make for the **Palo Colorado Recreation Area** at km 11.8, the hub of a network of trails shooting off all over the forest. The **information centre** is a small hut with a shop, basic maps and a ranger on hand to provide advice, with two small car parks on either side. La Mina Trail zips off to the falls

Tours and activities

Birdwatching: Ornithologists should contact AdvenTours (☎787/530-8311, ⓦwww .adventourspr.com) for custom-made **bird-watching tours** ($90/person or $175 for one person). Tours run 7.30am to 3.30pm and must be booked 48 hours in advance.

Canyoning & abseiling: If you are more of a thrill seeker, get in touch with Aventuras Tierra Adentro (☎787/766-0470, ⓦwww.aventuraspr.com), which arranges **canyoning** trips to El Yunque every Sunday ($160), with abseiling, a couple of *via ferratas*, rock climbs and zip-lines across the river – on-the-spot training is provided and expert guides are on hand throughout. Tours run from 5.45am to 5pm.

Hang-gliding: Team Spirit Hang Gliding (☎787/850-0508, ⓦwww.hangglidepuertorico .com) is based southwest of El Yunque, on PR-9948 (near the end of PR-186), offering various **hang-gliding** options from four-hour beginner classes ($50) to four-month programmes ($750) and intensive ten-day courses ($999). Paragliding is $100.

Hiking: The Forest Service run **Forest adventure tours** (1hr; $5 adults, $3 children) which are available on a first-come-first-served basis from 10.30am until 3.30pm daily, from the Palo Colorado Visitor Center (☎787/888-1810). Guides lead short, fairly easy hikes around the area, providing background on local history and ecology. Ecoquest Adventures and Tours (☎787/616-7543, ⓦwww.ecoquestpr.com) arranges **hikes** through sections of El Yunque (half-day $62; full day $75) accompanied by informative, experienced guides, not a bad option if you are staying in San Juan and don't want to drive (they'll pick you up from your hotel).

If you're staying in the area, try knowledgeable local **Robin Phillips** (☎787/874-2138, mobile 787/414-9596, ⓔphillips@east-net.net), who organizes illuminating hiking excursions on the south side of the forest, usually starting at 10am and taking in several rivers, the falls on the Río Prieto and the Taíno petroglyphs (minimum $125 for up to five people, $25/additional person; exclusive tours $180). Shorter tours of just the petroglyphs are available for $53.

Swimming: Though **swimming** in rivers and mountain pools is one of the most popular activities in the reserve, especially in the summer, heavy downpours can cause flash floods and turn the water an uninviting muddy-brown colour. **Fishing** is banned throughout the forest.

(see p.99) from here, while the **El Yunque Trail** starts opposite (see opposite). Before tackling the latter, take a look at the forlorn waters of the **Baño Grande**, up the steep flight of steps opposite the information centre. Another legacy of the 1930s, this 5m-deep swimming pool was created by a stone and masonry dam, with the old bathhouse beyond. It has been out of use since 1976.

South of Palo Colorado and higher up the mountain, PR-191 is blocked by a metal gate just beyond km 13: you can continue on foot from here (see El Toro, opposite), making sure your car doesn't block the road, but you'll have to return the same way unless you're attempting to cross the whole forest. Just before the metal gate, cars can turn right on PR-9938 for another 400m to the parking area at the end of the road. This is the trailhead for the **Mount Britton Trail** (1.29km), popular as the shortest route to one of the loftiest observation points in the forest (see opposite) – you can continue on to El Yunque from there, but it's best to start back at Palo Colorado.

Climbing El Yunque

Although it's only the second highest peak in the forest, the Taíno holy mountain of El Yunque (1055m) dominates the region, making a tempting target for an exhilarating half-day hike. The well-marked trail to the summit is lined with some of the richest forest in the reserve, a mostly gentle climb rewarded by scintillating views from the top.

From the Palo Colorado Visitor Center you have two options: the direct route via the Baño Grande along the **El Yunque Trail** (3.86km), or the small detour via the **Baño de Oro Trail** (500m), which starts further up PR-191 at km 12.2. The latter passes the sadly dilapidated Baño de Oro bathhouse and pool (which the Forest Service is planning to rehabilitate), built in the mid-1930s as a children's swimming pool (it means "bath of gold") and long since closed to the public. The gravel path rejoins the main Yunque trail beyond the abandoned fish hatchery pools (a failed attempt to introduce trout farming to the forest), further up the hill. From here El Yunque Trail climbs slowly through lush sierra palm forest for just under two miles and you should reach the spur to the rugged peak of Los Picachos ("the peaks") in a leisurely sixty to ninety minutes. It's just 320m to the top, reached by 45 short, steep steps at the end of the trail. The flat grassy summit of **Los Picachos** (926m) is enclosed by a concrete wall built in the 1930s, providing a taste of what's to come – practically the whole of eastern Puerto Rico is visible on a clear day. Hawks hover above the precipitous drops on all sides and the peaks of El Toro and El Yunque loom beyond. Return to the main trail and you should reach the peak of El Yunque itself, sprinkled with communication towers, in under thirty minutes. On the way up you'll understand why the cloud forest is also known as dwarf forest, as the vegetation is increasingly twisted, stumpy and wind-blown. When you reach the road on top, turn left for the summit, marked by a stocky observation tower also built in the 1930s. Clouds often submerge the peak, but you'll see a stunning panorama unfold through the mist, including stellar views of San Juan to the west.

Rather than retrace your steps, make a loop by returning along Forest Road 10, which drops past the police communication towers. Follow the road and you'll eventually come to the trailhead for **Mount Britton** (the short path that veers off to the right of the information board), a 918-metre peak topped with a turret-like observation **tower** built in 1935. It's named after US botanist Nathaniel Lord Britton (1859–1934), founder of the New York Botanical Gardens and keen student of Caribbean ecology. Return to the road and continue down to the next trail that drops off to the left (the lower section of the Mount Britton Trail), snaking down the mountain to the parking area below. Though maps suggest otherwise, you cannot turn left at the parking area – follow the road back to where it meets PR-191 and walk another 1.6km down to Palo Colorado. The whole loop can be completed in three hours, depending on stops and fitness level.

El Toro

Crowned with dense cloud forest and grand vistas that take in half of Puerto Rico, **El Toro** (1076m) is the highest peak and most challenging hike in the reserve, though unless it's exceptionally wet, not as draining as some rangers make out.

The path is sometimes overgrown, so dress accordingly and get an early start. The **Trade Winds Trail** (6.3km), which begins on PR-191, around 400m beyond the metal gate at km 13, is the best route up. The path should be easy to follow, but does get muddy and strenuous in places, making for an arduous three- to four-hour ascent. It's possible to pitch a tent near the summit and you can continue down the other side of the mountain on the steep and generally unmaintained **El Toro Trail** (3.5km) to PR-186, assuming you have some way of getting picked up. Otherwise the hike back to PR-191 should take under three hours: if you start in the morning it's easy to complete the return trip in one day.

Cubuy

The southern section of El Yunque, known as **Cubuy**, offers a completely different experience to the busy northern half, with PR-191 slicing through a wilder, more rugged landscape of steep river valleys, raging waterfalls and towering trees. To appreciate this area you really need to spend the night in one of the local guesthouses: places such as *Casa Cubuy* and *Casa Flamboyant* are a wealth of information and have their own network of trails across the four mountain streams that water the **Río Blanco**: the Cubuy, Sabana, Icacos and Prieto rivers.

If you just want a taste of the area, drive half a kilometre beyond *Casa Cubuy* to where PR-191 is blocked by a metal gate on the bridge over the Río Cubuy (park on the roadside). From here a narrow, short concrete path leads upriver to a series of invigorating pools fed by the stream, popular for swimming and barbecues at the weekends. You can also continue walking along the road, which remains in surprisingly good condition and is lined with great clumps of bamboo and sierra palm forest, to the **Río Sabana**, around 1km further on. This area was covered in coffee plantations before the 1930s and what you see today is almost all secondary-growth forest. Beyond here, the road rises and is quickly gobbled up by the giant landslide that destroyed it in the 1970s. Hardy climbers with a decent map can negotiate the landslide and rejoin the road on the other side, from where it's a long slog to the El Yunque Recreation Area, but you'll need to camp or arrange transport before making the return journey. Don't try it in wet weather.

Other highlights include the enigmatic Taíno **petroglyph sites** located along the **Río Icacos** and **Río Blanco** (inscribed onto large boulders in the river) and the secluded falls on the **Río Prieto**, but these are hard to find on your own – ask at your guesthouse or join a tour (see p.100).

Eating and drinking

Eating options within El Yunque might seem limited at first, but there are several places to fill up on local food and plenty of restaurants nearby offer a smarter experience. You can get snacks within the forest on PR-191, but once you hit the trails you're on your own.

North side

El Bosque Encantado PR-191 km 7.2. Convenient pit stop halfway into the forest, a no-nonsense food shack that serves fresh *batidas*, juices and fried snacks such as *alcapurrias* and tacos stuffed with beef, chicken and shrimp ($2). In the summer, Puerto Ricans tend to hit this place in the late afternoon, on the way home. Park your car along the roadside nearby. Daily 9am–5pm.

La Muralla PR-191 km 7.4. Just up the hill from *Bosque Encantado*, this canteen and souvenir shop sells similar fare, with a wider range of fried treats: beef or crab *alcapurrias* ($2), *empanadillas* and occasionally *bacalaítos*. Lunch is usually busiest here: park on the road nearby if you can. Daily 9am–5pm, closed Thurs.

Yuquiyú Delights Sierra Palm Recreation Area, PR-191 km 11.3. This welcome food shack sits in what used to be the forest visitor centre, with a popular picnic site nearby. Handy for lunch, it knocks out decent burgers (from $6.95), fruit shakes (from $3.95) and grilled meats from its outdoor barbecue, as well as local *frituras*, pizza and hot dogs (from $2.50). Daily 11am–5pm.

Cubuy

El Bohío ☎787/874-3802 or mobile 787/463-6640. This little culinary gem is a private dining room attached to *Casa Picaflores*, not far from PR-191. Inside you'll find a table which seats ten, a small bar and nourishing, home-style cooking. The dinner menu is set daily: the person who makes the first reservation (you must call in advance, before noon on the same day) decides the time and the main dish to be served (usually from a choice of five dishes such as spare ribs, steaks and salmon). Open daily by appointment, dinner $30 (children $10; no credit cards) and breakfasts for $10 (children $5).

Restaurant Casa Cubuy PR-191 km 23 ☎787/874-7766, ⓦwww.casacubuy.com. Much needed local diner halfway up the mountain, with a fabulous open terrace overlooking the valley at the back. The menu features mostly Puerto Rican classics, such as an excellent *mofongo* ($10.95), can can pork chops ($12.95) and strip skirt steak ($12.95). Thurs–Mon 2–9pm.

Luquillo and the northeast coast

Perched on the balmy Atlantic coast in the shadow of El Yunque, 45km east of San Juan, **LUQUILLO** combines three of Puerto Rico's most appealing pastimes: lounging on palm-fringed **beaches**, world-class **surfing** and gorging on celebrated *cocina en kiosco*. While it can get insufferably busy on weekends, it's well worth a pit stop during the week and a couple of attractive hotels mean you can stay the night (and use it as a base for El Yunque). **Getting here** involves a straightforward 45-minute drive from San Juan along PR-3, or a shorter twenty-minute hop from El Yunque. Taxis from San Juan's Aeropuerto Internacional Luis Muñoz Marín will charge $70.

Accommodation

Much of Luquillo's seafront is dominated by holiday homes and condos, rented primarily by *sanjuaneros* on weekends or over the summer. **Rental apartments** can be a good deal, especially if you stay a week or longer (the minimum stay is usually a weekend). Check ⓦwww.playaazulpr.com or call ☏787/435-1825 for a current sample of what's available. The north coast between San Juan and Luquillo is also the preserve of the most luxurious **resorts** on the island. These giant five-stars monopolize some of the best stretches of **beach** in the region and often feature top-class **restaurants**. Many visitors like to end their trips to Puerto Rico with a night or two of pampering here, within caviar-throwing distance of El Yunque and Luquillo, but unless you're an avid **golf** fan with plenty of cash, it's not worth visiting for the day (non-guest parking fees are often exorbitant).

If you have a tent, you can **camp** at the Balneario de Luquillo (☏787/889-5871), facing the beach ($17 with or $13 without utilities in camping area, or $10 in open areas).

Luquillo

Luquillo Sunrise Beach Inn Costa Azul A2, ☏787/409-2929, ⓦwww.luquillosunrise.com. The best place to stay in town, with twelve clean, smart rooms with tiled floors, TV, a/c and balconies overlooking the ocean. Full breakfast is included. The location is perfect, facing La Pared beach on the edge of the town centre. ❺

Yunque Mar Beach Hotel Calle 1, no. 6, Playa Fortuna ☏787/889-5555, ⓦyunquemarhotel .com. This hotel is also right on the seafront, but several kilometres west of town at Playa Fortuna. It's still a great deal though, with spacious rooms equipped with cable TV, a/c and balconies, so book ahead. ❸

Beach resorts

Bahía Beach Resort PR-187 km 4.2, ☏787/809-8000, ⓦwww.bahiabeachpuertorico.com. This luxurious A-list retreat, operated by St Regis Resorts, is Puerto Rico's most exclusive hotel, embellished by a Robert Trent Jones Jr golf course, personal butler service, a world-class spa,

oceanfront swimming pools, Jean-Georges restaurant and a magnificent three-kilometre arc of sand. Rooms cost around $1000. ❾

Gran Meliá Golf Resort Puerto Rico Coco Beach 200, PR-968 ☏787/809-1770, ⓦwww.gran -melia-puerto-rico.com. This all-inclusive resort at the end of a spur off PR-955 lies on Coco Beach, one of the most alluring stretches of sand on the north coast. You get suites not rooms, set in two-storey villas on the beach with flashy contemporary design and all the extras. Despite the 11 percent resort fee (and $15 parking), online deals can reduce prices considerably. ❼

Río Mar Beach Resort Blvd Río Mar 6000, 3.5km off PR-3, ☏1-877/636-0636, ⓦwww .wyndhamriomar.com. This Wyndham-owned hotel is like a self-contained island covering five hundred acres, with a secluded beach, six hundred rooms with balconies and luxury baths dripping with marble and eleven restaurants and entertainment venues. Again, despite the hefty 14 percent resort fee, deals on the web can make this surprisingly affordable. ❼

The beaches

Luquillo's town centre lies around Plaza Jesús T. Piñero, just off PR-3, but other than a few places to eat, contains little to see and the **beaches** are spread out for several miles either side of here. If you're coming from San Juan the first is **Balneario de Luquillo** (daily 8.30am–5pm; parking $5.35), the main beach and one of Puerto Rico's most beguiling strips of sand, formally known as Balneario de Monserrate. Look for the brown sign to "Balneario" and "Kioscos" on PR-3, just after you pass the line of *kioscos* on the left (if you reach the Luquillo exit on PR-3, you've missed it).

With a wide swathe of honey-gold sand, plenty of palm trees and El Yunque for a backdrop, it's definitely one of the top beaches on the island, best enjoyed on weekdays when you'll avoid the crowds (and the rubbish). As an official public beach, it has a vast car park, toilets, changing facilities, showers and clear, calm water, perfect for **swimming**. It even has a staffed ramp for wheelchair users known as the **Mar Sin Barreras** ("sea without barriers", see p.42). Luquillo itself is 1km east of the *balneario* on the other side of a headland and quite separate from it – you have to rejoin PR-3 and take the next exit to reach the centre (you can follow one-way PR-193 in the other direction).

The northern half of Luquillo town is almost completely given over to condos and known as Vilomar or just "Condominio" – it backs **Playa Azul**, a narrow but reasonably clean beach where you can park for free on the street and doze under the palms. Central Luquillo lies beyond the small headland ("La Punta") further along, a slightly shabby, sleepy place fronting the rougher beach of **Playa La Pared**, popular with **surfers** (see below). To the southeast you'll see the sand stretching away into the distance: known as **La Selva**, this is hard to access by car and often sprinkled with debris, but almost always deserted. Conservationists managed to get the undeveloped stretch of coast between here and Balneario Seven Seas (dubbed "the **Northeast Ecological Corridor**") designated a nature reserve in 2008, but just over a year later Governor Fortuño rescinded the decision. With **turtle** nesting sites threatened by the construction of mega resorts, the area has attracted a coalition of various groups campaigning for its protection: see Ⓦwww.sierraclub.org/corridor for more details.

Eating and drinking

Luquillo contains a handful of decent **restaurants** and **bars**, but is more famous throughout Puerto Rico for its **kioscos**, sixty *friquitines* (food stalls) that stand along the north side of PR-3, just before the turning to the *balneario* (coming from San Juan, exit the highway as if heading to the latter and turn left at the beach).

Luquillo watersports

Surfers flock to Luquillo's **Playa La Pared** ("the wall") on weekends for its fairly consistent left beach-break, though it can go flat in the summer: it's fine for beginners, with a fairly gentle swell and a sandy bottom. **Board Riders Luquillo Surf Shop** (Mon–Fri noon–midnight, Sat & Sun 10am–2am; ℡787/599-2097, Ⓦwww .boardridersinc.com) overlooks La Pared at c/Veve Calzada 25, not far from the main plaza and rents **surfboards** for $40 per day ($10/hr) and bodyboards for $20 per day ($6/hr); lessons are $60 per hour. Ask here about current conditions, or stop by **La Selva Surf Shop** (daily 9am–5pm; ℡787/889-6205) at c/Fernández García 250, one block inland from the plaza, where boards are usually slightly cheaper and owner Bob Roberts also offers **lessons**. The reefs around La Punta dividing Playa Azul and La Pared offer some good **snorkelling**, but you'll need your own gear.

Kioscos

Only a handful of *kioscos* are open in the mornings or early in the week; you'll get a bigger choice later in the day or on weekends.

Ay Bonito Grill (no. 21) ⓦ www.aybonitogrill.com. This is a smarter place that serves great seafood (*mahi-mahi*, pan-seared halibut; $16–22) and even has a website.

🏃 **Dieguito & Markitos** (no. 44) ⓣ 787/355-0875. This *kiosco* serves up a more sophisticated dinner menu such as red snapper, conch *mofongo* and mouthwatering shrimp *pastelitos* (reckon on $45/head).

🏃 **El Jefe Burger Shack** (no. 12, towards the San Juan end). Serves tasty rib, jalapeño and chorizo burgers ($5–12) in addition to the usual choices (and a spectacular ginger *mojito*).

La Roca Taina (no. 60, at the Luquillo end). Solid choice for fried snacks ($1–2), including *dorado*- and marlin-stuffed *pastelitos*.

Restaurants and bars

Board Riders Rum Shop c/Veve Calzada 25, not far from the main plaza ⓣ 787/599-2097, ⓦ www .boardridersinc.com. This casual surf bar overlooks Playa La Pared, doubling as a surf shop (see box opposite). It's the best place to grab a drink or snack in town, with the breeziest ocean views and congenial surfer-dude staff. Brunch costs $5–10. Mon–Fri noon–midnight, Sat & Sun 10am–2am.

Brass Cactus Bar & Grill PR-193 km 1.3, ⓣ 787/889-5735, ⓦ www.thebrasscactus.com. This Tex-Mex grill is a good choice for lunch or evening drinks. The seven types of juicy half-pound burger (from $6.95) and tender baby-back ribs in home-made sauce ($10.50) are highlights and the margarita menu is well worth sampling. Take the first exit into Luquillo and turn left on the main street. Sun–Thurs 11am–midnight, Fri & Sat 11am–1am. Happy hour Mon–Fri 5–7pm.

Erik's Gyros & Deli c/Fernández García 352 ⓣ 787/889-0615. Handy for a last-minute stop on the way out of Luquillo (it's just off PR-3, on PR-193 at the southern end of town), this cheap diner serves all the Greek favourites (*gyros*, lamb kebabs and lots of feta cheese) but also burgers, sandwiches and breakfasts ($5–10). Mon–Sat 7am–6pm, Sun 8.30am–2pm.

King Seafood PR-193 (c/Fernández García 1) ⓣ 787/889-4300, ⓦ kingseafoodpr.com. Just down the road from *Brass Cactus,* this is one of the best places in town for fresh seafood. With its own car park, the small dining room with wooden tables is packed at lunch with a loyal clientele. The freshly cooked fish dishes are superb, as is the *mofongo*, crammed with lobster, prawns, octopus and fish broth (mains from $10). Tues–Fri 11am–10pm, Sat & Sun noon–10pm.

🏃 **Pasta y Pueblo** c/14 de Julio at Playa La Pared ⓣ 787/909-2015. This ramshackle shack overlooking the northern end of the beach has just five tables but serves some of the best food in the region. Favourites include the perfectly grilled skirt steak and the curry shrimp with pesto pasta and coconut rice. Service is slow but friendly. Mains cost $12–15 and you can bring your own bottle. Tues–Sun 5–10pm.

Fajardo and around

Justly regarded as the boating capital of Puerto Rico, it's no surprise that the real appeal of **FAJARDO** lies along the coast. Numerous boat operators provide ample opportunity to explore the glittering waters and islets of **La Cordillera** just offshore, while the nearby **Reserva Natural Cabezas de San Juan** is an unexpectedly wild reserve containing one of the island's extraordinary **bioluminescent bays**. The city itself has become something of a boomtown in recent years and is best avoided; a wholly unattractive mess of strip malls, clogged highways and rampant property development.

Coming by car, it's easy to drive right through all this and most *públicos* will drop you elsewhere if you ask – get a taxi or another bus if you get stuck at the downtown terminal. The *reserva* is 5km north of the city on PR-987, near the fishing village of **Las Croabas**, which also contains some of the best places to stay and eat. Most boat excursions depart from **Villa Marina**, just east of the centre on PR-987, or **Puerto del Rey**, several kilometres to the south. For the ferries to Vieques and Culebra (see p.110), head straight to the grubby port district of **Puerto Real** (referred to locally and on *públicos* as "La Playa").

FAJARDO & AROUND

EATING & DRINKING

Blue Bahía Seafood Restaurant	1
Cremaldi Ice Cream	4
La Estación	3
Ocean View	2

0 — 500 m

ATLANTIC OCEAN

RESERVA NATURAL CABEZAS DE SAN JUAN

El Faro

Laguna Grande

Plaza El Convento

Laguna Aguas Prietas

Balneario Seven Seas

Road closed

LAS CROABAS

Ⓐ

987

Ⓟ

❶ ❷

Las Croabas Pier

Ⓟ

987

❸

Ⓑ

Entrance to El Conquistador

CARIBBEAN SEA

N

AV. EL CONQUISTADOR

Sun Bay Marina

RAFAEL BERMUDEZ

CAMINO CABEZAS

Supermarket   **Villa Marina**

Isleta Marina

A

Cayo Zancudo

194

AV. GENERAL VALERO

OSVALDO MOLINA

PUERTO REAL

NAVARRO

Ⓒ

UNIÓN

Ferry Terminal

SIERRA

195

AV. A

966

FAJARDO

❹

MORALES

MUÑOZ RIVERA

AGUILERA

MARCELITO GOTAY

DEL CARMEN

Río Fajardo

194

3

La Cordillera ▶

St Thomas (Virgin Islands) ▶

Culebra ▶

Vieques ▶

Luquillo (11km) & San Juan (50km) ◀

Ⓓ, Ceiba Airport & Puerto del Rey ▼

ACCOMMODATION

Ceiba Country Inn	**D**
El Conquistador Resort	**B**
Fajardo Inn	**C**
Passion Fruit Bed & Breakfast	**A**

Accommodation

Fajardo's budget hotels were hit hard by the 2008–2009 recession and choices are now limited and often overpriced. You can always **camp** at *Balneario Seven Seas* (☎787/863-8180) for $10 if you have your own tent: there are toilets, showers and 24-hour security, making this one of the safest places to pitch tents on the island.

Ceiba Country Inn PR-977 km 1.2 ☎787/885-0471, ⓦwww.ceibacountryinn.com. This former hacienda lies on a wonderfully scenic and tranquil ridge surrounded by forest. The nine rooms are simple, clean and comfortable and each has a/c and fridge, but no TV. Breakfast is included and there is free w-fi in the lounge. Take PR-975 from the highway (exit 5), then follow the signs on PR-977. ❸

El Conquistador Resort Avda Conquistador 1000 ☎866/317-8932, ⓦwww.elconresort.com. This vast resort sprawls over the cliffs above Puerto Real, with a casino, a spa, five "villages" including the luxury *Las Casitas Village* (ⓦlascasitasvillage .com), 21 restaurants and lounges and its own private island. All the rooms have balconies and five-star amenities, though staying here sometimes feels too isolated. ❽

Fajardo Inn c/Parcelas Beltrán 52, Puerto Real ☎787/860-6000, ⓦwww.fajardoinn.com. Despite looking like a big motel, this is more like a mini-resort. All rooms are sparsely decorated but clean and relatively spacious, with queen-sized beds, ironing boards, a/c and basic cable TV. The free wi-fi is only guaranteed around the lobby and pool areas (you can also check email in the computer room). ❹

Passion Fruit Bed & Breakfast PR-9987 km 4.8 (off PR-987), Las Croabas ☎787/801-0106, ⓦpassionfruitbb.com. The best of the budget hotels in Las Croabas, this three-storey villa just off PR-987 has large, simply furnished rooms with tiled floors and satellite TV, great breakfasts, super-friendly owners and a small pool. Free wi-fi, though not always in-room. ❺

Around Fajardo

Lingering in Fajardo itself is pointless; focus instead on the varied ecosystems of the **Reserva Natural Cabezas de San Juan** and **Laguna Grande** before exploring the reef-encrusted islands of **La Cordillera**. While plenty of travellers visit on day-trips from San Juan, staying in the area means you won't have to pay additional transport charges or get up at the crack of dawn.

Balneario Seven Seas

The only public beach in the Fajardo area, **Balneario Seven Seas** (daily 8am–6pm; parking $5.35) is 4.85km north of the city centre on PR-987, a sheltered arc of sand famed for its brilliant, multi-hued waters, though you'll need a vivid imagination to identify all seven colours alluded to in the name. With a reef just offshore, it's better for snorkelling than swimming and because it's generally calm, popular with families. The facilities here tend to be more run-down than at Luquillo and the sand not as clean (it has lots of seaweed year-round and rubbish on public holidays). Alternatively, hike to the western end of the beach (left side) where the rocky area begins and look for an overgrown trail up to the left. Follow this short trail until it ends (around 10min), and turn right to reach **Playa El Convento**, a more remote, secluded beach, home to turtle nesting sites and the location of the governor's beach house. It's also part of the **Northeast Ecological Corridor** (see p.104).

Reserva Natural Cabezas de San Juan

Wonderfully preserved by the Conservation Trust (ⓦwww.fideicomiso.org) since 1975, the **Reserva Natural Cabezas de San Juan** (Wed–Sun, tours 9.30am, 10am, 10.30am, 2pm; $8, over-65s and 5- to 11-year-olds $5; weekdays ☎787/860-2563 or 787/722-5834, weekends ☎787/860-2560) comprises 321 acres of untamed scrub and mangroves and 8km of reef-lined coast on the north-eastern tip of the island. You'll pass the gated entrance to the reserve just beyond the Balneario Seven Seas car park, but the guard will only let you in if you have a reservation: **reserve a tour** in advance, by phone or online: English tours depart at 2pm.

Laguna Grande (see below) dominates the lower half of the reserve, while the bush-smothered hill that rises over the northern section is topped by **El Faro**, the old Spanish lighthouse completed in 1882. It now houses a small visitors' centre with exhibits showcasing the reserve's marine and coastal ecosystems, including the bio bay – the highlight being bags of dinoflagellates (see p.132) that glow in the dark when shaken. Be sure to soak up the magnificent views from the observation deck on top.

General tours (by trolley bus; 2hr 30min) provide a brief taste of some of the diverse environments preserved here, starting with the **mangrove forests** that surround the lagoon (30 percent of the reserve), where a short boardwalk passes red, black, white and buttonwood mangroves and hordes of crab scuttle for cover. At Playa Lirios you get a chance to see the **rocky coast** and scrub and the three headlands that give the reserve its name (*cabeza* means "head"), before ending up at the lighthouse. Other than birds and insects, the only other wildlife you may encounter are giant **iguanas**, plodding through the undergrowth.

Laguna Grande

Lying just inside the reserve, the placid waters of **Laguna Grande** look fairly ordinary by day, but when night falls everything changes. Thanks to creatures known as dinoflagellates (see p.132), kayaks and boats leave glowing trails in the dark, while water falls like sparks of light from paddles and trailing arms. Puerto Rico has several places where heavy concentrations of microscopic plankton create this mesmerizing phenomenon: Vieques is home to the most celebrated example, but on a dark (and moonless) night, Laguna Grande is almost as magical. Optimum days for viewing are based not only on the phases of the moon but also the actual time the moon rises – check before you go.

The only way to experience the lagoon is to take a **tour**, preferably by **kayak**. It is forbidden to swim in the bay, so cutting through the mangroves by kayak is the best way to appreciate its bizarre luminescence – it's not as taxing as it looks and easy for beginners. One of the most eco-friendly and informative operators is **Yokahú Kayak Trips** (☎787/604-7375, Ⓦwww.yokahukayaks.com), which runs 2hr tours at 6pm and 8pm daily ($45). Kayaking Puerto Rico (☎787/435-1665, Ⓦwww.kayakingpuertorico.com) is another professional outfit that can arrange trips also for $45 per person (daily 6.30pm & 8.30pm; 2hr). Try to book at least three days in advance for both companies.

Captain Charlie Robles's electric boat at **Bio Island** (Mon–Sat at 6pm, 8pm & 9.30pm; $49/person; ☎787/422-7857, Ⓦwww.bioislandpr.com) is an eco-friendly alternative to kayaking. **Captain Suárez** (☎787/655-2739 or 787/556-8291) is the only operator licensed to pilot actual motorboats in the lagoon (Mon–Sat at 7pm, 9pm & 11pm; $45/person), and though he's a knowledgeable guide, his boat isn't really helping the lagoon. All tours start at the Las Croabas quay, last 90 minutes, and guides are all bilingual.

La Cordillera

While the modern city of Fajardo has all the charm of a giant shopping mall, the real Caribbean starts in earnest just offshore. La Cordillera is a chain of

Diving La Cordillera

Join any dive trip from Fajardo and you'll almost certainly be heading for **La Cordillera**. Unless conditions are perfect, experienced divers may be disappointed with the coral and marine life on display, much reduced in the last twenty years or so – hardcore divers should head to **Cayo Diablo** (or Culebra, p.142). For casual or beginner divers, it's worth a look and it's not overly expensive.

La Casa del Mar Dive Center (daily 8am–6pm; ☎787/860-3483, ⊛www.scuba puertorico.net) inside *El Conquistador Resort* is open to non-guests and offers two-tank dives for $99 ($69 for one tank). Trips to Culebra start at $125 for two tanks, while the Discover Scuba programme for beginners is $139. They also run daily **snorkelling** trips to Lobos ($60) and Culebra ($95), and offer a popular **kids' programme** (for 8- to 9-year-olds) known as Bubblemakers – call for details.

Sea Ventures Dive Center (Mon–Sat 8am–noon & 1–5pm, Sun 8am–1pm; ☎787/863-3483, ⊛www.divepuertorico.com) at Puerto del Rey is the other main operator in the area, charging $119 for two-tank dives with equipment and $109 if you bring your own ($55–65 for one tank). Non-certified beginners can dive for $150.

   Where you end up diving is largely in the hands of your divemaster and the weather/sea conditions on the day – heavy rain in El Yunque can decrease visibility dramatically, as heavily silted rivers flow into the sea near here. Beginners usually end up at **Pyramid** (9m), a coral rise teeming with small fish and reef lobsters, but often disappointing for seasoned divers. **Cayo Lobos** has three main sites, with **Lobos** itself (up to 10m) having the greatest variety of fish: yellowtail snapper, blue tang, the ubiquitous sergeant major and sometimes dolphins and stingrays. **Isla Palominos** has five main dive sites, with **Sandslide** (4.5–21m) one of the most popular, a gentle sandy slope that leads to a large reef crawling with enormous lobsters and all sorts of coral. You might also see dolphins, turtles, barracudas, small tuna and octopus here. Finally, **Cayo Diablo** (13–15m) has several sites and some of the best diving on the east coast, though swells and high winds often prevent visits. The island is surrounded by brilliant hard and soft corals, schools of barracuda and occasional rays – the water is extremely clear.

around ten uninhabited, reef-encrusted white sand cays, paradise for anyone interested in snorkelling, diving or lazing on the beach. Turtles nest here each year and the sprawling coral reefs are home to a variety of marine life. Many of the islands are protected within the **Reserva Natural La Cordillera**, managed by the DRNA.

   To reach the islands you'll need a boat: the easiest way to get one is to find or call Captain Domingo "Mingo" Nieves (☎787/383-6509) at the Las Croabas pier. He'll take you to **Icacos** or **Palominitos** for $100 (maximum 6 people) and pick you up anytime. For $30 per person (minimum 4 people) he'll take you snorkelling off Palominitos for a couple of hours. If you're lucky enough to be a guest at the *El Conquistador Resort* (see p.107), you'll get ferried over to Isla Palominos for free and failing that, numerous boats operating out of Villa Marina and Puerto del Rey (see p.110) visit the islands every day.

The islands

Cayo Icacos (163 acres) is the biggest island in the chain, coated in a thick layer of scrubby bush, seagrape and coconut palms, and fringed by incredibly seductive beaches of floury white sand and vivid, turquoise waters. Being relatively close to shore (though still 7km from Villa Marina), it's a particular favourite of boat operators, which means the best beach areas (on the calmer, leeward side) can get crowded on weekends, but at other times it's easy to find a secluded spot. The ocean side of the island is rough and rocky, while the reefs between Icacos and the rock known as "Cucaracha" have the best snorkelling.

From here, smaller islets stretch east towards Culebra: **Cayo Ratones**, **Cayo Lobos** and, further out, **Cayo Diablo** (30–40min by boat), are popular dive and snorkel sites (see p.109), and it's rare to go ashore. Five-acre Lobos is 2.7km east of Icacos and actually a private island, though it's permitted to dive or snorkel off its reef. A posh hotel was built here in the early 1960s, but went bankrupt soon after and now serves as a luxury vacation home for the owners.

To the south is the larger, rockier **Isla Palominos** (4.8km offshore and 15min by boat). Most of the island is leased by the *El Conquistador Resort* and officially off-limits to everyone else, though people do come here to snorkel off the northern shore and dine in the restaurant. Resort guests get whisked across in minutes to enjoy the lavish facilities on the 104-acre island, which include swimming, snorkelling, diving, windsurfing and horse riding. It also has a bar, a café and plenty of loungers on the smallish but pristine beach. **Isla Palominitos** covers just one acre, 460m off the southern tip of Isla Palominos, and surrounded by a reef perfect for snorkelling. Though it's tiny, it also has wide, sugary-sand beaches – a real desert island.

Boat trips

The boats listed below depart from either **Villa Marina** in Fajardo or **Puerto del Rey** further south, most offering similar routes and services: departing at around 10am, most head out to the reefs of La Cordillera (invariably Icacos) before a buffet lunch and afternoon snorkelling further offshore, returning at 3–4pm. Many locals refer to these boats disparagingly as "cattlemarans": that's a little harsh, but at peak times on big boats you might find yourself sharing the deck with over forty people.

Moving on from Fajardo

Ferries

Ferries to Culebra and Vieques depart from the run-down port area of **Puerto Real**, at the end of PR-195. You'll see the ample, secure **car park** (daily 6am–midnight; $5/24hr) on the right as you arrive at the wharf. The **Terminal de Lanchas** (ferry terminal) is a basic affair with a snack bar, toilets and some seating, while tickets are sold on the other side of the road. Ferries can fill up quickly at weekends or holidays – you can reserve tickets (daily 8–11am & 1–3pm; ☏787/860-2005 or 1-800/981-2005), but you can also buy them in advance at the ferry pier. Schedules do change, so check times before arrival.

Ferries to Vieques ($2 one-way, kids and seniors $1) depart Mon–Fri at 9.30am, 1pm, 4.30pm and 8pm, and 9am, 3pm and 6pm Sat & Sun. Coming back, ferries leave Vieques at 6.30am, 11am, 3pm and 6pm weekdays, and 6.30am, 1pm and 4.30pm Sat & Sun. The journey takes around 1hr 15min.

Ferries to Culebra ($2.25 one-way) depart daily 9am, 3pm and 7pm daily, returning 6.30am, 1pm and 5pm. The trip takes around 1hr 30min.

Flights

Flying to Vieques or Culebra from **Ceiba Airport** (aka Aeropuerto José Aponte de la Torre) is relatively cheap and much faster than the ferry. But the airport is rather isolated – it's not convenient for the Fajardo hotels (some 10km north), and taxis from San Juan will charge $80. You are better off leaving your own car in the car park ($8.50/24hr). The airport is signposted 2.5km off on PR-3 just south of Puerto del Rey (take PR-53 exit 2 from San Juan). Avis (☏787/885-0505) has a car rental outlet nearby, and inside the terminal there is a Banco Popular ATM and a café.

Villa Marina

Villa Marina (☎787/863-5131, ⓦwww.villamarinapr.com) occupies a small harbour just off PR-987 at km 1.3. Assuming you've made a reservation, the guard will open the gate and you should be able to park inside. The marina is barebones, but you'll find a small row of shops, including a supermarket, on the road before the main entrance.

Caribbean School of Aquatics ☎787/728-6606, ⓦwww.saildiveparty.com. Captain Greg Korwek organizes snorkelling trips on his self-built catamaran *Fun Cat* ($69, extra $20 for pick-up) and diving for certified divers.

Fajardo Tours Traveler ☎787/863-2821 or 787/396-0995, ⓦwww.travelerpr.com. Fajardo native Captain Antonio and family take their catamaran *Traveler* out to Icacos and other islands, providing new snorkelling gear and a "snorkelling instructor" on board. The salad-style lunch buffet with cold cuts and cheeses is top-notch, accompanied with plenty of cocktails and the fun crew is popular with families. Day-trips are $65/person including lunch and drinks. Maximum 48 people.

Salty Dog ☎787/717-6378, ⓦwww.saltydreams.com. This 14-metre catamaran makes regular trips out to Icacos, Lobos and Palominitos, its young and enthusiastic crew, led by Captain Saso, making it something of a party boat popular with twenty-somethings. Snorkelling breaks up the cocktails and salsa. Day-trips are $59/person.

Spread Eagle II ☎888/523-4511, ⓦwww.snorkelpr.com. This 15-metre catamaran is one of the most popular in Fajardo, running daily trips out to Icacos for snorkelling and dive trips, with gargantuan sandwich buffet lunches. All tours includ e complimentary *piña coladas* and tropical fruit punch, as well as snorkel equipment. Daily trips (10am–3.30pm) are $70 ($50 for under-12s) and they'll provide return transport from San Juan for $12. Maximum 49 people.

Puerto del Rey

Puerto del Rey (☎787/860-1000, ⓦwww.puertodelrey.com) is the largest marina in the Caribbean, a few kilometres south of Fajardo at PR-3, km 51.4: take

Vieques Air Link (☎787/534-4221, reservations ☎1-888/901-9247) flies from Ceiba to **Vieques** and Culebra on demand for around $30 one-way: though you can just turn up, it's best to call ahead to check the current schedule.

Air Flamenco (☎787/801-8256) offers charter flights (you rent the whole plane) from Ceiba to various destinations and can be economical if you have a group. One-way fares are: Culebra ($350); Vieques ($250); St Thomas ($700); St Croix ($780); and Tortola ($800).

Taxis

Though taxis and *públicos* do typically wait for ferry and air arrivals, **moving on to San Juan** from either the ferry terminal or the airport, it's best to arrange transport in advance. Reliable drivers include Mary and Ángel (☎787/863-8224 or 787/649-9155). The latter have minibuses with air conditioning and charge $65 to Old San Juan and just $50 to San Juan's **Aeropuerto Internacional Luis Muñoz Marín** (plus a few dollars extra for additional people, luggage and evening drives).

To the Virgin Islands

At the time of writing you could take a fast ferry to **St Thomas** and **St John** in the **US Virgin Islands** from Fajardo: the Saturday 8am departures on *M/V Caribe Cay* are designed to accommodate day-trips and return by 7pm; the ferry arrives at St Thomas (Charlotte Amalie) at 10am, heads on to St John before returning to St Thomas for the 4pm departure back to Fajardo. Reservations are required at the office near the pier or by phone (☎787/863-6582), but only Mon–Fri 7.30am–4.30pm. One-way is $70, return is just $90.

exit 2 off PR-53. The large free car park is just inside the main entrance, with a convenience store, ATM and a couple of places to eat nearby.

East Island Excursions ☎787/860-3434, ⓦwww.eastwindcats.com. One of the most professional operations in the area, the 62ft sailing catamaran *East Wind* visits Icacos and La Cordillera for $69, while speedy power catamarans are used for excursions to Culebra, Culebrita (both $89), Vieques (for the bio bay; $109) and St Thomas ($109, minimum twenty people) – these boats are the most efficient way to visit the outer islands for the day.

Erin Go Bragh Charters ☎787/860-4401, ⓦwww.egbc.net. Captain Bill Henry (who has been here since 1990) sails to Palominos, Icacos, Lobos and Palominitos for snorkelling and a sumptuous barbecue lunch of chicken, ribs and salad, with the real draw being the small groups of two to six people on board his 50ft Gulfstar Ketch yacht. He also offers charters to Vieques, Culebra and the Virgin Islands. Day-trips $85/person.

Eating and drinking

The scruffy waterfront in **Las Croabas** has the greatest concentration of Puerto Rican seafood restaurants in the area, while cheap fast-food chains are scattered all over central Fajardo and easy to spot from the highways. **Nightlife** is fairly subdued, with many of the restaurants listed here and in Las Croabas doubling as bars and venues for live music on weekends only. If you really want to splurge, you're better off heading to the **casino** and posh **restaurants** like the *Strip House* or *Piccola Fontana* inside the *El Conquistador Resort* (see p.107).

Blue Bahía Seafood Restaurant Las Croabas ☎787/863-6509. This indoor dining room overlooking the park and harbour beyond is a sound choice for seafood: try the *camarones de ajillo* (garlic prawns), filling *arepas rellenos* (all $7–8) or the *ruedas de mero* (red grouper). Mains $9–18. Sun–Thurs 11am–10pm, Fri & Sat 11am–11pm.
Cremaldi Ice Cream c/Unión 62 ☎787/801-1770. This venerable ice cream parlour is the best reason for a detour into downtown Fajardo, where home-made ice cream in tangy fruit and chocolaty flavours ($1.75–3.50) are sold beneath faded historical photos of the town and swinging bench chairs. It's really famous for its fried ice cream (vanilla only). Mon–Fri 11am–10pm, Sat & Sun 3–10pm.

La Estación PR-987 km 4 ☎787/863-4481, ⓦwww.laestacionpr.com. This humble-looking place is justly celebrated as one of the best restaurants in the region. Local produce and freshly ground spices are simply grilled over charcoal and salads feature seasonal native fruits and vegetables. Even the fish (such as local shark *pinchos* and pepper-crusted tuna) is caught locally. Mains $14–35. Mon–Wed 5pm–midnight, Fri–Sun 3pm–midnight.
Ocean View Las Croabas ☎787/863-6104. Another harbourfront restaurant, with a lime-green open-fronted terrace, specializing in fresh fish, *mofongo*, grilled lobster and prawns – a worthy alternative to *Blue Bahía* if you prefer sitting outside. Open 11am–11pm, closed Tues.

The east coast

Heading south along the east coast, you eventually lose the cars, condos and tourists and enter a rural, slower-paced and infinitely more appealing part of Puerto Rico. The main towns here, Naguabo and Humacao, hold little interest for most visitors and once again, it's the coast that provides the real allure. Highlights include the boat trip to **Monkey Island** (Cayo Santiago), some exceptional seafood **restaurants** at **Playa Naguabo** and **Punta Santiago** and the **beaches** and staggering vistas of **PR-901**, one of the most scenic roads on the island. Along the way, nature lovers should check out the thoroughbred Paso Fino **horses** at Palmas del Mar.

Playa de Naguabo

The first place of any interest south of Fajardo, the laidback seaside village of **PLAYA DE NAGUABO** (not to be confused with Naguabo town, and also known as **Playa Húcares**, after the local tree), is a welcome reminder than Puerto Rico isn't all shopping malls, cars and fast-food chains. Other than soaking up the soporific atmosphere (though as always, it gets busy on weekends), the main draw is the plethora of seafood **restaurants** on the small *malecón* (promenade), and the celebrated local snack, **chapín** (deep-fried turnovers usually stuffed with local trunkfish).

Playa Naguabo is on PR-3 a short drive off the PR-53 *autopista* (exit 13; once off the highway, don't take the right fork on PR-31 to Naguabo itself). You can park along the main road that runs along the harbour, or in the car park behind the *kioscos* at the end of the *malecón*. The helpful **Oficina de Turismo** (Mon–Fri 8am–4.30pm), where PR-3 hits the *malecón* , usually has English-speakers on hand and plenty of information on Naguabo municipality, but little else.

Monkey Island (Cayo Santiago)

The main reason to visit Playa Naguabo is to take a trip out to **Monkey Island**, just offshore. In 1938, the University of Puerto Rico established a colony of 409 Indian rhesus **monkeys** on the 39-acre cay (now thought to number at least 1000) to study their behaviour. It's the oldest monkey colony in the world.

Trips (2hr 30min) on *La Paseodora*, the motorboat captained by the sprightly Frank (Paco) Lopez (☎787/316-0441 or 787/850-7881), cost just $35–40 per person, a real bargain (the boat can take up to twenty people, but he prefers to take groups of between six and ten; groups smaller than six will pay more per head). Though it's forbidden to actually go ashore, Lopez regales his passengers with facts and amusing yarns about the island throughout the voyage, summoning the monkeys on the beach by blowing a conch shell. Trips also include snorkelling nearby, spiced up by the wreck of a cargo ship that sank in 1944 and is now a haven for tropical fish; you might see anything from a manatee to huge starfish and small octopus out here. Lopez goes out every day, but make sure you call in advance to reserve a space

Eating and drinking

Each February Playa Naguabo hosts a **Festival del Chapín** to honour its savoury fish *empanadas*. You'll find them all over Puerto Rico but this is where they were first created and the festival features boat races, market stalls and arts and crafts, as well as the tasty snack itself. At other times, most of the restaurants on the seafront offer their own versions of *chapín*, and if you have access to a kitchen, you can buy freshly made, raw versions at *Pastelillos Marca Nitza* (daily 8am–6pm; ☎787/530-0799), a short walk back up PR-3 from the waterfront ($8 for fourteen, but you need to cook them before eating). They also sell sweet *arepas de coco* ($5 for sixteen).

The best **restaurants** are to the left as you hit the waterfront, while those that face the *malecón* itself are a little dilapidated and tend to function as **bars** that open later in the day. *El Makito* (Wed–Sun 11am–11pm; ☎787/874-7192) occupies the second floor of the building above the dock (turn left when you reach the seafront on PR-3), with air conditioning and rustic decor. It specializes in lavish plates of lobster or *mofongo* stuffed with seafood and offers a range of fresh fish and Puerto Rican staples – you also get sweeping views of the bay and Monkey Island. If you fancy something cheaper, *El Botecito* (☎787/630-0994), opposite *Makito*, sells filling tacos ($2), hamburgers ($4) and *chapín* ($2). Failing that, at the far end of the *malecón* (heading south out of the village), *kioscos* deliver all the classic *frituras* for $1–3, usually open weekends only.

Punta Santiago

Five kilometres south of Playa Naguabo lies the small seaside town of **PUNTA SANTIAGO**, another former fishing village now home to some top-notch **seafood restaurants**, but with little else in the way of attractions. Around 3km further south at PR-3 km 72.4, **Balneario Punta Santiago** (Wed–Sun 8.30am–5pm; $3 parking; ℡787/852-1660) is a long strip of public beach also known as Balneario Público de Humacao. The beach is relatively clean and usually empty during the week, if you fancy a quick swim.

Eating

The most inviting **place to eat** in Punta Santiago is *Daniel Sea Food* (℡787/852-1784; closed Tues) at c/Marina 7, the road that runs along the seafront parallel to PR-3. It has a terrace and indoor seating, though views of the sea are blocked by thick vegetation here. The menu features fresh fish and local specialities such as *arroz con jueyes* (crab rice), *salmorejo de jueyes* (stewed land crabs) and *pastelillos de chapín*. Call ahead to be sure it's open. *Panaderia La Familia* (℡787/852-5273) on the main road in the centre of town sells lip-smacking barbecue chicken and fresh bread daily, if you want something cheaper for a picnic.

One local speciality is **shark meat**: at weekends, *kioscos* north of the town sell *pastelillos de tiburón* (shark turnovers), a surprisingly rich and tasty snack best experienced at the ⚓ *Bajo El Arbol de la Frescura* (a *kiosco* on the right side of PR-3 as you enter the town from the north). They don't always have shark, but everything else (lobster, crab) is generously sized and excellent tasting ($1.50–2). Open from around 11am till early evening most days.

Palmas del Mar

Just over 11km south of Humacao lies the high-end "club community" of **PALMAS DEL MAR** (ⓦwww.palmasdelmar.com), a 2700-acre Neverland of landscaped putting greens, pristine condos, country clubs and 9km of beaches. More like an affluent suburb of southern Florida than Puerto Rico, it's neverthe-less one of the best places to go **horseriding** on the island and the local **dive** and **boat** operators tend to be less swamped than their Fajardo rivals.

Arrival and information

The gate-guarded main entrance is on PR-906, a short drive from *autopista* PR-53 (exit 35). Grab a map at the **information centre** (daily 8am–5pm) just beyond here. To get to the **marina** (formally known as Anchor's Village Marina) and the best restaurants, follow Palmas Drive (the main road) past Candelero Drive, turn left on Coral Way, then right on Harbour Drive.

Accommodation

More resorts are planned, but at the time of writing the suitably opulent *Four Points by Sheraton* (℡787/850-6000, ⓦwww.starwoodhotels.com; ⑥–⑦) at 170 Candelero Drive was the only **hotel** on site, replete with casino and super-luxurious rooms. Although it might not look it, the pleasant (and generally deserted) **beach** here is open to the public and you can simply walk through the hotel grounds and stake out a spot on the sand (follow the signs for "3 Tee Palm Course" from the hotel entrance).

Rancho Buena Vista

Tucked away on the edge of Palmas del Mar (turn left on Academy Drive opposite the information centre), **Rancho Buena Vista** (℡787/479-7479,

Los Caballos de Paso Fino: the horses with the fine walk

Puerto Ricans are among the most passionate horseriders in the world, immensely proud of their unique, island-bred **Paso Finos**. Despite rapid modernization, you'll come across locals (often sporting baseball caps and mobile phones) steering their horses along busy roads in towns and villages all over the island, families joining *cabalgatas* (group day rides) organized on weekends in mountain towns and serious international competitions held here every year.

Horses were introduced to Puerto Rico by the Spanish, the Paso Fino evolving as a cross-breed of the Andalusian, North African Barb and Spanish Jennet. Although the horse also emerged in Colombia, only the Puerto Rican Paso Fino has the tantalizing **four-phase gait** that makes it so valuable: other show horses have to be taught the walk, but Paso Finos are born with it. Bred all over the world today, Paso Finos are fast learners and extremely responsive, making them a pleasure to ride.

Unless you have local horse-loving friends, the best way to experience the smooth, fine walk of a Paso Fino is to visit a ranch such as Rancho Buena Vista (see opposite), where experienced guides take groups out on well-trained horses. You can also check out *4 Tiempos* (☎1-888/4843-6767, ⓦwww.4tiempos.com), the world's largest Paso Fino magazine, for the latest reviews of horses, shows, and events from around the world, and including what's going on in Puerto Rico.

ⓦwww.ranchobuenavistapr.com) provides a fabulous opportunity to ride **Paso Fino horses** along tropical sandy beaches. The **regular trail rides** (10am, 1pm, & 3pm; $45) are perfect for beginners, lasting around one hour and covering 6.5km (no minimum, but maximum thirty people). Experienced riders can opt for the **expert trail ride** (9am; $75, minimum two people, maximum ten), which lasts two hours and covers over 9.5km of trail. Both routes include local beaches where turtles nest (the beaches are regularly inspected so that nothing is disturbed). Riders must be eight years or older, but ponies are available for children aged three to seven. The ranch is open daily from 8am, but sometimes closes in September and October. Christmas is peak season, so book ahead.

Diving, snorkelling and fishing

Palmas del Mar is a worthy alternative to Fajardo as a base from which to explore the rich waters of the east coast, with local operators here less focused on the San Juan day-trip brigade and diving more suited to intermediate and advanced levels. The water tends to be clearer and the corals healthier: there are 35 recognized dive sites within 8km of the marina, most located along the 3km **Basslet Reef System**. **Red Hog** is the highlight for seasoned divers, an awe-inspiring wall that drops from 24m to 350m.

The only dive outfit here is **Sea Ventures Dive Center** (Mon–Sat 8am–noon & 1–5pm, Sun 8am–1am; ☎787/863-3483, ⓦwww.divepalmasdelmar.com), which organizes daily trips to all the primary dive sites and snorkelling trips to Monkey Island (p.113). Two-tank dives are $119 ($100 with your own equipment). They also offer Discover Scuba dives for non-certified divers for $150.

The other main attraction is **fishing**. **Karolette Charters** (☎787/850-7442, mobile 787/637-7992, ⓦwww.puertoricodeepseafishing.com) is run by Captain Bill Burleson, who has been fishing these waters since 1964. He offers fishing and snorkelling trips to Vieques ($640 whole boat). Ocean fishing is $680 for a half-day and $1140 for a full day. **Maragata Charters** at Slip 14 (☎787/850-7548 or mobile 787/637-1802, ⓦwww.maragatacharters.com) is run by Captain Matthew, who leads daily snorkelling trips to a variety of destinations, according to demand: Monkey Island (8am & 1pm; 3–4hr; $65 per person), Vieques (4hr; $75), and Culebra (8hr; $175): and also four-hour fishing charters (7am & 1pm) from $105 per person in his 11.5m power catamaran. Minimum two people required for all trips. All the operators are based at the **Anchor's Village Marina** at the end of Harbour Drive, though they work off their boats and there are no offices or dive shops here, so call in advance to arrange trips.

Eating and drinking

Being a self-contained universe, it's no surprise Palmas del Mar has twenty **restaurants** on site. For something special, visit *Chez Daniel* (Mon, Wed & Thurs 6.30–10pm, Fri–Sun noon–3pm & 6.30–10pm; ☎787/850-3838), a French restaurant run by acclaimed chef Daniel Vasse, right on the marina at 110 Harbour Drive (near the charter boats), with indoor and terrace seating.

Coastal highway PR-901

Coastal highway **PR-901** winds around the rugged southeast corner of the island, where the mountains of the Central Cordillera collapse gracefully into the sea. Though only a short drive south of Palmas del Mar, the towns and villages here seem unusually remote and despite jaw-dropping vistas and a smattering of windswept beaches, see far fewer tourists.

Autopista PR-53 ends abruptly at the long causeway over the Río Guayanés wetlands, near the former sugar town of **Yabucoa**. Follow PR-901 along the coast from here, towards **Maunabo** and the heart of sugar country (see p.230). You can also head inland on the **Ruta Panorámica** (see p.237) – the first section of this mountain highway actually follows PR-901, before looping back to Yabucoa on PR-3.

Playa Lucia

Your first stop heading south should be **PLAYA LUCIA**, off PR-901 on PR-9911 just 5km from Yabucoa, a thin arc of reddish sand backed by coconut palms and cooled by the brisk trade winds that whip across the waves from the Virgin Islands. The beach is often deserted on weekdays and has a slightly rougher, raw feel – Playa Lucia is a natural debris basin and sometimes the washed-up timber, seaweed and assorted jetsam can be quite extensive. The beach is cleaned on a regular basis, however, and with a couple of decent hotels it makes an inviting place to break a journey or use as a base for longer stays.

Practicalities

The Playa Lucia area makes a pleasant stopover heading along the south coast, with a choice of three places to stay. The *Parador Palmas de Lucia* (☎787/893-4423, ⓦwww.palmasdelucia.com; ❹) is the oldest hotel on the beach, offering reasonable rates for standard doubles and package deals that include meals. It has a small pool and tends to get very busy with families at weekends and holidays.

Just off the beach ⅀ *Lucia Beach Villas* (☎787/266-1111, ⓦwww.luciabeach villas.com; four people ❻, six people ❼) is a series of luxury two-floor villa units tastefully furnished and equipped with air conditioning, satellite TV, DVD players, kitchenette (microwave, cutlery/plates, fridge and stove) and balcony with sea views. The landscaped garden features a lovely pool and ornamental waterfall.

A short drive further along PR-901 at km 5.6, the *Costa del Mar Guest House* (☎787/266-6276, ⓦwww.tropicalinnspr.com/costa-del-mar.php; ❹) is a convenient alternative, a bright three-storey place perched on the hillside with sixteen simple but comfortable doubles. The real highlight here is the spectacular view down to the coast: twelve rooms have sea views and you can see Vieques from the small pool and sun deck.

Eating options at Playa Lucia are restricted to *Coco Mar*, the beach bar, usually open from noon Thursday to Sunday for snacks and drinks, with live salsa on Sundays, and the mediocre restaurant in the *Parador Palmas de Lucia*: open daily from breakfast through till early evening, the lunch menu comprises basic American comfort food (such as burgers and ribs) while dinner sees a greater choice of fish and Puerto Rican dishes from around $12. Better **restaurants** are scattered further along PR-901 (see below).

For **self-catering**, Ralph's Food Warehouse (Mon–Sat 7am–10pm, Sun 11am–6pm) is a big supermarket on PR-901, back on the edge of Yabucoa. *Walgreens* and several **fast-food** options are on the same stretch of road.

Punta Yeguas and El Cocal

Beyond Playa Lucia, PR-901 temporarily cuts inland across the headland of **Punta Yeguas**, rising high above the Caribbean and away from the actual coastline. **El Cocal** is a local secret and can be tricky to find, but being well off the beaten path, it's a secluded, wild and undeveloped beach. Popular with surfers, it's also a favourite with Puerto Rican families who like to lounge on the reddish sand in between the palm trees and scrub, especially in summer.

To reach it, take the narrow, unmarked lane off PR-901 at around the 8.5km mark, opposite *Club Tropical*, a snack stall and bar. Follow the lane steeply down towards the coast, for almost 3km to the end, before turning left just before it becomes a private drive – this side road ends a short distance ahead, at a craggy, potholed parking area behind the beach.

For spectacular views across the headland, nothing beats *El Nuevo Horizonte* (☎787/893-5492; Wed–Sun noon–10pm) at km 8.8, 4km from Playa Lucia and a bit further along from the turning to El Cocal. It's worth stopping here for a quick look, even if you don't intend to eat, as it's the highest point on the road with magical vistas all along the coast. The seafood is usually fresh, but the steep prices primarily reflect location: six types of *mofongo* range $16–25, while mains such as *dorado* fillet or marlin start at $24 and the house special, the aromatic *asopao de langosta* (lobster rice soup), is $45 for two people. You can also grab a quick drink at the small terrace bar overlooking the cliffs by the restaurant car park, the *Balconcito del Cielo*, which also does high-quality *pastellilos* stuffed with chapín (trunkfish), crab and shrimp ($2.50) at the weekends.

Emajaguas

Around 12km from Playa Lucia, PR-901 rejoins the coast at the *barrio* of **Emajaguas**, part of Maunabo municipality. The beach here is relatively tranquil and fringed with trees, but often littered with seaweed.

It does, however, contain the best budget **accommodation** in the area, *Playa de Emajaguas Guest House* (☎787/861-6023; ❷) at PR-901 km 12.6, signposted off the road just before the village. Overlooking the sea in rustic gardens replete with overgrown tennis courts and with roosters ambling around, this milky-white guesthouse offers simple, clean and very peaceful studio apartments with kitchenettes. In the centre of the village the *Mauna Caribe* (☎787/861-3330, ⓦwww.tropicalinnspr.com/mauna-caribe.php; ❹) looks a bit like a dreary holiday camp, but the rooms have all been brightly renovated and equipped with all the latest amenities and overlook an inviting infinity pool. Nearby, *Aqua Mar* (Mon & Wed 11am–10pm, Thurs–Sun 11am–11pm; ☎787/861-1363) is the best place **to eat**, just off the beach, serving decent steaks and seafood from $10 a plate.

Faro Punta Tuna

Just under 2km further along the PR-901 from Emajaguas is the turning to the **Faro Punta Tuna** (Wed–Sun 9am–4pm; free), a striking 27-metre Neoclassical lighthouse completed in 1893 – take left along PR-7760 and then left again along PR-760 to the end of the road (parking is limited). It's one of the most attractive Spanish-era lighthouses on the island, but as it's still working, you can't go inside. Instead, you can wander around the grounds, admiring the French-designed octagonal tower and lantern, as well as the views of the coast and overgrown **Playa Larga** to the north: you can reach this beach by taking the path to the left of the lighthouse entrance, along the fence, but though it's a pleasant place to relax, swimming is not advisable due to **strong currents**. Better is **Playa Los Bohíos**, 2.5km from the lighthouse on PR-760, a 2km stretch of greyish sand shaded by palms with the *faro* standing guard in the distance. Though plenty of seaweed and flotsam gets blown onto the beach, the cooling breezes and lack of people make this an attractive spot, and *Los Bohíos* (☎787/861-2545; Fri–Sun 11am–8pm), the restaurant overlooking the beach is a chilled-out restaurant that specializes in Puerto Rican seafood. Dishes are satisfying but standard fare (fried fish, *mofongo* and the like), and the main attraction is the chance to relax in the open dining area facing the beach, soaking up a truly languid Caribbean atmosphere. The turning to the beach is signposted on PR-760 at the 2.7km marker, but easier to spot coming from Maunabo.

On to the Porta Caribe

PR-901 ends in Maunabo, where PR-3 continues west into the Porta Caribe region (see p.209). From here the south coast stretches towards Arroyo and Ponce, a quiet, thinly populated area reminiscent of sleepier Caribbean islands. In the *barrio* of Guardarraya, 6km west of Maunabo at km 112.1, the ⚘ *Caribe Playa Beach Resort* (☎787/839-6339, ⓦ www.caribeplaya.com; ❺) faces a narrow strip of sand, with a sun deck right over the waves and an excellent café. The spacious beachfront studios have fridges, air conditioning, cable TVs and a balcony or patio, and you can use the pool and barbecue grills. Two kilometres further along PR-3 at km 114.3, the *Parador Caribbean Paradise* (☎787/839-5885, ⓦ www.caribbean paradisepr.com; ❸) is a cheaper alternative, set on the hillside above the coast just off the main road. It's a bit like a motel, but has a nice enough pool, landscaped grounds and a restaurant.

The most inviting place to eat or spend a lazy afternoon on this stretch of road is *El Mar de la Tranquilidad* (Tues & Wed 11am–5pm, Thurs & Sun 11am–8pm, Fri & Sat 11am–10pm; ☎787/839-6469), a beachside restaurant in *barrio* Bajos, at PR-3 km 118.9. The wooden terrace sits over a rocky, crab-infested shoreline: unsurprisingly, crab rice ($8.50) is the house speciality, served with beans and plantains. The food is OK considering the price, but the main appeal is the laidback vibe and location.

Vieques and Culebra

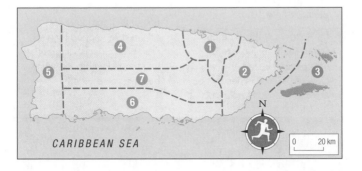

CARIBBEAN SEA

N

0   20 km

CHAPTER 3   # Highlights

* **Museo Fortín Conde de Mirasol** This distinctive museum was one of the last Spanish forts to be built in the New World, with superb views across Isabel II. See p.127

* **Horseriding on Vieques** You'll see the famed horses of Vieques grazing all over the island, and the beaches and trails are perfect for riding excursions. See p.130

* **Beach-hopping** Rent a car and explore the pristine coastline of Vieques, from the silky sands of Sun Bay to the reef-rimmed coves of Green Beach. See p.131

* **La Reserva Natural de La Bahía Bioluminiscente** Be mesmerized by the otherworldly glow of the bioluminescent bay at Puerto Mosquito. See p.132

* **Diving Culebra** The offshore cays and rugged coastline of Culebra shelter some of the finest reef dives in the Caribbean. See p.142

* **Playa Flamenco** Lounge on one of the world's most spellbinding stretches of sand. See p.144

* **Kayaking the Reserva Natural Canal de Luis Peña** Paddle through the calm, clear waters of this marine reserve, home to multicoloured reefs, rays, turtles and tropical fish. See p.145

* **Isla Culebrita** Take a water-taxi to this gorgeous cay off Culebra, topped by a crumbling Spanish lighthouse and fringed with bone-white beaches. See p.146

▲ Sun Bay, Vieques

3

Vieques and Culebra

T he offshore islands of **Vieques** and **Culebra** are in many ways the most alluring parts of Puerto Rico. If you're yearning for laidback, tropical islands and dreamy landscapes of empty, palm-fringed beaches, this is where to find them. The US Navy occupied both islands for over half of the twentieth century and as a consequence they have avoided the rampant development endemic to much of the region. Today you'll find some of the most unspoiled **beaches** in the Caribbean and a chilled-out mix of locals and *Americanos* running a simple but sophisticated infrastructure of guesthouses and restaurants. Both islands are surrounded by vivid coral and tropical fish, with Culebra in particular a haven for sea turtles.

High season is between November and May, but Vieques goes into semi-hibernation over the summer, while Culebra sees a second boom in domestic tourists – rental cars and hotels can be booked solid in July.

Vieques

Lying just 12km off the east coast of Puerto Rico, **VIEQUES** is blessed with great sweeps of savagely beautiful **beaches** and the world's brightest and healthiest **bioluminescent bay** (or just "bio bay"). Most of Vieques was occupied and sealed off by the **US Navy** in 1941 and by the time the military was forced out sixty years later, much of the coastline had reverted to a wild, natural state. Despite a steady stream of new arrivals from the US mainland, Vieques has been spared large-scale resort and condo development – for now.

Vieques is undoubtedly one of the highlights of Puerto Rico, but as with many seemingly idyllic islands, life here has a darker side. Although the public beaches are clean and perfectly safe, much of the island remains contaminated and off-limits, and while the small scale of tourism is appealing for outsiders, it has had little impact on the **local economy**, the poorest in Puerto Rico. Petty crime is a problem and unemployment regularly hits sixty percent. You'll rarely see any expression of these frustrations on the streets, however: *Viequenses* are a friendly, easy-going bunch who welcome visitors.

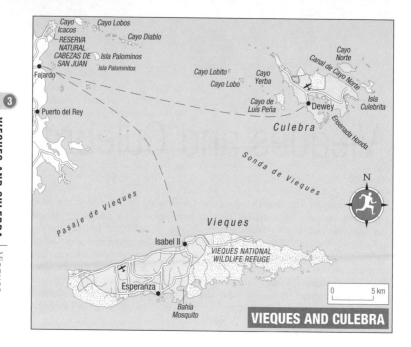

Most travellers arrive at **Isabel Segunda** (or just Isabel II), the workaday capital of the island, with its spread of modest sights and shops guarded by the old Spanish fortress, **Museo Fortín Conde de Mirasol**, now an absorbing history museum. From here the windswept north coast is sprinkled with a series of rougher, thinner beaches, broken up by the **Rompeolas** (Mosquito Pier), a World War II folly that juts into the sea like a road to nowhere. **Esperanza**, on the south coast, is more geared up for tourists, with its lazy *malecón* lined with restaurants and bars, and excellent snorkelling just offshore. Nearby, the sands at Sun Bay, Media Luna and Playa Navío offer an enticing introduction to the island's southern coastline, while more beaches lie within the **Vieques National Wildlife Refuge**.

Some history

Vieques has been inhabited by humans for at least three thousand years, colonized by a series of **Arawak** migrations much as Puerto Rico itself (see p.261). "Vieques" comes from a Spanish transliteration of *bieques* or **Bieké** in the Taíno language, meaning "small island". Initially ignored by the Spanish, the Taíno of Bieké, led by *cacique* **Cacimar**, aided the rebels on the main island in 1511 (see p.263). Cacimar was killed on Puerto Rico and in the aftermath a punitive Spanish force was sent to Vieques, where his brother and successor **Yaureibo** was also killed along with most of his warriors. The Taíno villages on Vieques were razed and the island virtually abandoned. For much of the subsequent three hundred years the island remained the domain of fugitives and pirates such as **Captain Kidd**.

The Spanish established their first formal outpost on Vieques in 1811, but the governor was ineffectual and order was eventually restored by an enterprising Frenchman, **Don Teófilo Le Guillou**. A former plantation owner from Haiti, he arrived on Vieques in 1823 and persuaded the governor in Puerto Rico to allow him complete authority in return for bringing the island under control. By 1828 he had achieved his aim and introduced **sugar cane** to the island, retaining the position of military and political governor until his death in 1843. **Sugar plantations**, manned mostly by slaves from Tortola, soon dominated the island's economy and the forests that had once covered the island were gradually cleared.

In 1941, with war looming, the **US Navy** essentially occupied Vieques, a cataclysmic event that led to three-quarters of the island being sealed off. Thousands of locals emigrated to St Croix and many were resettled, many forcibly with minimal notice, on just over three square kilometres of razed sugar-cane fields in the centre of Vieques: 89 percent of the population was squeezed into just 27 percent of the land.

Formal **resistance** began in the 1970s, when the **Vieques Fishermen's Association** successfully sued the navy for accidentally destroying fish traps and protested against navy war games off Playa de la Chiva. In May 1979, Puerto Rican activist **Ángel Rodríguez Cristóbal** – who was supporting the fishermen – was arrested along with twenty other protestors and was murdered in his prison cell in Florida later that year, a case that remains unsolved.

The navy clung onto Vieques throughout the 1990s, the end coming only after the **Navy–Vieques protests** triggered by the 1999 death of **David Sanes**, a local employed by the navy as a security guard. Sanes was accidentally killed by two bombs dropped by a US jet during target practice (for more on the protests, see p.271). After a prolonged campaign of civil disobedience, the navy **withdrew** from the island in 2003.

Arrival, orientation and information

Flights arrive at tiny **Aeropuerto Antonio Rivera Rodríguez**, around 7.5km west of Isabel II. *Públicos* operating like taxis usually meet flights, but you can also arrange a pick-up in advance. Drivers waiting at the airport usually charge $5 per person to Isabel II or Esperanza. The airport has no bank or ATM and nowhere much to eat. Rental car offices are based elsewhere on the island, but will usually pick you up if you arrange it in advance.

The **ferry** from Fajardo docks in the centre of Isabel II. If you haven't arranged a pick-up in advance, minibus *públicos* will drive you to Esperanza for around $5 per person, or anywhere in town for $3, but unless you want to hire the whole vehicle, buses are shared and leave when full.

Orientation

Vieques has an area of around 134 square kilometres, but large swathes of the island within the **Vieques National Wildlife Refuge** remain off-limits to the public due to military contamination – only the central third of the island is open land, much of it covered with small farms and *barrios*. On the north coast, the capital **Isabel II** is home to the ferry port, most services and businesses, and plenty of decent places to eat and stay. The south coast lies beyond the central ridge of tropical highlands, with tourist-oriented **Esperanza** closer to the best beaches and the bioluminescent bay.

Information

The **tourist information office**, at c/Carlos Le Brum 449 (daily 8am–noon & 1.30–4.30pm; ☎787/741-0800), faces the main plaza in Isabel II, with plenty of

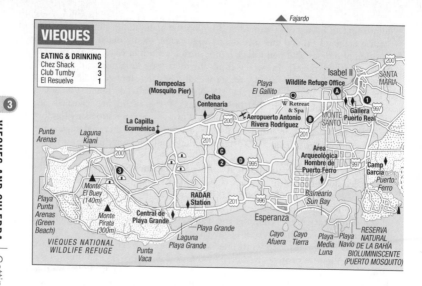

local information and English-speaking staff inside (though English is widely spoken on the island in any case). There is a profusion of **websites** on Vieques, including Ⓦwww.islavieques.com and Ⓦwww.enchanted-isle.com. **Gay travellers** should check out Ⓦwww.gayvieques.net.

Getting around

Vieques has no public transport as such, so visitors are reliant on *públicos* (which act more like taxis than on the main island) and rental cars and scooters. **Car rental** in Vieques can be expensive, but it's the most efficient option if you want to see a lot of the island. If you're staying in one of the towns and plan to visit just one or two beaches, *públicos* can be economical. Drivers typically charge $5–6 between Isabel II and Esperanza, $3 for journeys within the Isabel II area and $20 per hour to visit the principal beaches – in practice, it's much cheaper to rent a car if you intend to do a lot of exploring. See p.138 for a list of reliable *público* drivers.

Car rental

Renting a car is a good idea on Vieques, though charges can be steep ($50–60/ day) and **insurance** can add on $15 per day. All the rental firms are locally owned (there are no major chains), offer a similar standard of service, and are scattered across the island, but they will usually pick you up from the airport if you call in advance (see p.137 for numbers). To access the wilder beaches, you'll need an off-road Jeep or SUV and a steely disposition – some of the dirt roads (*camino de tierra*) are bone-jarringly rocky when dry, or scarred with potholes knee-deep in water when it rains.

Otherwise driving is easy and hassle-free – just take care at night and watch out for **horses**. There are two Total **petrol stations** on the island, opposite each other halfway to the airport on PR-200 in Playa Monte Santo district. Speed limits are usually 35mph outside built-up areas. Never leave any **valuables** in your car.

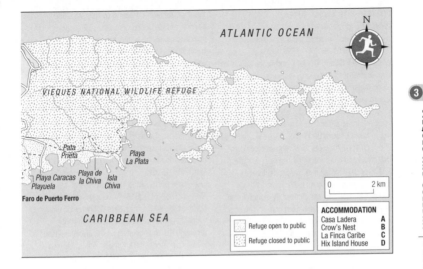

ACCOMMODATION

Casa Ladera	A
Crow's Nest	B
La Finca Caribe	C
Hix Island House	D

Refuge open to public

Refuge closed to public

Accommodation

There's plenty of **accommodation** on Vieques, ranging from fairly basic budget options (though there are no hostels), to smart, boutique hotels. **Apartment and villa rentals** can be a good deal for groups, or for those looking to stay one week or longer. Contact Vieques Realty (☏787/741-0330, ⓦwww.viequesrealtyand rentals.com) for a wide selection.

Many hotels are clustered in or around **Esperanza**, convenient for the southern beaches, though staying on the *malecón* itself can be noisy, especially on weekends. Hotels in **Isabel II** are more convenient for the airport, ferry and services, while the handful of options in **central Vieques** offer a quite different, more rustic experience, surrounded by hills and tropical forest. You can **camp** right on the beach at *Balneario Sun Bay*, near Esperanza (☏787/741-8198; $10), with showers and toilets.

Wherever you stay, **advance reservations** are essential for high season (Dec–April), when every hotel on the island can be booked solid.

Central Vieques

Crow's Nest PR-201 km 1.6 ☏787/741-0033, ⓦwww.crowsnestvieques.com. A Vieques institution with a homely atmosphere, tucked away in the foothills and set in tropical flower-filled gardens. The rooms come with kitchenette, bathroom, TV and Spanish touches such as alcoves and arches. Rates include breakfast, beach chairs, boogie boards and towels. Rates are $30 less in summer. ❺

La Finca Caribe PR-995 km 2.2 ☏787/741-0495, ⓦwww.lafinca.com. This rustic option is a wilderness lodge located in the jungly hills in the middle of the island. Life here is basic: rooms and *cabañas* have fans, mosquito nets and little else. The hammocks and solar-heated outdoor showers

add to the *Survivor* feel. It's on a narrow lane signposted off the main road and has a small pool and communal kitchen. Rooms (three-night min) ❸, *cabañas* (five-night min) ❻

Hix Island House PR-995 km 1.6, ☏787/741-2302, ⓦwww.hixislandhouse .com. This is the most original hotel in Puerto Rico. Tucked away in a forest (up a dirt track off PR-995), these thirteen modernist and spartan solar-powered open-plan studios have one side open to the forest (the modest can roll down a screen). Each room has a kitchenette, outdoor shower and mosquito nets. Grey cement interiors are brightened by art. Yoga classes are offered and the isolated location is magical at night. ❻

Isabel II and the north coast

Casa de Amistad c/Benítez Castaño 27, Isabel II ☎787/741-3758, ⓦwww .casadeamistad.com. The best mid-range option in town, a charming two-storey guesthouse with seven modern, cosy rooms, all with a/c, and a shared lounge with TV. Outside there's a small pool, patio garden and wooden roof deck. You can also use the kitchen and internet (free wi-fi). ④

Casa Ladera Off PR-200, Playa Monte Santo ☎917/570-7558, ⓦwww.casa-ladera.com. This bright and comfortable modern villa is a great deal, especially for families, containing three two-bedroom self-catering units. There's a large pool and tranquil gardens (shaded by mango trees), as well as a TV and DVDs in each unit. The owners will pick you up on arrival and get you oriented. Normally rented for the week ($1000–1500), but ask about nightly rates for shorter stays. ⑦

SeaGate Hotel c/El Fuente ☎787/741-4661, ⓦwww.seagatehotel.com. This hotel is set within a pretty hilltop garden with stupendous views of the Fortín Conde de Mirasol and Puerto Rico beyond. Rooms vary in price and size, but all are clean and simple with modern bathrooms, kitchens and terraces. Families and pets are welcome, and breakfast and ferry/airport pick-up are included. Free wi-fi. ③

Tropical Guest House E41 c/Apolonia Gittings, off c/Progreso ☎787/741-2449, ⓦwww.vieques tropicalguesthouse.com. The cheapest option in Vieques and a bit hostel-like; a plain, two-storey block in a quiet residential area off the main road. Singles ($5 cheaper) or doubles are basic but adequate and clean, and come with private shower, a/c and TV (Spanish channels only). ③

Esperanza and the south coast

Bananas Guesthouse c/Flamboyán 142 ☎787/741-8700, ⓦwww.bananasguesthouse.com. This long-standing guesthouse retains a backpacker feel, though the twelve basic rooms (with bath and fridge) are more comfortable than a hostel. Set at the back of the bar and restaurant on the ground floor, it's the best place to stay for easy access to the main strip. Non-a/c rooms are just $70. ③

Casa Alta Vista c/Flamboyán 297 ☎787/741-3296, ⓦwww.casaaltavista.net. A small hotel at the far end of the strip, but not as noisy at night. The eleven comfortable rooms offer plenty of choice: all have bath, fridge and tiled floors, some with balcony and the larger family rooms (for up to five people) have TV and microwaves. The cheapest are singles with no TV ($75). ③

Casa de Tortuga c/Hucar 6 ☎787/741-2852, ⓦwww.casadetortuga.com. One of the newest guesthouses on the island, just off the strip, with plush studio, two-bedroom and three-bedroom units, a small pool and bright contemporary furnishings. ③

Hacienda Tamarindo PR-996 km 4.5 ☎787/741-8525, ⓦwww.haciendatamarindo.com. Gorgeous colonial plantation house (named after the giant tamarind tree in the lobby), on a bluff high above the south coast, offering sixteen rooms with a charming, nineteenth-century theme. Rates include breakfast and use of an attractive pool. No TVs or kids under 15. ⑥

Inn on the Blue Horizon PR-996 km 4.2 ☎787/741-3318, ⓦwww.innontheblue horizon.com. With a magnificent, breezy location overlooking the sea, this is a perfect romantic getaway. The colonial-style rooms are embellished with four-poster beds, art and antiques. It's off the main road at the end of a dirt track, all very exclusive and extremely quiet, with no phones or TVs (and no a/c). Three-night minimum (much cheaper in low season). ⑥

Jaime's Escondite c/Magnolia 239 ☎787/741-7937, ⓦwww.enchanted-isle.com/byowner/jaimes .htm. This is the best of several appealing rental properties in the area, a tranquil *casita* for two, but unmarked from the street – you must reserve in advance. The tiny modern cottage has a queen-sized bed, bathroom, a/c, fridge, microwave and coffee maker. Genial owners Mimi and Joe Popp live nearby and offer a wealth of information about the island. ③

Malecón House c/Flamboyán 105 ☎787/741-0663, ⓦwww.maleconhouse .com. Stylish ten-room inn steps from the strip, with a small pool and sun deck. Rooms have been decked out in an elegant contemporary style with a/c and some have balconies and views of the sea. Breakfast included. ⑤

Trade Winds Guest House c/Flamboyán 107 ☎787/741-8666, ⓦwww.tradewindsvieques.com. This solid-looking house perched at the western end of the *malecón* is another budget favourite on the strip. Rooms are rather plain, but come with fans (some with a/c), mini-fridges, free wi-fi and private bathroom. Singles pay $10 less. Ask for a front room with a balcony overlooking the sea and eat breakfast (included) on the open-air veranda. ③

Villa Coral c/Gladiola 485 ☎787/741-1967, ⓦwww.villacoralguesthouse.com. One of the best bargains on the island, this high-end guesthouse has six compact but luxurious rooms with a/c, fridge, fans and stylish bathrooms. You get fine views of Sun Bay from the roof deck. Minimum three nights in winter. ③

The Island

Most travellers arrive at **Isabel II** – home to a handful of sights associated with the island's rich past, notably the **Museo Fortín Conde de Mirasol** – but soon gravitate towards a tempting array of **beaches** for the rest of their stay on Vieques. The south coast boasts the most spectacular stretches of sand, as well as the laidback village of Esperanza, with the **Vieques Conservation and Historical Trust** and nearby **Area Arqueológica Hombre de Puerto Ferro** offering a break from the surf and sun. Further east, the **bioluminescent bay** is one of the highlights of Puerto Rico.

Isabel II

The island's main town, **ISABEL II** is a mishmash of modern low-rise buildings and Spanish Neoclassical houses thrown up around the harbour. Though the ferry dock sees more action these days, the historic heart of the town is **Plaza Luis Muñoz Rivera**, bounded by the old city hall or **Casa Alcaldía** (dating from 1844), the tourist office, venerable *Bar Plaza* (see p.137), several ageing schools and a dull, modern church. Note, opposite the tourist office, the bust of South American liberator **Simón Bolívar**, whose ship ran aground here in 1816 while escaping from Venezuela – Vieques was the only part of Puerto Rico visited by the legendary general.

The fort (see below) is a short stroll uphill from the plaza, but it's also worth wandering north to Calle German Rieckehoff, beyond the ferry dock, and the **Siddhia Hutchinson Gallery** (daily 9am–3pm, closes 2pm in summer; free; ☎787/741-1343), which showcases the exuberant work of one of the island's gifted artists – Hutchinson's typical subject matter is the people and landscapes of Vieques.

Standing on a hill above the ferry pier, a short walk beyond the gallery, the **Faro de Punta Mulas** was completed in 1896, a fine example of the squat but elegant Neoclassical Spanish lighthouses constructed all over Puerto Rico just before the US occupation. The interior is closed, but a stroll up here will reward you with a fine view across the rooftops and bay beyond.

Museo Fortín Conde de Mirasol

Completed in 1855 and named after the governor of Puerto Rico at the time (the Count of Mirasol), the **Museo Fortín Conde de Mirasol** (Wed–Sun 8.30am–4.20pm; free, donations suggested; ☎787/741-1717) served as a barracks and prison before ending up as a beautifully restored museum, surrounded by gardens and battlements offering distant views of the cloud-topped peaks of El Yunque.

Although the collection inside is fairly modest, displays are enhanced by original wooden floors, exposed brick walls and timbered ceilings. Upstairs you'll find local artwork and artefacts from the prehistoric and Taíno periods: ceramics and stone tools, the esoteric *cemí* and striking jade amulets. Other exhibits include historic photos of the town, local art, old Spanish weapons and coins and an explanation of the fort's restoration. From the plaza take PR-989 up the hill to get to the fort – you can park on site.

The north coast

The Atlantic-facing **north coast** of Vieques tends to be rougher than the Caribbean south coast and its beaches less enticing, though there are a few attractions dotted along PR-200 before you reach the snorkelling haven of Punta Arenas (see p.134). Beyond the airport, you'll pass the **Ceiba Centenaria**, an

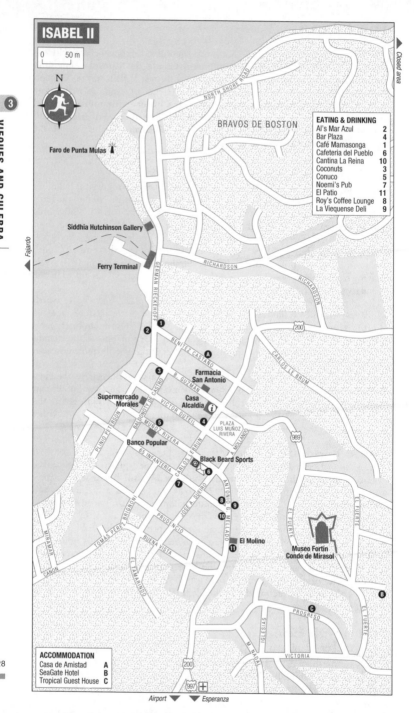

ISABEL II

0 50 m

N

BRAVOS DE BOSTON

EATING & DRINKING
Al's Mar Azul	2
Bar Plaza	4
Café Mamasonga	1
Cafeteria del Pueblo	6
Cantina La Reina	10
Coconuts	3
Conuco	5
Noemi's Pub	7
El Patio	11
Roy's Coffee Lounge	8
La Viequense Deli	9

NORTH SHORE ROAD

Faro de Punta Mulas

Siddhia Hutchinson Gallery

Ferry Terminal

RICHARDSON

RICHARDSON

GERMAN RIECKEHOFF

BENITEZ CASTAÑO

200

CARLOS LE BRUM

Farmacia San Antonio

B. GUZMAN

BALDORIOTY DE CASTRO

VICTOR DUTEIL

Casa Alcaldia

PLAZA LUIS MUÑOZ RIVERA

Supermercado Morales

PLINIO PETERSON

MUÑOZ RIVERA

Banco Popular

65 INFANTERIA

CARLOS FEBRIN

A. MILANO

989

Black Beard Sports

ANTONIO G. MELLADO

JOSE A. SUERO

PRUDENCIO

TOMAS PEREZ BRIGNON

MIRAMAR

CAÑON

BUENA VISTA

EL TAMARINDO

El Molino

Museo Fortín Conde de Mirasol

EL FUERTE

EL FUERTE

PROGRESO

IGLESIAS

N. NAVAL

VICTORIA

200

997

Airport ▼ ▼ Esperanza

ACCOMMODATION
Casa de Amistad	A
SeaGate Hotel	B
Tropical Guest House	C

Closed area

Fajardo

ancient kapok tree in a grassy clearing on the right side of the road. Said to be over 400 years old, the short but incredibly distended trunk is buttressed by broad, ridge-like roots, its thorny branches heavy with a dense canopy of leaves.

Not far from here is Mosquito Pier, more accurately known as **Rompeolas** in Spanish, meaning "breakwater" – it's actually a solid sea wall of rubble and stone jutting 1.6km into the ocean. The breakwater is the vestige of what now seems a ludicrous scheme to create a giant naval base linking Vieques with the main island during World War II, in part to create a safe haven for the British Navy should the Germans occupy the UK. Today it's a convenient staging post for divers and fishermen, with particularly good **snorkelling** towards the end. The pier lies off PR-200, about 1.5km beyond the airport, though the turning is not signposted: look out for a wide road branching off to the right, passing an abandoned car park.

Continuing west on PR-200, the road passes through a wide, grassy clearing containing **La Capilla Ecuménica** (open 24hr) the simple wooden chapel and bell tower built by activists during the Navy–Vieques protests (see p.271). The original chapel was built on Playa Icacos in 1999 (which is still off-limits), becoming the spiritual centre of the protest movement before being bulldozed by the authorities in May 2000. In 2002, a replica was built in front of the Capitolio in San Juan, but this was transported to Vieques a year later to mark the departure of the navy: the chapel was supposed to be erected in Camp García, but due to a logistical foul-up it ended up here. Heading west, it's a short drive to the Vieques National Wildlife Refuge (see p.133).

Area Arqueológica Hombre de Puerto Ferro

The **Area Arqueológica Hombre de Puerto Ferro** (daily; free) is a mystifying circle of giant boulders: whether they were assembled into a mini-mountain of rock by prehistoric man, or just fell that way naturally, is still a matter of fierce debate. The discovery of **El Hombre de Puerto Ferro** here in 1990 (the remains of a 35- to 40-year-old man who lived on the island around four thousand years ago), added weight to the theory that the site had mystical or ceremonial significance in prehistoric times, though it seems impossible that such bulk could be manoeuvered by anything less than a twenty-ton excavator.

The site can be reached from PR-997 via a heavily rutted dirt track marked by a sign: it's just under 1km from Esperanza, on the left just after the turn to the bio bay.

Esperanza

Facing the Caribbean on the south side of the island, the village of **ESPERANZA** is far more inviting than the capital, its cheerful *malecón* (Calle Flamboyán, or just "the strip") the preserve of independent travellers since the 1980s. With its guesthouses remaining low-key and bars and restaurants ranging from casual to super-hip, it just about retains its backpacker ethos, though Esperanza attracts a far more eclectic range of visitors these days, with prices to match.

The narrow beach in front of the *malecón*, **Playa de Esperanza**, is a little scruffy, with some mildly interesting snorkelling around the rusting **Muelle de la Caña**, the old sugar-cane pier. Things get much better if you wander east towards **Cayo de Tierra** (you can stroll to the tip of the headland, or cut across to Sun Bay), or snorkel in the calm waters around **Cayo Afuera** just offshore, where you might see turtles. You can leave your car in the parking area at the eastern end of the beach.

If lazing on an empty beach isn't enough, Vieques offers a wide range of **watersports**. For **bio bay** tours see p.132.

Diving

Vieques isn't as rewarding as Culebra when it comes to **diving**, but there are plenty of worthy options offshore, particularly around Rompeolas (Mosquito Pier), the headland near Playa El Gallito (Gringo Beach) and in the shallow lagoons on the south coast (perfect for beginners).

Black Beard Sports (Mon–Fri 8am–5pm, Sat 8am–4pm, Sun 10am–3pm.; ☎787/741-1892, ⓦwww.blackbeardsports.com), at c/Muñoz Rivera 101 in Isabel II, runs night dives ($100) or two-tank day dives for $120 and half-day "discover scuba" PADI courses for $150. They also rent snorkelling gear for $15 per day. **Nan-Sea Charters** (☎787/741-2390, ⓦwww.nanseacharters.com) offers half-day two-tank dives for $120 (maximum six people), one-tank beach dives for $60 and 2hr snorkelling trips from $60.

Fishing

The waters around Vieques are rich in tarpon, bonefish, permit and snook, with marlin, barracuda, kingfish and amberjack also common. **Caribbean Fly Fishing** (☎787/741-1337, ⓦwww.caribbeanflyfishingco.com) is managed by fishing veteran Captain Franco González. He charges $350 for a half-day excursion and $550 for a full day.

Kayaking

Blue Caribe Kayaks at c/Flamboyán 149 in Esperanza (☎787/741-2522, ⓦwww.bluecaribekayaks.com), rents kayaks for $15 per hour or $45 for 4hr – perfect for the cays and mangroves just offshore. Garry Lowe at **Vieques Adventures** (☎787/692-9162, ⓦwww.viequesadventures.com) rents top-of-the-line kayaks for $75 per day and will drop you off at the best locations – he also leads guided fishing trips by kayak for $150 per half-day. **Fun Brothers**, at the tiki hut in the car park at the eastern end of the Esperanza *malecón* (daily 7am–5pm; ☎787/435-9372, ⓦwww.funbrothers-vieques.com) rents kayaks for $35 (9.30am–5pm) or $45 for 24hr.

Sailing and jet skiing

Kris and Barbara Dynneson run **Marauder Sailing Charters** (☎787/435-4858, ⓦwww.viequessailing.com) with the 10-metre yacht *Marauder*, charging $100 per person for day-trips (2 to 6 people only; 9.30am–3pm; includes visits to two offshore reefs, snorkel gear and gourmet lunch). **Captain Bill Barton** sails the 9-metre *Willo* out of Isabel II (☎787/508-7245, ⓔbillwillo@yahoo.com), offering half-day cruises ($50 per person) and all-day excursions ($110 per person, minimum 4 people), which include snorkelling, a beach visit and lunch. **Fun Brothers** (see above), rents **jet skis** for $100 for one hour or $60 for thirty minutes.

Snorkelling

Abe's Snorkelling Tours (☎787/741-2134, ⓦwww.abessnorkeling.com) organizes two-hour trips (by kayak) to Cayo Afuera off Esperanza ($35) and two-hour excursions off Mosquito Pier ($30) for beginners. **Blue Caribe Kayaks** (see above) also organizes short snorkelling trips from around $35. **Fun Brothers** (see above), rents snorkels for $10 per day and runs tours for $35.

Horseriding

If you want to ride horses on Vieques contact the **SeaGate Hotel** (see p.126), which can arrange a two-hour jaunt around the island ($65/person) through local expert **Penny Miller**. Call the hotel (☎787/741-4661) or Penny directly (☎787/667-2805) a few days in advance.

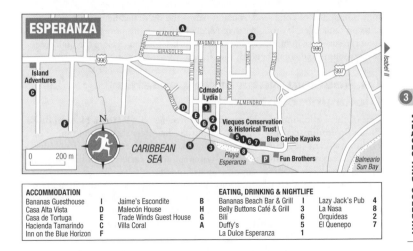

ESPERANZA

ACCOMMODATION				EATING, DRINKING & NIGHTLIFE			
Bananas Guesthouse	I	Jaime's Escondite	B	Bananas Beach Bar & Grill	I	Lazy Jack's Pub	4
Casa Alta Vista	D	Malecón House	H	Belly Buttons Café & Grill	3	La Nasa	8
Casa de Tortuga	E	Trade Winds Guest House	G	Bili	6	Orquideas	2
Hacienda Tamarindo	C	Villa Coral	A	Duffy's	5	El Quenepo	7
Inn on the Blue Horizon	F			La Dulce Esperanza	1		

On the *malecón* itself, the **Vieques Conservation and Historical Trust** (shop & museum Tues–Sun 11am–4pm, office Mon–Thurs 8am–1.30pm; free; ℡787/741-8850, Ⓦwww.vcht.com), at c/Flamboyán 138, was founded in 1984 to preserve the bioluminescent bay and delicate coral reef systems that surround the island. Inside, the **Museo de Esperanza** houses a collection of Taíno bracelets, ritual masks and tools, as well as old photos and other artefacts. At the back there's a mini-aquarium and a room highlighting the ecology of Vieques (targeted principally at children). The **gift shop** sells books, local crafts and jewellery. You can also bring in your seashells for identification and use the **internet** here ($5/hr).

Balneario Sun Bay

Just east of Esperanza on PR-997, **Balneario Sun Bay** (summer daily 8.30am–5pm, winter Wed–Sun 8.30am–5pm; parking $3) is a dazzling 1.6km-long crescent of sugary white sand, perfect for swimming and easy to reach. The only official public beach on Vieques, the Compañía de Parques Nacionales upgraded the facilities in 2007, including the cheap cafeteria *(Arena y Mar)*, showers and toilets, along with gazebos on the beach to escape the sun – the handful of coconut palms add character but little shade. You can use the main car park or drive along the tracks to park at the eastern end of the beach.

Playa Media Luna and Playa Navío

Keep driving along the bumpy sand road at the eastern end of Sun Bay and you'll find the route to two of the best beaches on Vieques. After another stretch of spine-jarring track, **Playa Media Luna** (Half Moon Beach) is signposted to the right (the left fork cuts across to the bio bay), a beguiling cove of fine, powdery white sand and shallow water – ideal for paddling and swimming, especially for families. Portia trees with bushy yellow flowers, bay cedar and sea grape bushes provide limited shade, while underwater the outer reaches of the bay are thick with turtle grass.

Playa Navío lies at the end of the dirt road, 400m or so beyond Media Luna, another gem of a beach and location for the final scenes of Peter Brook's powerful movie *Lord of the Flies* (1963). It retains the same wild, raw appeal captured in the film, a small bay of coral sand, coconut palms and sea grape, hemmed in by jagged cliffs on both sides. It's rougher than Media Luna, so a bit more fun for swimmers (you can surf here in summer), and with a snorkel you can explore the underwater caves, sponges and corals beneath the cliffs.

La Reserva Natural de La Bahía Bioluminiscente

One of the world's most enchanting natural wonders, **La Reserva Natural de La Bahía Bioluminiscente** at Puerto Mosquito is definitely the richest example of a **bioluminescent bay**. Boats leave glowing trails in the darkness, while swimmers are engulfed by luminous clouds, the water spilling off their hands like glittering fireflies – it's like something out of a fantasy movie.

The effect is produced by millions of harmless microscopic **dinoflagellates**, most commonly a protozoa known as *pyrodinium bahamense*. These release a chemical called luciferin when disturbed, which reacts with oxygen to create light. Experts think that this is a defence mechanism (the glow drawing bigger predators that will eat the creatures feeding on the protozoa) or a way to attract food. Dinoflagellates are found all over the tropics, but Puerto Mosquito has a particularly intense concentration: it's shallow, has a narrow mouth that acts like a valve, the salinity is perfect (with no freshwater source or human contamination), and the mangroves provide a crucial nutrient boost. Though you can visit the bay on your own, it's much wiser to use one of the local **tour operators**, at least at first, to get a thorough introduction to the site.

Surprisingly, most of the land around the bay is private and the main threat for now is **artificial lighting**, which limits the bioluminescent effect: the Vieques

Bio bay tours

Tours of the bay run all year, but **moonlight** has a huge impact on bioluminescence – it's crucial to avoid full moon cycles, when it's impossible to appreciate the effect. Though most operators don't run tours when the moon is full, they tend to play down its impact. Another problem is **jellyfish**, which collect in the bay and sometimes sting hapless swimmers. Again, tour operators are reluctant to make too much of this, though to be fair, the stings are rarely serious, affect only a handful of visitors and are easily treated with vinegar spray.

Conservation-minded **Island Adventures** ($32.10; ☏787/741-0720, ⊚www .biobay.com) is the best operator and has a useful **moon calendar** on its website. Tours begin at their office, west of Esperanza on PR-996 (near *Inn on the Blue Horizon*), with an informative talk, followed by a rickety bus ride to the waterside. From here one of their expert guides takes a boat around the bay (around 1hr), stopping for at least twenty minutes for a swim and pointing out all the major stars and planets along the way, with plenty of local history and botany thrown in. They have a café (daily 5.30–11pm) at the office serving Puerto Rican and Mexican food and plenty of parking.

Abe's Snorkelling Tours (☏787/741-2134, ⊚www.abessnorkeling.com) in Esperanza organizes daily **kayak trips** to the bay at 2pm, paddling through the mangroves for just over an hour, followed by snorkelling and a beach visit, before returning to the bio bay after dark ($100). They also do night trips around the bay only (with swimming; 1hr 30min; $30). **Blue Caribe Kayaks** (☏787/741-2522), at c/ Flamboyán 149 in Esperanza, also organizes kayaking trips for $30 per person. **Vieques Adventures** (☏787/692-9162, ⊚www.viequesadventures.com) offers unique tours in their clear polycarbonate canoes for $50.

Conservation and Historical Trust (see p.131) is leading the campaign to reduce public and private light sources nearby.

Vieques National Wildlife Refuge

Vieques National Wildlife Refuge (daily: May–Aug 6am–7.30pm, Sept–April 6.30am–6.30pm; free), a trove of spellbinding beaches, tropical forest and flourishing mangroves, covers almost two-thirds of the island, though much of it remains closed for fear of contamination. Nevertheless, the public areas are well worth exploring, epitomizing the raw, untouched aspect of Vieques that makes it so special.

Visit the **refuge office** (Mon–Fri 8am–3pm; ☏787/741-2138), just outside Isabel II at PR-200 km 0.4, for the latest information. It's not signposted on the road and can be irritatingly hard to find: look for the long, single-storey, light-green building on the left as you leave Isabel II, after the junction with PR-997 (opposite a small electricity booster station on the edge of a housing estate). Inside you'll find information on the varied **habitats** in the reserve, including beaches, lagoons, mangrove wetlands and upland forest areas, as well as some of the best examples of subtropical dry forest in the Caribbean. The refuge is also home to at least five plants and ten animals on the **Federal Endangered Species list**, including the Antillean manatee, the brown pelican and four species of sea turtle (green, loggerhead, hawksbill and leatherback). Reserve security guards have been known to dish out stiff **fines** ($100–200) for sunbathing nude and driving or parking on the sand.

The southern beaches

The only part of the vast eastern section of the refuge open to the public lies along the ragged **south coast**, sprinkled with wonderfully peaceful beaches. Many have English names based on colours, a legacy of when the navy used them for assault practice. All the beaches can be accessed from the former entrance to **Camp García** on PR-997, halfway between Isabel II and Esperanza. Most of the beaches are signposted off the main road that runs through the camp, many along much rougher potholed mud tracks.

The first right turn off the main camp road, 2.7km from the entrance, is a surfaced road that leads another 1.2km to **Playa Caracas** (Red Beach), a small bay north of Punta García. Justifiably popular with locals, its shady pavilions and palm trees face a wide arc of ivory sand – waves tend to be weak and with a soft sand bottom throughout the bay it's excellent for swimming and safe for small kids. You can **snorkel** around the small cay about 90m offshore.

Before you reach Caracas you'll see another turn to the right: take this gravel road and it splits again, the right-hand track ending up at a landing site on Puerto Ferro known as **Tres Palmitas** (an excellent tarpon fishing spot), while the left branch ends at **Playuela** (García Beach), a wilder strip of sand with choppy waves, backed by a thick screen of scrub and bushes and flanked by rough limestone cliffs – it's often deserted.

Beyond the Caracas turning the main road through the camp reverts to gravel, with the next right turn a narrow, steep track littered with jagged rocks, ending happily at **Pata Prieta**, an exceptionally isolated beach: take the right fork when you get to the end of the track. Also known as **Secret Beach**, this is one of the prettiest spots on the island and also good for swimming.

At the end of the main road through the camp (5.6km) is Bahía de la Chiva, a wide, sun-drenched bay facing Isla Chiva just offshore. The set of three beaches here is known collectively as **Playa de La Chiva** (Blue Beach) or Manuelquí (after a man who once lived on the island), another wild and windy stretch of coast and the place to come for glorious isolation. The beach is very scrubby, but the long, narrow stretch facing the island is a fine place to lounge. The second, middle section is the only one with shady *bohíos*, or "huts", but no other cover. Isla Chiva is a prime snorkelling spot, with turtles and rays often gliding through the waters nearby and plenty of pelicans, egrets and herons nesting onshore (the island itself is off-limits as live munitions were still being found here in 2010). **Playa La Plata** (also known as Silver or Orchid Beach) is as far as you can go beyond here, another idyllic splash of bleached-white sand and almost always empty.

Laguna Kiani

Rich in mangrove forests, the **Laguna Kiani** conservation zone covers four square kilometres and is the first point of interest in the western section of the refuge. The lagoon itself is around 1.5km along a gravel road at the end of PR-200, just after the metal bridge. Park at the information boards here and take the short **boardwalk** to lookout points on the murky stretch of water and through a dense forest of red, black, white and button **mangroves**, the muddy floor carpeted with swarms of **land crab**. Fishing and swimming are forbidden (though some locals flout the former rule) as the water may still be contaminated by toxic waste.

Punta Arenas (Green Beach)

Continue west from Laguna Kiani for around 1.5km and the road ends at the coast – turn right to **Punta Arenas** itself or left to run behind **Playa Punta Arenas**, also known as Green Beach. In reality the "beach" is just a series of thin strips of sand shaded by clumps of coconut palms and the real attraction is world-class **snorkelling**. The reef starts right off the beach (which makes it a bad place to swim), with patches of rare soft corals you'd normally only see on much deeper scuba dives: delicate Christmas tree coral and elegant, wavy fan corals, swaying with the current. Plenty of tropical fish dart around the reef and spiny sea urchins are also plentiful, so be careful. Lying on the sheltered leeward side of Vieques, the beach also unfortunately attracts swarms of **sand flies** in the early mornings and evenings.

Monte Pirata

The slopes of **Monte Pirata** (300m) are open to the public, but the summit itself is sealed off (the communications tower is used by the US Coast Guard), though locals regularly ignore this ban. The road to the top (turn left just before you enter the Laguna Kiani conservation zone) is blocked halfway up, so you must leave the car and walk up: it's an energetic but pleasant hike along the paved road and the view from the summit takes in both sides of Vieques, the Puerto Rico mainland and Culebra. The conservation zone around the summit covers just over seven square kilometres of rare and unusual trees, but it's the land below (actually just outside the reserve) that has the most appeal. A loop road cuts through this area from PR-200, passing over a hundred concrete **bunkers**, mostly abandoned navy stores and munitions depots. Most are eerily empty or locked, like overgrown relics of a lost civilization, but some have been decorated by local artists and are occasionally used for exhibitions. Adding to the sense of surrealism, you might also encounter herds of Vieques' famed "wild" horses in the jungles around here.

Playa Grande

The southwest corner of Vieques is mostly barred to visitors, save for the desolate stretch of **Playa Grande**, at the end of PR-201. This steeply inclined beach runs for around 3km between the sea and swampy Laguna Playa Grande. Strong currents, choppy water and submerged rocks make this a poor choice for swimming, but it's perfect for *de vagabundo*, or **beachcombing**. You can hike all the way to rugged **Punta Vaca**, the sea cliffs that mark the most southerly point on the island, but don't stray any further west. The really adventurous can explore the decaying, jungle-covered ruins of the once-mighty **Central de Playa Grande** sugar mill, which lie behind the lagoon near the navy radar station (by car, the ruins are best approached from the north coast). The largest and last mill to be built on the island, the crowning glory of the Benítez sugar empire closed in 1942.

Eating and drinking

Traditional **food** on Vieques is identical to the *cocina criolla* found on the main island, with a handful of cheap but enticing diners knocking out rice and beans, *frituras* and fresh seafood, with an eclectic choice of creative **restaurants** catering primarily to visitors. Things quieten down in the summer, when many places operate at reduced hours (most are closed on Monday or Tuesday throughout the year), and several shut down altogether between September and October.

For **self-catering**, try El Molino (Mon–Sat 7am–11pm, Sun 10am–11pm) in Isabel II at c/Antonio G. Mellado 342 (next to *El Patio*), or the Supermercado Morales (Mon–Fri 6.30am–9pm, Sat 6.30am–6pm, Sun 6.30am–noon) at c/ Baldorioty de Castro 15. In Esperanza, Colmado Lydia on Calle Almendro sells a good selection of groceries.

Central Vieques

Chez Shack PR-995 km 1.8 ☎787/741-2175. This ramshackle wooden house with an open terrace is literally in the middle of nowhere, surrounded by lush, tropical forest. Booths and benches provide fittingly rustic surroundings for slabs of barbecued pork, ribs and *mahi-mahi* – portions are big, but still a bit pricey ($20–24). Don't miss the signature crab cakes. Owner Hugh Duffy is a real character, so expect steel drum bands and other eclectic entertainment on weekends. Mon & Wed–Sun, 6–11pm, Sun 6.30–11pm.

El Resuelve PR-997 km 1 ☎787/741-1427. This open-air roadside diner between Isabel II and Esperanza is justly acclaimed for its hearty plates of Puerto Rican food, such as *arroz con pollo* and crab *empanadas*. You can eat well for around $10 (with beer). Locals congregate here to dance salsa and play the slot machines on weekends. Wed 9am–6pm, Thurs–Sat 9am–9pm, Sun 9am–7pm.

Isabel II and around

Café Mamasonga c/German Rieckehoff ☎787/741-0103. Isabel II stalwart, with an upper deck providing picture-perfect views of the bay. Breakfast features fluffy omelettes and more exotic German apple or potato pancakes created by the German-born chef and owner Ute (*Mamasonga* to the locals). Lunch offers American staples such as burgers, nachos and quesadillas (all under $10). Wed–Sun 7am–5pm.

Cafeteria del Pueblo c/Muñoz Rivera. A real hole-in-the-wall place popular with locals looking for tasty fried snacks and coffee that packs a punch, right at the top of the main street. The chicken tacos are a good choice for lunch ($2–3). Daily 8am–6pm.

Cantina La Reina c/Antonio G. Mellado 351 ☎787/741-2700. The best Mexican food on the island: tacos of course, but the mahi wraps, chicken tortilla soup ($5.50) and fresh salads (from $9) set this apart. Tues–Sat 5–10pm, Sun 11am–2pm.

Coconuts ☎787/741-9325. Excellent and innovative food served on a pleasant patio in the heart of town. Try the superb truffle steak fries ($24), spare ribs ($18) or justly lauded sushi pizza ($20). Fri–Tues 5–10pm.

Conuco c/Muñoz Rivera 110 ☎787/741-2500. Classic Puerto Rican food served in a lovely old dining room with ceiling fans. Service can be hit and miss, but the staples – *mofongo*, roast pork and rice – are always tasty options. Wed–Fri 11am–2pm & 6–10pm, Sat 6–10pm.

El Patio c/Antonio G. Mellado 340 ☎787/741-6381. Cheap, no-frills *criollo* food, cooked up in a roadside diner with exposed brick walls, TV blaring all day, and a small veranda. Local workers swarm here for breakfast ($3–6) and lunch ($5–20): lots of seafood, fried snacks and plates of richly stewed rice and beans grace the menu. Daily 7am–10pm.

Roy's Coffee Lounge c/Antonio G. Mellado 355 ☎787/741-0685. Expat favourite and the closest thing on the island to an American coffee house, with snacks (including the only decent bagels on Vieques), cocktails and free wi-fi complementing the full range of coffees ($2–5). The pink Neoclassical exterior is easy to spot, a gorgeous colonial building with an outdoor patio at the back. Daily 8am–8pm, closes 2pm in summer.

La Viequense Deli c/Antonio G. Mellado 352 ℡787/741-8213. Best bakery on the island, serving fresh bread, a choice of 25 different sandwiches and hamburgers for $4–6 and specials such as sweet cheese bread and sugar doughnuts. Mon–Sat 6am–3pm, Sun 6am–2pm.

Esperanza and the south coast

Bananas Beach Bar & Grill c/Flamboyán 142 ℡787/741-8700. This wooden beach house with an open front is a Vieques institution, always packed with expats and travellers. The menu is crammed with juicy US staples such as chicken wings and the celebrated half-pound Paradise, and spiced up with hearty Caribbean comfort food like crab cakes and jerk chicken (mains $6–15). Daily 11am–1am, Fri–Sat 11am–2am.

Belly Buttons Café & Grill c/Flamboyán 62 ℡787/741-3336. Great open-air place for a cheap breakfast of *pan de agua* sandwiches and pineapple pancakes. Lunch features a wider choice of sandwiches, cheap American diner food and zesty home-made lemonade. Daily 7.30am–2pm.

Bilí at *Amapola Inn*, c/Flamboyán 144 ℡787/741-1382. This oceanfront restaurant with a bright, cheerful interior offers a flamboyant take on Puerto Rican classics, but stands out for its vegetarian options. Try the yucca salad with bay leaves or

cheese-stuffed enchiladas; seafood highlights include fresh sea scallops, crab pasta and crispy red snapper (mains $8–20). Becomes a salsa-soaked bar at night. Daily 11am–11pm.

Duffy's c/Flamboyán 140 ℡787/741-7600. This relaxed bar and restaurant is named after the son of the *Chez Shack* owner and serves a solid choice of deli-style sandwiches such as the *cubano* and reuben, as well as meaty, flame-grilled burgers (from $7.50), and tasty veggie burgers. At night, sip a fresh *piña colada* or *parcharita*, a margarita made with *parcha* juice (passion fruit). Daily 11am–11pm.

La Dulce Esperanza c/Almendro btw c/Hucar and c/Tintillo ℡787/741-0085. This local bakery, a short walk behind the *malecón*, sells breakfast sandwiches (egg, ham and cheese), slices of pizza, calzones and larger subs, as well as basic bread, muffins and cakes, though opening times vary. Usually open daily 7.30–11am and 5–9pm, and occasionally lunchtimes Wed–Sat.

Orquideas c/Orquideas 61 ℡787/741-1864. Stop by this elegant restaurant for healthy fusion-inspired cuisine such as salmon, avocado BLT sandwich for lunch ($9), or one of the carefully dinner dishes such as seared scallops with Thai red curry and vegetables ($18), and roasted pork loin with mango butter sauce ($16). Tues, Wed & Sat 10.30am–4pm; Thurs, Fri & Sun 10.30am–4pm & 5.30–9.30pm.

El Quenepo c/Flamboyán 148 ℡787/741-1215. The most stylish bistro on the strip and a fabulous place for dinner, with a tantalizing menu inspired by local and Caribbean cuisine: dishes include conch chowder, shrimp and lobster *mofongo* and tuna with noodles in a shellfish broth. At least $200 for dinner for two with wine. Tues–Sun 5.30–11pm.

Nightlife

Nightlife on Vieques is low-key and tends to centre on restaurants and a cluster of **bars** in Isabel II and Esperanza – the latter is favoured on holidays and weekends by bar-crawling locals as much as tourists. Most nights out involve at least a few drinks at *Bananas Beach Bar* and *Duffy's* on the *malecón* in Esperanza (see above). The adventurous might consider an outing to *Club Tumby*, set among the abandoned bunkers in the far western part of the island at Magazine 404, Barrio Mosquito, PR-200 (Wed, Thurs & Sun noon–10pm, Fri & Sat noon–2.30am; ℡787/420-3257, ⓦclubtumby.com). Part club, sports bar and grill, it can be a fun place to visit, but check the schedule in advance before heading out there.

Isabel II

Al's Mar Azul c/German Rieckehoff 577 ℡787/741-3400. One of the most popular bars on the island, with an enticing wooden deck overlooking the ocean and ferry pier nearby, pool tables and a notorious karaoke night (known locally

as "scareoke"), from 9pm on Sat (the more you drink, the more the singing improves). The best place for rum cocktails at sunset and mingling with locals and tourists on weekends. No food, just snacks. Mon, Wed, Thurs, Sun, 11am–1am, Fri & Sat 11am–2.30am.

You can usually pick up a **flight** back to **Ceiba** (10min) or **San Juan** (30min) with a few hours' notice, though you'll need to book ahead for services at peak times (weekends and holidays). Cape Air (☎1-800/352-0714), Seaborne Airlines (☎866/359-8784) and Vieques Air-Link (c/Antonio G. Mellado 358, ☎787/741-8331) operate several scheduled daily flights to **Aeropuerto Internacional Luis Muñoz Marín** in San Juan, with the latter also flying five times a day to Isla Grande Airport and to Ceiba. Single prices are around $30 to Ceiba, $90–122 to San Juan international and just $63 to Isla Grande. All three airlines fly twice a day to **St Croix** (US Virgin Islands) for around $75 (30min).

Air Sunshine (☎787/741-7900) also flies to San Juan International Airport and St Croix, as well as **St Thomas** (US Virgin Islands; 35min) twice a day on demand (minimum 3 to 4 persons required). Air Flamenco (☎787/741-8811) runs charter flights on demand (you rent the whole plane) to Ceiba and **Culebra** (both $250).

You can buy **ferry** tickets to Fajardo (1hr 15min) at the *embarcadero* in Isabel II (daily 8–11am and 1–3pm; $2 single; ☎787/741-4761). Ferries depart Mon–Fri 6.30am, 11am, 3pm & 6pm; Sat, Sun & holidays 6.30am, 1pm & 4.30pm. Note that other than chartering a plane from Air Flamenco, the only way to travel between Vieques and **Culebra** is to go by ferry via Fajardo.

Bar Plaza Plaza Luis Muñoz Rivera. Exuding a run-down, raffish charm, this dive bar in the centre of town is a classic Spanish cantina, with peeling murals, high ceilings and nothing but local beer on the menu ($3). Savour the atmosphere with the motley group of locals slumped at the bar or around the ageing pool table. Built in 1903, the bar was originally a pharmacy, amusing considering the state of its patrons most Friday nights. Daily 9am–9pm.
Noemi's Pub c/Carlos Lebrum 434, at c/65 de Infanteria ☎787/741-8200. Traditional bar set in an old house with bright blue shutters (no sign) and a big TV for sports events. Also serves decent food and Sunday brunch 10am to 2pm. Daily 7am–11pm.

Esperanza

Lazy Jack's Pub c/Orquideas 61 at c/Flamboyán ☎787/741-1447. Congenial bar that faces the seafront, with cold beers and comforting slices of pizza. There's something happening here most nights, from karaoke on Tuesdays, Nintendo Wii games on Wednesdays and DJ parties on Fridays. Daily noon–2am.
La Nasa c/Flamboyán. It doesn't get more local than this shack on the beach side of the *malecón*. Entertainment alternates between live music and DJs each week. The name hasn't anything to do with the space programme – it means "fish trap". Sat & Sun 5pm–2am.

Listings

Banks Banco Popular (☎787/741-2071) at c/ Muñoz Rivera 115, open Mon–Fri 8am–4.30pm, Sat 9am–1pm, has the island's only ATM (24hr) that accepts foreign cards. The wait for the ATM can be very long in the morning and occasionally it runs out of cash over weekends.
Bicycle rental Black Beard Sports (☎787/741-1892, ⓦwww.blackbeardsports.com), at c/Muñoz Rivera 101 in Isabel II, rents mountain bikes for $25–35/day ($20 drop-off fee). Open Mon–Fri 8am–5pm, Sat 8am–4pm, Sun 10am–3pm. Vieques Adventures (ⓦwww.bikevieques.com) runs excellent guided cycling tours around the island for $95 for a half-day and also rents bikes for $25/day.

Car and scooter rental Extreme Scooters (☎787/741-8141); B&E Car Rental (☎787/435-6488); Coqui Car Rental (at *Hotel Vieques Ocean View*, c/German Rieckehoff, near the ferry; ☎787/741-3696); Marco's Car Rental (☎787/741-1388); Maritza's Car Rental, PR-201, Barrio Florida (☎787/741-0078, ⓔmaritzas carrent@aol.com); Martineau Car Rental, PR-200 km 3.4 (☎787/741-0087, ⓦwww.martineau carrental.com); and Vieques Car and Jeep Rental (☎787/741-1037, ⓦwww.viequescar rental.com).
Emergencies For serious emergencies call ☎911, for fire ☎787/741-2111.

Hospital The Centro de Salud de Familia is south of Isabel II on PR-997, open Mon–Fri 7am–3.30pm, with a 24-hour emergency room.

Internet Black Beard Sports (see p.137) offers high-speed access for $5/hr (Mon–Sat 8am–5pm, Sun noon–3pm). Also in Isabel II, Roy's Coffee Lounge (p.135) offers free wi-fi for customers. Free wi-fi is also usually available around the main plaza. In Esperanza, you can access the internet at the Vieques Conservation and Historical Trust (Tues–Sun 11am–4pm) for $5/hr.

Laundry Familia Ríos (☎787/556-5158) was looking for new premises at the time of writing – call for new location (number unchanged).

Pharmacy Farmacia San Antonio is at Avda Benítez Guzmán 52 in Isabel II (Mon–Fri 8.30am–6pm, Sat 9am–noon & 1.30–6pm; ☎787/741-8397).

Police The police station is at PR-200 km 0.2 (intersection with PR-997 in Isabel II), ☎787/741-2020.

Post office The post office (Mon–Fri 8.30am–4.30pm, Sat 8am–noon) is at c/Muñoz Rivera 97 in Isabel II.

Taxi Recommended *público*/taxi drivers include Ana Robles (☎787/313-0599 or 787/385-2318), Ángel (☎787/484-8796), Eric (☎787/741-0448), Henry (☎787/649-3838), and Luis González (☎787/608-6894).

Culebra

Effectively occupied by the US Navy until the 1970s, **CULEBRA** is an unapologetically raw Caribbean island that has resisted high-impact tourism and shrugged off attempt at large-scale development. There are no casinos, tour buses, mega-resorts or traffic lights, crime is virtually unknown and the **beaches** are simply staggering – **Playa Flamenco** is consistently voted one of the world's most awe-inspiring stretches of sand, while the turtle-rich sapphire waters and shallow reefs offshore make **diving** and **snorkelling** a real treat.

But behind the calm veneer – and *Culebrenses* are undeniably chilled out – paradise has an edgier side. Though the US Navy was chased out in 1975, the spirit of **activism** remains strong, vividly expressed in the energetic campaigns to protect the local **reef ecosystems** and **turtle populations**, as well as resistance to looming **development** and attempts to limit **beach access**. Indeed, more and more land is sold for posh condos and **tourism** is booming, making parts of the island uncomfortably busy, especially in July. For now, though, it's still easy to avoid the crowds and the island remains untainted by **cruise ships** – just make sure you bring plenty of bug spray, as the flies and mosquitoes can be voracious.

Some history

Little is known about the early inhabitants of Culebra, though evidence has been found of a prehistoric people known as the **Cuevas** (part of the Igneri culture; see p.261), who settled here in around 640 AD. It wasn't until Spanish adventurer Don Cayetano Escudero founded the village of **San Ildefonso de Culebra** in 1880 (in honour of the then Bishop of Toledo, Spain) that a formal Spanish presence was established. The name Culebra, meaning "snake", was eventually applied to the whole island (although there are no snakes and its shape bears no resemblance to a serpent).

The colony was short-lived, as the US assumed control in 1898 and the US Navy took charge of the island five years later, promptly sealing off large areas for marine exercises and forcing the abandonment of San Ildefonso, or "Pueblo Viejo". The majority of islanders were resettled on the other side of Ensenada Honda: leaving no doubt as to who was now in charge, the new town was named **Dewey** after Admiral George Dewey, a US Navy hero from the 1898 campaign. The island was dominated by the navy thereafter.

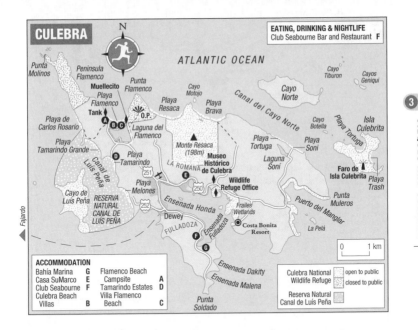

CULEBRA N

ATLANTIC OCEAN

EATING, DRINKING & NIGHTLIFE
Club Seabourne Bar and Restaurant **F**

Punta Molinos
Peninsula Flamenco
Muellecito
Punta Flamenco
Playa Flamenco
Tank
O.P.
Playa de Carlos Rosario
Playa Tamarindo Grande
Laguna del Flamenco
Playa Resaca
Cayo Motojo
Playa Brava
Canal del Cayo Norte
Cayo Tiburon
Cayos Geniqui
Cayo Norte
Cayo Botella
Isla Culebrita
Playa Tortuga
Monte Resaca (198m)
Museo Histórico de Culebra
LA ROMANA
Playa Tortuga
Playa Soni
Laguna Soni
Faro de Isla Culebrita
Playa Trash
Playa Tamarindo
Playa Melones
Wildlife Refuge Office
Cayo de Luis Peña
RESERVA NATURAL CANAL DE LUIS PEÑA
Canal de Luis Peña
Ensenada Honda
Dewey
FULLADOZA
Frailes Wetlands
Ensenada Fulladora
Costa Bonita Resort
Punta Muleros
Puerto del Manglar
La Pelá
Fajardo

0   1 km

ACCOMMODATION
Bahía Marina **G**
Casa SuMarco **E**
Club Seabourne **F**
Culebra Beach Villas **B**
Flamenco Beach Campsite **A**
Tamarindo Estates **D**
Villa Flamenco Beach **C**

Ensenada Dakity
Ensenada Malena
Punta Soldado

Culebra National Wildlife Refuge — open to public / closed to public
Reserva Natural Canal de Luís Peña

In 1970 the formal campaign to remove the US Navy began with a feisty coalition of locals known as the **Culebra Committee**, led by **Mayor Ramón Feliciano**, **Rubén Berríos**, the leader of the Puerto Rican Independence Party (PIP), and several US senators. Finally, in 1973, with the help of Governor Colón, a coalition of respected ex-governors, and US Senator Howard Baker, the US government agreed to **withdraw** the navy from Culebra – all navy activity ended in 1975.

Arrival and information

Culebra is an exhilarating ten-minute **flight** from Ceiba or thirty minutes from San Juan, ending up at tiny **Aeropuerto Benjamín Rivera Noriega**, around 1km north of the main settlement, **Dewey**. Inside the terminal you'll find the small *Café Delizioso*, the main airline desks and the Carlos Jeep desk (often unmanned – call ahead). If you are not renting a car and your accommodation is not providing a pick-up, you'll need to take a *público* to your hotel for $3–5, depending on where it is: if none is around, call one (see p.148). The airport has no ATM – you have to go into Dewey for cash.

Ferries from Fajardo dock in the centre of Dewey and are met by a cavalcade of *públicos* that will take you to any of the hotels ($3–5) when full, though at peak times their main business is running back and forth between here and Playa Flamenco.

Information

The friendly **tourist information office** (Mon–Fri 8am–4.30pm; ☎787/742-3521) faces the harbour close to the ferry pier, and can supply basic information and maps. Staff usually speak English, but note that they sometimes close at lunch

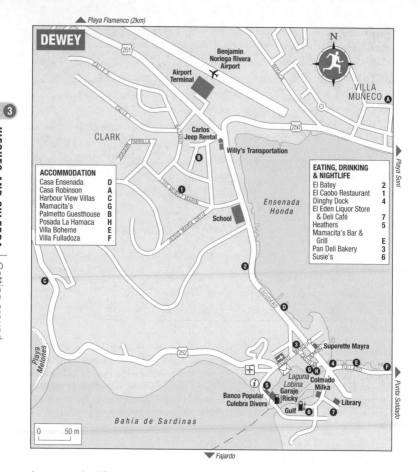

Playa Flamenco (2km)

DEWEY

N

251

Benjamin
Noriega Rivera
Airport

Airport
Terminal

VILLA
MUÑECO **A**

CALLE 2

CALLE 1

250

CLARK

Carlos
Jeep Rental

Willy's Transportation

Playa Soni

PEDRO

PARRILLA

B

1

LUIS MUÑOZ MARIN

Ensenada
Honda

ACCOMMODATION
Casa Ensenada   **D**
Casa Robinson   **A**
Harbour View Villas **C**
Mamacita's   **G**
Palmetto Guesthouse **B**
Posada La Hamaca   **H**
Villa Boheme   **E**
Villa Fulladoza   **F**

EATING, DRINKING
& NIGHTLIFE
El Batey   2
El Caobo Restaurant   1
Dinghy Dock   4
El Eden Liquor Store
& Deli Café   7
Heathers   5
Mamacita's Bar &
Grill   **E**
Pan Deli Bakery   3
Susie's   6

JESUS MARIA MARIN

School

2

C

ESCUDERO

D

Playa Melones

252

3

PEDRO MARQUEZ

Superette Mayra

6 H

4

FULLADO

F

Laguna
Lobina

Colmado
Milka

Banco Popular
Culebra Divers

Garaje
Ricky

5

i

Gulf

6

Library

7

Bahía de Sardinas

Punta Soldado

0   50 m

Fajardo

(noon–2pm). When you arrive, try to pick up a copy of the island newspaper, *Culebra Calendar* (Ⓦwww.theculebracalendaronline.com), published monthly. **Online resources** are plentiful and include Ⓦwww.gotoculebra.com.

Getting around

Culebra is a compact island, but unless you want to spend all your time near your hotel, you'll need some form of transport to get around. The main island has an area of around 25 square kilometres, and is easily covered in a couple of hours by car. If you're feeling fit, you can **rent a bike**, though considering the heat and swarms of flies on the island in summer, cycling is definitely the most uncomfortable option – see p.148 for numbers.

Públicos

Privately operated **públicos** (usually minibuses) serve as buses and taxis on Culebra, and can be useful if you just want to get into town or go to the beach a couple of times – if you're staying in Dewey, you might prefer this much cheaper option over renting a car. Daily buses run between the ferry pier and Playa Flamenco ($3 one-way) via the airport (also $3) when full, but will make detours to drop off at hotels ($3–5) near Dewey. The last *públicos* start to leave Flamenco at around 4pm.

At other times, most drivers will pick up on demand, charging $3 per person for most trips to the airport or ferry and $15 per person for longer trips around the island – travelling in the evening requires advance reservations and is much less reliable. See p.148 for numbers.

Car and scooter rental

If you want to really explore it's best to **rent a car or scooter**, though the latter can be uncomfortable on bumpier roads. **Golf carts** are also available and cheaper than cars. The main operator is Carlos Jeep Rental (daily 8am–5pm; ℡787/742-3514, ⓦ www.carlosjeeprental.com). New Jeep Wranglers are around $60 per day; golf carts are $40. **Insurance** can add up to $15 per day (even with insurance, you are usually liable for the first $500 in damages). Driving rules are casually enforced by Culebra's police department, but limits are 25mph in town and 40mph elsewhere. There are only two **petrol stations**: Garaje Ricky (8am–6pm) opposite the ferry pier, and Gulf (8am–noon & 1–3.30pm) on the south side of Dewey, across the canal.

Water taxis

To reach Culebra's more isolated beaches and islets, you'll need to take a **water taxi**, operated by a handful of private boat owners. Pick-up points are usually near Dewey, but in theory you can ask to start anywhere. Call at least a day in advance. Guillin's Water Taxi (℡787/314-6163) offers various day-trips to **Ensenada Dakity** as well as services to Playa Carlos Rosario, Cayo de Luis Peña and Isla Culebrita ($45 per person). The healthy alternative is to rent a **kayak** (see p.142).

Accommodation

Accommodation is plentiful in Culebra and you are unlikely to have problems finding a place other than on major holidays and weekends in July. Most of the options are family-owned **guesthouses** and many are operated by long-term expat residents. There's also a handful of small, high-end **hotels** and a varied choice when it comes to **apartment and villa rentals**: these tend to be a better deal than the relatively overpriced alternatives. Culebra Vacation Planners (℡787/742-3112, ⓦ www.culebravacationplanners.com) is a local real estate agent that also helps with hotel bookings and a large choice of rental properties – check their website for a full listing.

In terms of **location**, Dewey is convenient for food, transportation and services – if you want to save on renting a car, it's best to stay here. Staying on Playa Flamenco has an obvious plus side, though it can be busy on holidays and weekends, and if you prefer more solitude the island is littered with hideaways featuring equally magnificent ocean views.

Central Culebra and Dewey

Casa Ensenada c/Escudero 142 ℡787/742-3559, ⓦ www.casaensenada.com. A cute rental home overlooking the bay on the north side of Dewey, divided into three units (all with a/c, TV, internet and kitchens). It's a little worn in parts, but Jackie and Butch Pendergast are thoughtful hosts, offering use

Culebra watersports

The inviting cays and reefs off Culebra are ideal for **diving**, **snorkelling** and **swimming**, but remember to check the latest tide and weather reports before setting out – currents, waves and riptides offshore can be **treacherous** and people drown here every year. One of the best sites is **Ensenada Dakity** (Dakity Bay), a sparkling stretch of cobalt blue water at the mouth of the Ensenada Honda, accessible only by boat.

Diving

With no freshwater runoff, the pellucid waters off Culebra offer some of the best **diving** in the Caribbean and are certainly its best-kept secret. With up to fifty sites to choose from, including a plethora of shallow locations perfect for beginners and plenty of more challenging dives, you won't get bored. Everywhere you'll see forests of fan coral, sponges, sea urchins and great clouds of tropical fish; turtles, barracuda, stingray and puffer fish are also common.

Culebra Divers, just across from Dewey's ferry terminal at c/Pedro Marquez 14 (daily 9am–1pm & 3–5pm; ☎787/742-0803, ⓦwww.culebradivers.com) offers daily **dive trips** (8.30am–2pm; $65 one tank, $98 two tanks, plus $15 gear rental) for a maximum of six divers. In the afternoons they offer **snorkelling trips** (2.30–4.30pm; $50, minimum two people). You can **rent** snorkelling equipment for $15 per day.

Friendly competition is supplied by **Aquatic Adventures** (☎787/209-3494, ⓦwww.diveculebra.com), operated by Captain Taz Hamrick, with morning and afternoon dive trips ($100 two tanks), as well as snorkelling excursions for $45.

Kayaking

Jim Petersen's Oceans Safaris, at c/Escudero 189 (☎787/379-1973), rents **kayaks** for $60 per day for two (first time, $40 thereafter), usually starting at Playa Tamarindo. Rates include orientation and instruction if necessary.
Culebra Bike Shop (☎787/742-2209, ⓦwww.culebrabikeshop.com) rents kayaks for $50 per day and snorkels for $10 per day.

Fishing

Contact local expert Chris Goldmark at **Culebra Fly Fishing** (☎609/827-4536, ⓦwww.culebraflyfishing.com) for boat and off-beach fly fishing for bonefish, permit and tarpon (equipment included). He charges $60 per hour on the boat, $50 for the beach and $400 for a full day.

---

of the waterside patio and barbecue, free kayaks and beach chairs. Prices vary considerably. ⑤

🏃 **Casa Robinson** La Romana, off PR-250 ☎787/742-0497, ⓦwww.casarobinson.com. Modern, super-comfortable, three-storey house on a fabulous hilltop perch overlooking the Ensenada Honda and Vieques beyond. The immaculate rooms come with kitchenette and TV, while your host, Elias Robinson, is a mine of information and will usually pick you up from the dock or airport. ④

Casa SuMarco La Romana, off PR-250 ☎917/848-0054, ⓦwww.casasumarco.com. Another panoramic, breezy deck overlooking the *ensenada*, this cosy two-bedroom, one-bath rental home is a great deal for families, comfortably sleeping up to four people. Amenities include kitchen, washing machine, a/c in bedrooms (fans in

all other rooms), indoor and outdoor showers, TV (DVD only), and stereo. Three-night minimum. ⑥

Harbour View Villas PR-252, Barrio Melones 1 ☎787/742-3855, ⓦwww.harbourviewvillas.com. Flowing down the hillside above Playa Melones, these A-frame chalets have been rented out since the 1970s. Town is a short walk away, but the real draws are the gorgeous views and sunsets. Be warned, however: this is a rustic experience, with ageing open-air kitchens and showers. Hot water can be erratic and because it's so open there are plenty of bugs. ⑤

Mamacita's c/Castelar 64–66 ☎787/742-0090, ⓦwww.mamacitasguesthouse.com. Small guest-house with rooms overlooking the canal in the centre of town, above the celebrated bar of the same name. Each has a veranda, though Room 3 is at the top (third storey) and has by far the best views. Though you get TV, DVD, a/c and spotlessly clean rooms, this is fairly basic, hostel-like accommodation and a bit pricey unless you expect to be hanging out in town most nights. Be prepared for noise on weekends. ❹

Palmetto Guesthouse c/Manuel Vasquez 128 (behind Carlos Jeep Rental) ⓣ787/742-0257, ⓦwww.palmettoculebra.com. This comfy inn has been fully renovated by its friendly owners and the compact but spotless rooms have tiled floors, a/c, fridge and sparkling bathrooms. There are two shared kitchens and a lounge, free bikes and boogie boards, and a DVD and book exchange. ❸

Posada La Hamaca c/Castelar 68 ⓣ787/742-3516, ⓦwww.posada.com. Albert and Mary Custer run this guesthouse next door to *Mamacita's*, with a deck overlooking the canal, small doubles and larger apartments for two to eight people. Rooms have clean tiled floors, a/c, TVs and kitchenettes, and the free beach towels, coolers and ice are nice touches. ❸

Villa Boheme c/Fulladoza 368 ⓣ787/742-3508, ⓦwww.villaboheme.com. This modern and cheery place on the waterfront south of the centre is the best deal in town. It's run by the amiable Rafy, with eleven spacious, bright and clean rooms (all with a/c and bath), three of which have kitchens (others have access to a shared kitchen). The second-floor rooms have balconies and the waterside sun deck also has stellar views across the Ensenada Honda. It's right next to *Dinghy Dock*. ❹

Villa Fulladoza c/Fulladoza ⓣ787/742-3576. Seven self-catering apartments set within a pretty, white wooden house with pink and blue trim, in a tranquil spot at the end of town, right on the Ensenada Honda near *Boheme*. This is more like a villa rental – you get clean sheets and towels and are left more or less to yourself. Rooms are simple but cheap – they start at just $490 for the week. ❸

Playa Flamenco and around

Culebra Beach Villas ⓣ787/754-6236, ⓦwww.culebrabeachrental.com. Whether you stay at this unique hotel depends on how much you value the incredible location, right on the beach. Though the views are spectacular and the chalets running back to the car park are slightly better, rooms in the four-storey wooden beach house are spartan and showing their age. Avoid public holidays (especially the summer), when it's overrun with families. Options range from studios to three-bedroom apartments. ❺

Flamenco Beach Campground Enchanting Playa Flamenco is the only legal place to camp on the island. Avoid July, weekends and holidays if you value solitude, however, as a party scene ensues on the beach, despite the segregation of "teenage" campers by the warden. You need to fill in an application form for the Culebra Conservation and Development Authority (6am–7pm; ⓣ787/742-0700), which you can do on arrival at the beach, though it's best to reserve a space in advance. Tents are $20 (maximum six people), with a seven-day maximum. There are toilets, barbecue pits and showers (4–7pm) on site. Don't forget the bug spray.

Tamarindo Estates c/Tamarindo Final ⓣ787/742-3343, ⓦwww.tamarindoestates.com. These hillside villas sit on the west side of the island facing Playa Tamarindo (and the sunset), three minutes' drive from Playa Flamenco and 1km off PR-251 at the end of a sealed road. It's a high-end place, but not as luxurious as Culebra's newer hotels – the twelve villas are neat and simply furnished. Staff are rarely around; if you just turn up you'll have to use the phone at the entrance to call the manager. ❻

Villa Flamenco Beach ⓣ787/742-0023, ⓔflamenc6@aol.com. These six units, all with kitchenettes, in a two-storey pink concrete building just off the beach, are much nicer and quieter than the *Culebra Beach Villas*. Maintained by the sociable Max and Esmeralda Gutiérrez, there are two large apartments for four people each and four studios upstairs that accommodate two people. Note the one-week minimum Dec 15–May 30, four-night minimum June 1–Dec 14 and closure Oct–Nov. ❺

Fulladoza

Bahía Marina c/Fulladoza km 2.4 ⓣ787/742-0535, ⓦwww.bahiamarina.net. This luxury "condo-resort", tucked away in the hills above Ensenada Dakity, offers fabulous views over the water and real tranquillity, with sixteen plush one- or two-bedroom apartments with balconies, TV, kitchens, tiled floors and lounge areas. At the end of a narrow lane off the main road, opposite *Club Seabourne*. ❻

Club Seabourne c/Fulladoza km 1.5 ⓣ787/742-3169, ⓦwww.clubseabourne.com. Culebra's first luxury hotel and the one with the most character, overlooking the Ensenada Honda amid lush, landscaped gardens and a fine pool. With just fourteen units, it feels exclusive and the Spanish plantation-style rooms are decked out with dark wood furniture, sofas and vintage fixtures, though some rooms are showing their age. Rates include breakfast, airport and ferry pick-ups and beach towels. ❻

The Island

The real charms of Culebra are its rugged coastline, wild beaches and warm, enticing waters – other than services and shops, there's little to see in Dewey, the main settlement. The justly celebrated highlight is **Playa Flamenco**, but there are plenty of other empty and equally appealing stretches of sand, notably **Playa Soní**. Some of the most precious parts of the island are contained within the **Reserva Natural Canal de Luis Peña** and the **Culebra National Wildlife Refuge**, but to really appreciate your surroundings, you need to get onto the water. Aim to explore at least one of the offshore islands by kayak or water taxi – **Isla Culebrita** has the most to offer.

Playa Melones

The only **beach** within easy walking distance of Dewey is **Playa Melones**, near the end of PR-252, a fifteen- to twenty-minute hike west of the centre The sand here is meagre and the primary appeal is the easy **snorkelling** just offshore; watch out for the giant **long-spined sea urchins** here (reef shoes are essential). Melones, which gets its name from the abundance of melon cactus in the area, is the southernmost section of the protected **Reserva Natural Canal de Luis Peña** (see opposite) and perfect for sunset watching.

Playa Flamenco

A brilliant white crescent of coral sand, lapped by glittering waters of turquoise and azure blue, **Playa Flamenco** (24hr; free) is fringed with the same low-lying scrub and palm trees that Columbus would have seen five hundred years ago. Staggeringly beautiful, it's worth a day of swimming, lounging and simply soaking in the idyllic scenery. The beach can get busy at the weekends, but it's wide enough to handle the crowds and at other times is remarkably tranquil. Check out the rusting **Pershing tank** half-buried in the sand at the northwestern

---

Save the turtles!

Culebra is one of the few places on earth where the nesting population of **giant leatherback sea turtles** is on the increase, as well as hawksbill and a smaller number of green turtles. Leatherbacks can nest at any time between February and August, though the peak season runs April to July, while hawksbills visit the beaches from September to December. Watching one of these ancient reptiles crawl up the beach and lay eggs in the middle of the night is a truly magical experience, but never go wandering around turtle beaches on your own: contact **CORALations**, an innovative NGO founded in 1995 that's dedicated to conserving the turtle population through **Proyecto Tinglado**. For a small donation (suggested $10, children $5), you can help patrol nesting beaches at night. After making camp (usually on Playa Brava, Resaca or Soní), you'll take turns scouring the beach in groups until dawn, notifying one of the experts on hand of any activity: you'll usually be able to watch the turtles digging a nest from a safe distance, before coming in closer to watch them lay eggs. Leatherback females are huge, averaging 1.5m in shell length and weighing 450kg. Participation is limited to ten people per night and kids must be over ten years old.

CORALations also works to conserve Culebra's **coral reef ecosystems**, through establishing marine reserves, supporting relevant legislation, using artificial concrete reefs such as Reef Ball (ⓦwww.reefball.org), and by growing corals more resistant to thermal stress. For more **information** and **volunteer** opportunities, contact CORALations (☏787/556-6234, ⓦwww.coralations.org).

end of the beach. Once used as target practice, it's decorated with murals (there's another tank just inland). At the far eastern end of the beach is the **"Muellecito"**, where an old pier has formed a sheltered pool popular with families.

Flamenco lies about 2.5km north of **Dewey** at the end of PR-251, with the large car park behind the sands home to a series of tempting **kioscos** selling drinks, snacks and more substantial meals from around 7am to 6–7pm every day; the best is number 6, *Meson de Goyita* (T 787/642-1101), selling fresh fish, shark nuggets and garlic shrimp ($4–11). For information about **camping** here, see p.143. To access beach **hotels** (see p.143), turn right along the signposted dirt track just before the car park.

Reserva Natural Canal de Luis Peña

To escape the relative hustle of Flamenco, you can walk to the **Reserva Natural Canal de Luis Peña** on the western side of the Flamenco peninsula. The reserve was established in 1999 to protect the fragile **reefs** here. You are free to **snorkel** on your own, but take care: the slightest touch of hands, feet or fins can damage the coral.

Playa Tamarindo and Playa de Carlos Rosario

From the back of the Playa Flamenco car park look for the trail on the other side of the metal fence – the gate is chained, but it's never closed and there's a sizeable gap to squeeze through (it is acceptable to walk here). It takes about fifteen to twenty minutes to walk up the hill and down the other side. The trail is easy to follow despite the lack of signs, but can be overgrown.

The first beach you'll reach is **Playa Tamarindo Grande**, usually deserted – you can see the **mooring buoys** marking the coral just offshore, used to deter anchor damage. Walk a little further north, past the headland and you'll reach **Playa de Carlos Rosario**, the best **snorkelling** site on the island, with a far larger reef stretching out from the shore. Flitting among the brain and pink fan coral are angelfish, stingrays, blue tangs and the occasional green sea turtle.

If you follow the coast south of Tamarindo Grande you'll reach **Playa Tamarindo**, also accessible via the road to *Tamarindo Estates* (see p.143). Information boards here describe the **Ruta de Snorkel**, marked by yellow and green buoys, that takes a safe passage through the delicate offshore reef and constructed **coral farms**.

Culebra National Wildlife Refuge

Covering 25 percent of the archipelago, the **Culebra National Wildlife Refuge** is divided between several different areas on the main island and many of the offshore cays. Only some of this is accessible to the public, however, so to find out what's currently open, stop at the **visitor centre** (Mon–Fri 7.30am–4.30pm; T 787/742-0115), signposted on the right off PR-250 at km 4.2. Take the second left and follow the gravel road to the end. Set in an area of the reserve known as Lower Camp, it has plenty of information and usually has helpful English-speakers on hand.

Birds are the big draw in the refuge: more than fifty thousand sea birds from thirteen species breed on Culebra each year and Peninsula Flamenco contains one of the largest **sooty tern** nesting sites in the Caribbean. **Sea turtles** are also important visitors. Areas open to the public include Isla Culebrita and Cayo de Luis Peña; Laguna del Flamenco and Laguna Soní for birdwatching; and the Puerto del Manglar wetlands on the eastern side of the island. Visitors aren't normally permitted to enter the rest of the refuge, including Peninsula Flamenco, all of Monte Resaca (the island's highest point at 198m), and Punta Flamenco. **Live bombs** still litter these areas, jammed into the reefs or buried in sand. The public areas are open daily sunrise to sunset.

Cayo de Luis Peña

Cayo de Luis Peña is a 1.5-square-kilometre island off the west coast of Culebra, topped by a small hill and crisscrossed by a couple of hiking trails. Other than **snorkelling** the reef-rich channel between here and the main island, you can relax on one of the cay's narrow beaches. The most popular is **North Beach**, though the southwest side of the cay also has a sandy beach bordered by coral, and you'll see **tropicbird** nesting sites all over the island.

Isla Culebrita

Don't leave Culebra without spending some time on **Isla Culebrita**, the inviting cay off the east coast. Like Luis Peña, the 1.2-square-kilometre island is only accessible via water taxi or kayak (see p.142). The main attraction here is the **beach**, but you can also hike up the 90-metre hill in the centre to the half-ruined **Faro de Isla Culebrita**. The Spanish lighthouse opened in 1886 and after a spell as a navy observation post, was closed in 1975.

The best beach on Culebra is actually on Culebrita: **Playa Tortuga** is a cove on the northern side of the island and one of the most picturesque arcs of milky white sand you'll ever see, backed by the odd coconut palm and scrub. It's often deserted and never crowded (though boats from Fajardo do come here, especially on weekends), and you'll often spy stingrays and turtles playing in the water just offshore, the latter munching on seagrass beneath the surface. Nearby are the **Jacuzzis**, shallow pools of warm saltwater big enough to bathe in.

Museo Histórico de Culebra

The **Museo Histórico de Culebra** (Fri–Sun 10am–3pm; $1; ☎787/742-3832) is housed in the barn-like Polvorín, the former US munitions warehouse, built in stone in 1905 on the edge of what was then the village of San Ildefonso. The area later became a camp for US troops, and all that remains of the village is the old cemetery. Inside the museum you'll find a core collection comprising over two hundred historic photographs, old navy items and Taíno artefacts discovered on the island. You'll pass the museum on PR-250 as you head towards Playa Soní – it's on the left just after the turn to the refuge office.

Playa Soní and Playa Tortuga

At the end of bumpy PR-250, on the eastern side of the island and below a hillside flowing with expensive, secluded condos, **Playa Soní** (or "Zoni") is a gorgeous beach that stretches for about 1.5km. It's another nesting site favoured by leatherback turtles, with nests roped off with yellow tape and the beach closed after dark from February to September. Try to avoid making footprints in the sand between June and September, which can trap hatchlings. If you wander to the far northern end of the beach and clamber over the rocky headland, you'll discover another pretty cove known as **Playa Tortuga**, a small but picture-perfect patch of sand that's usually deserted. As with most beaches on Culebra, shade is lacking on Soní, but you get fine views of Cayo Norte, Culebrita and St Thomas.

Cayo Norte

The only privately owned island in the archipelago, 2-square-kilometre **Cayo Norte** lies off the north shore of Culebra, and is the second largest cay in the chain. It was ceded to Don Leopoldo Padrón, one of the last of the Spanish special delegates to Puerto Rico, during the initial colonization of Culebra. In 2006, one of the family members managed to auction off Cayo Norte to property developer

Spanish Virgin Island Investments for $10.1m. The island is still technically closed to casual visitors, though its beaches (including the long, beautiful stretch of sand on the south side) are public and you can kayak, snorkel and fish just offshore. To visit, call Guillin's Water Taxi (☎787/314-6163), which charges around $45.

Punta Soldado

Beyond *Club Seabourne*, south of Dewey, PR-252 (also known as Calle Fulladoza) weaves along the banks of the Ensenada Honda towards the southern headland of **Punta Soldado** (Soldier's Point). After the surfaced road ends, follow the rocky track for another 800m to the small parking area: on the left, the reef just offshore is suitable for snorkelling (this bay is known as Ensenada Malena), while the stony coral beach on the right is known as Playa Punta Soldado. It's a tranquil if unspectacular spot, with decent views of the actual headland, topped with an old navy observation tower, and Vieques beyond. Come later in the day to swim with schools of trumpet fish off the beach and enjoy the blazing pinks, ambers and ruby-reds of a tropical sunset.

Eating, drinking and nightlife

Most of the **eating** options on Culebra are within Dewey or on the roads nearby, comprising a mix of American and Puerto Rican family-run diners and high-end restaurants serving more creative cuisine.

As you'd expect, **nightlife** is fairly subdued, but locals and tourists mingle at a few cheery bars, with plenty of salsa-inspired dancing on weekends. For **self-catering** try the Superette Mayra mini-market on Calle Escudero in Dewey (Mon–Sat 9am–1.30pm & 3.30–6.30pm), which sells groceries, bug spray and sun cream. Colmado Milka (Mon–Sat 7am–7pm, Sun 7am–1pm), across the canal near the petrol station at c/Escudero 374, also has a decent selection of groceries and booze.

Dewey

El Batey PR-250 km 1.1 on c/Escudero, towards the airport ☎787/742-3828. This roadside bar is little more than a wooden shack with a few tables, pool table and long bar inside, but it serves the best burgers and cheeseburgers ($3–5) on the island and is the closest thing to a club on Culebra, packed with a salsa-loving crowd late on Fridays and Saturdays. Sun–Thurs 11am–midnight, Fri & Sat 11am–2am.

El Caobo Restaurant c/Luis Muñoz Marín ☎787/742-0505. No-frills traditional *comida criolla* restaurant offering hefty grilled meats ($8–10) and seafood (mains $15) for dinner, and served in a small house in a residential area off the main road (turn left at the Escuela Nueva). Known locally as *Tina's*, highlights include the roast chicken and grilled pork cutlet, but don't pass on the aromatic rice and beans. It's cheap but bright and clean, with a tiny bar. Mon–Sat 4–10pm.

Dinghy Dock c/Fulladoza, just across the drawbridge ☎787/742-0233. Great restaurant and bar with a deck of plastic chairs overlooking the Ensenada Honda – check out the hungry tarpon gliding below – and a solid menu of Angus beefsteaks and fresh local seafood. The bar's theme nights pull in plenty of locals, with Thurs karaoke ever popular. Happy hour runs 3–6pm daily. Daily 8am–11pm.

El Eden Liquor Store & Deli Café ☎787/742-0509, @eledenculebra.com. The wooden shack exterior hides a hip, a/c-cooled deli-cum-bar with a fine wine cellar. Highlights are the deli sandwiches, freshly baked breads, salads, soups and espresso coffee (mains from $8). It also sells fresh cheddar, cold cuts and provolone. Dinner served from 6pm with conch salad and lasagnes ($12–20). Wed–Sat 9am–9pm.

Heathers c/Pedro Márquez 14 ☎787/742-3175. Best home-made pizzas on the island, with a wide variety of toppings, as well as subs, salads, pasta and scrumptious desserts (mains $9–12). The bar can be fun on weekends (rum punch $5), with satellite TV normally showing all the major US sports events. Thurs, Sun Mon 4–11pm, Fri & Sat 4pm–1.30am.

Mamacita's Bar & Grill c/Castelar 66 ☎787/742-0322. Bar and restaurant

Moving on from Culebra

You can usually pick up a **flight** back to **Ceiba** (12min) or **San Juan Isla Grande Airport** (30min) with a few hours' notice, though you'll need to book ahead for services at peak times (weekends and holidays). Vieques Air-Link (☏787/742-0254) is the only airline offering regular scheduled flights ($40 to Ceiba and $65 to San Juan), while Air Flamenco (☏787/742-1040) offers charter flights (you rent the whole plane) to Vieques (10min; $250), Ceiba (12min; $250) and St Thomas in the Virgin Islands (15min; $400). Get your hotel to arrange a *público* ride to the airport.

You can buy **ferry** tickets to **Fajardo** (1hr 30min; $2.25) at the dock in Dewey in advance; the office usually opens Mon–Fri 8–9.30am, 10.30am–noon, and 1–3pm (no reservations; ☏787/742-3161). Ferries depart daily at 6.30am, 1pm and 5pm and take around 1hr 30 min. Delays are common and during July and holiday periods the ferry fills up well in advance, so try to buy tickets ahead of time.

With the cancellation of the inter-island ferry, the only way to travel between Culebra and Vieques by boat is via Fajardo; take the 6.30am ferry from Culebra and you can catch the 9.30am departure from Fajardo to Vieques (buy both tickets in Culebra).

celebrated for the posse of iguanas that sunbathe on the deck every morning. The menu changes daily, but always features fresh local fish, salads, burgers, Puerto Rican classics and vegetarian dishes (mains $9–15). Things are livened up by DJs on Fri – the bar is justly acclaimed for its frozen cocktails: try the passion fruit *coladas* and bushwhackers (a toxic blend of Baileys, Kahlua, rum, Amaretto and vodka).

Pan Deli Bakery c/Pedro Márquez 17 ☏787/742-0296. Come here for a cheap early morning breakfast ($4–5) of buns, Danish, *mallorcas*, *quesitos* and *pastellitos*, or sandwiches ($2.75–5.95) and salads ($4.25–5.95) for lunch. Welcome a/c, free wi-fi and seating inside. Mon–Sat 5.30am–5pm, Sun 6.30am–5pm.

Susie's c/Sardinas 2 (next to the Gulf petrol station) ☏787/742-0574,

ⓦsusiesculebra.com. Susie is noted for her superb, filling plates of modern Puerto Rican food fused with Asian and European influences – think egg rolls with pork and octopus salad in Seville orange vinaigrette. Mains $17–24. Wed–Sun 5–10pm.

Fulladoza

Club Seabourne Bar and Restaurant c/Fulladoza km 1.5 ☏787/742-3169. The Caribbean gourmet cuisine concocted by Chef Yamil Sanchez keeps discerning *sanjuaneros* happy at this posh hotel restaurant overlooking the bay. The lobster bouillabaisse and award-winning duck *patacón* are sublime, but leave room for the chocolate spring rolls. Count on spending at least $40/head, without wine, and follow up with a *mojito* at the bar (open from 3pm) – it tends to attract an older, well-heeled clientele. Wed–Sun 6–10pm.

Listings

Banks Banco Popular is at c/Pedro Márquez 10 (Mon–Fri 8.30am–3.30pm; ATM 24hr).
Bicycle rental Culebra Bike Shop (☏787/742-2209; ⓦwww.culebrabikeshop.com) rents mountain bikes for $15/day. You can also try Dick & Cathie's Bike Rentals (☏787/742-0062).
Emergencies ☏911; police ☏787/742-3501; fire ☏787/742-3530.
Hospital The small island clinic (☏787/742-3511) is in Dewey on the road to Playa Melones (c/ William Font) and open Mon–Fri 7am–4.30pm. It has a 24-hour emergency service (serious cases are airlifted to the main island).

Internet Central Dewey and *Pan Deli Bakery* offer free wi-fi.
Laundry Ricky's Laundry is behind the gas station opposite the ferry pier ($1.50/wash).
Pharmacy The clinic has the only official pharmacy, but Superette Mayra and Colmado Milka (see p.147) stock basic over-the-counter remedies.
Post office At c/Pedro Márquez 26 (Mon–Fri 8.30am–4.30pm, Sat 8.30am–noon).
Taxi The following *públicos* serve as taxis: Fontañez Transportation (Adriano, ☏787/590-1375); Kiko's Transportation (☏787/648-5863); and Willy's Transportation (☏787/449-0598).

4

The north coast and karst country

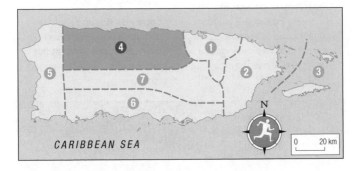

CHAPTER 4 **Highlights**

✳ **Playa Mar Chiquita** Swim, snorkel or just laze in the sun on the north coast's most dazzling beach. See p.156

✳ **Hacienda La Esperanza** Tour the beautifully restored buildings of this nineteenth-century Spanish sugar plantation. See p.156

✳ **Bosque Estatal de Guajataca** This forest reserve is one of the best on the island for hiking, with well-maintained trails snaking past jungle-smothered outcrops of limestone karst See p.159

✳ **Observatorio de Arecibo** Take a dizzying look at the world's biggest radio telescope, a vast window into outer space suspended above the tropical forest. See p.161

✳ **Parque de Las Cavernas del Río Camuy** Tour the largest cave system on the island, a maze of gaping sinkholes, dimly lit caverns and twisted pillars of limestone. See p.162

✳ **Lares** Soak up the spirit of independence at this proudly Puerto Rican town, home of the *Grito de Lares* and some of the best ice cream in the region. See p.163

✳ **Centro Ceremonial Indígena de Caguana** A series of ancient ball-courts inscribed with mystifying petroglyphs, this is an important Taíno site. See p.163

✳ **Lago dos Bocas** Feast on superb Puerto Rican food overlooking the water at this picturesque, mountain-ringed lake. See p.165

▲ The Observatorio de Arecibo

The north coast and karst country

B eyond the sprawling suburbs of San Juan, much of northern Puerto Rico remains refreshingly rural, a region of small coffee towns, untouched nature reserves and dozing cattle. The **north coast** is endowed with spectacular **beaches** and a ragged coastline punctured by blowholes, caves and lagoons, while **karst country**, its hilly hinterland, is a sparsely populated, ethereal landscape of overgrown limestone peaks, quite unlike anything else on the island.

The north remained a relative backwater until **Operation Bootstrap** (see p.269) brought rapid industrialization to the coast after World War II, and today many of its larger communities are dominated by pharmaceutical plants and serve as little more than overspill towns for the capital. Proximity to San Juan partly explains the lack of hotels in the area, and though day-tripping *sanjuaneros* flood the coast at weekends and holidays, fuelling a mini-construction boom in condos and second homes, large stretches of oceanfront remain wild and unspoiled. The small settlements tucked away in the folds of karst country are far more inviting, remnants of the island's once great **coffee** industry, while the hills themselves are best experienced on foot, hiking in one of several pristine **forest reserves**. This region also contains three of Puerto Rico's most popular attractions: the gigantic radio telescope at the **Observatorio de Arecibo**, the subterranean wonderland of the **Cavernas del Río Camuy** and the **Centro Ceremonial Indígena de Caguana**, an evocative remnant of ancient Taíno culture.

The north coast

The secret to making the most of Puerto Rico's rugged **north coast** is to skip the towns and head straight for the **beaches**: the exceptions are **Dorado**, which boasts a modest collection of museums and galleries, and **Vega Baja**, a gracious old colonial town. *Autopista* PR-22 is a fast and efficient route west, but if you have time you're better off following the coast roads, a leisurely alternative rewarded by long, deserted stretches of sand. The trinity of Balneario Cerro Gordo, Playa Los Tubos and Playa Mar Chiquita represent the best of Puerto Rican **beach life**, while the Reserva Natural de Hacienda La Esperanza and Bosque Estatal de Cambalache offer some wilder, off-road relief. **Quebradillas** is the gateway to the Porta del Sol (see p.169), well off the beaten track despite some celebrated culinary

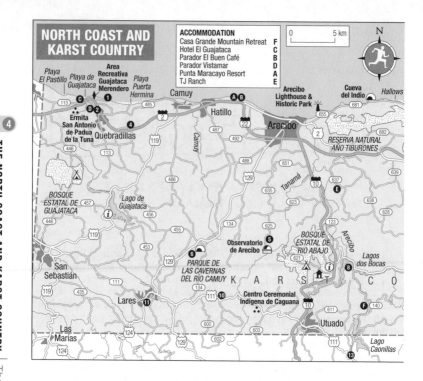

attractions, a compelling beach area and some low-key but enigmatic ruins. Toa Baja, Toa Alta, Vega Alta and Manatí hold little appeal, while even the region's largest city, **Arecibo**, offers little in the way of sights and is best avoided.

Dorado

DORADO means "golden" in Spanish, but **golf** adds the lustre here these days, with four of the town's superlative courses designed by Robert Trent Jones and the other conceived by Chi Chi Rodríguez, the legendary Puerto Rican golfer. As the first coastal town beyond Greater San Juan (27km from Old San Juan), it's worth a look even if you're not into thwacking balls between bunkers, as beyond the condos, clubs and resorts lies a compact historic core with a cluster of absorbing museums.

Condo-land stretches out along PR-693 west of downtown Dorado, principally a playground for rich *sanjuaneros* and well-heeled North American tourists, following in the footsteps of billionaire **Laurance Rockefeller**. The wealthy conservationist arrived in 1955, and three years later created the first of several mega hotels along the coast, the original *Dorado Beach Resort*.

Other than downtown, which is small enough to explore on foot, Dorado is spread out and you'll need a car to get around. From San Juan, the fastest way to get here is to take PR-22 to junction 22 then PR-165 north, but you can also follow PR-165 along the coast.

Accommodation

There are a couple of **places to stay** in Dorado, making it a more convenient base than San Juan to explore the north coast. Coming direct from San Juan's

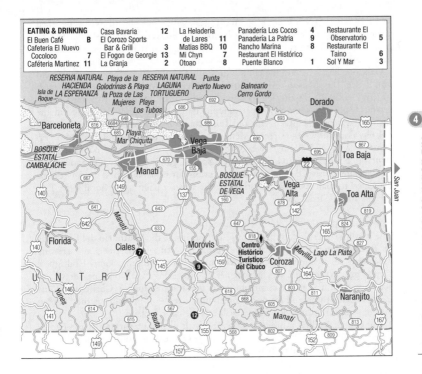

EATING & DRINKING		Casa Bavaria	12	La Heladería		Panadería Los Cocos	4	Restaurante El	
El Buen Café	B	El Corozo Sports		de Lares	11	Panadería La Patria	9	Observatorio	5
Cafetería El Nuevo		Bar & Grill	3	Matías BBQ	10	Rancho Marina	8	Restaurante El	
Cocoloco	7	El Fogón de Georgie	13	Mi Chyn	7	Restaurant El Histórico		Taíno	6
Caféteria Martinez	11	La Granja	2	Otoao	8	Puente Blanco	1	Sol Y Mar	3

Aeropuerto Internacional Luis Muñoz Marín or anywhere in San Juan, taxis will take you to any of these hotels for $60.

The *Hyatt Vacation Homes Hacienda del Mar* (☏787/796-3000, ⓦhyatthacienda delmar.hyatt.com; ❼), is on PR-693 at km 12.8, a collection of luxury condos rather than a traditional hotel, but with units rented to temporary visitors. Amenities include kitchen, balcony, washer and dryer, TV and DVD player, but the real highlight is the astonishing 500m **freshwater river pool** with fourteen waterfalls, hot tub and slides. The beach here is fabulous.

Embassy Suites (☏787/796-6125, ⓦwww.embassysuitesdorado.com; ❼) is the only conventional resort hotel in town, a sprawling property on the seafront in a gated community off PR-693 (at the end of Dorado el Mar Blvd).

The Town

Founded in 1842, the tidy centre of Dorado is **Plaza de Recreo**, a compact zone of old buildings, shops and businesses that makes quite a contrast to the invasive sprawl of development nearby. Parking here can be a problem, especially in the mornings, but at other times downtown Dorado seems more like a village, with a correspondingly small chapel-like church, **Iglesia de Parroquia San Antonio de Padua**, dating from 1848. The town's patron saint, San Antonio, is honoured with a bronze statue in front of the church, while in the centre of the plaza is the grander **Monumento a las Raíces**, commemorating the *criollo* heritage of the island with bronze life-size statues of a proud Taíno, "El Africano Negro", and a Spanish conquistador. On the north side of the plaza is the enchanting birthplace and former home of **Don Marcos Juan Alegría** (1916–1992), the respected painter, maintained as the **Museo Marcos J. Alegría** (Mon–Fri 8am–noon &

153

1–4pm; free; ☎787/796-1433). With pale yellow clapboard walls, polished wooden floors and ceilings and the bedroom preserved in 1920s simplicity, the *criollo*-style residence is immaculately kept, though apart from some odd bits of memorabilia, paintings and a bust of the artist, has little to see inside.

Walk one block behind the church on Calle Méndez Vigo, the main street, and you'll see the **Museo Histórico del Dorado** (Mon–Fri 8am–4pm; free; ☎787/796-1030) on the left, a tiny storehouse of historical treasures; Taíno artefacts, notably some vivid petroglyphs dating from 1200 to 1500, and the skeletal remains of a fifteen-year-old Taíno found at nearby Ojo de Buey in 1984.

A few doors down the street c/Méndez Vigo 292 is the **Casa del Rey** (Mon–Fri 8am–noon & 1–3.30pm; free; ☎787/796-1030), an exquisite colonial stone structure built in 1823 to house the local Spanish garrison. Today it's a modest but immaculately restored gallery of rooms, simply furnished in period style, with one dedicated to Juan Alegría, and others to the abstract paintings of local artist Taly Rivera (for sale from $800).

Santuario del Cristo de la Reconciliación

The world's largest indoor image of Jesus rests inside the **Santuario del Cristo de la Reconciliación** (Tues–Sat 8am–5pm, Sun 9am–6pm; free), an arresting 7.6-metre-tall creation by well-known Puerto Rican sculptor, Sonny Rodríguez. Cast in grey cement and acrylic polymer, the towering installation measures 2.7m across and 12m high. It commemorates the resurrection of Christ, including images of his tomb and four accompanying angels – it probably is the "biggest indoor sculpture suspended from a wall", as the church claims.

The church itself is a modern structure with plenty of parking at the end of Paseo del Cristo, off PR-693 just west of the centre – the paseo is marked by the bronze **Monumento al Cristo**, another striking statue of Jesus.

Eating and drinking

There are plenty of options when it comes to **eating** in Dorado, with the cheapest Puerto Rican food concentrated near Balneario Manuel Nolo Morales (mid-May to mid-Aug daily 8am–6pm; mid-Aug to mid-May daily 8.30am–5.30pm; free; parking $3) at the end of PR-697, also known as Playa Sardinera, or just "playa".

Antojitos de Kitrinche (aka Katrina Restaurant) C/146, Balneario Manuel Nolo Morales (where PR-697 hits the seafront), ☎787/278-3183. This large wooden bar and restaurant has a big menu of home-cooked Puerto Rican food to eat in or take to the beach. Locals go for the freshly caught fish, exceptional *carne fritas*, king crab and octopus. It's an appealing spot, with a kids' menu, lots of space, pool table and terrace. Daily 11am–10pm.

Grappa c/Méndez Vigo 247 (PR-693) ☎787/796-267. This unassuming Italian/Mediterranean restaurant is the best place to eat in Dorado, with culinary gems such as champagne and strawberry risotto topped with grouper and tasty seafood pasta on the menu. Wed–Thurs 5–10pm, Fri & Sat 5–11pm.

El Ladrillo c/Méndez Vigo 334 (PR-693) ☎787/796-2120. This attractive old villa features prime Angus beef and lamb steaks, with perfectly grilled sirloin and T-bones, as well as Puerto Rican seafood such as rich shrimp and lobster stews (mains around $20). Sun, Tues–Thurs noon–10pm, Fri noon–11pm, Sat 5–11pm.

Seyer's ☎787/278-1282. Simple canteen right on the main plaza, knocking out tasty home-made burgers and Puerto Rican food for under $10. Mon–Sat 6–11pm, Sun 1–10pm.

La Terraza c/Marginal C-1, PR-693 ☎787/796-1242. This is the best of a small strip of restaurants on the north side of PR-693, next to the PR-697 turn-off, with a wooden terrace and a menu of upmarket versions of Puerto Rican classics such as *mofongo* (stuffed with octopus and lobster) and fat, juicy steaks ($20–45). The second floor acts as a sports bar on weekends, with live music. Open daily from 5pm.

Balneario Cerro Gordo

The first **beach** that merits attention as you head west from Dorado is **Balneario Cerro Gordo** (mid-May to mid-Aug daily 8am–6pm; mid-Aug to mid-May Wed–Sun 8.30am–6pm; free; parking $3), a small curving bay with thick golden sands, clumps of palm trees and a rocky headland at the end of PR-690. You can snorkel along the reef just offshore, and the usually calm, crystalline waters are perfect for swimming: in the summer it gets mobbed on weekends. You can also **camp** here (☎787/883-2515; $13 per night); there are showers and toilets on site.

To **eat**, try *Sol Y Mar* opposite the beach on the main road, a bar and restaurant that does a good trade in cold beers and Puerto Rican staples ($5–15), and has a couple of pool tables to boot. Further back along PR-690 (km 6.9), at the junction with PR-6690, the stylish *El Corozo Sports Bar & Grill* (☎787/270-1770) is an open terrace bar and restaurant with pool tables, open every day. Grilled meats such as *churrasco* are the speciality here ($7–10), as well as succulent roast chicken dishes.

Vega Baja

Established in 1776, **VEGA BAJA** is one of the few towns worth seeing along the PR-22 corridor, its gracefully ageing centre enhanced by the **Museo Casa Alonso**, a charming museum. At the heart of Vega Baja is **Plaza de Recreo José Francisco Náter**, the animated central square containing the imposing **Casa Alcaldía** (town hall). Built in US Neoclassical style in 1925, it boasts a precious clock beneath the dome on top, created by master New England clockmaker Seth Thomas. Next door is **Teatro Fénix**, a Greek Revival theatre built in 1917 with slender Doric columns, occasionally still used for performances and events. The **Iglesia Nuestra Señora del Rosario**, a simple colonial church dating from 1867, sits on the other side of the plaza near the **Teatro América**, an Art Deco cinema completed in 1942 – renovated in 2000, it's still used to show movies in the evenings (in Spanish and English). Both theatres are usually locked up during the day. The real highlight of the town, however, is the **Museo Casa Alonso** (Tues–Sat 9am–noon; $2; ☎787/855-1364), a sumptuous nineteenth-century townhouse with typical *criollo* touches: wooden doors and shutters, a tranquil inner patio, timbered ceilings and ornate wrought-iron railings along the verandas. Originally owned by Don Pablo Soliveras, a former mayor, it was bought in 1912 by Don Ramón Alonso Dávila and the Müller family and finally acquired by the city in 1982. The interior has been restored in flawless nineteenth-century style, with one room honouring satirical writers **José Gualberto Padilla** (who died in Vega Baja in 1896) and **Trina Padilla de Sanz** (born in the town in 1863) with a few personal effects and assorted memorabilia. The Sala de la Música contains a collection of dusty 78rpm vinyl records, and the first guitar of **Fernandito Alvarez**, born in Vega Baja in 1914 and leader of the Trío Vegabajeño, one of the most beloved Puerto Rican *bolero* groups (see p.274). The entrance is on Calle José Julián Acosta, a short walk east of the plaza.

Practicalities

The **Casa de Cultura y Turismo** (Mon–Fri 8am–4.30pm; ☎787/858-6447), at the junction of Calles Betances and Calles Tulio Otero, is an attractive colonial house but usually has very little English information. You'll find plenty of **parking** at the western end of Vega Baja, off PR-155 beyond the modern Plaza del Mercado building, but there are no **hotels**. The Plaza del Mercado itself, on Calle Betances, is the best place for cheap **food**, cooked up at the snack stalls facing the street – *Cafeteria Pabon* on the western side does the best *bacalaítos*. Otherwise the choices in town are fairly uninspiring – head to Punta Puerto Nuevo instead.

Punta Puerto Nuevo

Jutting into the Atlantic a few kilometres north of Vega Baja, the pockmarked headland of **PUNTA PUERTO NUEVO** also gives its name to the adjacent beach and seaside village, best known for its enticing snack stalls. The action takes place at the junction of PR-692 and PR-686 (km 12), where a huge car park lies behind the beach. Known as the **Playa de Puerto Nuevo** (or just Playa de Vega Baja), the beach is backed by pine trees, faces a calm bay with gentle waves, clear water and a small reef offshore, all said to be inspiration for a much-loved song by local crooner Fernandito Alvarez. *Kioscos* serve everything from crispy fried tacos to crab *alcapurrias* and potent "coco whiskey" cocktails for under $5, but you won't find much open in winter (Oct–April).

Playa Los Tubos and Playa Mar Chiquita

The stretch of coast north of **Manatí** is graced by some of the most memorable beaches in Puerto Rico. Heading west along PR-686, the first is **Playa Los Tubos** (Wed–Fri 8am–4pm, Sat & Sun 9am–5pm; free), a thick, beautiful wedge of sand with a big car park and basic amenities. Los Tubos gets some heavy **surf** in winter, while for the week of July 4 the beach plays host to the **International Playero Los Tubos de Manatí Festival**, featuring a series of concerts by well-known artists from Puerto Rico and all over Latin America.

Beyond here the road follows a narrow strip of beach known as **Playa Tortuguero**, enticing on weekdays when the lack of people means you can simply pull over and stake out your own private stretch. Keep driving west along PR-685 and you'll come to PR-648, the road to stunning **Playa Mar Chiquita**. This cove is an almost perfect horseshoe shape, hemmed in by jagged arms of coral on both sides and lined with a silky strip of sand. The water here is calm and perfect for swimming in summer, though in winter bigger waves surge through the narrow gap into the lagoon. The beach remains wild and undeveloped, with no facilities or food on site, though you'll be sharing it with the usual hordes on weekends and holidays.

To find two much quieter beaches, return to PR-685, turn right and make the short drive to the right-hand turning for PR-6684. Bear left at the next junction, then follow the road around 2km to where it dead-ends. Walk across the fence at the end of the road and turn right at the sign for the Reserva Natural de Hacienda La Esperanza: you should reach **Playa de Las Golondrinas** in around five to ten minutes. This is home to La Cueva de Las Golondrinas (Cave of the Swallows), a small tunnel at the edge of the beach, cutting through the rocks to the bay on the other side. You'll find **Playa La Poza de Las Mujeres** is off to the right, with no actual well (*poza*), but a tiny, sheltered cove.

Reserva Natural de Hacienda La Esperanza

Formerly one of the largest sugar plantations on the island, holding 152 slaves at its peak, the **Reserva Natural de Hacienda La Esperanza** (Fri–Sun 8am–6pm; free) contains over eight square kilometres of unsullied grassy plains, karst forest, wetlands and coastline, as well as a Taíno ceremonial site and the original hacienda building in the centre.

The plantation was established by the Spanish Fernández family in the 1830s, but it's been owned by the Conservation Trust since 1975. The main entrance is at the end of PR-616, off PR-685 and inland from Playa Mar Chiquita. From here a bone-jarring dirt track leads 6km through the reserve, before ending at a small **beach** zone, the most accessible area for visitors. You'll pass several places to pull off along the way, but be warned that on weekends it can get jam-packed, making it hard to find a space (despite the 175 vehicle limit). The two principal beaches are rocky coves, making natural pools ideal for swimming and snorkelling, with a thick bank of trees and tropical bush right up to the water providing plenty of shady cover.

Enlightening guided tours ($8; 1.5hr) of the renovated **sugar mill** and actual hacienda are available in English (Thurs–Sun 8.30am, 10.30am, 1pm & 3pm; ☎787/722-5882), if you reserve in advance. The tour gets you a closer look at these fine colonial buildings dating from the 1860s, with outhouses containing a rare beam steam engine constructed in New York State (at the West Point Foundry) in 1861, and sobering reminders of the hundreds of slaves that once worked here.

Barceloneta to Arecibo

The former port of **Barceloneta** was founded in 1881, one of the last towns to be established by the Spanish on the island. Today it's surrounded by ugly pharmaceutical plants and, though the centre is pleasant enough, bereft of attractions. Instead, aim for coastal road PR-681, which winds between here and Arecibo, a less-travelled route that in part resembles southern California. Beyond the pineapple groves just inland, the beaches start to get emptier and the waves get bigger. At km 16.2 to 16.6 you'll pass the **Isla de Roque**, actually a rocky promontory with some good places to swim, a beach and *kioscos* selling snacks on weekends. Beyond here there are numerous places to pull over and lounge on the sands: at around km 9.7 you'll find another secluded beach protected by a headland, behind *La Poza de Don Guelo* café. Nearby, at km 9.4, the *Gasolina Beach Club* ($5 parking) hosts a variety of DJ and live acts at weekends, turning a once tranquil section of coast into a slightly surreal San Juan by the sea (see ⓦwww.facebook.com/gasolina for more information).

At around km 7.8, the **Reserva Natural Cueva del Indio** is a sea cave filled with ancient Taíno **petroglyphs**, though when the waves are fierce, the dramatic surroundings are more thrilling than the symbols themselves, and it's easy to believe that this was a sacred Taíno site. The cave is signposted on the right around 50m before the Total petrol station. Drive up the sandy trail (where there's a small café) and you can park for $2 on land owned by the affable Richard, who will usually offer to give a quick introduction and point you in the right direction. The site itself is public property (the DRNA has yet to decide what to do with it), and if you drive on to the next bay, you can park just off the road for free and clamber along the rocky coastline back to the cave, though this will take much longer. Beyond the trees at the back of Richard's house you emerge onto a headland honeycombed with dead coral arches and blowholes. The cave is essentially a large overhang underneath the headland, a spectacular location with waves slamming into the rocks and roughly hewn steps leading down to the water. You need a flashlight and a good sense of balance to explore the cave properly, but you can spot some of the petroglyphs without going too far down: a series of simplistic, almost alien-like figures and shapes, daubed in white paint.

Arecibo Lighthouse and Historic Park

The coastal city of **Arecibo** is one of the fastest growing in the region, but with little to offer in the way of sights, with the exception of the **Arecibo Lighthouse and Historic Park** (Mon–Fri 9am–6pm, Sat & Sun 10am–7pm; $10, children 2–12 $8, parking $2; ☎787/880-7540, ⓦwww.arecibolighthouse.com), a theme park probably only worth a look if you're travelling with kids. The park hinges around the old lighthouse, the **Faro de Los Morrillos de Arecibo**, built in 1898, and now containing a small exhibition on marine life – it's one of the few lighthouses on the island that you can explore inside, and offers stellar views of the coastline from its upper deck. The park also includes a small petting zoo and five areas with historical themes, notably the recreation of a small Taíno village, a fairly candid reproduction of a barebones nineteenth-century slave quarters and replicas of the *Niña*, the *Pinta* and *Santa María* (one-third of the actual size), the first fleet of Columbus, ideal for clambering around and exploring (with small displays about the admiral inside). Finally, kids will love the creepy pirate's cave and Blackbeard's pirate ship. The park is at the end of PR-655, off coastal road PR-681, just before you hit Arecibo proper.

Practicalities

The most convenient **places to stay** on this stretch of coast lie just beyond the end of the PR-22 *autopista*, on the other side of Arecibo. *Parador El Buen Café* (☏787/898-1000, ⓦwww.elbuencafe.com; ❹) at PR-2 km 84 is a busy roadside hotel with comfortable but rather pricey rooms considering the motel-like standard. The hotel has two **places to eat** in the building opposite: the cheap buffet-style cafeteria (daily 5.30am–10pm) on the right, serving great breakfasts (from $4), sandwiches and hearty Puerto Rican dishes (under $10), and the posh *mesón gastronómico* and bar on the left, *El Buen Café* (daily 11am–10pm), noted for its *carne mechada* (stuffed pot roast), chicken rice and red snapper (mains $18–28). The Sunday buffet is $16.95 (11am–5pm).

A newer alternative is the *Punta Maracayo Resort* (☏787/544-2000, ⓦhotelpunta maracayopr.com; ❹) on the other side of the highway (km 84.6), which despite the name, is a fairly standard modern hotel. Rooms come with all the amenities (fridge, DVD players), and the pool is a decent extra – you can see the ocean from second- and third-floor rooms.

Quebradillas and around

Few visitors make it to **QUEBRADILLAS**, a typically languid provincial town best known in Puerto Rico for its legendary basketball team, the Piratas. While the centre holds little interest, the town makes a decent base for visiting the surrounding countryside, packed with offbeat attractions and enhanced by some unusual places to eat – the overall lack of tourists makes this a fun place to explore.

From here you can head east into karst country via **Lago de Guajataca**, a peaceful lake, or head into the Porta del Sol (see p.169) on PR-2: it's just 7km to Isabela from Quebradillas and 28km to Aguadilla.

Accommodation

The most expensive **place to stay** in Quebradillas is *Hotel El Guajataca* (☏787/895-3070, ⓦwww.hotelelguajataca.com; ❹), signposted off PR-2 at km 103.8, above Playa de Guajataca. You get relatively compact but classy rooms (some with antique-looking beds), balconies overlooking the sea and a nice pool, popular with local day guests. The *Restaurante Casabi* on site is a slightly overrated *mesón gastronómico*, but it does have stellar views across the choppy waves below.

Parador Vistamar (☏787/895-2065, ⓦquebradillas-paradorvistamar.com; ❸) is slightly better value, perched high above the coast on PR-113 (just over 1km from PR-2, north of town), with spectacular views across the whole of Guajataca bay and plenty of parking. The property itself is a modern, fairly characterless place with basic motel-like units that are showing their age, but all well maintained, with cable TV and air conditioning – you'll pay $30–40 extra for the larger rooms with ocean views. Wi-fi is free but available in the lobby only.

Guajataca

The Taíno kingdom that covered this part of the north coast was known as **Guajataca** (Taíno for "the water ladle"), commemorated in a host of place names including the Río Guajataca, the main river. When locals refer to Guajataca however, they're usually talking about the **beach**, a popular strip of sand 1km from PR-2, west of Quebradillas. **Playa de Guajataca** is hemmed in by cliffs on one side and fringed by a line of palms, though its location is more appealing than the shell-strewn beach itself, which has coarser sand and rough waves – swimming is discouraged thanks to strong currents. On the west side, the **Tunel del Guajataca** – an old sugar-cane railway tunnel built in 1911 – cuts through the cliffs for around 20m. You can continue walking along the trail for 200m to a more secluded beach, and if you have time, on to Playa El Pastillo, a beautifully wild, often empty beach just off PR-113, a few kilometres west of Guajataca.

Although you can access Playa de Guajataca from both directions on PR-2, coming back you can only rejoin the highway heading west, away from Quebradillas. Just up the hill from the junction, at the intersection of PR-113 and PR-2 at km 105, the **Monumento Cacíque Mabodomaca** or *Cara del Indio* ("Face of the Indian"), is a giant image of the last ruler of Guajataca carved into the rocks, facing north towards the sea. Mabodomaca was a key member of the 1511 rebellion (see p.357), and though this is a powerful reminder of Puerto Rico's Taíno roots, it can be tough to stop with traffic racing down the hill.

A short drive east along PR-2 from Playa de Guajataca, the **Area Recreativa Guajataca Merendero** (daily 8am–5.30pm; free) is a fabulous viewpoint just off the highway, in gardens overlooking a vast swathe of the north coast – keep driving down this turn-off to reach the *Puente Blanco* restaurant.

Eating and drinking

Quebradillas has some intriguing places **to eat**, relics of the island's *criollo* and colonial past. *La Granja* at PR-2 km 101.9 (Mon–Fri 8.30am–6pm, Sat & Sun 8.30am–7pm; ☎787/895-2614) is hard to spot – a large wooden shack on the southwest side of PR-2 – heading towards Hatillo (eastbound), you should see it just after the PR-4484 turn-off (it can't be accessed safely from the other side of the road). Just pull off and park nearby. It is packed with Puerto Rican sweets, cakes, fried snacks and local *queso de hoja* (white cheese), all for well under $10.

Panadería Los Cocos at PR-484 km 0.2 (☎787/895-6932) is reputed to be the oldest bakery on the island, though the current premises look like typically modern Puerto Rico. It's also the only one still baking bread in wood-fired ovens, according to an original nineteenth-century recipe. Standout items include bread stuffed with *lechón asado* (roast pork), and the locally produced *queso del pais* (white cheese). You'll find the bakery on PR-484, just north of PR-2. For a sit-down meal try the *Restaurant El Histórico Puente Blanco* on Calle La Estacion, at PR-4484 km 1.9, some 2km east of PR-2 (daily 11.30am–10pm; ☎787/895-1934). Noted for its vast menu of steak, seafood and Italian dishes (mains $13–20, pastas around $10), the restaurant is particularly lively at weekends and has stunning views of the ocean below. It's named after the "white bridge" built in 1922 to carry a railway over the nearby gorge – you can walk over the concrete replacement at the end of the road, 200m further east.

Bosque Estatal de Guajataca

Head inland to the **Bosque Estatal de Guajataca** and you start to penetrate karst country (see p.160), the forest characterized by giant sinkholes and oval-shaped hills covered with a thick carpet of trees. Unlike many of the island's sadly under-used forest reserves, this one is well organized, with a network of 46 short, interlinked trails making it one of the best for hikers. Like all state forests in Puerto Rico, entry is free.

The **information centre** (☎787/724-3724) is 9km south of PR-2 on PR-446, in the heart of the forest: for the last 2km after the junction with PR-476 the road narrows to a single track. The centre supplies basic **trail maps** and information, and is usually open Monday to Saturday 7.30am to 4pm, though the rangers occasionally step out for short periods. The **campground** is along Vereda 9 (trail 9), a short walk from the information centre – you'll need the usual permit from the DRNA to camp here ($5; see p.26).

The most popular and accessible trail is the **Vereda Interpretiva** (3.2km), an interpretive trail incorporating parts of Vereda 1 (2.6km) and others, which can be hiked at leisure in an hour and starts near the information centre – grab an English leaflet here pointing out all the main flora and fauna along the way. You'll pass through groves of *pino Hondureño* (Caribbean pine), *majó* (blue mahoe), *moralón* and *María* trees and see bunches of white scented flowers sprouting from *cupey* trees in the summer, but to hear one of the 45 species of birds in the forest, get here early. Make sure you make the short detour to the **Torre de Observación** (400m from the start), providing magnificent views of haunting karst formations, before continuing onto the **Cueva del Viento** (2.5km and around 40min). The entrance to the cave itself is partially blocked by wire mesh and a staircase now takes you down into the cavern, along with several vines and hefty tree roots that reach right into the cave. If you have a flashlight, you can explore the large boreholes that lead off left and right: the latter contains spectacular dry limestone formations and flowstone walls, ending in around 120 metres.

Karst country

Squashed between the north coast and the peaks of the Central Cordillera, **karst country** is quite unlike anything else in Puerto Rico, a haunting landscape that resembles parts of China more than the Caribbean. Stretching between Quebradillas and Corozal, this is a region of crumbling limestone hills smothered in dense jungle, flashes of white stone poking through the vines like a lost city, the narrow gorges (*sumideros*) in between pockmarked by cavernous sinkholes. These striking formations, known as *mogotes*, were created over millions of years, the limestone bedrock worn away by seeping water: Kras (or "karst" in German) is the region in Slovenia where the phenomenon was first studied. Gazing over Puerto Rico's karst country from lofty viewpoints on the Ruta Panorámica (see p.237), it's easier to appreciate their surreal uniformity – a bit like a roughly made egg carton spreading across the horizon.

Hard to believe today, but by the 1940s much of the area had been deforested to make way for coffee plantations and fruit farms. By the 1960s most of these had closed and with the forests restored, you'll find plenty of tranquil **reserves** nestled among the peaks, as well as some major attractions: you might recognize the vast **Observatorio de Arecibo** from movies such as *Contact* (1997) and *GoldenEye* (1995), while the **Parque de las Cavernas del Río Camuy** shows what happens beneath the surface and the **Centro Ceremonial Indígena de Caguana** is an evocative reminder of the Taíno past. Make time for **Lares** if you can – spiritual home of Puerto Rico's independence movement – and the small hill towns further east, with **Ciales** a charming introduction to the island's lauded **coffee-growing** traditions.

Accommodation

You can see much of karst country on day-trips from the coast, assuming you have a car, but there is a handful of **places to stay** in the mountains.

One of the most popular, especially with jaded North American city dwellers, is *Casa Grande Mountain Retreat* (℡787/894-3939, ⓦwww.hotelcasagrande.com; ❸), a former coffee plantation with twenty spotless rooms in five wooden chalets, tucked away in a quiet valley engulfed by lush vegetation. Each room has a private bath, fan, balcony and hammock, but not much else – you're paying for the serene location. The hiking trails, freshwater pool and 8am yoga sessions ($12) enhance the calm atmosphere, and at night you'll be serenaded by the sound of a hundred *coquís*. Its restaurant, *Casa Grande Cafe*, serves high-quality Puerto Rican food and has a veranda with sublime valley views; on offer are hearty breakfasts, dinner daily, plus lunch on weekends. The hotel is on PR-612, just off PR-140 to the north of placid **Lago Caonillas**.

Another former coffee plantation, *TJ Ranch* (℡787/880-1217, Ⓦwww.tjranch .com; ❸) lies in the foothills off PR-22 between Arecibo and Utuado, with just three cosy *casitas*, all with bathrooms, a pool and a restaurant offering a mix of international and local dishes. You can also **camp** in the grounds of the Parque de Las Cavernas del Río Camuy (℡787/898-3100; $5 per person), which has showers and toilets.

Observatorio de Arecibo

The world's largest radar and radio telescope, the **Observatorio de Arecibo** (Aug to mid-Dec & mid-Jan to May Wed–Sun 9am–4pm; June, July & mid-Dec to mid-Jan daily 9am–4pm; $6, kids $4; ℡787/878-2612, Ⓦwww.naic.edu) is an immense 300-metre concave dish surrounded by jungle-drenched limestone peaks. Scientists come here to gaze into the deepest corners of the galaxy and the giant installation has an appropriately serene, isolated feel.

The **visitor centre** contains an illuminating series of exhibits that explain the pioneering research that takes place here, with sections on the Earth and our solar system, stars and galaxies and tools and technology. Short **videos** look at the Big Bang Theory, the birth and death of stars and finally the Solar System, a mind-blowing imaginary journey that starts with the telescopic protons of a human being and ends at the outer limits of the universe.

Step outside onto the viewing deck and the vast size of the **reflector dish** is brought home. Below, 38,778 aluminium panels hang just over the jungle canopy, supported by a network of steel cables. Suspended 137m above the dish is a monitoring station and a series of precarious-looking walkways, held up by eighteen cables strung from three reinforced concrete towers (the tallest is 110m). The whole site is surrounded by a typical karst landscape, thick with verdant outcrops of limestone and enveloped with an almost eerie calm.

The telescope was conceived by Dr William E. Gordon at Cornell University and constructed between 1960 and 1963, making it one of the oldest still in use. The location was chosen principally because of its proximity to the equator (which provides the clearest views of the night sky) and the surrounding limestone forma-tions, which provided a natural shell in which to build it. Unlike optical telescopes, it works by collecting radiation in the radio region of the electromagnetic spectrum – the dish concentrates the radio waves so that scientists can detect all sorts of objects in space, from pulsars and quasars to black holes and, one day perhaps, signs of extraterrestrial life. Cornell University still operates the telescope, under contract with the National Science Foundation.

Practicalities

The observatory is tucked away in the heart of karst country at the end of PR-625, 20km from Arecibo, and not hard to find – just follow the brown signs from PR-22. From the car park it's a short but steep walk up to the visitor centre. The **gift shop** sells freeze-dried astronaut food, mugs that light up when hot liquids are added and plenty of educational games and toys.

The only place **to eat** around here is the *Restaurante El Observatorio* at PR-625 km 1.1 (closed Mon & Tues; mains $8–22), a short drive from the main entrance. You'll get solid if unexceptional local food – the fried pork is a good choice and the *mofongo* worth sampling – but there's a pleasant open-air deck with views across the karst landscape.

Parque de Las Cavernas del Río Camuy

Tapping into one of the largest cave systems in the world, the **Parque de Las Cavernas del Río Camuy** (Wed–Sun 8.30am–5pm, last entry 3.45pm; ☎787/898-3100 ext 405) makes a dramatic contrast to the world of palm trees and beaches on the coast, a series of cool limestone caverns packed with dripping stalactites, flowstone walls that seem to collapse into the rock and giant stalagmites crumpled like melted wax.

The caves were known to the Taíno, but rediscovered by speleologists in 1958 and only opened to the public in 1986. The park is a tiny portion (1.2 square kilometres) of a vast cave system that includes 15km of caverns, created by the world's third longest underground river, the Río Camuy, but most of this is inaccessible to casual visitors.

Practicalities

Operated by the Compañia de Parques Nacionales, the caves are clearly signposted at PR-129 km 18.9, with plenty of **parking** ($3). Once inside, you must buy tickets for a **tour** (adults $12, children 4–12, $10) at the **visitor centre** (which has a basic cafeteria and gift shop), the only way to visit the site (around 1.5 hours). You also rent mandatory **audio tour guides** ($3) here, available in English (guides accompany the group, but don't provide commentary).

From the visitor centre a trolley bus takes you down to **Cueva Clara**, a vast cavern hidden beneath a soaring wall of white limestone at the bottom of a jungle-clad gorge, pockmarked with holes and straggling plants. The entrance is strewn with ivy- and vine-covered stalactites, with guides leading you down into the **Hall of Sculptures**, the dimly lit main chamber, 50m high and 60m wide. Plenty of **bats** live inside the caves, but you are unlikely to see them during the day. The trail runs for around 200m, past some dimly lit but garish rock formations, and ends at the bottom of the **Sumidero Empalme** (127m), and a look at the Río Camuy.

For something **to eat** nearby, try *Restaurante El Taino* (Wed–Sun 10.30am–7pm; ☎787/897-7417) at PR-129 km 20, a short drive south of the caves, a large, simple dining room just off the road. The best things on the menu are the speciality of the house, *arroz con guinea* (guinea hen with rice; $11.25) and *mofongo*, which comes in large wooden goblets with a variety of fillings ($16.25).

Caving and abseiling

Karst country is riddled with caves, but most of them should only be tackled by professional spelunkers or on organized tours. Ecoquest Adventures and Tours (☎787/616-7543, ⓦwww.ecoquestpr.com) runs standard trips to the Camuy caves and the Arecibo observatory (Wed–Sun; $99), but thrill-seekers should get in touch with Aventuras Tierra Adentro (☎787/766-0470, ⓦwww.aventuraspr.com), which arranges **caving** trips to the Río Camuy every Saturday ($170). Tours (5.45am–5pm) involve an exhilarating 76-metre abseil into Angeles Cave. Expediciones Palenque (☎787/823-4354, ⓦwww.expedicionespalenque.com) also runs caving excursions to the Camuy (Cueva Resurgencia; $90) and Ciales (Cueva Yuyú; $85) areas, as well as expeditions along the Río Tanamá ($90).

Lares

The mountain town of **LARES** is often bypassed by foreign visitors, its shabby centre and weathered buildings evidence of prolonged hard times. Yet its citizens are some of the most welcoming on the island, proud of their central role in the **Grito de Lares** of 1868 (see p.265), the most significant Puerto Rican rebellion against the Spanish and commemorated solemnly here every year on September 23. Indeed, revered independence activist Pedro Albizu Campos is supposed to have said "Lares is Holy Land, and as such, it must be visited kneeling down." Lares isn't all serious, however: Campos would no doubt be mortified by the monument honouring the slightly less heroic (but equally famous) local girl **Denisse Quiñones**, who in 2001 became the fourth Puerto Rican to win the Miss Universe title, and even if the history doesn't interest you, the town's celebrated **ice cream** more than justifies a visit.

The town is centred around the **Plaza de la Revolución** and its large Spanish Colonial-style church, the **Iglesia de Parroquia San José de la Montaña** (usually open daily). Its wide vaulted interior has antique tiled floors and a beautifully carved wooden *retablo* – the rebels placed their revolutionary flags here to signal the beginning of the 1868 revolt. After the well-attended Mass on Sundays, worshippers eat fried snacks ($1–2) at the *Kiosko de la Iglesia*, beneath the church on the plaza, only open on Sunday mornings. In front of the church are the main memorials to the *Grito*: the all-white **Obelisco**, an austere pillar flanked by flagpoles honouring the six heroes of 1868; the **Arbol de Tamarindo** behind it, a tamarind tree from Simón Bolívar's estate in Venezuela, symbol of the struggle for freedom in Latin America; and the **Monumento a Betances**, a statue of the leader of the rebels, Ramón Emeterio Betances (see p.265).

Walk down the hill from the plaza (north along Calle Campos) and a couple of blocks on the right is the **Museo de Lares** (Mon–Fri 8am–noon & 1–4pm, Sat 11am–4pm; $1; ℡787/563-7883), with an odd collection of photos, documents and bric-a-brac relating to the history of Lares, as well as local contemporary art.

Lares is also home to one of Puerto Rico's "Coffee Zone" haciendas, **Café Lareño** (℡787/897-3643), south of Lares, at PR-128 km 40. Call in advance to be given a tour of the premises (Mon–Sat 7am–5pm).

Practicalities

Drive straight into the centre of Lares and park if you can near the main plaza, where you'll also find Banco Popular and Santander ATMs. The friendly **tourist office** (Mon–Fri 8am–4pm; ℡787/897-3290) is in the old Casa Suau Fiol at the southern end of the plaza, The best of the local snack bars around the plaza is *Caféteria Martinez* at the south end, a small place popular for its breakfasts and Puerto Rican snacks and cakes. The real culinary highlight here is ⅍ *La Heladería de Lares* (Wed–Fri 10am–5pm, Sat & Sun 9am–6pm) a venerable **ice cream** parlour at c/Vilella 10, on the plaza, selling some of the strangest flavours ever devised: bean, avocado, rice, *bacalao* (cod) and even *arroz con pollo* (chicken rice). Scoops from $1.25.

Centro Ceremonial Indígena de Caguana

One of the few remnants of Taíno civilization on the island, the **Centro Ceremonial Indígena de Caguana** (daily 8.30am–4.20pm, closed public holidays; $2; ℡787/894-7325) was established between 1200 and 1270, and used well into the sixteenth century. Hidden within a tropical forest and backed by a majestic karst ridge known as *Montaña Cemí*, a Taíno holy mountain, the site's palpable sense of antiquity, unusual in Puerto Rico, is just as appealing as the ruins themselves. As with Tibes (see p.221), you'll find none of the awe-inspiring monuments of Mesoamerica here, just stone foundations and outlines of a series of **ball-courts** known as *bateyes*, as well as some valuable **petroglyphs**, but thought-provoking nonetheless. The true purpose of Caguana remains a mystery, though it's evidence of a level of social complexity brushed over by early Spanish accounts, a sort of Caribbean Olympia, built purely for ceremonial games rather than as a settlement: people would gather here at special times, but very few lived here. The **ball game** (also known as *batey*), which was played with two teams of ten to thirty males and a rubber ball, is thought to have had great symbolic significance, the outcome influencing important tribal decisions – some experts believe the site was also used to make **astronomical observations**. If you've seen any of the ancient ball-courts in Central America, the similarities will be obvious and though most academics agree that the ball game probably spread across the Caribbean from Mesoamerica, it remains a contentious theory.

Ten courts have been excavated, including the central plaza, a circular plaza and eight smaller *bateyes*, revealing thick paving stones around the edges and some remnants of walled enclosures. Some of the **standing stones** are engraved with worn **petroglyphs**, geometric designs and arcane depictions of human faces and animals. The largest plaza, the **Batey Principal**, is also known as the *Batey del Cacique Agüeybana* in honour of the last great overlord of the Taíno (see p.261), though it seems unlikely he spent time here. The small **museum** at the entrance exhibits Taíno artefacts garnered from all over the island – very little has been found at Caguana itself.

Practicalities

Caguana is around 14km east of Lares, at km 12.4 on PR-111. On the way you can grab something **to eat** at *Matias BBQ* (Sat & Sun 9am–4pm), which sells fabulously crispy roast chicken ($4–10) from a roadside stall just before the junction with PR-602. From Caguana it's another 11km to the dreary mountain town of **Utuado**, along an increasingly windy road. From here you can head to *Casa Grande* and **Lago Caonillas**, picking up some sumptuous *lechón* (roast pork) at *El Fogon de Georgie* (Thurs–Sun 9am–9pm), along with other grilled meats, veggies and bananas for under $10 – it's at the junction of PR-111 and PR-140. To continue your tour of karst country, head north from Utuado on PR-10 towards Arecibo (27km), stopping at the **Bosque Estatal de Río Abajo** (8km) and **Lago dos Bocas** on the way. Adjuntas (see p.253) on the Ruta Panorámica is 20km south of Utuado via PR-10.

Bosque Estatal de Río Abajo

For a slice of sylvan tranquillity and the chance to see karst country on foot, visit the **Bosque Estatal de Río Abajo**, a reserve of dense woodland created in 1943 from old logging plantations. You'll see it signposted on the west side of PR-10 – note that this route (PR-6612) is the only way into the forest from the main highway. A short drive from PR-10 you'll hit PR-621: turn left into the forest or right to the **Centro de Visitantes** (hours are erratic). Head into the forest and you'll pass the ranger station (call in for maps here), and around 3km further on, beyond a small village, the road ends at the *Area de Acampar María Soto* (☎787/817-0984), where you can pitch a tent for $4 a night (per person) assuming you have a DRNA permit (see p.26). You'll also find picnic tables and several trailheads nearby. There are supposed to be 24 hiking trails in the area, but only two are recommended by rangers, both offering a fine introduction to the inner forest: **Las Perdices** (around 2km one-way), which starts at the campground and **La Juanita**, which makes a shorter loop around the same area. Note that the photocopied trail maps are very poor and on weekdays you won't see a soul. Beyond the camping area is the **José L. Vivaldi Aviary**, created in 1993 as an extension of the El Yunque programme to save the endangered **Puerto Rican Parrot** (see p.97), but currently off-limits to visitors. Back at the Centro de Visitantes, if you keep driving along PR-621 you'll eventually hit PR-123, the main road down to **Lago dos Bocas**.

Lago dos Bocas

Puerto Rico doesn't have many mountain lakes, but **Lago dos Bocas** is one of its most captivating, hemmed in by karst cliffs draped with tenacious fern-green vegetation. Created as a reservoir in 1942, its three snaking arms cover 25 square miles, making it the third largest lake in Puerto Rico. You might see a few pelicans on the water, but other than soaking up the impressive scenery, the main reason for a visit is to dine at one of several inviting lakeside **restaurants**, only accessible by boat and open only on weekends.

Practicalities

The lake is signposted at PR-123 km 68, a short drive from PR-10. Park your car at the *embarcadero* (dock) and catch a *lancha* (small boat) across the lake to a restaurant of your choice. At weekends the restaurants will ferry you across in their own boats, but you can also use the public *lanchas* that operate from 6.30am and run every hour between 10am and 5.30pm (free; ☎787/879-1838), though it's supposed to be locals only from 3pm. These boats also run on **weekdays** and you can enjoy a free spin around the lake, a round trip taking around an hour.

On weekend mornings you'll be amiably accosted by representatives of each **restaurant** at the *embarcadero*: all offer a similar experience, but the best is ⚓ *Rancho Marina* (☎787/894-8034, ⓦ www.ranchomarina.com; Sat & Sun only 10am–6pm), set in tropical gardens on a quiet stretch of the lake, with a friendly, rustic atmosphere and fresh food cooked in nouvelle Puerto Rican style. Try the *albondigas* (meat balls in creole sauce, $5.50) or fried cheese with guava sauce ($6) to start, followed by breaded rabbit in tropical sauce ($15.95), or mashed plantain stuffed with chicken ($12.95). *Otoao* (☎787/312-7118; Fri–Sun) comes a close second, specializing in *fricasés* (thick stews served with rice; $13.50) of rabbit, lamb and veal.

Ciales

The first of three beguiling hill towns on the eastern side of karst country, **CIALES** straggles attractively over a hillside above two rivers, encircled by low karst peaks. Despite increasing modernization, Ciales remains remarkably old-fashioned; farmers in straw hats chat at street corners, vendors knock out rice and beans for a couple of dollars, and the paint peels gracefully off brightly coloured *criollo* homes. The town is particularly well known for its high-quality **coffee**, the main reason for a stop today.

From the car park, walk up Calle Betances towards the main plaza and turn right along the main street, Calle Palmer to the **Museo del Café** (daily 8am–5.30pm; free), next to the indoor market (look for the **Paseo Aroma de Café** signs). The museum is part of an ambitious community project to chart the history of coffee production on the island and also to catalogue a library of forty thousand precious documents associated with two local coffee giants: **Café Pintueles**, which operated between 1850 and 1967 and **Café Cialitos**, established in 1939 and closing in 1983. The museum is run by the English-speaking Maldonado family, founders of the latter company. Inside you'll find a café selling a wide range of freshly ground beans and free cups of superb coffee and a small display room with all sorts of ageing coffee paraphernalia.

Around 250 farmers in the area still contribute to local gourmet brand **Café Cibales** (ⓦ www.cafecibales.com), sold at the museum along with **Finca Cialitos**

(☏787/807-5248, ⓦ www.fincacialitos.com), another exceptionally fine coffee produced locally. Contact friendly owner Joaquin Pastor González to visit the plantation and buy direct.

Practicalities

Ciales lies 27km east of Lagos dos Bocas along PR-146. Use the **free parking** near the Mercado Agricola (agricultural market) building on PR-649, which runs into the centre from PR-146, on the west side of town.

Restaurant options are limited in Ciales, but *Mi Chyn* (daily 10.30am–10pm) on the plaza offers a break from Puerto Rican food with its Chinese staples, ranging $5–20. For cheap and cheerful *comida criolla*, try *Cafeteria El Nuevo Cocoloco* (Mon–Sat 6am–6pm) at the indoor market on Calle Palmer, which sells bargain ham and cheese sandwiches ($2.50), various *frituras* (from $1.50) and burgers ($2.75). It has a small bar-style counter and a few chairs facing the street.

Morovis

If you're really feeling hungry, make for **MOROVIS**, another hill town 14km east of Ciales via PR-145 and PR-156. *Panadería La Patria* (daily 5am–10pm; ☏787/862-2867) is one of the **oldest bakeries** on the island, said to have roots in 1862, and much admired for its *pan de la patita echá*, freshly braided French bread ($0.75), crunchy on the outside and pillowy soft inside. You'll find the disappointingly modern premises on PR-155 in the centre of the town. Squeeze your car into a space right outside or further south on the same road, where you'll find **free parking**.

The best **restaurants** in the area can be found on PR-155 south of town. *Casa Bavaria* (PR-155 km 38.3, ☏787/862-7818; Thurs, Fri & Sun noon–8pm, Sat noon–10pm) is around 8km south of Morovis in the *barrio* of Perchas. As the name suggests, the theme here is German, with an eclectic menu featuring *schweinshaxe* (pork knuckles) and hearty *goulasch* (stew), as well as classics such as *bratwurst* and *schnitzel*.

Corozal

A swift 14km drive from Morovis on PR-159, **COROZAL** is the last hill town of any interest before hitting the dreary San Juan suburbs, a much busier place surrounded by karst outcrops swamped in emerald green.

The town's premier attraction, however, is a small theme park 2.5km outside the centre on PR-818, the **Centro Histórico Turístico del Cibuco** (Thurs–Sun 9am–5pm; $5, under-12s $3; ☏787/859-8079), a firm favourite with Puerto Rican families and once part of a large sugar plantation. Facing the car park is **Hacienda Aurora**, a handsome wooden mansion built between 1934 and 1940 in colonial style for the wealthy Bou family (maker of the much-loved Melao Cibuco syrup). The rooms inside have been decked out with nineteenth-century furniture and also house two museums. The **Museo de La Caña de Azúcar** is an enlightening exhibition on the history of sugar cane, as well as the back-breaking process of sugar extraction in the nineteenth century, while the **Sala de la Historia de Corazal** is a collection of old photos and documents relating to the history of the town – note the bills of sale used for slaves in 1850 and the wooden bowl used to pan for gold.

Beyond the house is a kids' playground and a rather provocative bronze **statue** symbolizing Puerto Rico's creole roots: a Taíno warrior and a Spanish man holding an African slave by the chain. A trolley bus runs through the park's grounds, where you can stroll on a nature trail through woods of graceful *ceiba*, *guayacán* and *panapén* trees, see Taíno petroglyphs and paddle boats on an artificial lake.

Porta del Sol

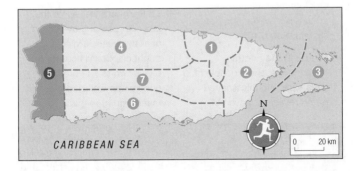

CARIBBEAN SEA

0   20 km

CHAPTER 5 # Highlights

✳ **Playa de Jobos** The northwest coast is littered with exceptional surf breaks, but this is the best for beginners, a picture-perfect bay with soft sand and consistent waves all year round. See p.171

✳ **Rincón** The surf capital of the Caribbean boasts killer waves, spectacular sunsets and Isla Desecheo, an underwater paradise just offshore. See p.177

✳ **Mayagüez** Soak up the colonial charm of this once grand city, best known for its stock of majestic buildings, cream-filled cakes and potent *sangría*. See p.186

✳ **Isla de Mona** For true adventure, spend a couple of days exploring this isolated island reserve, a haven of unique wildlife and untouched beaches. See p.196

✳ **Cabo Rojo** This scenic cape topped by a Spanish lighthouse looms high above pounding waves, a seductive beach and a shimmering expanse of salt flats. See p.198

✳ **San Germán** Wander the beguiling streets of this remarkably well-preserved town, its mansions, churches and neat plazas frozen in seventeenth-century splendour. See p.200

✳ **La Parguera** Delve into the labyrinth of mangrove cays near this seaside village of bright clapboard houses, or dive down to La Pared, an underwater wall smothered in marine life. See p.204

▲ The Faro de Los Morrillos de Cabo Rojo

Porta del Sol

W
hen Christopher Columbus reached Puerto Rico in 1493, he staggered ashore somewhere on the balmy west coast, a sun-soaked region known today as the **PORTA DEL SOL** (Ⓦwww.gotoportadelsol .com), or "gateway to the sun". This is Puerto Rico's playground, with an enticing coastline rimmed by low-key resorts offering sensational snorkelling, diving and surfing. Yet tourists rushing to the beaches miss out on a traditional hinterland steeped in colonial history, with rickety old towns, crumbling ruins and a diverse landscape that runs from the forest-drenched northern mountains to the arid saltpans of the south.

The **northwest coast** begins at Isabela and **Playa de Jobos**, a gorgeous arc of sand and the perfect place for surfers to get warmed up. **Punta Borinquen** marks the start of Puerto Rico's prime **surfing** real estate, a chain of nonstop breaks that peaks in **Rincón**, one of the world's most revered surf centres but just as inviting for divers, horse riders and beach bums. Inland, the French elegance of the **Palacete Los Moreau**, the delicate lace of **Moca** and the historic towns of **Aguada** and **Añasco** provide aesthetic relief from the coast, while serious divers and adventure seekers should target **Isla Desecheo** and **Isla de Mona** further offshore. **Mayagüez** is the underrated capital of the west, slowly recovering some of its former glitz and loaded with fine colonial architecture, plus the best zoo on the island. The southwest is vacation central for Puerto Ricans, dominated by unpretentious resorts with heaps of character: **Playa Joyuda** has the seafood, **Playa Buyé** and **Boquerón** the beaches, and **La Parguera** an intriguing patchwork of canals and mangrove cays. Towering **Cabo Rojo** and its nineteenth-century lighthouse guards an otherworldly landscape of lifeless salt flats and reserves thick with bird life, while **San Germán** is a colonial pearl of a city with quiet, narrow streets and cobbled plazas, perfect for idling away an afternoon.

The northwest coast

The windswept **northwest coast** of Puerto Rico is redolent of Hawaii's North Shore, a series of empty **beaches** and sandy dunes set between small, laidback beach communities. In the winter, the **surfing** here rivals Rincón, and as always, you'll need a car to enjoy the best breaks. Many pros claim that the municipality of **Aguadilla** contains the finest surf on the island, though the city itself holds little appeal unless you're travelling with kids (see p.42). Towns are not major attractions here, so stick to the more rural stretches of coast, pulling over wherever you see a tempting sweep of sand.

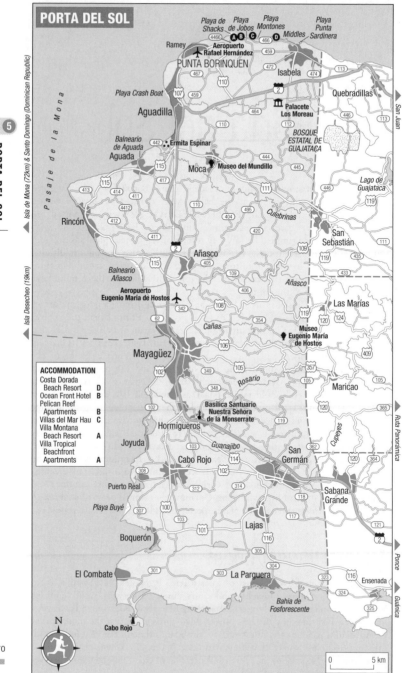

PORTA DEL SOL

Playa de Shacks · Playa de Jobos · Playa Montones · Playa Punta Sardinera
4466 **A** **B** **C** 466 **D** Middles

Ramey
Aeropuerto Rafael Hernández ✈
PUNTA BORINQUÉN
459
472 Isabela 474 113

4466

467 110

Playa Crash Boat
107 459
464
Aguadilla

110
Palacete Los Moreau 🏛
112
446 113

Balneario de Aguada 442 ● Ermita Espinar
Aguada
115
BOSQUE ESTATAL DE GUAJATACA

444
Moca ● Museo del Mundillo
445

413 115
414 411
4412 111 446 Lago de Guajataca
412 110 404 495 119
420 Culebrinas

Rincón
411
San Sebastián 111

2
115 109 119 435
Añasco
405 433
Balneario Añasco 109 Añasco
406
Aeropuerto Eugenio María de Hostos ✈
62 342 108 Las Marías
Cañas 354 120 124
106 Museo Eugenio María de Hostos ●
Mayagüez 105 409
102 349 357
348 Rosario 105 Maricao 105
102 120 365

Basílica Santuario Nuestra Señora de la Monserrate ✝
Hormigueros 119
103 Guanajibo Culpeyes
Joyuda
Cabo Rojo 114 San Germán 362
308 102 120 364
Puerto Real 312 314 118 Sabana Grande
Playa Buyé 307 100 117
103 121
101 Lajas 116 2
Boquerón 305
301 303 La Parguera 304 323 116 Ensenada
El Combate 324
Bahía de Fosforescente 325

N
Cabo Rojo

0   5 km

ACCOMMODATION

Costa Dorada Beach Resort	**D**
Ocean Front Hotel	**B**
Pelican Reef Apartments	**B**
Villas del Mar Hau	**C**
Villa Montana Beach Resort	**A**
Villa Tropical Beachfront Apartments	**A**

Pasaje de la Mona

◄ Isla de Mona (72km) & Santo Domingo (Dominican Republic)

◄ Isla Desecheo (19km)

San Juan ►

Ruta Panorámica ►

Ponce ►

Guánica ►

5

PORTA DEL SOL

Arrival and information

The only **international airport** in the region is **Aeropuerto Rafael Hernández** in Punta Borinquen, 5km north of Aguadilla and part of the former Ramey Air Force Base. Arrivals are primarily from the mainland US (New York, Fort Lauderdale and Newark) and the Dominican Republic (Santo Domingo); there are no domestic flights.

Inside you'll find **car rental** desks (Avis, Budget, Charlie Car Rentals, Hertz and Thrifty), a Banco Popular ATM and a café. The regional **tourist office** (daily 8am–4.30pm; ☏787/890-3315) is also located here. Some **taxis** do meet flights, but it's best to call ahead if you're not renting a car: Boriquen Taxi (☏787/431-8179) is a reliable operator. **Driving** is straightforward, with most of the roads around the coast blissfully free of heavy traffic as far as Punta Borinquen and the airport, though the main highway, PR-2, is often badly congested.

Playa de Jobos and Playa Montones

The coast is littered with dazzling beaches west of Isabela, but the most appealing is **PLAYA DE JOBOS**, a sumptuous crescent of sand facing a shallow, protected bay perfect for swimming and surfing. Though the beach avoids a serious hammering, even in winter, heavier waves roll steadily into the bay throughout the year, making Jobos hands down the best **surf** beach for beginners on the island.

Sadly, a couple of restaurants have blocked access to the best part of the beach at the eastern end; you'll have to park on the road or opt to eat/drink at the restaurants to use their private car parks.

Surfing the northwest coast

Northwest Puerto Rico is **surf** heaven, its numerous breaks catching more swell than Rincón during the peak Nov–March season, and some decent waves lingering through summer. The best spots lie to the north of Aguadilla in the area known as **Punta Borinquen**, host to the 1988 world surfing competition, and closer to Isabela at challenging **Middles**, site of the 2010 Rip Curl Pro Search (**Playa de Jobos** is also a magnificent beach for beginners). Assuming you have a car you could base yourself at any of the beaches or towns covered in this section, as distances are short – make sure you visit one of the following shops if you intend to spend a lot of time in the area.

Aquatica Dive & Surf PR-110 km 10, near Gate 5, Ramey Base ☏787/890-6071, ⓦwww.aquatica.cjb.net. This small shop rents boards for $25 per day and offers 90min lessons for around $65. Mon–Sat 9am–5.30pm, Sun till 3pm.

Playa Brava Surf Underground Calle E, no. 135, Ramey Base ☏787/431-8055, ⓦtupicabrera.com. Managed by veteran surfer Tupi Cabrera, who offers lessons ($40/person, or $35/person for two) and board rentals ($20/24hr). A good choice for beginners. Call daily 9am–10pm.

El Rincón Surf/Beach Shop Ramey Shopping Center ☏787/890-3108, ⓦwww .elrinconsurfshop.com. The friendly English-speaking staff here have been assisting surfers for over thirty years, selling gear, handing out surf maps and tide charts, advising on current conditions, and offering rentals and lessons. Mon–Sat 9am–6pm, Sun 11am–5pm.

Surf Zone Cliff Road Bldg 704, on the way to Playa Surfers ☏787/890-5080. Compact but hip place for gear, owned by surf pro Rebeca Taylor – also has the best website for up-to-date surf conditions. Mon–Sat 9am–6pm, Sun till 4pm.

The Punta Jacinto headland near here is a jagged cape of dead coral, with sweeping views across Playa Jobos and **PLAYA MONTONES** on the other side, a long expanse of honey-gold sand usually deserted during the week. From the Jobos side you can clamber up to the tip of the headland, where you should spy the natural arch and blowhole known as **Foso Jacinto** (or El Pozo de Jacinto), a few precarious centimetres from the crashing waves below.

Not far from the beach at PR-466 km 6.3, the friendly and experienced crew at **La Cueva Submarina Dive Shop** (Mon–Sat 9.30am–5.30pm, Sun 9am–4pm; ☎787/872-1390, ⊛www.lacuevasubmarina.com) offer **snorkelling** ($25) and various **dives** in the area from $45 (9.30am and 1.30pm), as well as diving certification courses.

Accommodation

Playa de Jobos makes an attractive base for touring the region, with plenty of options when it comes to accommodation.

Costa Dorada Beach Resort PR-466 km 0.1 ☎787/872-7255, ⊛isabela-costadoradaresort .com. Just west of Isabela, this hotel is a bit past its prime, catering primarily to Puerto Rican families on weekends. Rooms range from standard pool-side suites (❹) to the posh *Villas de Costa Dorada* (❺), fully equipped apartments with partial sea views, overlooking a palm-fringed beach.

Ocean Front Hotel PR-4466 km 0.1 ☎787/872-0444, ⊛www.oceanfrontpr.com. This budget option is just a short walk from the western end of the beach and is popular with surfers, offering simple rooms equipped with a/c, shower, cable TV (only a few channels), free wi-fi and small balcony. ❸ ($15 extra Fri & Sat).

Pelican Reef Apartments PR-4466 km 0 ☎787/830-0984, ⊛www.pelicanreefapartments .com. Near the *Ocean Front* but a step up in comfort, this spacious one-bedroom apartment is available for long or short stays. It comes with a full kitchen, wi-fi, cable TV, fridge, a/c and a terrace that faces the sea, though it's a short walk away from the actual beach. ❸

Villas del Mar Hau PR-466 km 8.9 ☎787/872-2627, ⊛www.hauhotelvillas.com. Cluster of flower-studded *cabañas* facing their own wild stretch of sand at Playa Montones. The cheapest rooms are basic doubles, but other cabins have kitchens and the most expensive sleep six. All are decked out with slick, modern furnishings, a/c and decent cable TV, while extras include a pool and laundry. ❹

Eating and drinking

The best places **to eat** line the coastal road behind the beach, particularly the strip known as Punta Jacinto on PR-4466.

Happy Belly's PR-466 km 5.3, Playa de Jobos ☎787/872-6566. This Jobos institution is little more than a large wooden shack right on the sand, serving cheap drinks and a voluminous menu of US and Puerto Rican comfort food (such as burgers, buffalo wings, fajitas, and *mofongo*) for under $10, with a raucous party scene and dancing till 4am Thurs–Sat nights. Unless it's raining most people lounge on the open-air deck on the beach.

Mi Casita Tropical PR-466 km 5.3, Playa de Jobos ☎787/872-5510. Next door to *Happy*

Belly's, with a similar but slightly younger crowd on weekends and regular karaoke nights (Wed). The speciality is seafood, including stuffed *mofongo* and fresh fish. Closed Mon & Tues.

Ocean Front Restaurant *Ocean Front Hotel*, PR-4466 km 0.1 ☎787/872-3339. This smart hotel restaurant offers a surprisingly sophisticated menu of Puerto Rican fusion cuisine, such as dumplings *de langosta* (filled with lobster) and grilled salmon (mains $12–20). Closed Mon & Tues.

Playa de Shacks

With a wide reef riddled with tunnels and underwater caves just yards offshore, **PLAYA DE SHACKS** is perfect for **snorkelling** and **diving**, a quiet coral beach backed by unassuming private villas. Note that while you can happily sunbathe here, swimming is difficult. To explore the reef, contact Aquatica Dive & Surf (see p.171) in Punta Borinquen: two tanks are $75 for non-certified and $60 for certified divers, while you can rent snorkelling equipment for $35 per day.

Practicalities

Playa de Shacks is at the end of a narrow road off PR-4466 km 1.9, a short drive west of Jobos – look out for signs to *Villa Montaña* and Tropical Trail Rides. As you approach the sea you'll come to a crossroads: the beach is straight ahead. Note that **parking** is extremely limited at the end of the road – most of the seafront is occupied by private homes, so park on the verge further back. Turn right at the junction and you'll come to *Villa Tropical Beachfront Apartments* (☎787/872-7172, ⓦwww .villatropical.com; ❹) right on the beach, all with full kitchens, cable TV, free use of snorkelling equipment, surfboards and kayaks. Tropical Trail Rides and *Villa Montaña Beach Resort* (☎787/872-9554, ⓦwww.villamontana.com; ❼) are left at the junction, the latter a plush **resort** on the best stretch of sand, with rooms decorated in colonial plantation style. The resort's *Eclipse* **restaurant** (open daily for breakfast, lunch and dinner), with its open terrace, is the best place to splurge on Caribbean-European fusion cuisine (mains $19–26), while Asian-influenced food (mains $9–19) is served Tuesday to Saturday evenings at the hotel's *"O"* restaurant. The only other option for drinks is the *Ola Lola's Garden Bar* (Fri–Mon 3–9pm; ☎787/872-1230; ⓦwww .ola-lolas.com), set in blooming gardens on the road coming in.

Punta Borinquen and Aguadilla

Best known today for its network of dreamy **beaches**, plunging cliffs and slamming winter waves, between 1939 and 1973 **PUNTA BORINQUEN** was occupied by **Ramey Air Force Base**, home to B-52 bombers and hundreds of US airmen. Since closing, most of the base housing has been sold off to locals and ex-Federal employees, creating a slightly institutional-looking community that retains the layout and road system of the old base.

Along the jagged coast between Punta Borinquen and the city of **AGUADILLA** there are many enticing **beaches**. **Playa Crash Boat** is the best and most accessible, with a festive atmosphere on weekends and some decent surfing. Despite a spate of beautification projects along its seafront in recent years, downtown Aguadilla itself has a justly unglamorous and gritty reputation.

Arrival and orientation

Heading west on PR-110 you'll enter the Ramey area through Gate Five, and here it gets a little confusing. Within the former base signs are rare, but follow traffic through the maze of streets and you'll eventually emerge on the west side and PR-107, which heads south towards Aguadilla. This west side is where you'll find the golf course and the airport (see p.171). Other landmarks include the **Ramey Shopping Center**, off Belt Road in the centre of the base (where you'll find Banco Popular, shops and restaurants).

Accommodation

Given the slightly odd surroundings, staying in the base is less appealing than Playa de Jobos or points south, but there are plenty of **hotels** and all are extremely convenient for nearby beaches.

Casa Caribe Avda Borinquen 131 (in front of the tennis club) ☎787/314-3227, ⓦwww.casa caribepr.com. This three-bedroom property (❺) comes with kitchen, a/c, washer/dryer, phone, outdoor shower, TV, barbecue and plenty of parking. You can also rent the adjacent studio, *Casa Sunset* (❸) or much newer two-bedroom *Villa Caribe* (❺).

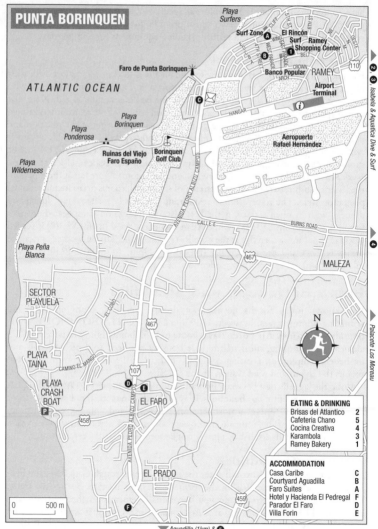

Aguadilla (1km) & ⑤

Courtyard Aguadilla West Parade at Belt Rd ☎787/658-8000, ⓦwww.marriott.com. This Marriot-run hotel opened in 2008 and is a more expensive but far more appealing alternative to the nearby *Faro*, with spacious rooms, free internet and plush facilities (though parking is $1.25/hr or $8/day). ⑥

Faro Suites West Parade at Wing St ☎787/890-9000, ⓦwww.ihphospitality.com. This is a fairly characterless but cheap business hotel behind the Ramey Shopping Center. Rooms are comfortable

enough, with the usual cable TV, free wi-fi, a/c and plenty of free parking on site, as well as an attractive pool. ③

Hotel y Hacienda El Pedregal Calle Cuesta Nueva, PR-111 km 0.1 ☎787/891-6068, ⓦwww .hotelelpedregal.com. This is a better budget choice, with cable TV, a/c, clean tiled floors, bright decor and small balconies overlooking landscaped gardens on a hillside. ③

Parador El Faro PR-107 km 2.1 ☎787/882-8000, ⓦwww.ihphospitality.com. This is a comfy but standard business hotel with pleasant gardens right on the highway and a very convenient choice. Cable TV and a/c included. ❸

Villa Forin PR-107 km 2.1 ☏787/882-8341, ⓦwww.villaforin.com. Another cheapish roadside motel on the other side of the highway from *Parador El Faro*, two minutes from Crash Boat. Rooms are simple but adequate (free wi-fi), and singles pay $20 less. ❷

Playa Surfers

Some of the wildest waves can be found at **Playa Surfers**, a classic reef break rather than a beach, on the rugged northern side of the old base. Surfers is sometimes compared to the legendary break point at Lower Trestles (in California), with a long right and a short, hard-hitting left, but unless things are unusually fierce, it should be OK for beginners. **To get here**, drive behind Ramey Shopping Center and *Faro Suites* on 4th Street, turn right on Cliff Road and pass Surf Zone: where the road appears to end at a residential estate, turn left through the metal fence and follow the road downhill.

Playa Borinquen to Wishing Well

The secluded **beaches** that lie west of the base offer some of the best **surf breaks** on the island, as well as the chance to laze on usually empty swathes of sand. **To get here**, take the unmarked narrow lane that cuts across the golf course from PR-107, just beyond the turning for the club house and opposite the airport runway – this winds through bunkers and sombrero palms before dropping steeply through the cliffs to the shoreline. As you near the sea you'll pass a small turn-off to **Playa Borinquen**, a soothing carpet of fine sand – the water is ideal for swimming in the summer. The main road continues along the coast for a short distance until it's replaced by an extremely battered dirt track laced with potholes. The beach here is known as **Playa Ponderosa**, and you should be able to spot the remains of **Las Ruinas del Viejo Faro Españo** poking through the scrub – the old lighthouse was constructed in 1886 but flattened by the earthquake and tsunami of 1918. The two breaks offshore are known as **Ruinas** and the hard-to-forget **Shithouse**. More intrepid (or well-insured) drivers rattle a little further along to **Playa Wilderness**, a solid long right pro surf beach where groundswells of 7m are possible. At the end of the track lies the equally challenging **Wishing Well** break, just north of Playa Crash Boat (see below) – you'll have to return to PR-107 to reach the latter, however.

Playa Crash Boat

Sandwiched between two rocky headlands and plummeting cliffs, **Playa Crash Boat** is a wide, fine stretch of sand at the end of PR-458. The concrete piers that jut into the sea here are an unsightly remnant of Ramey Air Force Base, built in 1956 for fuel tankers, when "crash boats" (fast rescue launches) would speed out to save pilots who had overshot the runway. Today, multicoloured fishing boats are dragged up onto the sand, tables and snack stalls lodge between the palm trees, and the lively weekend scene attracts plenty of families, and sadly, a fair amount of litter. The surprisingly clear waters around the piers make for diverting if unspectacular **snorkelling**, while further offshore, an artificial reef 18 to 30m down provides a greater spread of marine life for **divers** (contact Aquatica Dive & Surf – see p.171, or La Cueva Submarina Dive Shop – see p.172).

Eating and drinking

Ramey Bakery inside the Ramey Shopping Center is best for cheap cakes, coffee and bread, while plenty of **restaurants** line PR-110 just east of the base. Further south, PR-107 is also lined with fast-food chains and local bakeries. For a decent coffee try the lobby café at the *Courtyard* hotel (see opposite).

Brisas del Atlantico PR-110 km 7.4 (opposite the junction with PR-4466) ⓣ787/890-1441. This bright diner serves a side-splitting *criollo* buffet lunch for just $6.95, a real bargain – expect roast chicken, pork, rice and beans, and a couple of desserts. Daily 11am–5pm.

Cafeteria Chano Avda Victoria (PR-111) ⓣ787/891-3055. This small shack at the northern end of Aguadilla serves legendary fried chicken.

Cocina Creativa PR-110 km 9.2 ⓣ787/890-1861. Justly popular

European-Caribbean fusion restaurant-cum-surf shack, serving everything from a lip-smacking lasagne to huge green salads (rare in these parts) and sausage stuffed mushrooms, all made with organic produce where possible. Mains rarely top $10. Sun–Wed 9am–5pm, Thurs–Sat till 6pm.

Karambola PR-110 km 8.7 ⓣ787/890-1392. On PR-110, midway between the base and the junction with PR-4466, this is a popular roadside shack serving local staples from $4, with a small area for parking.

Aguadilla to Rincón

Most visitors zip between the surf breaks and beaches of Aguadilla and Rincón without stopping, but there are a handful of enticing historical diversions along the way, including a traditional lace-making town, a handsome mansion and a holistic health institute.

Moca

Founded in 1772, 8km inland from Aguadilla, **MOCA** is best known for its delicate, handmade bobbin **lace** or *mundillo*, used to embellish collars and handkerchiefs, linens, pillows, bridal veils and baby clothes. The town's *mundillo*-making roots are hazy: the craft was imported from Spain and became popular among the island's elite in the nineteenth century, when it seems to have become the established trade of the town.

Though lace-making remains an important cottage industry here, you won't see much evidence of this on the streets: it's a fairly typical Puerto Rican country town, with a sleepy centre of ageing clapboard houses and newer concrete buildings. The busy main square, Plaza Don José de Quiñones, contains a small statue of female lace workers, the **Monumento a la Tejedora de Mundillo**, but is overshadowed by the pretty pink Spanish Colonial-style church.

The **best place to buy** *mundillo* nearby is Artesanía Leonides and Pequeño Angelito, both at c/Blanca E. Chico 200 (Mon–Sat 9am–5.30pm, Sun noon–5pm) just south of the plaza. You can pick up lacy purses, place settings (from around $15), and cute dresses and booties for babies here ($30–40). Otherwise the **Festival del Mundillo** (ⓣ787/818-0105) is held at the end of June, when stalls in the main plaza overflow with fine lace products.

Museo del Mundillo

To learn more about the craft and history of *mundillo* visit the **Museo del Mundillo** (Wed–Sun 9am–4pm; free; ⓣ787/877-3815, ⓦwww.museodel mundillo.org), a short walk east of the plaza at c/Barbosa 237. The modest collection of antique bobbins from nineteenth-century shirts, dresses, lace patterns and baby clothes is primarily for aficionados, but retains a degree of quirky charm nonetheless. Labels are in Spanish only (with English leaflets available). Be sure to pick up the museum's list of local **lace-makers** in the municipality – you have to call ahead to arrange a viewing of their work, but prices are much cheaper than retail outlets. The museum is forbidden to recommend individual lace-makers, but two of the most respected are Gladys Hernández (ⓣ787/877-2285) and Ada Hernández Vale (ⓣ787/877-3800).

Palacete Los Moreau

Further inland along PR-2 from Aguadilla is the **Palacete Los Moreau** (daily 8am–3.30pm; free; ℡787/830-2540), lording it over a swathe of parkland like a mini French castle. The house is tucked away 2–3km along PR-464 from the highway (follow the signs), and is now the artfully restored cultural centre and museum for Moca municipality.

This enchanting mansion was once at the heart of one of Puerto Rico's largest **coffee plantations**, established by the Peugeot family in the nineteenth century. The estate was inherited by Frenchman **Juan Labadié** in 1860, but it wasn't until 1905 that the house you see today was completed, a grand *criollo* adaptation of French château style. The mansion appeared in the 1935 best-selling novel *La Llamarada* by **Enrique Laguerre** – it was renamed in 1993 to honour the fictional Moreau family from the book, and the author was buried in the garden on his death, twelve years later. Inside, the first-floor museum contains bits and pieces related to Moca, while a more absorbing collection of black-and-white plantation photographs can be found on the second floor. The house and grounds are far more engaging than the collections on display, however, and the beautifully restored wooden floors, stairs, rails and upstairs bedrooms give a rough idea of what it must have been like to live here.

Aguada

Travelling west on PR-115 towards Rincón you'll pass the **Ann Wigmore Natural Health Institute** (℡787/868-6307, ⓦwww.annwigmore.org) at km 20 on the edge of **AGUADA**. The centre is dedicated to teaching the late Dr Ann Wigmore's "Living Foods Lifestyle" through its two-week programme – see the website for details. **Wiggie's Shop** (Mon–Fri 9am–4pm, Sat 10am–2pm) on site sells all sorts of health foods, books and related products.

Near the Ann Wigmore Institute, don't miss the celebrated roadside stall on PR-115 at km 20 known as *El Original Kioskito de la 115* (℡787/868-3124), a popular vendor of sweets, cakes and snacks for over 25 years. Try the *limber de coco*, frozen coconut milk cake, (or the *piña*, *uva*, *maiz* or "cheez-cake" versions) for less than $1.

Central Aguada has little to offer, but the town's quirky **eating** options are worth a try, with *El Plátano Loco* (℡787/868-0241, ⓦwww.platanoloco.com; Sun & Thurs 11.30am–10pm, Fri–Sat till 11pm) top of the list. You'll find it south of town off PR-411 at km 5 – look out for the signs to "Universidad del Plátano" and turn right beyond "Parada 5". As befits the name, everything on the menu features **plantains**, the savoury green banana: a bizarre but satisfying array of lasagne, pizza, sandwiches and the *isla de plátano*, the signature *mofongo* shaped like Puerto Rico and stuffed with meat. Try the sweet *flan de plátano* for dessert.

Rincón and around

Hemmed in between the coast and a ridge of lush, flower-strewn hills, **RINCÓN** has managed to hang onto its small town roots, despite being one of the most popular resorts in Puerto Rico and justly celebrated for its *bellos atardeceres* (beautiful sunsets). Perhaps best known to outsiders as the premier **surfing** destination in the Caribbean, its northern *barrio* of **Puntas** is a maze of narrow lanes and steep slopes dotted with chilled-out guesthouses, bars and cafés, all booming thanks to "surf tourism". US expats (many of them surfers) dominate businesses in the area, providing an easy-going, international feel similar to

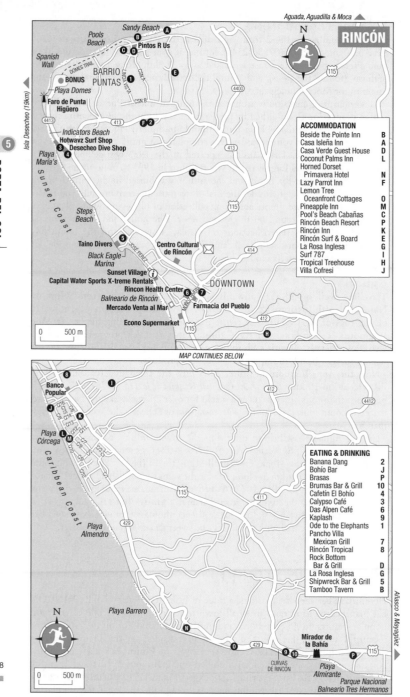

RINCÓN

Aguada, Aguadilla & Moca

N

Isla Desecheo (19km)

Sandy Beach **Ⓐ**
Pools Beach
Ⓑ Pintos R Us
Spanish Wall
Ⓒ Ⓓ
Ⓔ
BARRIO PUNTAS
● BONUS
❶
Playa Domes
▲ **Faro de Punta Higüero**

115

4400

413

Ⓕ ❷
Indicators Beach
Hotwavz Surf Shop
❸ Desecheo Dive Shop
❹
Playa María's
Sunset Coast

413

Ⓖ

Steps Beach

115

Taino Divers
❺
Black Eagle Marina
Sunset Village ⓘ
Capital Water Sports X-treme Rentals
Rincón Health Center
Balneario de Rincón
Mercado Venta al Mar
Econo Supermarket

Centro Cultural de Rincón ✉

414

DOWNTOWN

❻ ❼
Farmacia del Pueblo

412

Ⓗ

0   500 m

MAP CONTINUES BELOW

ACCOMMODATION	
Beside the Pointe Inn	B
Casa Isleña Inn	A
Casa Verde Guest House	D
Coconut Palms Inn	L
Horned Dorset Primavera Hotel	N
Lazy Parrot Inn	F
Lemon Tree Oceanfront Cottages	O
Pineapple Inn	M
Pool's Beach Cabañas	C
Rincón Beach Resort	P
Rincón Inn	K
Rincón Surf & Board	E
La Rosa Inglesa	G
Surf 787	I
Tropical Treehouse	H
Villa Cofresí	J

Ⓗ
ⓘ

Banco Popular
Ⓙ
Ⓚ
Playa Córcega
Ⓛ
Ⓜ
Caribbean Coast

412

4412

115

411

Playa Almendro

429

N

Playa Barrero

Ⓝ

Ⓞ
429
CURVAS DE RINCÓN

Mirador de la Bahía
❾ ❿
115
Ⓟ
Playa Almirante

Parque Nacional Balneario Tres Hermanos

Arrasco & Mayagüez

0   500 m

EATING & DRINKING	
Banana Dang	2
Bohío Bar	J
Brasas	P
Brumas Bar & Grill	10
Cafetín El Bohío	4
Calypso Café	3
Das Alpen Café	6
Kaplash	9
Ode to the Elephants	1
Pancho Villa Mexican Grill	7
Rincón Tropical	8
Rock Bottom Bar & Grill	D
La Rosa Inglesa	G
Shipwreck Bar & Grill	5
Tamboo Tavern	B

Vieques. In contrast, the southern beaches of the **Caribbean Coast** area are lined with gleaming beach resorts, condos and hotels attracting thousands of overseas and Puerto Rican sun-seekers. This area in particular has been experiencing a mini-construction boom, prompting some disapproving locals to refer to the town as "**Rin-condo**". Development has not gone unprotested however, and thanks to environmental groups, particularly the local chapter of the **Surfrider Foundation**, Rincón is at the forefront of ecological activism on the island.

In addition to some serious surfing, you can do just about any outdoor activity here, with nearby **Isla Desecheo** offering some of the best **diving** in the region, and **horseriding** along the beach for those who prefer to stay dry. During the **winter season** hordes of surfers descend on the town, while the blazing **summer** months are dominated by Puerto Rican vacationers who tend to huddle in the southern resorts – with the waves flattening off, this is the best period for **snorkelling** and **swimming**.

Arrival and information

The nearest airport to Rincón is at Aguadilla (see p.171), about 25km and thirty minutes' drive to the north – San Juan is 150km and around two and a half hours by car. Most visitors drive here, but depending on the time of year and on what day you arrive, the roads into Rincón can be frustratingly congested, particularly around Aguada and Añasco. PR-115 is the main route from PR-2 heading south or north, making a loop along the coast.

Rincón's **tourist office** (Mon–Fri 8am–noon & 1–4pm; ☏787/823-5024) is in the Sunset Village complex, right on the public beach in downtown. It doesn't have much information, but English speakers are usually on hand and you can park nearby. When it comes to English-language information sources, Rincón is the best served of any destination in Puerto Rico: in addition to the free *El Coqui of Rincón* newspaper (Ⓦ www.coquirincon.com), you'll find a plethora of excellent websites, notably the **Rincón Online Guide** (Ⓦ www.rinconpr.com), and the official **tourism association** site (Ⓦ www.rincon.org).

Accommodation

Rincón's laidback vibe is genuine enough, but this is no backpacker paradise and prices can be steep in peak season (Nov–April). **Barrio Puntas** offers an informal mix of small hotels, cottages, apartments and private houses, while more traditional resorts and beach hotels line the **Caribbean Coast**, along with condos, beachfront villas and inns. As always, consider **renting** private homes or apartments if you're staying for more than five days or have a big group: try Property Resources West (☏787/420-5227, Ⓦ www.prwest.com) and Island West Properties (☏787/823-2323, Ⓦ www.rinconrealestateforsale.com).

Barrio Puntas

Beside the Pointe Inn PR-413 Interior km 4.4 ☏787/823-8550, Ⓦ www.besidethepointe.com. Basic inn accommodation on two floors above the *Tamboo Tavern*: it's ideal for Sandy Beach but can be noisy at night. Rooms are spacious and airy with plenty of murals and tropical colours to brighten things up, and all units come with a/c, free wi-fi, cable TV, fridge and bathroom. ❹

Casa Isleña Inn PR-413 Interior km 4.8 ☏787/823-1525, Ⓦ www.casa-islena.com. One of the nicest properties in the area, with an attractive pool terrace and alluring Spanish-style beach villas overlooking the ocean. Rooms are light and breezy, with shiny red Mexican tiled floors, a/c, wooden beds and cable TV. Rates include breakfast. ❺

Casa Verde Guest House PR-413 Interior km 4.4 ☏787/823-3756, Ⓦ www.enrincon.com. Just back from Sandy Beach, with eight simple but comfy, spotlessly clean rooms and the *Rock Bottom Bar & Grill* on site: the studios are a real bargain off-season, while the three-bedroom apartments with kitchen (⑥) are a good deal for groups. ❸

🏃 **Lazy Parrot Inn** PR-413 km 4.1, ☎787/823-5654, ⓦ www.lazyparrot.com. Popular hotel with eleven rooms whimsically dressed in bright tropical colours and art, all with a/c, cable TV, fridge and spotless tiled floors. Breakfast is included. Perched high on La Cadena ridge, 5km from town, its lush back terrace slopes down to a restaurant, pool and bar – the parrot lives in a cage at the entrance. Can be pricey, but the "budget pod" room is discounted (❸), and they will do deals for longer stays in summer. ❺

Pool's Beach Cabañas PR-413 Interior ☎787/823-8135, ⓦ www.poolsbeach.com. Mid-range accommodation for a mostly hardcore surf crowd, off the narrow road that fronts Pool's Beach – turn left at Puntas Bakery on PR-413. Choose from two-, and three-bedroom cabins with a/c, kitchenettes and basic cable TV. Extras include a laundry and even a small pool (free wi-fi here) with bar and grill. Great weekly rates. ❻

Rincón Surf & Board PR-413 Interior ☎787/823-0610, ⓦ www.surfandboard.com. Laidback guesthouse doubling as a surf school, managed by Dez and Garret Bartelt, and the only place with dorms ($20). Other rooms are simple but equipped with a/c and TV, all set in a ramshackle but comfy three-storey clapboard house high in the hills above Sandy Beach. Note that it can be tricky to find, and parking is tight. From PR-413 heading west, take the lane next to the *Vista de la Bahia* signs, past Colmado Bonet. ❷

🏃 **La Rosa Inglesa** PR-413 Interior km 2 ☎787/823-4032, ⓦ www.larosainglesa .com. The winding, potholed lane up to this enticing B&B is rewarded by mind-blowing views of the coast and the best breakfast in town. The hilltop property has just three suites with satellite TV, free wi-fi, sparkling tile floors and basic kitchenettes, 1.5km from PR-413: the road up starts opposite the turn-off to Playa Escalera, and rejoins PR-413 on the other side of Puntas, just beyond the Speedway petrol station. ❹

🏃 **Tropical Treehouse** ☎541/499-3885, ⓦ www.tropical-treehouse.com. The most original and eco-friendly lodging in Puerto Rico is a real jungle fantasy, with a central bamboo treehouse (that sleeps eight) and two separate bamboo "hooches" sheltered by mango trees. Once a private home, the Scheer family now rent out the main house (❼) with two bathrooms, a kitchen, two doubles and two singles; and the two treehouses with bathrooms and basic cooking facilities (❹).

The Caribbean Coast

Coconut Palms Inn Calle 8, no. 2734 ☎787/431-4313, ⓦ www.coconutpalmsinn.com. This modest white villa offers one studio and a one-bedroom apartment right on the beach, without the glitz or fuss of a resort: it's set in a quiet residential area, with plenty of terrace space for lounging and a garden full of palms, while the beach is narrow but usually empty. ❸

Horned Dorset Primavera Hotel PR-429 km 3 ☎787/823-4030, ⓦ www.horneddorset.com. Exclusive resort of Mediterranean-style villas set in cliff-top gardens overlooking a very thin strip of secluded beach. Thanks to a recent upgrade, guests can choose between "non-electronic" rooms and suites with all the extras: LCD TVs, iPod docks and Bose speakers, internet and phones. All rooms feature luxurious old world Puerto Rican interiors, but this remains a pricey option, even for the Caribbean. ❾

Lemon Tree Oceanfront Cottages PR-429, km 4.1 ☎787/823-6452, ⓦ www.lemontreepr.com. The best thing about these seven apartments is their waterside location, with spacious terraces literally hovering right over an extremely peaceful stretch of sand. Rooms are fitted out with flat-screen TVs, DVD players, free wi-fi, contemporary furniture and soothing lights. ❻

Pineapple Inn Calle 11, no. 2811 ☎787/823-1430, ⓦ www.thepineappleinn.net. Charming family-owned place, with extra-helpful owners and enticing pool, just behind a beach shaded by a giant mango tree. Prices differ according to room size, but all contain plenty of amenities, including a handy microwave and free wi-fi, and there's fresh coffee, pastries and fruit for breakfast. ❹

Rincón Beach Resort PR-115 km 5.8, Almirante Beach ☎787/589-9000, ⓦ www.rinconbeach.com. Another exclusive seaside resort that looks like a modern condo, with plush facilities and a swanky infinity pool overlooking a beach that's effectively private to the hotel. It's just off the main road, but a bit of a trek from Rincón's main drag. Rooms come with smart antique furniture, giant beds, tiled floors and lots of drapes. ❽

🏃 **Rincón Inn** Avda Pedro Albizu Campos 2231 (PR-115 km 11.6) ☎787/823-7070, ⓦ www.rinconinn.com. Best of the budget options, with comfy dorm beds (four/room; $25/person) as well as basic singles and doubles – stay more than two nights for discounts. All rooms come with a/c, basic cable TV, bathrooms, free use of internet, cheap surfboards ($12/day) and access to the small pool, making this exceptionally good value, though the road can be noisy. Doubles ❷

Surf 787 off PR-115 (right at *Angelo's*) ☎787/448-0032, ⓦwww.surf787.com. This newish guesthouse doubles as surf school and resort, with packages including full board and lessons – you can also just stay at one of the six simple but clean and spacious rooms (one with private bath), cooled by mountain breezes, and enjoy the stellar ocean views. Includes breakfast. ❹

Villa Cofresi PR-115 km 12 ☎787/823-2450, ⓦwww.villacofresi.com. Grand dame of Rincón resorts and still popular with Puerto Rican families, though it's struggling to match the posh new resorts nearby. Rooms are large but standard motel fare, though most bathrooms have been renovated. The staff are helpful and you get access to a lovely beach and lively bar. If you're looking for a resort-style experience, this is good value out of season or on weekdays. ❻

The town and beaches

Downtown Rincón has little to offer in the way of sights, and the real allure lies along the coast. Assuming you have transport it's not hard to get around, and though the narrow and generally unmarked lanes of Puntas can be confusing at first, you won't get lost if you keep heading downhill. **Downtown Rincón**, known simply as *pueblo*, is the busy commercial heart of the area, though the *barrios* of most interest to visitors lie several kilometres to the north and south along the coast. North of downtown, along PR-413, the most venerated stretch of surf has been dubbed the **Sunset Coast**, and also includes the lighthouse and old nuclear power station. **Barrio Puntas** extends around Punta Higüero and covers the plunging northern coast off PR-413, the closest Rincón comes to a stereotypically bohemian surf community. South of downtown, along PR-115 and the PR-429 loop, the **Caribbean Coast** incorporates some hotels and restaurants that are technically inside the Añasco municipality.

Downtown

Downtown Rincón is a concentrated area of shops and services lining the main plaza and congested PR-115 for several kilometres. If you turn off PR-115 and

Surf Rincón

Rincón is surf central between October and April, though come in summer (May–Sept) and the waves are a lot calmer. **Beginners** should start at María's Beach or Parking Lot, though when the swell gets up, even these require caution: surfers die almost every year in Rincón. Unsurprisingly, the town is loaded with **surf instructors** and **surf shops**: learners should also consider **Surf 787** (see above) and **Rincón Surf School** (ⓦwww.rinconsurfschool.com) at *Rincón Surf & Board* (see opposite).

The latter is a good place to make friends, though classes tend to be bigger here in peak season, so it doesn't appeal to everyone ($95 for 1 day). Elsewhere, entertaining (and qualified) **teachers** include Ramses Morales ($72/2hr; ☎787/617-4731, ⓦwww.surflessonspuertorico.com), and Puntas Surf School run by Melissa Taylor, a certified lifeguard and surf instructor (☎787/823-3618 or 787/366-1689, ⓦpuntassurfschool.com) who runs lessons from $45 per hour ($75/2hr) with groups of a maximum of four people.

At Playa María's **Desecheo Surf & Dive Shop** (☎787/823-0390, ⓦwww.desecheo surfshop.com) is usually open daily 9am–7pm, for rentals of snorkel gear ($10/4hr, $15/8hr, $20/24hr), and short, long and fun boards from $20–25 for 4 hours, $30–35 for 8 hours and $35–45 for 24 hours.

Hotwavz Surf Shop (daily noon–6pm; ☎939/697-8045; ⓦwww.rinconsurflessons .com) was opened by veteran surfer Cindie Rice in 1989 as part of *Calypso Café* (see p.184) and sells all the surf and beach accessories as well as offering lessons ($55/2hr; $135/day).

keep following the coast, you'll pass the **Balneario de Rincón** (free parking), the town's modest public beach, backed by a strip of condos. At the far end of the beach, **Sunset Village** is a modern shopping centre, which contains the main **tourist office** (see p.179), a decent seafood restaurant, and watersports and beach rentals (see opposite).

Steps Beach and the Reserva Marina Tres Palmas

Heading north from downtown, PR-413 shoots towards the Sunset Coast, passing Playa Escalera or **Steps Beach**, named for the unsightly stub of concrete steps washed up on the sands (look for the turning opposite the sign for the *English Rose*). In winter this is prime surf country, with both Steps and the adjacent outside break of **Tres Palmas** generating some of the meanest waves around, with 6m swells over a rocky reef bottom. In summer the beach is much calmer, ideal for **snorkelling** the precious waters of the **Reserva Marina Tres Palmas**. Established in 2004 after years of local activism, the reserve stretches along the coast from La Marina to Dogman's Beach, protecting its endangered banks of **elkhorn coral**. You can swim, snorkel, surf and dive in the reserve, as long as you don't touch anything.

In addition to the dominant elkhorn, you'll see clumps of brain, star and mustard hill corals along a dense reef that begins about 4.5m offshore and extends seaward 18 to 30m. Fish life is gradually increasing, and the deeper you get the more sea fans, soft corals and shellfish you'll see, as well as the occasional hawksbill and leatherback **sea turtle**.

The Sunset Coast

The biggest, gnarliest winter waves slam into the **Sunset Coast** north of Steps Beach, where the Atlantic meets the Caribbean at Rincón's "corner", the **Punta Higüero**. The action takes place off PR-4413, a short, clearly signposted spur of PR-413, which dead-ends at the old power station, 2.5km from downtown. Surf central is **Playa María's** behind the *Calypso Café*, a reef break with long, right, fast waves, and though it can get rough, usually OK for beginners because of its depth. Just to the south is the break known as **Dogman's**, named after the dog-loving old man who once lived here and for experienced surfers only. In summer things are completely different, with waves at María's becoming much calmer.

Faro de Punta Higüero

Drive a little further and you'll reach Rincón's beloved lighthouse, the **Faro de Punta Higüero** (daily 8am–midnight; free), built by the Spanish in 1892 and reconstructed in 1922 after a big earthquake and tsunami. The unstaffed *faro* is something of a local landmark, though it's fairly stubby and not particularly impressive – the lighthouse is still in use so the inside is closed, but the surrounding gardens and low-rise cliffs make ideal viewing points for the surfers at Domes (right) and Indicators (left). Just below the lighthouse is one of the most famous surf breaks in Rincón, known as **Deadman's** for the jagged rocks jutting out from the cliffs.

Playa Domes

Beyond the lighthouse, PR-4413 eventually dead-ends at **Playa Domes**, named after the dome of the **decommissioned nuclear power plant** looming behind it, and another legendary surf break: it's also one of the most crowded beaches, as the waves are normally very consistent. Often littered with seaweed and bits of trash, Domes nevertheless remains popular for swimming in the summer, and there's usually enough space for parking.

Activities and watersports

In addition to surfing, Rincón offers **diving, snorkelling, yacht cruises, humpback whale watching** (Jan–April, but peaks in Feb), **fishing** and **horseriding** along the beaches. Many outfits are based at Black Eagle Marina (or just La Marina) off PR-413, now almost completely silted up with sand – boats depart from a concrete slip nearby.

Taino Divers at 564 Black Eagle Marina Rd, La Marina (daily 9am–6pm; ℡787/823-6429, ⓦwww.tainodivers.com) offers daily **scuba and snorkelling** excursions to **Isla Desecheo** (two-tank dives $129, snorkelling $95) and sunset whale watching ($55). For a pleasant day of **cruising** by catamaran, contact **Katarina Sail Charters** (cruises from $50–70; ℡787/823-7245, ⓦwww.sailrinconpuertorico.com). **Fishing** enthusiasts should contact **Makaira Fishing Charters** (℡787/823-4391, ⓦwww.makairafishingcharters.com), which runs half- ($575) or full-day ($850) excursions.

You'll find **Capital Water Sports X-treme Rentals** (℡787/823-2789) at Sunset Village on the public beach downtown, renting **bikes, kayaks** and **windsurfers** (from $35/day). Landlubbers can try **Pintos R Us**, PR-413 Int (daily 8.30am–5pm; ℡787/516-7090), which organizes daily **trail rides** ($55–185) on high-spirited Paso Fino horses; find them near Sandy Beach. Finally, for $60 you can zip above the waves with **Flying Fish Parasail** (daily 9am–5pm; ℡787/823-2359, ⓦwww.parasailpr.com).

Hard to believe given its precious natural surroundings, but the nuclear plant, known as **BONUS** ("Boiling Nuclear Superheater"), was a sort of experiment, a prototype nuclear station built between 1960 and 1964. Decommissioned in 1970 after technical difficulties terminated operations, many contaminated materials were simply entombed in concrete on site, and additional clean-up activities were conducted in the 1990s and early 2000s. The site has been slated to open as a nuclear museum for years (it even has an official name, "Dr. Modesto Iriarte Technological Museum"), but nothing is likely to happen in the near future.

Barrio Puntas

Beyond Punta Higüero, PR-413 climbs into the hills above Rincón's alluring northern **beaches**, a labyrinth of lanes known as **Barrio Puntas**. It's not quite Goa, but the low-rise community that clings to the slopes all the way down to the shore exudes a tropical languor wholly distinct from the downtown area. The **beach breaks** here are perfect for beginners, though the swells can really thicken up in winter and it pays to seek local advice before paddling offshore.

Sandy Beach, the main Puntas strip, is where most of the action takes place. With a sandy bottom, it's justifiably enticing for beginner surfers, but be careful – it has a brutal undertow and a steep drop-off. The beach itself is one of the widest in town and a mellow place to simply loll in the sun. Sandy Beach ends at **Parking Lot** (in front of *Casa Isleña*), another fine and less crowded spot for beginner surfers, with waves breaking over a flat reef.

The Caribbean Coast

South of downtown, the **Caribbean Coast** is far calmer than the northern beaches, marked by long swathes of palm-lined beaches and serene turquoise waters. You can access **Playa Córcega** at *Villa Cofresí* (p.181) though a better place to spend an afternoon is **Playa Almendro**, off PR-429 just after it splits from PR-115 – look for the lane next to the Sol y Playa condo. Named after almond trees nearby, the beach is wide and usually clean, the favourite haunt of local families enjoying the gentle waves and palms in between the condos. It can be a squeeze, but you can usually park at the end of the road.

Back on PR-115, just beyond the collection of restaurants at km 6.7, the road passes the **Mirador de la Bahía** (daily 7am–6pm; free), a three-storey lookout tower over Añasco Bay. The tower is often locked up despite the listed opening times, but it's still worth stopping to gaze over the glassy waters of the bay, distant Mayagüez and the hazy mountain-choked interior on the other side.

If you're looking for a wider beach with easier access and more facilities, drive on to the **Parque Nacional Balneario Tres Hermanos** (summer daily 8am–5pm; winter Wed–Sun 8.30am–5pm; parking $3; ☎787/826-1610) at Tres Hermanos, a sleepy village at PR-401 km 1, off PR-115, a few kilometres beyond the Mirador. Usually empty on weekdays, it's a dazzling stretch of sugary sand, the Caribbean feel augmented by lilting palm trees and striking views across the bay towards the hills of Rincón – you can also **camp** here ($10–17).

Isla Desecheo

Clearly visible around 19km off the coast of Rincón, **Isla Desecheo** is a barren 370-acre hunk of rock that became a national wildlife refuge in 1983, off-limits to casual visitors. The real draw lies beneath the sapphire waters that surround the island, an underwater wonderland with consistent 30–45m visibility, open for **diving** and **snorkelling**. Amid the shimmering corals, swim-through tunnels and caverns just offshore you'll spot nurse sharks, giant lobsters and a plethora of tropical marine life: porcupine fish, spiky scorpion fish, and schools of flounder, snappers and triggerfish. Boats take around 45 minutes to reach the island – see p.183 for details.

Eating and drinking

Most **restaurants** in Rincón double as bars, ranging from simple Puerto Rican canteens to American-style diners with full international menus. The scene gets lively during peak season, fuelled by an amicable mix of locals and tourists, though things quieten down considerably in the summer. The coolest surf bars and cafés lie, not surprisingly, in **Puntas** or along the **Sunset Coast**, while **downtown** and especially along PR-115 is where you'll find all the chains and a cheaper range of options. On the **Caribbean Coast**, head for the cluster of restaurants on the hilltop at PR-115 km 7 (known as **Las Curvas de Rincón**), perfect for cheap snacks and spectacular views. For **self-catering**, Econo supermarket (Mon–Sat 7am–9pm, Sun 11am–5pm; ☎787/823-1051) is at PR-115 km 13.2, just south of downtown.

Downtown

Das Alpen Café Rincón Plaza South, at c/Muñoz Rivera and c/Comercio ☎787/233-8009, ☜www .dasalpencafe.com. Authentic restaurant offering German and northern Italian specialities; think dumplings, schnitzel, *bratwurst* and Italian sausages and plenty of creative pastas (including pumpkin ravioli). Real ales on tap also available here. Mains average $17. Thurs–Mon 5–10pm, Sun 3–9pm.

Pancho Villa Mexican Grill Rincón Plaza, c/ Progreso 157-B ☎787/823-8226, ☜panchovilla rincon.com. Excellent Mexican food in the heart of town, with classics such as sizzling chicken fajitas ($14.95) and burritos ($9–16), as well as fish wrapped in banana leaf ($15.89) and a decent kids' menu. Listen to live *mariachi* bands on Sundays, or sample the cheap tequila on Tuesdays. Tues–Sun 5pm–midnight.

Shipwreck Bar & Grill 564 Black Eagle Rd, La Marina ☎787/823-0578, ☜www.rinconshipwreck .com. This large shack-like place near the marina is becoming a Rincón institution, with an open-air deck and fabulous pig roast on Sundays. At other times try the local fish specials, or indulge in the $2 rum punch and beers at happy hour (3–6pm). Daily noon–2am (June–Dec closed Mon).

Sunset Coast

Cafetín El Bohío PR-4413, Playa María's ☎787/823-0509. A shack next to *Calypso* that serves bargain beers ($1.50 Medallas) and stiff rum punch ($2.50). Wash it down with some tasty *pinchos* (kebabs). Daily 5pm–midnight.

Calypso Café PR-4413, Playa María's ☎787/823-1626. Surfer bar just off the beach. The legendary happy hours run 5–7pm to take in the sunsets, with the special calypso rum punch just $2.50. Food highlights include fresh *dorado ceviche*, jalapeño cheeseburger and guava barbecue wings. Fri & Sat see live music and dancing 10pm–2am, with full moon parties every month, and you can order a range of grilled snacks throughout the day. Sun–Wed 11am–midnight, Thurs–Sat 11am–2am.

Barrio Puntas

Banana Dang PR-413 km 4.1 ☎787/823-0963, ✺www.bananadang.com. Chilled-out coffee house near *Lazy Parrot*, serving the best organic coffee (all Puerto Rican) and tea in town, scrumptious smoothies from $4 (try the "nutty dang", a blend of banana, chocolate and peanut) and moist pumpkin and zucchini breads ($3.50). Espressos start at $2, but you can also order Vietnamese coffee ($3) and bagels ($3.50). You can check the internet here (free wi-fi; terminals $3/30min). Wed–Mon 7am–4pm.

Ode to the Elephants c/Vista Linda (Sandy Beach Apartments), PR-413 km 3.3 ☎787/424-8707, ✺odetotheelephants.com. Who can resist a name like this? Chef Kevin Ngosuwan certainly delivers with exquisite Thai food, enhanced with great sea views. Excellent staples (*Pad Thai*, curries) complement Thai riffs on Puerto Rican favourites such as *churrasco* (skirt steak), served with lime chilli sauce here). Daily 5–10pm.

Rock Bottom Bar & Grill *Casa Verde Guest House*, PR-413 Interior km 4.4 ☎787/823-3756. Another surfer stalwart, this "treehouse-style" bar offers different themes every night: Wednesday is "margarita madness" (drinks $3), Thursday is "jam night", and on Sunday they show surf videos and there are *sangría* pitchers for $16. The menu of finger-licking bar snacks like chilli cheese fries ($7.95) is irresistible, and the Rock Bottom Burger ($7.95) is legendary. Rum punch is $2.50 every day. Daily 9am–late.

La Rosa Inglesa PR-413 Interior km 2 ☎787/823-4032, ✺www.larosainglesa.com. Best place for a full breakfast in Rincón (and possibly Puerto Rico), at the B&B that bakes its own bread, fries bubble and squeak and stuffs its own sausages. The winding ride up is rewarded with a fabulous menu: Encore Eggs Benedict (eggs Benedict with salmon, $9), the Full Monty (full English, eggs, bacon, sausage, bubble and squeak; $7) and classic American with pancakes ($6). See p.180 for directions. Mon–Sat 8am–noon, Sun till 1pm (June–Dec closed Mon–Wed).

Tamboo Tavern PR-413 Interior km 4.4 ☎787/823-8550. This legendary beach bar and surfers' haunt has a wide wooden deck jutting over the beach. Cocktails cost $5.14 to $7 (the Tamboo Mojito is one of the best on the island), while the *Tamboo Seaside Grill* serves high quality steaks and seafood ($12–20) and sandwiches ($6.78–9.35). Live music gets things fairly animated on Fri while DJs spin Sat – happy hours run 7–9pm weekdays. Mon–Thurs & Sun noon–midnight, Fri & Sat noon–2am.

Caribbean Coast

Bohío Bar *Villa Cofresí Hotel*, PR-115 km 12 ☎787/823-2450. This venerable resort hotel has one of the best beach bars in town, with heart-melting sunset views, pool tables and an awesome line-up of drinks, including the infamous "Pirata Special", a blend of four kinds of rum, cacao milk, coconut juice and milk, served in a coconut shell for $7.50. Free salsa lessons Wed 8–10pm; happy hours Mon–Fri 5–7pm (wine $3, beers $2.50). Daily 9am–midnight.

Brasas *Rincón Beach Resort*, PR-115 km 5.8 ☎787/589-9001. For a splurge, try this posh hotel restaurant overlooking the water, a romantic location with delectable seafood and fresh fish – try the fresh snapper fillet with coriander (cilantro) and tomato sauce or Chilean sea bass with lemon caper sauce. You can even order a super-swish seafood *mofongo* for $22. Mains $23–27. Daily 7am–10.30am & 5–10pm.

Brumas Bar & Grill PR-115 km 7 ☎787/826-6315. Large bar with spectacular balcony, big TVs and pool tables. Wed is ladies' night ($1 drinks), Fri karaoke, and Sat live music and salsa. The menu is heavy on comfort food such as fish bites, *empanadillas*, *tostones*, burgers and a delicious shrimp basket, and there are several other places to try within stumbling distance. Tues–Thurs 5–10pm, Fri 2pm–2am, Sat noon–2am, Sun till 11pm.

Kaplash PR-115 km 7, next to *Brumas* ☎787/826-4582. No-frills diner tucked away in the cluster of restaurants here (on the bay side of the road) and extremely popular for its seafood *empanadillas*. For $1.50–2.95 you can feast on lobster, crab, octopus or prawn fillings; or join the genial mix of locals and expats in the evenings as they enjoy beers on the back terrace, with fabulous views of the ocean. Mon–Wed 11am–9pm, Thurs–Sun till 11pm.

Rincón Tropical PR-115 km 12.4 ☎787/823-2017. One of the best Puerto Rican restaurants in town, in a small residential block just off the main road, with its own car park and open-front dining area. Plenty of fresh fish gets fried up here, along with all the *criollo* favourites, and in case you're missing it, decent *mofongo*. Mains under $10. Daily 11am–9pm.

Añasco's brandy cakes

Heading south from Rincón towards Mayagüez it's worth making a brief detour to Añasco, a small town "where the gods died". Taíno *cacique* (chief) Urayoán had a Spanish soldier drowned in the nearby Río Grande de Añasco to prove the white men weren't gods, precipitating the rebellion of 1511 (see p.263), but today Añasco is a hard-working blue-collar town some 17km from downtown Rincón.

The best reason for a pit stop is to try the local speciality, **hojaldre** cakes (literally "puff pastries", made with brandy and spices), sold from a tiny shop east of the main plaza: **Fábrica de Hojaldres** (Tues–Fri 7am–1pm, Sat 7.30am–noon; bags of cakes from $1.34; ☎787/826-5011) is tucked away in a commercial building off Calle 65 Infantería (PR-109) opposite the old Plaza de Mercado – walk through the passage towards the car park at the back and look for the yellow sign. The official address is c/65 Infantería no. 50.

Listings

Banks Banco Popular (Mon–Fri 7.30am–5pm, Sat 8.30–11.30am) has a branch and 24hr ATM on the central plaza in downtown Rincón (c/Muñoz Rivera and Unión). It has another branch at PR-115 km 12.4 (Mon–Fri 8am–4pm, Sat 9am–noon).

Car rental B-Smart Rent a Car (☎787/823-3438, ⓦwww.b-smartrentacar.com) at PR-115 km 12 is a local outfit that rents cars from $45/day.

Hospital Rincón Health Center (Mon–Fri 8am–4.30pm, Sat & Sun till 4pm emergency only) is on PR-115 (c/Muñoz Rivera 28) in the middle of downtown.

Internet Wi-fi is widely available in Rincón, but internet cafés with computers are thin on the ground. Try the Banana Dang (see p.185).

Laundry Try the coin laundry at Plaza Bonet, south of downtown on PR-115. Open daily 8am–7pm ($2.50/load; ☎787/823-3504).

Pharmacy Farmacia del Pueblo (Mon–Sat 8am–9pm, Sun 10am–6pm) is opposite the Rincón Health Center on PR-115 in the centre of downtown.

Post office The post office (Mon–Fri 7.30am–4.30pm, Sat 8.30am–noon; ☎787/823-2625) is north of downtown on PR-115.

Taxi Rincón Tours & Taxi ☎787/823-0454.

Mayagüez and around

After years of decline, **MAYAGÜEZ** is finally starting to feel like Puerto Rico's third city again, a wilfully provincial place that has always stuck its nose up at posh Ponce and the brash wealth of the capital, desperately proud of its historic reputation as "La Sultana del Oeste" (Sultan of the West). Long ignored by tourists, central Mayagüez is a surprising treasure-trove of ornate **architecture**, a legacy of the boom years of coffee and sugar, and home to some endearing edible attractions: the cream-stuffed *brazo gitano* and zesty home-made *sangría*. Now just the eighth most populous city on the island after years of migration, the city's impressive centre has been spruced up, and a palpable sense of optimism pervades the streets.

Some history

Mayagüez was founded in 1760 by a group of settlers from the Canary Islands, the name deriving from the Taíno word for the Río Yagüez, "Maygüex". In the nineteenth century the city became a major port and commercial centre serving the rich **coffee** plantations in the western mountains. This was despite a series of catastrophic **natural disasters**: the great fire of 1841 destroyed most of the city, while the **1918 earthquake** and tsunami levelled it yet again with seven hundred stone buildings and over a thousand wooden homes destroyed – much of what you see today dates from the massive rebuilding programme that followed. The

University of Puerto Rico Mayagüez Campus (UPRM) was founded in 1911 (Ⓦwww.uprm.edu), and today the city remains a major **education** centre, students making up a large proportion of its population.

The city was an important **rum producer** between the 1930s and 1970s, and Cervecería India (now Cervecera de Puerto Rico), which opened in 1937, still produces **Medalla beer** here. After World War II, **textile** factories boomed, and between 1962 and 1998 Mayagüez was a major **tuna-canning centre**, supplying 80 to 90 percent of all tuna consumed in the US – now only one factory remains, supplying the Bumble Bee brand. The city's recent renaissance was in part inspired by its selection to host the 2010 **Central American and Caribbean Games** – the games were a big success and gave a welcome boost to the local economy.

Arrival and information

Mayagüez's tiny airport, **Aeropuerto Eugenio María de Hostos**, is located 6.4km north of the city on PR-342 (off PR-2); there are five daily flights from San Juan (35min). Only Thrifty (Ⓣ787/834-1590) has a car rental desk at the terminal – they'll transport you by minibus to where the cars are. Otherwise take a taxi into the city ($10); if none is around, get the Cape Air desk to call one.

Ferries from the Dominican Republic (3 weekly from Santo Domingo; 12hr), dock at the **Puerto de Mayagüez** (Mayagüez Port), north of the city off PR-64 on PR-3341. Inside the terminal you'll find a small shop, toilets and a basic café (no bank or ATM). American Ferries (see p.192) can arrange for Línea Sultana *públicos* to meet you at the terminal before driving on to **San Juan** (Río Piedras), but only when you buy the ferry ticket. Take a **taxi** ($7) into the city – if you can't find any call one (see below) or ask the ticket office to help.

Most **públicos** should pull in at the **Terminal de Vehículos Públicos** at the end of Calle Peral, a few blocks north of the plaza and a short walk from most of the central hotels. **Driving** into Mayagüez is fairly straightforward, though there is a one-way system and the streets in the city centre tend to get clogged with traffic during the week. The **car park** ($1.25 first hr, $0.90/hr thereafter) on Calle Méndez Vigo, near Calle Del Río and the *Howard Johnson* hotel, is convenient for the plaza, but most hotels have their own parking.

The helpful **tourist office** (Mon–Sat 8am–4.30pm; Ⓣ787/832-5882) is in the centre of the city on Plaza Colón at c/Candelaria 53.

City transport

Public transport in Mayagüez is limited to a free **trolley bus** (Mon–Fri 6am–6pm) that trundles between the north side of Plaza Colón (Calle Peral) and the Palacio de Recreación y Deportes (sports stadium) every thirty minutes or so, which is useful for the Tropical Research Station but not much else.

Taxis are easy to find downtown: White Taxi (daily 6.30am–midnight; Ⓣ787/832-1154) operates from the *público* terminal and a small office at c/José de Diego 18 Este, while Westernbank Taxi (daily 6am–midnight; Ⓣ787/832-0562) is based just south of the plaza on Calle Del Río. Both usually charge $10 for the airport, $7 for the ferry terminal and $5 for the zoo.

Accommodation

Staying in Mayagüez can be good value, its hotels ranging from basic but comfortable one-star inns to luxurious mini-resorts. Your options fall into two principal groups: the collection of hotels in **downtown**, all handy for the central sights and restaurants; and the two smart hotels on PR-2 north of the centre, convenient for drivers but a little isolated from the rest of the city. All the hotels

▲ ❸ & Museo Eugenio María de Hostos ▲ Maricao

MAYAGÜEZ

0   250 m

ACCOMMODATION
Colonial	E
Holiday Inn Mayagüez & Tropical Casino	B
Howard Johnson Inn	C
Downtown Mayagüez	A
Mayagüez Resort & Casino	A
Western Bay Mayagüez	D

▲ ❶ (2km), ❶ (5km) & Rincón Airport (6km)

▲ Mayagüez Zoo (1km)

▲ Puerto de Mayagüez (2km)

Palacio de Recreación y Deportes

Supermarket

Parque Atlético de París

Tropical Agriculture Research Station

Parque de los Próceres

Entrance

Terminal de Vehículos Públicos

Universidad de Puerto Rico

Cervecera de Puerto Rico

Río Yagüez

Radio Centro Laundromat

Hospital San Antonio

Farmacia de Diego

Banco Popular

Museo Casa Grande ❾

Farmacia Luciano ❻

Catedral Nuestra Señora de la Candelaria

Banco Popular

Teatro Yagüez

Casa Alcaldía

Oficentro Express

Plaza Colón

Plaza de Mercado

Casa de los Cinco Arcos

Laundry Puerto Rico

Taxi ★

Taxi ★

N

▶ Ponce, Mayagüez Mall & Hormigueros

Bahía de Mayagüez

EATING & DRINKING
La Biblioteca	4	Mia Bistro	8
Bleu Bar & Tapas	6	Restaurant Vegetariano	9
Brazo Gitano Franco	5	La Familia	11 & 12
Chilín	1	Rex Cream	10
Fido's Sangría Garden	3	Ricomini Bakery	7
Friend's Café	13	Siglo XX	7
El Garabato	2	Stoa's	C

listed here have free **wi-fi** unless otherwise stated, but only the *Holiday Inn* and *Mayagüez Resort* have computers for guests' use.

Colonial c/Iglesia 14 Sur ☎787/833-2150, ⓦwww.hotelcolonial.com. This excellent budget option is a charming pinkish red building built around 1920, and used as a convent for forty years. Its 29 rooms include triples and quads, and all come with a/c, cable TV and bathroom; private parking is available nearby. Breakfast is included and singles get great deals (from $49). ❷

Holiday Inn Mayagüez & Tropical Casino PR-2 km 149.9 ☎787/833-1100, ⓦwww.holidayinn .com/mayaguezpr. Sizeable mini-resort 5km north of downtown, popular with American business travellers and locals attracted by the casino (24hr). Rooms are comfortable and spacious, with cable TV and a/c, while the fitness centre and outdoor pool make pleasant extras. ❹

🏃 Howard Johnson Inn Downtown Mayagüez c/Méndez Vigo 70 Este ☎787/832-9191, ⓦwww.hojo.com. This five-storey building oozes historic charm, with wide balconies that wrap each level and 39 comfortable rooms with cable TV. The stately building was constructed in 1902 by a Catholic order, and survived the 1918 earthquake. Extras include a 24hr self-service laundry, free parking across the street and breakfast at *Ricomini Bakery*. ❹

Mayagüez Resort & Casino PR-104 km 0.3, Barrio Algarrobo ☎787/832-3030, ⓦwww .mayaguezresort.com. Another large resort hotel, just off PR-2, 3km north of the city and set in twenty acres of gardens. In addition to a fabulous river pool, fitness centre and tennis courts, you get breezy sea views and a posh restaurant, *El Castillo*, on site. Rooms are showing their age, however, and are a bit overpriced; guests pay $5.35 per tube slide in the pool, a $9 per day "resort" fee and $4.50 for parking. ❻

Western Bay Mayagüez c/Santiago Riera Palmer 9 Este ☎787/834-0303, ⓦwww.westernbay hotels.com. This old hotel offers a variety of modern rooms from singles to quads (prices go up $10 each size), each with spotless tiled floors, a/c and cable TV. The hotel has a small pool and private parking. ❸

The City

Downtown Mayagüez, centred on **Plaza Colón,** is the oldest and most interesting part of the city to explore. To the north, across the Río Yagüez, lies the sprawling campus of the **Universidad de Puerto Rico**, the **Tropical Research Station** and the **city zoo** (Puerto Rico's best), while 2km west of downtown, at the end of Candelaria and Méndez Vigo, the old, run-down port area (known as **Mayagüez Playa**) is also being slowly revitalized with new shops and businesses, though there's not much to see other than *Brazo Gitano Franco* (see p.191).

Plaza Colón and around

The heart of downtown Mayagüez has been **Plaza Colón** since the foundation of the city in 1760, though the current name and elegant design date from 1896. The area around the plaza remains shabby in places, but life is returning and many of the old buildings have been restored. The **Catedral Nuestra Señora de la Candelaria** (Mon–Sat 6.30am–5pm, Sun services only) dominates the plaza, its majestic twin towers and Neoclassical facade dating from 1922 and the lavish restoration completed in 2004 – the city's first church was constructed of wood on this spot in 1763. The interior is relatively opulent for Puerto Rico, with timbered ceiling, marble floors and an impressive *retablo* depicting scenes from the life of Jesus. Don't miss the statue of Mary to one side, always surrounded by reverent worshippers and known here as **Nuestra Señora de la Candelaria**.

The flamboyant building on the southeast corner of the plaza is the **Antiguo Casino Español**, a blend of Neoclassical, Mudéjar and *modernisme* elements. Constructed in 1874, it was rebuilt after the quake and completed in 1930 by Francisco Porrala Doria, one of the key architects of the post-1918 city. On the western side of the plaza stands the impressive **Casa Alcaldía**, a US-inspired Neoclassical building with a clock tower dating from 1926. The original was constructed in 1845 but, like almost everything else, was destroyed in 1918.

One block west of the plaza on Calle Candelaria is one of the most exuberant buildings on the island, **Teatro Yagüez** (Mon–Fri 8am–noon & 1–4.30pm; free; ☎787/833-5195), the city's main theatre and a playful concoction of Neoclassical pillars and elaborate, multi-patterned Art Nouveau windows and dome. Completed in 1909, it survived the quake only to get tragically (and suspiciously) gutted by fire in 1919. The latest restoration project was completed in 2008.

Museo Casa Grande

Two blocks east of the plaza at c/Méndez Vigo 104 Este, the **Museo Casa Grande** (Mon–Fri 8am–4.30pm; free) was built in 1890 and is a rare survivor of the quake, a pristine example of nineteenth-century "Neoclassical *criollo*" architecture. Built as the private home of Don Guillermo Santos de la Mano, it temporarily hosted the Audiencia de Mayagüez (the judicial court), and is now a museum and cultural centre, retaining much of the original interior – wooden floors, ornate plaster ceilings and odd pieces of period furniture. You'll see paintings of former mayors and various Puerto Rican politicians on the walls (many by respected portrait artist Tulio Ojeda), and a room dedicated to **Oscar Garcia Rivera**, the first Puerto Rican to hold public office in the US – he was born in Mayagüez in 1900 and served in the New York State Assembly 1937–1940. Note that the museum is **closed for renovation** until sometime in 2012.

Tropical Agriculture Research Station

If you've always wondered what cocoa, vanilla, ginger or coffee looks like before ending up in the supermarket, check out the US Department of Agriculture's **Tropical Agriculture Research Station** (Mon–Fri 7am–noon & 1–4pm; free; ☎787/831-3435), a series of beautifully maintained gardens north of downtown. As the staff are likely to emphasize, however, this is not a botanical garden or public park; the 127-acre estate was once part of the Hacienda Carmen, but since 1902 it's been a centre for experimental research, and you must stick to approved paths at all times. On arrival you have to check in at the information centre in the historic main building. A pamphlet details the best route around the grounds, passing 76 tropical trees, shrubs and bushes including sugar palms, cacao, nutmeg, fig, lychee, camphor, teak and breadfruit. The route takes thirty minutes to one hour, and you must sign out before leaving. The research station is next door to the university (but is completely separate from it) at Avda Pedro Albizu Campos 2200 on PR-65. It's a short 1km walk or cab ride from the plaza.

Zoológico de Puerto Rico Dr. Juan A. Rivero

More simply referred to as Mayagüez Zoo, the **Zoológico de Puerto Rico Dr. Juan A. Rivero** (Tues–Sun 8.30am–5pm, also closed Tues in low season; $13, $8 children 5–11, free for under-5s, seniors $6.50; ☎787/834-8110, Ⓦwww.parquesnacionalespr.com) is the only real zoo in Puerto Rico, and has tried hard to get away from cages by constructing "savannah-style" enclosures, protected by moats and walls. Some of its 75 species are native to the island and the Caribbean (including birds such as the red-tailed hawk and wide-eyed owl), and you will also find the usual crowd-pleasers: lions, tigers, leopards, elephants, snakes, rhinos and giraffes. The **Aviario** (aviary) has a high walkway through tropical forest, and features macaws, parrots and flamingos, while the **Mariposario** is an enchanting butterfly house. You'll find the zoo 2km northeast of the city centre, off PR-108, and too far to walk – drive or take a taxi. Parking is an additional $3.

Eating and drinking

The most famous Mayagüez snack and certainly the most addictive is the **brazo gitano** (literally "gypsy arm"), a sweet and slightly crumbly Swiss roll (or jelly roll), loaded with a variety of creamy fruit fillings. You can buy it from several sources in town, as well as roadsides all over the west coast. For cheap eats, try the stalls in and around **Plaza del Mercado**, between calles Pablo Casals and Muñoz Rivera. For **self-catering**, Mr Special Supermarket (Mon–Sat 7am–9pm) is on Calle Balboa at the eastern end of downtown, just across the Río Yagüez.

Brazo Gitano Franco c/Méndez Vigo 276 at Manuel Pirallo ☎787/832-0070, ⓦwww .brazogitano.net. Bakery and cafeteria founded in 1850 by Don Enrique Franco Rey, best known for bringing the *brazo gitano* to Mayagüez from Spain. The shop and small eating area occupy the end of an old brick warehouse; the kitchen doles out all the *criollo* staples for lunch (rice and beans, grilled meats, sandwiches and *frituras*) while the shop sells cakes, cheap coffee ($0.50), and other snacks: the *brazo gitano* comes in 29 flavours ($5.05–8.50). Daily 6.30am–5pm.

Friend's Café Plaza Colón. This simple *kiosco* on the plaza has the best location in town, offering al-fresco snacking and drinking throughout the day. Espressos from $0.79, and bagels, cakes, healthy wraps and sandwiches from $1.25. Free wi-fi. Daily 8am–midnight.

Mia Bistro c/Del Rio Norte 13 ☎787/831-6100. Justly popular restaurant with a simple, cosy dining room and creative menu of European dishes such as champagne risotto ($16), *filet mignon* ($17) and osso bucco ($18), all served with fresh vegetables. They also serve craft beers and ales – rare in Puerto Rico. Mon–Wed 11am–6pm, Thurs & Fri till 10pm, Sat 6–10pm.

Restaurant Vegetariano La Familia c/José de Diego 151 Este ☎787/833-7571. Only real vegetarian restaurant in town and a no-frills place that offers outstanding value: for $6–10 you can stuff yourself with rice, tofu, fresh salads, lasagne, pasta and *empanadas* from the sumptuous daily lunch buffet. Mon–Fri 10.45am–3pm.

Rex Cream c/Méndez Vigo 60 ☎787/265-6250. Established by Chinese immigrants in the mid-1960s, this ice cream chain has two branches in the city (the other one is on c/ Candelaria near the plaza), each knocking out a plethora of refreshing and often imaginative natural flavours ($1.50–1.85/cone): *parcha* (passion fruit), *piña colada*, maize, *guanabana* (soursop), *uva* (grape) and the bitter-tasting *tamarindo*. Daily 9am–midnight.

Ricomini Bakery c/E. Méndez Vigo 101 ☎787/833-1444. Bakery and basic canteen open for over 100 years, selling its trademark *brazo gitano* (large/small $7/$4.50) and *pan de flauta* (fresh bread), in addition to offering breakfast and light meals from $4.75. The *brazos* come in cream, cheese, pineapple, coconut or regular guava jam flavours. Order at the counters first and then grab one of the tables. Daily 5am–1am.

Siglo XX c/Peral 9 Norte ☎787/833-1370. This old-fashioned café was founded in 1973 in another handsome building oozing character, with a wooden upper deck, cosy booths and stools at the bar. You can get all the usual *criollo* dishes for under $10: stews, *chuletas*, *pechuga*, snapper, *mofongo* and vanilla *flan*, as well as filling sandwiches. Mon–Sat 6am–8.30pm.

Bars and clubs

Mayagüez has a somewhat mixed reputation when it comes to **nightlife**, reflecting the fact that much of it depends on its large but restless population of students. It's also true that places tend to go in and out of fashion fast, though there are always plenty of pubs and clubs in the streets between the university and the plaza, especially on Calle Betances (formerly c/Post). Wednesday and Thursday nights tend to be the most animated during term time. Other than grabbing a locally produced Medalla beer, don't leave Mayagüez without sampling the local **sangría**, a snappy cocktail which has an almost cult following in Puerto Rico. The *sangría* is actually a potent blend of fruit juice, Bacardi 151 rum and red wine.

If you just fancy a night on the slots, check out the **casinos** at the two resort hotels north of the city, which also have lively bars and clubs that tend to attract an older local crowd on weekends.

La Biblioteca c/Betances 65 ☎787/832-5248. Casual student beer house, perfect for a mellow drink and a game of pool.

Bleu Bar & Tapas c/Jose de Diego 63 ☎787/831-1446. This popular club has a shiny industrial exterior and a big dancefloor bathed in appropriately azure lights, featuring live Latin sounds and DJs. Tapas ($5–8) are served with cocktails ($6) and beers ($2.50). Cover is $5 on Sat, but the busiest nights are Wed (ladies free) and Thurs (college night; free entry) when Medalla beer is $1. Wed–Sat from 7pm–late.

Chillin c/Betances 59 ☎787/265-1395. Super-hip bar and club, with a variety of specials each night; Medalla beer is just $0.75 on Tuesdays, Coors $1 on Wednesdays, sangría is $2 on Thursdays and DJs spin hip-hop and dance on Fridays. No cover charge. Tues–Fri 5pm–2am, Sat 8pm–2am.

Fido's Sangría Garden c/Dido 78, off PR-106, east of the plaza ☎787/833-4192. This small bar opened in 2009 to sell the acclaimed home-made *sangría* first bottled by Wilfrido Aponte aka Fido in the 1950s (he died in 2006 but his family still makes it). Choose from La Tradicional, Albina (white wine) or Juan 23 (non-alcoholic). Look for the sign on PR-106 beyond the Texaco petrol station on the right (c/ Belisario del Valle), then take the third right. Wed–Sat 11am–midnight, Sun 9am–6pm.

El Garabato c/Betances 102 ☎787/834-2524. If you just want a few beers, this is the most dependable choice in downtown and one of the few bars open all afternoon most days, marked by the unmistakeable grin of the yellow face outside. Beyond the wooden doors and shutters it has a laidback, sports bar feel, with TVs and plenty of older regulars mingling with student drinkers. Beers are $2. Closed Sun.

Stoa's c/Méndez Vigo 70 Este ☎787/832-9191. Café and wine bar in the lobby of the *Howard Johnson*, serving $6 wraps and pasta plates, and $5 pizzas to wash down the drinks. Huge wine list. Closed Mon & Sun.

Listings

Banks Banco Popular has a branch with an ATM on the plaza (c/Candelaria 53 Este; Mon–Fri 7.30am–5pm, Sat 8.30–11.30am), with its main branch at c/Méndez Vigo 15 (Mon–Fri 7.30am–6pm, Sat 8.30am–12.30pm).

Car rental Avis is at Sears at the Mayagüez Mall, 975 Avda Hostos (Mon–Sat 9am–1pm & 1.30–9pm, Sun 11am–5pm; ☎787/805-5911).

Cinema Try Caribbean Cinemas Western Plaza on PR-2 (☎787/833-0315, ⊛www.caribbean cinemas.com).

Consulate Dominican Republic, c/Candelaria 30, 2/F, ☎809/833-0007.

Hospital The main city hospital is Hospital Dr. Ramón Emeterio Betances with a 24hr emergency room and various day clinics, PR-2, Barrio Sabalos,

---

Moving on from Mayagüez

Cape Air (☎1-800/352-0714) operates several daily **flights** between Mayagüez and the international airport in **San Juan** ($79): you can buy tickets at Mayagüez airport, one hour before departure, though planes are small so it's best to reserve in advance.

American Cruise Ferries (☎787/832-4800 or 787/622-4800, ⊛www.acferries.com) runs two **ferries** a week (Wed & Fri 8pm) to Santo Domingo in the **Dominican Republic** from **Puerto de Mayagüez**, the port area north of the city ($7 by taxi). Voyages on the luxurious *Caribbean Fantasy* take 12 hours and tickets start at $169. Note you'll also have to pay $10 for the Dominican **Tarjeta de Turista**.

The **Terminal de Vehículos Públicos** is at the bottom of Calle Peral, a short walk north of the plaza, but as elsewhere on the island, long-distance services are becoming hard to find these days. The exception for now is Línea Sultana (☎787/832-1041), which operates a regular hourly service to **San Juan** (Río Piedras) for $15 (daily 7.30am–5pm). Taxi-type *públicos* charge $15 to Rincón, but are erratic. You can usually pick up a ride to **Añasco** ($10) and **Aguadilla** ($20), but aim to get to the terminal as early as possible, and definitely before 2pm.

Driving, the main route out of the city is PR-2, which can get gridlocked during rush hour. Ponce is 74km, Guánica 46km and Cabo Rojo (town) 14km. To the north it's 13km to Añasco, 27km to Aguadilla and 24km to Rincón. Mayagüez is the western terminus of the **Ruta Panorámica**; it's a winding 28km to the first major stop, Maricao (take PR-105 out of the city).

☎787/834-8690. In town, Hospital Perea (☎787/834-0101, 🌐www.hospitalperea.com) at c/ Basora 15 is more convenient.

Internet access You should have access to free wi-fi anywhere around the main plaza. Stationary store Oficentro Express at c/Candelaria 5 (between Basora and Betances) has a small internet café at the back (Mon–Fri 8am–5pm, Sat 9am–5pm; $4/ hr; ☎787/834-4688).

Laundry Try Radio Central Laundromat (Tues–Fri 10am–8pm, Sat & Sun 9am–6pm; ☎787/597-1540) on c/Del Bosque, just off c/Betances. It usually charges just $2 per load (drop-off). Further

out is Laundry Puerto Rico, c/Méndez Vigo 166, near PR-2) (☎787/832-4012), open Mon–Sat 8am–5pm.

Pharmacies Walgreens (24hr; ☎787/805-4805) is located on PR-2 (Avda Hostos 2097), north of the city (and at the Mayagüez Mall); in the centre try Farmacia Luciano (opposite the *Howard Johnson*), open Mon–Fri 8am–7pm & Sat till 5pm; or Farmacia De Diego (Mon–Fri 8am–6.30pm, Sat till 6pm; ☎787/832-1874) at c/Betances 17.

Police ☎787/831-2020.

Post office The main branch is at c/Candelaria Oeste 60 (Mon–Fri 7am–5pm, Sat 7.30am–1pm).

Cabo Rojo and around

Puerto Rico's rustic southwest corner is entirely taken up by the municipality of **Cabo Rojo**, a region of mellow seaside resorts, sprawling marshland and a coastline smothered in tangled mangroves. While El Yunque gets slammed with the full tropical force of the trade winds, Cabo Rojo is protected by the Central Cordillera and sees relatively little rain, making the area a prime target for sun-hungry tourists. The city of Cabo Rojo, known locally as *el pueblo*, boasts a few low-key historic attractions, but don't confuse this with the actual **cape** (the name means "Red Cape") further south, where crusty saltpans provide a startling contrast to the warmer tropical landscapes of the north.

The City

The languid centre of **CABO ROJO** retains a time-warped air despite encroaching modernization, its important monuments, clapboard houses and quaint if rambling examples of *criollo* architecture squashed among ugly modern development.

The eye-catching central square, **Plaza de Recreo Ramón Emeterio Betances**, is named after Ramón Emeterio Betances, the revered abolitionist, doctor and independence activist who was born here in 1827. Betances died in exile in France in 1898, but his ashes were taken back to Puerto Rico in 1920 and buried in the Cabo Rojo cemetery; two years later his remains were placed inside the **Monumento Ramón Emeterio Betances** on the plaza, topped with a bust of the great man by Italian sculptor Diego Montano, and backed by the Grito de Lares revolutionary flag (see p.265). Nearby is a striking steel sculpture of a broken chain by Alberto Fernandez Zequeira, commemorating the abolition of slavery in 1873.

The plaza is dominated by the pale yellow **Iglesia Católica San Miguel Arcángel** (Mon–Fri 8am–11.30am & 2.30–4.30pm), originally completed in 1783 but constantly added to and rebuilt since then. It retains its basic Spanish Colonial structure, and despite its relatively large size often overflows during Mass. Elsewhere on the plaza you'll see the **Monumento Salvador Brau**, a white marble statue of poet, historian and Cabo Rojo native Salvador Brau (1842–1912), backed by a soaring Art Deco pillar. The needle-like **Obelisco** in the southeast corner is a memorial to the 128 families (led by Arellano) who founded the town.

Just outside the centre, the **Museo de Los Próceres** (Mon–Sat 8am–4.30pm; free) is a grand memorial to famous locals (known as *Caborrojeños*), a bit overblown considering the modest nature of the displays inside, though every- thing is well presented and you can pick up useful information on the area here – it doubles as the headquarters of the local **culture and tourism department**

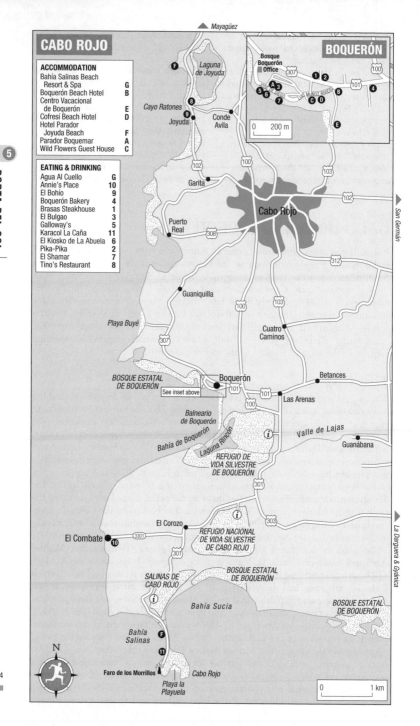

CABO ROJO

BOQUERÓN

ACCOMMODATION

Bahía Salinas Beach Resort & Spa	G
Boquerón Beach Hotel	B
Centro Vacacional de Boquerón	E
Cofresí Beach Hotel	D
Hotel Parador Joyuda Beach	F
Parador Boquemar	A
Wild Flowers Guest House	C

EATING & DRINKING

Agua Al Cuello	G
Annie's Place	10
El Bohío	9
Boquerón Bakery	4
Brasas Steakhouse	1
El Bulgao	3
Galloway's	5
Karacol La Caña	11
El Kiosko de La Abuela	6
Pika-Pika	2
El Shamar	7
Tino's Restaurant	8

Mayagüez

Laguna de Joyuda

Bosque Boquerón Office

Cayo Ratones

Joyuda

Conde Avila

Garita

Cabo Rojo

Puerto Real

Guaniquilla

Playa Buyé

Cuatro Caminos

BOSQUE ESTATAL DE BOQUERÓN

Boquerón

See inset above

Betances

Balneario de Boquerón

Bahía de Boquerón

Las Arenas

Valle de Lajas

Guanábana

Laguna Rincón

REFUGIO DE VIDA SILVESTRE DE BOQUERÓN

El Corozo

El Combate

REFUGIO NACIONAL DE VIDA SILVESTRE DE CABO ROJO

SALINAS DE CABO ROJO

BOSQUE ESTATAL DE BOQUERÓN

Bahía Sucia

BOSQUE ESTATAL DE BOQUERÓN

Bahía Salinas

Faro de los Morrillos

Cabo Rojo

Playa la Playuela

San Germán

La Darguera & G'ánica

N

0   1 km

(☎787/255-1560, ⓦwww.ciudadcaborojo.net). The building stands in parkland at PR-312 km 0.4, just south of the centre, with plenty of parking, and you can usually access the internet inside.

Practicalities

The city is best visited as a day-trip from Mayagüez or one of the nearby coastal resorts; try to park where you can in the centre, or aim for the ugly **multistorey** east of the plaza, on Calle Salvador Mestre between Betances and Baldorioty. Cabo Rojo's *público* terminal is a short walk from the plaza at the southern end of Calle Salvador Brau (PR-103). You can pick up taxi-type *públicos* from here to Puerto Real ($1.25) or Boquerón ($1.45) – Boquerón beach is five cents extra. Banco Santander has a 24-hour ATM on the main plaza.

Eating options are unexciting in Cabo Rojo, but the 🍴 *Kiosko Dulces Tipicos de Cabo Rojo* (Mon–Sat 8am–12.30am, Sun 4–10pm; ☎787/462-8797) in the central plaza serves up rich coffee and light snacks, while *Salvatore Bar & Tapas* on the south side of the square at c/Ruiz Belvis 25B is a welcoming Spanish/Venezuelan-style tapas bar (tapas $6–12; Thurs 7pm–2am; Fri & Sat till 3am; ☎787/638-5459) if you are here in the evening.

Playa de Joyuda and Cayo Ratones

One of several proudly traditional Puerto Rican seaside resorts on the southwest coast, **PLAYA DE JOYUDA** isn't really a beach but a string of seafood restaurants, fishing shacks and faded hotels. Running for 2km along PR-102 south of Mayagüez, between a ragged shore of bleached coral and the mangrove-fringed nature reserve of Laguna Joyuda, it's as unattractive as it sounds (most of the coral is dead and erosion has whittled away the seafront), but while its sobriquet of *Milla de Oro del Buen Comer* ("golden mile of good food") is a little exaggerated, some of the **seafood** restaurants are genuinely excellent value and the tiny islet of **Cayo Ratones** just offshore makes an appealing target for a lazy afternoon. The island is completely undeveloped and is actually part of the **Bosque Estatal de Boquerón** (see p.197), a protected nature reserve, with silky white sands and excellent snorkelling. You have to hire a boat to take you across: contact **Adventures Tourmarine** (☎787/255-2525, ⓦwww.tourmarinepr.com) at the small dock between the *Vista al Mar* and *Vista Bahía* restaurants, at PR-102 km 14.1. Captain Elick Hernández García ferries passengers to Cayo Ratones ($5, minimum four people). He also does fishing charters and diving/snorkelling day-trips to **Isla Desecheo** (see p.184) for $75 (minimum ten people) and **Isla de Mona** (see p.196).

Accommodation

There are plenty of **hotels** in Playa de Joyuda, but although you can get basic doubles for $75 to $100, none are a particularly good deal and you're better off staying elsewhere. If you do end up here, the best of the bunch is *Hotel Parador Joyuda Beach*, PR-102 km 11.7 (☎787/851-5650, ⓦwww.joyudabeach.com; ❸), at the more secluded north end of the strip, with simple but large and clean motel-style cabins, stretching back from a seafront of palms and a healthier reef just offshore. Rooms come with the usual cable TV and air conditioning, and plenty of parking, but it gets packed on weekends.

Eating

All the eating action takes place on PR-102, with the best **restaurants** jutting out over the rocky fringe for incredible sunsets and views of Cayo Ratones. The two top choices are *El Bohío* at PR-102 km 13.9 (☎787/851-2755), a wooden stilt house hanging right over the water, and venerable *Tino's Restaurant* at PR-102 km

Island adventure

One of the last true adventure destinations in the Caribbean, the **ISLA DE MONA** is a blessedly isolated nature reserve 72km off the west coast of Puerto Rico, and just 61km from the Dominican Republic. Staying on the island requires advance planning, though it's much easier to arrange day-trips to dive or snorkel off its deep, unbelievably clear waters and richly stocked barrier reef. It's worth the effort: although it's not quite the "Galapagos" made out in the tourist literature, it does offer the chance for a real wilderness, back-to-nature experience.

The island is roughly 11km long and 6.5km wide, and other than occasional groups of illegal immigrants from Cuba, completely uninhabited, though you can still see evidence of **Taíno** and early Spanish settlement. The island is essentially a raised plateau surrounded by 40m sea cliffs, with an extensive cave system and 8km of absolutely stunning pearly white beaches lining its southern shore. Other than enjoying the caves and these (usually) utterly deserted strips of sand, Mona's chief attraction is its wildlife. The Galapagos comparison was spurred chiefly by the **giant rock iguanas** that lounge on the shore, and can grow up to 1.5m long. There are also wild pigs, goats and cattle, left by Spanish colonists, and pods of humpback whales offshore in winter. Between May and October turtles nest on the beaches and there are over 100 species of bird zipping around the island, including hawks, red-footed boobies and pelicans. The DRNA maintains a basic ranger station, toilets and showers at Playa Sardinera on the west side of Mona, but otherwise you're on your own – you must bring a tent and all your food and drink.

Practicalities

To visit, you must obtain a **permit** from the DRNA (see p.26), usually good for up to three days. Camping is $5 per night and you need to apply at least 45 days in advance. In practice, the company taking you to the island should arrange this, and if you are just coming to dive or snorkel offshore, no permit is required – the trip takes about four to five hours by boat. Note, however, that most operators will be reluctant to take fewer than five people, so you may have to be flexible with dates (or cough up a hefty supplement).

Acampa (☏787/706-0695, ⊛www.acampapr.com) arranges all-inclusive packages from San Juan (four nights, three days, April–July only) for a around $1000 per person, but this does include all food, transport, tents, equipment and guided tours of trails and caves – you might be able to negotiate a cheaper price depending on the size of your group. You could also check with **COPLADET** (☏787/765-8595, ⊛www.copladet.com), which occasionally arranges tours to the island with an eco-friendly and educational angle. Other outfits arranging trips includes Adventures Tourmarine in Playa de Joyuda (see p.195), and Oceans Unlimited at the *Rincón Beach Resort* (see p.180).

13.6 (☏787/851-2976). Menus offer the usual range of seafood, plus steaks and tasty *criollo* sides such as yucca and *mofongo* ($15–17). Usually open Wed–Mon 11am–8.30pm.

Playa Buyé

One of the most alluring beaches in the southwest, **PLAYA BUYÉ** has a natural, unspoiled feel quite unlike anything else in the region. Though it can get crammed with families at weekends and the narrow strip of sand is backed by condos, development's low-key, the sea is a deep azure blue and bushy portia trees with bony limbs reach almost as far as the water, providing plenty of shade. You can **park** (summer $3) at the end of the potholed road to the beach, signposted at km 4.8 on PR-307, south of Cabo Rojo, and a small shop sells basic supplies and snacks.

Boquerón

The ramshackle fishing village of **BOQUERÓN**, with its jumble of clapboard houses and slightly shabby seafront, is a magnet for Puerto Rican tourists on weekends, who pile in to soak up the carnival atmosphere and fresh seafood. Apart from the food – particularly the **fresh shellfish**, sold raw from stalls on the main road through town – the real draw is the **Balneario de Boquerón** (facilities and parking summer daily 8.30am–8pm; low season Wed–Sun same hours; $4.28 with tax). One of the best beaches on the island, this 5km horseshoe-shaped curve of velvety white sand is backed by a thick crust of palm trees. You can park here or stroll along the coast from the main village. Other distractions include two **nature reserves** nearby and, in the summer (usually June), Boquerón's very own **gay pride parade**, which has regularly attracted over five thousand revellers since it began in 2003.

Central Boquerón is a compact area of shops, restaurants and hotels lining the bay and wharf area along PR-101, 6.5km south of Cabo Rojo – PR-101 makes a loop from PR-100 and rejoins PR-307 heading north to Playa Buyé. The **beach** is at the end of a wide road off PR-101, just before entering the main part of the village. Note that PR-101 is **closed** to traffic Friday to Sunday nights. The nearest **bank** is Banco Popular at Plaza Boquerón, PR-101 km 17.4, a ten-minute drive east of the village, but there's an ATM inside the *Boquerón Beach Hotel*.

Accommodation

Boquerón is overflowing with **hotels** and guesthouses, though it's best to call ahead on weekends and in summer. Note that anywhere on the central stretch of PR-101 (Calle José de Diego) will be **noisy** at weekends – in fact the whole village is best avoided at these times if you want peace and quiet, and weekday rates tend to be far cheaper. If your hotel doesn't have **laundry** facilities, try the public Laundromat (daily 7am–7pm) at the west end of the village, which has coin-operated machines ($1.50).

Boquerón Beach Hotel PR-101 km 3.3 ☎787/851-7110, ⊛www.westernbayhotels.com. Modern and characterless behemoth on the corner of PR-101 and the road to the beach, but worth considering for its proximity to the latter and its relatively cheap rates. Rooms are neat and tidy, with red-tiled floors and bright bedspreads, all equipped with fridge, clean bathrooms and TV. ❷

Centro Vacacional de Boquerón Balneario de Boquerón ☎787/851-1940. Despite the holiday-camp feel it's worth considering this government-run resort – it's the only place where you can literally stay right on the beach. Avoid weekends and summer holidays, though, when the place is overrun with families. Each basic cinderblock *cabaña* (❸) sleeps six (two bedrooms) and has a kitchenette and bathroom, but bring your own cooking utensils and sheets (or rent the latter from the centre) – it's all very sparse and a bit rough, but it's cheap and the proximity to sand and sunsets is priceless. Villas are slightly more comfortable (❹).

Cofresí Beach Hotel c/Muñoz Rivera 57 ☎787/254-3000, ⊛www.cofresibeach.com. Smart place with Art Deco facade on the main road into the village, containing a series of compact one-, two- and three-bedroom apartments, all with kitchens, tables and living rooms. The furnishings are standard mid-range fare, but clean and comfortable, and good value if you're looking for a self-sufficient base. ❺

Parador Boquemar c/Gill Buyé, just off PR-101 ☎787/851-2158, ⊛boquemar.com. Another nondescript, modern three-storey hotel, convenient for the bars and restaurants but noisy on weekends; rooms are a bit cramped, and it's worth paying $10–20 more for the top floor with views and balconies. The staff are adept at arranging activities such as kayak and snorkelling trips, *La Cascada* (daily 7.30am–noon & 5–8pm, closed Wed afternoon) is the only *mesón gastronómico* in town and it's relatively cheap considering the location. ❹

Wild Flowers Guest House c/Muñoz Rivera 13 ☎787/851-1793, ⊛www.wildflowersguesthouse.com. Two-storey renovated wooden house on the road into the village, far more appealing than most of the hotels, with just eight small but cosy rooms all with cable TV, fridge, a/c and attractive antique-style beds – ask for the rooms with outdoor seating and balconies overlooking the village ($25 extra), and check out the original artwork scattered throughout the hotel. ❹

Eating and drinking

After a trip to the beach, **eating** is perhaps Boquerón's most appealing activity, and despite appearances, hygiene standards are generally good. One of the best **kioscos** is *Happy Oyster*, usually found near the main pier: a dozen oysters or clams are sold raw, with a dash of lemon, for $4.50. It's open Friday to Sunday from around 11am till late, and occasionally on weekdays. Further along the main street you'll find more *kioscos* selling similar fare, along with *pulpo* (octopus), *carrucho* (conch) and *camarones* (prawns). *El Kiosko de La Abuela* sells tempting *pinchos de dorado y marlin* (*mahi-mahi* and marlin kebabs) for under $5.

Most **restaurants** double as bars, and come into their own on weekends when the village is usually crammed with revellers. Note it's illegal to drink from bottles or glasses in the street, but plastic cups or cans are OK.

Boquerón Bakery PR-101 km 18.3 ⓣ787/851-6003. Local favourite for an early breakfast, fresh bread and cakes on the edge of the village, but also conjures up extra-cheap burgers, hot dogs and Puerto Rican dishes for $2–3. Daily 7am–6pm.

Brasas Steakhouse c/Estacion 147, PR-307 ⓣ787/255-1000. Inviting restaurant located behind the seafront specializing in steaks and pasta. *Churrasco* steak is the main event here, but they also do pastas and local dishes (mains $13–25). Wed & Thurs 5–10pm, Fri till 11pm, Sat 3–11pm, Sun 1–10pm.

El Bulgao c/José de Diego 35 ⓣ787/547-5020. This shack is the self-proclaimed *casa de Viagra natural* for its libido-boosting *bulgao* (a conch-like shellfish also known as the West Indian Top-shell), as well as *pulpo* dishes (from $8) salads ($16) and lobster from $9; their whiskey and vodka cocktails mixed with *agua de coco* and *piña coladas* from $8 are more likely to leave you flat on the floor. Usually open weekends only.

Galloway's c/José de Diego 12 ⓣ787/254-3302, ⓦwww.gallowaysrestaurant.com. This wooden shack right on the water has an enticing open-air veranda and plenty of parking. Nominally an Irish pub (though US licence plates plaster the ceiling), the mix of *criollo* staples and comfort food isn't bad (mains $12–18): choose the sauce for your fresh *dorado*, snapper and prawns (creole, *fra diabla*, garlic butter or spicy creole). The main reason to visit is to enjoy the sunset over a cold beer or rum punch. Mon, Tues, Thurs & Sun 2pm–midnight; Fri & Sat noon–1am.

Pika-Pika c/Estacion 224, PR-307 ⓣ787/851-2440. Best bet for high-quality Tex-Mex food, with all the usual *burritos*, tacos and *fajitas* in a surprisingly refined dining room, though it's well behind the seafront. Mon 4–10pm, Wed & Thurs noon–10pm, Fri & Sat till 10.30pm, Sun till 9pm.

El Shamar c/José de Diego 1. Large, popular bar with pool tables, that erupts with people, salsa and *merengue* at the weekends, thanks in part to the cheap Medalla happy hours ($1) and friendly vibe. Also serves superb snack food: tacos, pizzas and plump *empanadillas* stuffed with juicy fillings – try the lobster or shrimp ($3–5). Daily 11am–midnight.

Refugio Nacional de Vida Silvestre de Cabo Rojo

Much of the actual cape area, south of Boquerón on PR-301, is a rolling landscape of empty grassland and dry scrub, once the domain of cattle farms and denuded of much of its native vegetation by years of overgrazing. Today it falls within the **REFUGIO NACIONAL DE VIDA SILVESTRE DE CABO ROJO**, managed by the US Fish and Wildlife Service, but given the rather drab terrain, principally of interest to **birdwatchers** – species such as the Puerto Rican tody, Adelaide's warbler and troupial thrive here.

The visitor centre, (Mon–Fri 7.30am–4pm; ⓣ787/851-7258), signposted off PR-301 at km 5.1, lies at the heart of the original section of the refuge, established in 1974 and once used as a CIA "listening" unit. The centre provides information about the ongoing work of the refuge, particularly the attempt to return the land to its original mature hardwood forest, and the twelve-mile network of trails that fans out across the plain: the two-mile interpretive trail provides a taster of the local ecosystem.

Centro Interpretativo de Las Salinas de Cabo Rojo

Scorched mercilessly by the sun, the final section of the cape is a haunting moonscape of gleaming *salinas* – arid **salt flats** – a bizarre contrast to the tropical flora so familiar on the rest of the island. Considered the most important stopover for migratory and **shore birds** in the eastern Caribbean, the pinkish waters and heaps of rock salt blur into the Bahía Sucia on the eastern side of the road, an inhospitable environment more typical of Utah or Arizona. Salt is still produced here, though in much reduced quantities, and in 1999 an additional 5 square kilometres were added to the Cabo Rojo wildlife refuge (see opposite), made accessible by the **Centro Interpretativo de Las Salinas de Cabo Rojo** (Thurs–Sat 8.30am–4.30pm, Sun 9.30am–5.30pm; free; ☎787/851-2999) at PR-301 km 11. Exhibits describe the ecology, history and geology of the area, including the rich **bird life** of the reserve: a nesting ground for snowy plovers, terns, brown pelicans and others, with 118 species recorded here in all. Outside, there is an interpretive trail, while the 12m-high **Torre de Observación**, a five-storey wooden tower, provides a bird's-eye view of the saltpans and actual cape beyond.

Faro de Los Morrillos de Cabo Rojo

Cape Rojo itself is a narrow promontory of scrubby heathland and brackish salt flats, crisscrossed with trails and crowned by the **FARO DE LOS MORRILLOS DE CABO ROJO**, an elegant Spanish lighthouse completed in 1882. The *faro* stands on jagged limestone cliffs with the pinkish hue that inspired the cape's name, 60m above the choppy waters below. PR-301 ends after 2km of bone-jarring unsealed road at a car park, from where it's a short walk to the lighthouse at the top of the headland. The lighthouse is still working and is closed to visitors, but you can wander around the grounds and drink in the blustery, dramatic views of the coastline.

Just east of the lighthouse, **Playa La Playuela** (sometimes referred to, incorrectly, as Playa Sucia) is one of the most scenic beaches on the island. Nestled between sheer cliffs, the short arc of floury sand is incredibly popular on weekends and in the summer, easy to reach from the lighthouse car park by following the dirt road that leads east – you can park behind the beach.

Practicalities

The 🕈 *Bahía Salinas Beach Resort & Spa* (☎787/254-1213, ⓦ www.bahiasalinas .com; ❺) is a real gem of a **hotel** and the best place to stay in this otherworldly end of the island. It faces Bahía Salinas, on PR-301 at km 11.5, just as it becomes a gravel track, and though you can't really swim here (the bay is too shallow and lined with mangroves), the narrow strip of sand is pretty and the sunsets magnificent.

The resort's swanky restaurant *Agua Al Cuello* is a lauded *mesón gastronómico* and the best place to eat in the region, serving contemporary Puerto Rican food with flair on a cosy wooden waterside terrace with rattan tables and chairs.

Alternatively, cheap *comida criolla* can be found at *Karacol La Caña* (Sat & Sun 10am–6pm), one of a series of *kioscos* down the road knocking out seafood *empanadillas*, *tostones gigantes*, *caldo de pescado* (fish broth), and the more creative *vasos de pulpo de mollejas* (octopus sweetbread in a glass).

El Combate

Though it does possess a sort of down-at-heel charm, the resort village of **EL COMBATE**, at the end of PR-3301, is scruffy and run-down, gets packed out with families in the summer, and its modern, unattractive buildings have little of the rustic appeal of Boquerón and La Parguera (see p.204). On calmer days, however, the long, palm-fringed **beach** that runs for several kilometres south of the village isn't bad, and the choice of cheap **restaurants** makes it a dependable choice for a budget lunch. Starting at the main beach car park, the **Cabo Rojo Refuge Bike Trail** leads south 8km through all the main sectors of the *refugio* (see p.198), though you'll have to come back the same way (enquire at the refuge visitor centre or *Bahía Salinas Beach Resort* for rentals).

For **food**, *Annie's Place* (daily 11am–midnight) is a solid bet, the first spot on the seafront as you drive into the village, serving a basic menu of *comida criolla* and morphing into a popular bar in the evenings.

San Germán

Steeped in colonial history, **SAN GERMÁN** boasts a ravishing centre of narrow streets and ornate mansions adorned with stained glass and elaborate stucco. It's certainly the most beautiful provincial town in Puerto Rico, equally as precious as Old San Juan, but with a fraction of the visitors. Chief among its rare collection of graceful homes, churches and museums is the **Museo Porta Coeli**, one of the oldest places of worship on the island and now an absorbing museum of religious art.

Some history

San Germán has an odd and rather confusing history, compounded by a lack of historical records and, as always, the intense competition among Puerto Rican municipalities for historic precedence. Villa Sotomayor, built in 1510 and destroyed a year later, is often considered the first incarnation of San Germán (at least by *Sangermeños*) – its successor, built in 1512, was actually named San Germán, but located in Aguada or Añasco, depending on whom you believe. After trying several different locations, it was the descendants of this town, consistently battered and pillaged by pirates and Taíno, who eventually abandoned the defenceless coastal plains and founded the current city kilometres inland between 1570 and 1573 (though a community had been growing here on the Santa Marta hills since the 1540s). At first it was called **Nueva Villa de Salamanca**, after the city in Spain, but nostalgic citizens insisted on calling it **San Germán el Nuevo**. Consequently, San

Germán, Aguada and Añasco all claim to be Puerto Rico's "second oldest city". The new San Germán flourished, and was the administrative centre for the western half of the island until 1692, with a greater population than San Juan until well into the 1700s. In 1856 the city was devastated by a **cholera epidemic** in which 2843 people died, and it gradually became more of a backwater.

Arrival, information and accommodation

Drive straight into the centre of town on PR-102 (Calle Luna) and pay for parking via meters on the street ($0.25/for/30min), or at the Estacionamento Municipal (first hr free; $0.75 second hr) next to the old Mercado. **Públicos** pull in at the terminal at the end of Calle Luna near PR-122, though as always, long-distance services are unusual: Línea Sangermeña (℡787/722-3392) makes runs on demand to Cabo Rojo, Mayagüez, Ponce and San Juan.

The only **hotel** in town is the faded *Parador El Oasis* at Calle Luna 72 (℡787/892-1175; ❸), which nevertheless retains plenty of colonial charm with old brickwork and a 400-year-old lobby area. Rooms are reasonably good value, with air conditioning, cable TV and tiled bathrooms, though the furnishings are getting very worn around the edges – check the rooms carefully before paying. The wooden cabins on the third floor are the cheapest rooms, but these are a bit smaller. The hotel comes with free parking, the mediocre *Oasis Restaurant* and a small pool. Outside town, the modern *Villa del Rey* (℡787/642-2627, ⓦwww.villadelrey .net; ❹) at PR-361 km 0.8, just north of PR-2, is a brighter, more comfortable option, though not as convenient.

The Antigua Casa Alcaldía on the main square contains the town's **tourist office** (Mon–Fri 8am–noon & 1–4pm; ℡787/892-3790), which can supply basic information and updates on current events. The **post office** (Mon–Fri 7am–4.55pm, Sat 8am–4.30pm) is opposite the *público* terminal, while there's **free internet** access at the **Biblioteca Pública** (June & July Mon–Fri 8am–5pm, Sat till 1pm & 2–4.30pm, Aug–May Mon–Thurs 8am–8.30pm, Fri till 6pm, Sat till 1pm & 2–4.30pm; ℡787/892-6820), the modern library at c/Acosta 11 on Plaza Quiñones.

The Town

The centre of San Germán is compact enough to explore on foot, and strolling its handsome streets is the best way to soak up the impressive architecture on show, a blend of local clapboard houses, various Neoclassical styles and plenty of flamboyant Art Nouveau and *modernisme* touches. The austere atmosphere is exaggerated by the lack of people: like many provincial Puerto Rican towns, traditional street life has been sucked out by malls and suburban development, and other than a steady flow of customers to the incongruously located Walgreens on Calle Luna, at times it can seem a bit of a ghost town. Start at Museo Porta Coeli, on the eastern edge of town, San Germán's oldest and most iconic building.

Museo Porta Coeli and around

Rare example of the humble Spanish Mission style employed by the island's early colonists, the **Museo Porta Coeli** (Wed–Sun 8.30am–noon & 1–4.20pm; $3) was Puerto Rico's oldest church outside San Juan. Once part of a larger Dominican convent, it was originally known as the Capilla de Santo Domingo de Porta Coeli and today houses religious art work and statuary from around the region.

The church was established in 1606, but what you see today dates from the 1690s. By 1874 the convent was so ruinous it was demolished. The chapel limped on until 1949, when the crippling costs of continued renovation led the Church to hand it over to the government. It reopened as a museum in 1961 and sits graciously above the plaza on steps of aged red bricks, its *ausubo* hardwood doors and weathered palm-wood pillars and beams making an atmospheric backdrop to the engaging collection inside. Highlights include a beautiful eighteenth-century wooden *retablo* (altarpiece), moved here from the cathedral and depicting the five patron saints of the city: Nuestra Señora del Perpetuo Socorro, San Germán, San Patricio, San Vicente Ferrer and Santa Rosa de Lima. Similarly impressive are the *Estaciones del Via Crucis*, nineteenth-century carvings of the Stations of the Cross, and a more simplistic image of the *Virgen de la Leche* painted in 1864. You'll also find a small exhibition about the foundation of the church and the Dominican order, while outside in the terrace garden are the meagre ruins of the convent.

Behind the church at c/Dr Santiago Veve 70, on the corner of Javilla, the **Casa Jaime Acosta y Florés** is a gorgeous example of late *criollo* architecture dating from 1917, a bright yellow clapboard house with veranda and ornate balustrade. Like most of the houses here, it remains a private home and can only be viewed from the outside (unless you eat at the *A2* restaurant, see opposite).

Walk back towards the church along Santiago Veve and you'll see **Casa de los Kindy** at no. 64 on the left, built to impress in the early twentieth century, with a marble staircase, grand Neoclassical facade of Doric columns and colourful *modernisme*-inspired glass in the windows. Before carrying on, nip down Calle Yamil Galib Frangie to peek at **Casa Juan Ortiz Periche** at c/Luna 94, constructed in 1920 in bombastic Palladian style, with a red and white entrance portico and staircase, the upper storey topped with a tin roof, and more delicate stained glass in the doors.

Plazuela de Santo Domingo

The long and slender plaza that slopes gently uphill from Porta Coeli is the **Plazuela de Santo Domingo**, one of San Germán's two central squares. Originally a marketplace, the plaza is paved with cobblestones, its central brick-lined walkway (Paseo de Los Proceres) bordered with cast-iron benches and busts of illustrious *Sangermeños*. Immediately opposite the steps below Porta Coeli is **Casa Morales**, San Germán's most photogenic house. Designed in an extravagant, gingerbread style, with turrets, pointed roof and delicate pillars, it was built in 1913 for the family of Don Tomás Vivoni and has been owned by Morales Lugo and his descendants since 1945. Note the multicoloured glass in the windows, providing a pearly, shell-like effect.

Plaza Francisco Mariano Quiñones

One block west of Plazuela de Santo Domingo is the town's principal square, **Plaza Francisco Mariano Quiñones**, a more traditional space with a few trees and lined with terraces of clapboard housing. The **Antigua Casa Alcaldía** (old town hall) on the eastern side was built in 1844 and modified over the years, an impressively stately Spanish Colonial building that still houses government departments (including the tourist office). The main feature of the plaza is the grandiose **Iglesia Católica San Germán de Auxerre**, which looms regally over the western end of the square. The original was completed in 1573, with many subsequent enlargements, notably in 1842 when the current structure took shape, blending Spanish Baroque and Colonial styles, a gleaming façade and decorative bell tower. Check out the stucco *trompe l'oeil* ceiling, restored in 1993 and mimicking wood beams, and the Carrara marble *retablo*, with a benevolent image of San Germán carved above it. The church is normally locked up and only opens for Mass (Mon–Sat 7am & 7.30pm, Sun 7am, 8.30am, 10am & 7.30pm), but you can try the parish office nearby on Acosta (Mon–Fri 8–11.30am & 1–3pm, Sat till 11pm; ☏787/892-1027) to see if someone will let you in at other times.

Back on the plaza, on the corner of Calle de La Cruz, **La Casona** was completed in 1871 as a luxurious home for Tomás Agrait, and for many years was the meeting place of local cultural foundation Círculo de Recreo, formed in 1880 and still going strong. It now houses *L'Auxerre* restaurant (see below).

Calle de La Cruz

South of the plaza **Calle de La Cruz** is lined with more venerable structures, notably the **Antigua Caja de Economías**, the old Banco San Germán building from 1880. Opposite is the captivating if slightly faded **Farmacia Domínguez**, originally a pharmacy founded in 1877, with walls of peeling pink stucco and heavy timber doors – the town hopes to restore it as a Museo de La Farmacia (pending fundraising). Heading south, you'll pass the **Logia Masónica** on Calle Luna, a typically Greek Revival Masonic lodge, now a small church on the lower floor but with the Masons' symbol still visible above. **Casa Cruz de La Luna** (Tues & Thurs 2–6pm) on the other side of the road (c/Luna 67) is a theatrical library and art space, with irregular events held on weekend evenings (check Ⓦwww .casacruzdelaluna.com or call ☎787/264-4402).

Museo de Arte y Casa de Estudio

The lavish French-influenced villa housing the **Museo de Arte y Casa de Estudio** (Wed–Sun 10am–noon & 1–3pm; free) was built in 1903. The museum displays the work of local artists and various aspects of the town's history – like many on the island, it has a small collection of Taíno artefacts, period furniture and assorted bric-a-brac from the Spanish period, including old documents, photos and religious items. The museum is a short walk west along Calle Luna from Calle de La Cruz, then south on Calle Esperanza to no. 7.

Eating and drinking

San Germán has a rather unfair reputation as being a poor place to **eat** and completely dead at night, but there are some exceptional restaurants in the centre and things are more animated on weekends. Businesses do seem to close with alarming frequency however, so call ahead to make sure.

A2 Tiempos c/Santiago Veve 70 ☎787/892-9600, Ⓦwww.a2tiempos.com. Housed in the elegant Casa Acosta y Forés, built in 1912, this restaurant is the perfect place to soak up old San Germán. The theme is "Puerto Rican revival", with a creative menu featuring sweet plantains stuffed with blood sausage; tostones and caviar; and codfish fillet dipped in *bacalaíto* batter. Sit in the tranquil gardens and enjoy live music at the weekends. Mains range $7–20. Wed–Fri 5–10pm, Sat 1–10pm, Sun 1–9pm.

L'Auxerre c/Estrella 16 at c/Cruz, ☎787/892-8844, Ⓦwww.lauxerre.com. Easily the most enticing place to eat in San Germán, housed in La Casona (entrance on c/ Estrella). Chef Pierre P. Saussy changes the menu weekly, but expect contemporary French and European cuisine: fresh *foie gras*, fragrant osso bucco and exquisite *filet mignon*. Set menus from $50. Wed & Thurs 6–10pm, Fri & Sat till midnight, Sun 11am–4pm.

Le Casa del Sandwich c/Luna 79 (opposite Walgreens). This classic hole-in-the-wall was established in 1930, with a weathered counter top and wobbly bar stools, crafting the eponymous sandwiches to order, with a variety of meat and egg fillings (from $3). Daily 9am–11pm.

Cattlemen Company c/Ruiz Belvis 34 ☎787/264-1010. Excellent steakhouse and cantina in one, right on the old plaza. Mains and steaks cost $15–20, and there's traditional live music Saturday 7–11pm. Mon–Thurs 5–11pm, Fri & Sat noon–11pm, Sun till 5pm.

Mr Snacks c/Luna (near junction with PR-122) ☎787/515-9051. Locals flock to this handy *kiosco* to gorge on fried breakfasts, industrial-strength coffee and lunches of gloriously deep-fried Puerto Rican favourites (around $0.75), pizza slices and ham and cheese sandwiches for under $2.

La Rumba c/Carro (near c/Santiago Veve) ☎787/922-3340. The only nightclub in the centre of town, with vibrant salsa and *merengue* pumped out by DJs and occasional live acts: drinkers nod their heads over cold beers at the back until the dancing kicks off later in the evenings. Wed–Sat.

🏃 Tapas Café c/Santiago Veve 48 ☎787/264-0610. Delicate tapas with an authentic Spanish feel, emphasized by the high ceilings, terracotta floors and small tables with Andalusian tile tops. Enjoy *jamón serrano*, spicy *chorizo* and *albondigas* (meatballs) from $6–15, washed down with tangy *sangría*. Things heat up with flamenco and salsa at the weekends. Wed & Thurs 5–10pm, Fri & Sat till 11pm, Sun 11am–9pm.

La Parguera

Despite the tourist veneer, the former fishing community of **LA PARGUERA** has managed to retain a modicum of rustic charm, especially on weekdays, with its weatherboard housing and tightly packed streets. But the real draw lies along the coast: Parguera's unique offshore environment, a patchwork of placid lagoons, extensive coral reefs and mangrove-smothered cays, is a water wonderland, known rather grandly as a "barrier reef-fringing mangrove ecosystem". Beyond this lies some of the best **diving** anywhere on the island, a huge drop-off known as **La Pared** ("the wall") that runs for 32km parallel to the south coast. A short drive to the east is the **Bahía de Fosforescente**, the island's most accessible bioluminescent bay, though thanks to pollution, the least impressive. And at the end of the day, the ensemble of down-to-earth pubs serving hearty Puerto Rican snack food, and punchy local **sangría** makes for entertaining eating and drinking, especially on weekends.

La Parguera's transformation has been rapid, even by Puerto Rican standards. In 1945 it was a tiny backwater of just 24 fishing families; the first hotel was built in 1955, but as recently as the early 1970s it was best known for its mud-spattered streets and cavorting feral hogs. It now welcomes over 100,000 visitors a year and, as elsewhere, flashy condo development has arrived on the outskirts. If you're here in summer, try to catch the **Procesión de San Pedro** on June 29, honouring the local patron saint. Headed by an effigy of St Peter, the procession begins on foot before taking to a flotilla of boats and making a festive tour of the nearby cays.

Arrival and information

La Parguera is essentially a big village, and PR-304 ends at the compact seafront, where you'll find most of the restaurants and boats. When you hit the waterfront, turn left to reach the free **car park**. With no local tourist office, hotels are the best source of up-to-date tour information and conditions.

Accommodation

Many visitors zip down to La Parguera for the day from other parts of the region, but if you intend to explore the coast more thoroughly it's worth staying the night. Much of the town is given over to hotels and restaurants, so there's plenty of choice, especially during the week, though overall the quality is not high – the smaller guesthouses are generally better value. On weekends, especially in summer, the town morphs into a full-on Puerto Rican family resort, and while this definitely adds spice to the place, especially at night, prices jump dramatically and it can get uncomfortably swamped with people.

La Jamaca Guest House Reparto La Borde, Colinas La Parguera ☎787/899-6162, ⓦwww.laparguerapuertorico.com. This welcoming 12-bedroom hotel is just outside town, a serene retreat with a small pool and an excellent on-site restaurant. Rooms are plain but come with a/c, cable TV and bathroom, and are very cheap. ➋

Lindamar Guest House Calle 7, no. 118 ☎787/899-7682, ⓔrosadolinda@hotmail.com. This cheap but pretty guesthouse is one of the best deals in the village, a two-storey family home with veranda set away from the waterfront in the sleepy residential area – rooms are plain but cosy, and helpful host Linda Rosado is a font of local information. ❷

Parador Villa Parguera PR-304 km 3.3 ☎787/899-7777, ⓦwww.villaparguera.net. This extensive clapboard property is the best hotel in the village, with comfortable if unspectacular rooms overlooking the water, and lush gardens that run around the pool and along the shore. As with most places here, check the rooms first: some are

showing their age, but you should get clean tiled floors and a balcony, the best feature. The old-fashioned cabaret show at the weekends can be fun (after a few *piña coladas*). ❹

Posada Porlamar PR-304 km 3.3 ☎787/899-4015. Opened in 1967, this waterside hotel looks like an old wooden warehouse, and is perennially popular with divers for the convenient dive shop on site. Ask for a room with a balcony on the third floor and check first: most are plain but adequate, and the real attraction is the location and outdoor deck, jutting over the water. ❹

Bahía de Fosforescente

The ethereal glow of Puerto Rico's **bioluminescent bays**, a mesmerizing night-time effect caused by microscopic dinoflagellates, is the island's most celebrated natural wonder, though pollution means that La Parguera's **Bahía de Fosforescente** is one of the poorest, and nowhere near as bright as those in Vieques (see p.132). The trade-off is that it's far cheaper to visit (around $6 per person), and if you skim across the bay on a cloudy or moonless night, the luminescent waves and sparkling drops of water are still magical – remember that any amount of moonlight can severely dilute the effect. Rampant development nearby has also had a major impact: over-fishing, the construction of almost two hundred summer houses (with marshland filled in to provide access), a sewage treatment plant and heavy boat traffic are all to blame. The **Parguera Nature Reserve** (☎787/899-7484) has been established to protect the bay and surrounding mangroves from further damage, but its powers are limited. Boats take around twenty minutes to get to the bay, and most stay for ten to fifteen minutes. **Johnny's Boats** and **Fondo de Cristal III** make trips (see below), as does **Paradise Scuba** (see p.206).

Exploring La Parguera's coast

The most pleasurable activities in La Parguera are exploring the more than thirty **mangrove cays** and winding channels (*Los Canales*) offshore, messing about on boats or swimming in the calm, balmy waters. You can take a tour, rent your own boat or simply pick an island and hang out for the day. To negotiate prices, aim for the booths and boat owners on the wooden pier and dock area in the centre of the village – at weekends you will be approached by ticket sellers in the car park, but don't sign up until you see the actual boat. The large island just offshore is **Isla Magüeyes** (or "Lizard Island"), owned by the Universidad de Puerto Rico and off-limits to casual visitors, its English nickname deriving from the giant Mona iguanas that can be seen lazing on its shores. Further round to the east are the smaller **Cayo Caracoles**, **Isla Mata de la Gata** and **Cayo Majimo**. Cayo Caracoles is fifteen minutes by boat, a popular choice for its protected swimming area and short boardwalk through the dense, creeping mangroves. Other options include **Playa Rosada**, a pleasant mainland beach accessed by boat, **El Laurel**, a wedge of reef and sand to the west of the village, and **Cayo Enrique**, a more secluded islet further offshore with a lagoon and coral sand beach.

Boat operators and activities

One of the more dependable operators is **Johnny's Boats** (☎787/460-8922), run by Johnny and Gina Cordero. They offer one-hour tours through the mangroves for around $25 per boat (or $6 per person), or tours of the bio bay at night for $6 (including time for a swim). Alternatively, for the same price you can have a boat drop you at the island or beach of your choice, and pre-arrange a time for pick-up, or rent your own motorboat ($35/1hr, $50/2hr).

Those short of time or requiring more comfort can try the **Fondo de Cristal III** (☎787/899-5891, ⓦfondodecristal.com), a 22m two-deck catamaran with part-glass hull. Trips around the bay and the underwater gardens of Isla Gata cost $35 to $65 per hour depending on the season and the number of passengers. They also do trips to the bio bay at 7.30pm.

For a more edifying tour of the mangroves, contact **Aleli Tours** (☎787/899-6086, ⓦwww.alelitours.com). Snorkelling tours ($50/hr) feature expert commentary from local ecologist Captain Ismael Ramos – they also arrange guided kayak trips ($50/person) and bio bay tours for $90 per trip (max 6 people). **Kayak rental** is $10 per hour or $50 per day and a fabulous way to explore the cays.

Diving

Lying just a few kilometres off the south coast, **La Pared** is an astonishing underwater shelf that runs for 32km, its 18 to 36m drop-offs, 30m visibility and teeming marine life making this one of the **best dive sites** in the region.

West Divers at PR-304 km 3.1 (☎787/899-3223, ⓦwww.westdiverspr.com), just up the main road from the waterfront, has modern gear and offers a full range of dive courses and snorkelling excursions. Dives off La Pared are $100 (for two tanks), while PADI courses start at $325. Competition is provided by long-established **Paradise Scuba and Snorkelling Center** (☎787/899-7611, ⓦwww.paradisescubasnorkelingpr.com), which offers two-tank dives from $85–100, PADI courses from $350 and snorkelling from $40 (daily 10am–1pm) or $60 including the bio bay. Trips around the bio bay by boat (with swimming) are $30 per person (minimum 6 people; daily 6.30–8.30pm) and they also do the full range of diving courses and rent snorkels from $15.

Eating and drinking

Like most seaside resorts La Parguera does a good line in **seafood**, but the real speciality is **sangría marca coño**, a potent blend of Argentine red wine and fruit juices that has a zestier kick than the usual Spanish version.

Los Balcones PR-304 (waterfront), ☎787/899-2145. This bar-cum-restaurant occupies the second storey of a modern building, popular for the views, pool tables, live rock music, frenetic dance-floor at the weekends, pitchers of *sangría* and fusion menu (mains average $7–16). Wed–Sun 4pm–midnight.

La Casita PR-304 km 3.3 ☎787/899-1681. Knocking out home-style Puerto Rican seafood dishes since the 1960s, always busy with regulars and families stuffing down the fresh whole fish (cooked in seven styles) and perfectly seasoned *asopaos*, particularly the lobster and shrimp versions, all finished off with the luscious coconut *flan*. Mains $10–25. July daily 11am–10pm, Aug–June Wed–Sat 11am–10pm, Sun 11am–9pm.

La Jamaca Reparto La Borde, Colinas La Parguera ☎787/899-6162, ⓦwww.laparguerapuertorico .com. This restaurant and guest house is hard to find but worth the hassle for its special *Chuleta Can-Can* (pork chops; $13.95) and tasty *criollo* food ($8.95–29.95) – follow the signs from the waterfront, west of the village, past all the new condos, and you'll eventually get there. Daily 5.30–10pm.

El Karacol behind the docks ☎787/899-5582. Operating since the late 1960s, the proud inventor of *sangría marca coño* ($4.75) also offers a range of fresh seafood dishes: the *pulpo* and *mofongo* are especially good, made daily and always fresh. Usually open for breakfast through till midnight.

Yolanda's Bar & Grill PR-302 km 3.2 ☎787/899-7676, ⓦyolandasbarandgrill.com. Just up the road from the waterfront this friendly bar in a wooden shack sells cheap beers, sandwiches, *empandillas*, hot wings, mozzarella sticks and nachos. Usually open 11am–midnight; closed Mon & Tues in winter.

Porta Caribe

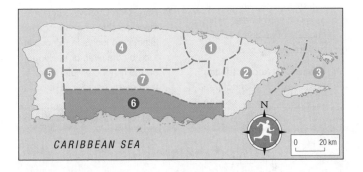

CARIBBEAN SEA

N

0   20 km

CHAPTER 6

Highlights

✳ **Ponce** This elegant city boasts romantic *criollo* architecture, an exceptional art gallery and grandiose Castillo Serallés, legacy of the Don Q rum empire. See p.209

✳ **Centro Ceremonial Indígena de Tibes** Highly organized and utterly mystifying, the ruined ball-courts of Tibes are a fascinating reminder of the island's hazy pre-Taíno past. See p.221

✳ **Hacienda Buena Vista** Tour the most perfectly preserved plantation on the island, a charming nineteenth-century mansion surrounded by cacao, coffee and tropical fruit trees. See p.223

✳ **Yauco** Best known for its illustrious brand of coffee, this beguiling rural town contains a gorgeous Belle Epoque villa and the creator of mouthwatering *"can-can"* pork chops. See p.224

✳ **Bosque Estatal de Guánica** Explore one of the world's most precious dry forests, a parched wilderness of gnarled trees and sandy hiking trails. See p.226

✳ **Guilligan's Island** Bask in the clear waters of this pristine mangrove cay encircled by reef, just off the south coast. See p.229

✳ **Baños de Coamo** Bathe in these soothing hot springs, joining the locals in the public tubs by the river, or soaking up the historic ambience of the nearby *parador*. See p.231

▲ Coffee sacks at Hacienda Buena Vista

Porta Caribe

Puerto Rico's balmy south coast is known as the **Porta Caribe** ("gateway to the Caribbean"), a designation that neatly sums up its laidback appeal. The only part of Puerto Rico that actually faces the Caribbean Sea, the waves here are calmer, the skies warmer and the air drier than elsewhere on the island, but the lack of beaches means you'll see far fewer visitors. As a result, traditional Puerto Rican culture remains vibrant here, towns and villages exuding a strong Spanish identity closer in spirit to that of Cuba and Central America.

Some of the most powerful **Taíno kingdoms** were based here, home to Agüeybaná himself, overlord of the island when the Spanish arrived in 1508, but the conquerors focused their efforts elsewhere and the south remained thinly populated until the eighteenth century. **Sugar** changed everything, with plantations rapidly colonizing the narrow strip between the Central Cordillera and the coast in the nineteenth century. By World War II the sugar industry had collapsed, and today great swathes of the south are empty, overgrown prairies, a haunting reminder of a lost era.

Ponce is the capital of the south, Puerto Rico's second city and peppered with ebullient architecture and museums, a poignant legacy of those heady days of sugar. Outside Ponce, make time for the **Centro Ceremonial Indígena de Tibes**, one of the most important archeological sites in the Caribbean, and **Hacienda Buena Vista**, a lush coffee plantation frozen in the nineteenth century. To the west, the humdrum town of **Yauco** boasts a number of less-visited treasures to complement its prestigious **coffee**, while **Guánica** is best known for its remarkable dry forest and series of enticing beaches, the only section of the south coast mobbed by tourists. To the east, the hot springs at **Coamo** are a pleasant novelty, but the town itself is a fine product of **sugar country**, with nearby **Guayama** another gracefully weathered example.

Ponce and around

Known as *La Perla de Sud* ("the pearl of the south"), **PONCE** is a glittering showcase of *criollo* architecture, its lavish buildings a legacy of the golden years between the 1880s and 1930s, when the city was the hub of vastly profitable trades in rum, sugar cane and shipping. Ponce remains the **second largest city** in Puerto Rico outside Greater San Juan, and sometimes fierce rivalry exists between the two, *Ponceños* often portraying themselves as a more sophisticated bunch than their money-minded northern cousins: as they say, "*Ponce es Ponce, lo demás es parking*" ("Ponce is Ponce, the rest is just parking"). Ponce feels surprisingly provincial despite its status,

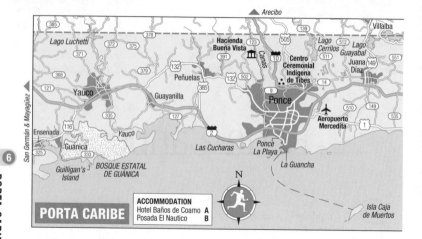

PORTA CARIBE

ACCOMMODATION	
Hotel Baños de Coamo	**A**
Posada El Nautico	**B**

retaining a relaxed atmosphere long lost in the capital. Several buildings act as small but fascinating museums, such as the exhibition commemorating the **Ponce Massacre**, while the collection of fine artwork on display at the **Museo de Arte** would be considered impressive in any European city. To get a feel for the old money that once dominated Ponce, visit **Museo Castillo Serallés** on the outskirts of town, monument to the great Don Q sugar and rum dynasty, and the sobering **Panteón Nacional Román Baldorioty de Castro**, the city's historic cemetery.

Some history

Ponce was little more than a village until the mid-nineteenth century, evolving around a hermitage established in 1670. Ponce de León y Loayza (or Loíza), Juan Ponce de León's great-grandson, obtained official recognition for the settlement in 1692, and the village was promptly named in his honour. Ponce remained a sleepy backwater until the 1820s, when the south became the centre of the burgeoning **sugar economy**. The good times lasted well into the 1930s, the city home to scores of artists, politicians and poets; *Ponceños* are justly proud of their musical traditions, and claim that *danza* and *plena* (see p.274) were invented in the city. Ponce was also the home of the growing independence movement. In 1937, seventeen civilians were killed by police during a march celebrating the 64th anniversary of the abolition of slavery, a tragic event known as the **Ponce Massacre** (see p.216). After World War II the agrarian economy collapsed, and the introduction of new factories did little to alleviate the decline of the city. The administration of Mayor **Rafael "Churumba" Cordero** began to turn things around in the 1990s, and although the popular leader died in office in 2004, his successors have continued to revive downtown Ponce.

Arrival

Flights (5 daily from San Juan; 25min) arrive at **Aeropuerto Mercedita**, 6km east of downtown Ponce. The terminal contains all the main **car rental** desks (see Listings, p.221) and a Banco Popular ATM, while the small **tourist information desk** (daily 3.30–8pm; ☎787/842-6292), supplying basic information and maps, is usually open to meet incoming flights. If you're not renting a car or getting picked up by your hotel, you'll have to take a **taxi**. Taxis tend not to use the meter; if you arrive late at night prices will double, but always fix the price first. Reckon

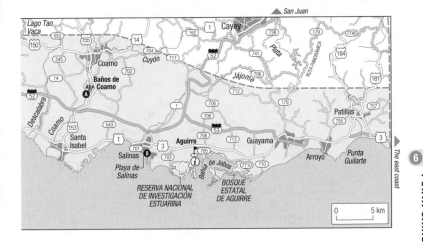

on around $15 into the centre, and up to $25 at night; the *Ponce Hilton* will be at least $20 and the *Howard Johnson* around $10 (more at night).

Ponce is 112.5km southwest of San Juan, around ninety minutes' **drive** along *autopista* PR-52 (there are four tolls along the way). Driving into the city is straightforward and traffic is far less congested than in the capital, especially in the centre. Around the plaza there is metered street parking ($0.25/for/30min, maximum 4hr), or you can try one of the central **car parks** – you'll find one on Calle Comercio east of the plaza (PR-133) and also on Calle Concordia south of the plaza under the *parque urbano*. **Públicos** pull in at Terminal Carlos Garay, four blocks north of Plaza Las Delicias on Calle Unión, between Calles Vives and Calle Estrella.

Information

The main **tourist information office** (daily 9am–5pm; ☎787/284-3338, ⓦ www .visitponce.com) is inside the Parque de Bombas on Plaza Las Delicias. The office sells tickets for **guided tours** of the city, which are good value if you're short of time: for $2 you get a ride on a **trolley-bus** around all the main sites (but not Museo Castillo Serallés), starting at the Casa Armstrong on Plaza Las Delicias (9am, 9.30am, 10am, 12.30pm, 1pm, 1.30pm and 4pm).

City transport

Ponce Centro is easy to explore on foot. If you don't have a car, take taxis or the trolley-bus tour (see above) for trips further afield.

The easiest way to get a **taxi** from the centre is to get the tourist office to call one for you, or find them near the central plaza, where you can set the fare in advance or persuade the driver to use the meter. Day-time rates to La Guancha and Castillo Serallés shouldn't be more than $10 (more at night), and $20 from Ponce Centro to the *Holiday Inn*, so use that as a guide when discussing fares elsewhere. Las Cucharas should be no more than $15.

Accommodation

Ponce offers two choices when it comes to **accommodation**: half of its hotels are within the central historic district, **Ponce Centro**, which has far more character and is more convenient; the other hotels are scattered around the outskirts near the

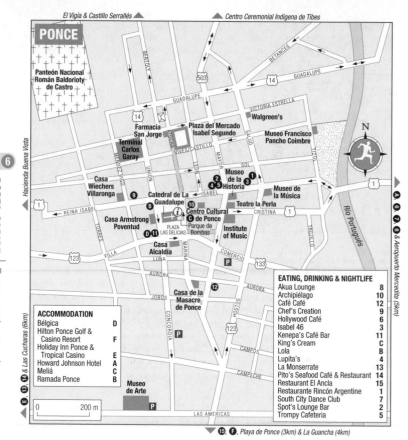

PONCE

El Vigía & Castillo Serrallés ▲   ▲ *Centro Ceremonial Indígena de Tibes*

Panteón Nacional
Román Baldorioty
de Castro

Farmacia
San Jorge
Terminal
Carlos
Garay

Plaza del Mercado
Isabel Segundo

Walgreen's

Museo Francisco
Pancho Coimbre

Casa
Wiechers
Villaronga

Museo
de la
Historia

Catedral de La
Guadalupe

Museo de
la Música

Casa Armstrong
Poventud

Centro Cultural
de Ponce

Teatro la Perla

Parque de
Bombas

Institute
of Music

Casa
Alcaldía

Casa de la
Masacre
de Ponce

Museo
de Arte

Hacienda Buena Vista ◄
& Las Cucharas (6km) ◄
& Aeropuerto Mercedita (5km) ►
Playa de Ponce (3km) & La Guancha (4km) ▼

N

ACCOMMODATION

Bélgica	D
Hilton Ponce Golf & Casino Resort	F
Holiday Inn Ponce & Tropical Casino	E
Howard Johnson Hotel	A
Meliá	C
Ramada Ponce	B

0   200 m

EATING, DRINKING & NIGHTLIFE

Akua Lounge	8
Archipiélago	10
Café Café	12
Chef's Creation	9
Hollywood Café	6
Isabel 46	3
Kenepa's Café Bar	11
King's Cream	C
Lola	B
Lupita's	4
La Monserrate	13
Pito's Seafood Café & Restaurant	14
Restaurant El Ancla	15
Restaurante Rincón Argentine	1
South City Dance Club	7
Spot's Lounge Bar	2
Trompy Cafeteria	5

main highways, PR-52 and PR-2, and include a couple of larger, more luxurious resort-style places. As with San Juan, there are few budget options, but the mid-range hotels are much better value here.

Ponce Centro

Bélgica c/Villa 122 ☎787/844-3255, ⓦwww
.hotelbelgica.com. Established in 1872, this
old-fashioned gem occupies a restored
Neoclassical building with heaps of charm, and
though it's fairly basic, the price makes it a good
deal overall. Rooms are scrupulously clean, with
high ceilings and wooden shutters, and some with
balconies overlooking the plaza (though choose a
windowless room to avoid noise at the weekends).
All have a/c and local TV. ❷

Meliá Plaza Degetau y c/Cristina ☎787/842-0260,
ⓦwww.hotelmeliapr.com. Facing Plaza Las
Delicias, this historic hotel was established by
Mallorcan émigré Don Bartolo Meliá in 1895, but
with no relation to the Spanish chain. The current

property dates from 1915, the elegant rooms are
tastefully decorated with smart bathrooms and
equipped with cable TV, free internet and wi-fi.
Breakfast on the rooftop sun deck is included, and
happily the small outdoor pool on the first floor is
empty during the day. ❹

Ramada Ponce c/Reina ☎787/813-5050,
ⓦwww.ramadaponce.com. Smart hotel
right on the main Plaza Las Delicias,
encompassing a beautifully converted townhouse
built in 1882 (only 6 rooms are located here). All
rooms are stylish and equipped with internet
connection and LCD TVs; the historical rooms
obviously have the most character. A fitness
centre, outdoor pool and *Lola* restaurant round
out the experience. ❹

Greater Ponce

Hilton Ponce Golf & Casino Resort Avda Caribe 1150 ☏787/259-7676, ⓦwww.hilton.com. The most luxurious resort on the south coast is an eighty-acre self-contained universe facing the water, though the black-sand beach is poor and it's certainly not five-star. Rooms are spacious, with balconies and internet access, and the relative isolation is compensated for by several restaurants, including the fêted *La Cava*, and a large palm-fringed pool, but the real draws for most guests are the 27-hole golf course and tiny casino. Given its distance from central Ponce, you'll need a car to get around (parking is $8/day). Resort fee is 12 percent. ⑥

Holiday Inn Ponce & Tropical Casino 3315 Ponce by-pass (PR-2) ☏787/844-1200,

ⓦwww.holidayinn.com/ponce. This is a comfortable if fairly characterless option, convenient for the highway but a long trek from town (west of the city). Rooms are modern, clean and comfortable, but the best features here are the stellar views of the ocean and huge pool (they also have a gym). Plenty of parking, but fills up with 24hr casino traffic. Free wi-fi. ⑤

Howard Johnson Hotel PR-1, 103 Turpo Industrial Park, just off PR-52 ☏787/841-1000, ⓦwww .hidpr.com. Convenient if you have a car (though it's still a good 15min drive into the centre), with free parking, slightly old-fashioned but clean and comfy motel rooms, a small pool and cable TV. Wi-fi is good in most rooms, and there's a laundry, basic gym and business centre with internet access. Book online for the best rates. ④

The City

Ponce is an enchanting old city with plenty to see, but much of the allure comes from its ravishing architecture, actually a mishmash of styles employed between 1880 and 1940. **Ponce Creole** style blends traditional clapboard *criollo* houses with exuberant balconies and layers of marble, while **Ponce Neoclassical** became vogue between the US occupation and the 1920s, a decorative form most associated with architect Alfredo Wiechers and influenced by Art Nouveau. You'll also see several Art Deco gems dotted around town, built in the 1930s.

Downtown Ponce, or **Ponce Centro**, is where most of the historic attractions are located. To the south, **Ponce La Playa** is the old port district while **La Guancha** is a flashy boardwalk and marina at the end of PR-12, both excellent places to eat but with not much else to do. West of town on PR-2, **Las Cucharas** is another cluster of inviting waterside restaurants, while overlooking Ponce Centro on the foothills to the north is **El Vigía** and **Castillo Serallés**.

Plaza Las Delicias

Ponce life once hinged around graceful **Plaza Las Delicias**, the central plaza that remains a hub of activity, though much of the commercial life of the city has migrated to shopping malls on the periphery. Anchored by Ponce's grand cathedral, the square is lined with Indian laurel trees, many dating back to the 1840s.

The most arresting building here, and probably in all of Puerto Rico, is the cartoonish **Museo Parque de Bombas** (daily 9am–5pm; free), a bright red and white timbered hall with Mudéjar (Moorish) elements, constructed for the 1882 trade fair. In 1885 it became the fire station, and now houses the tourist office and a small exhibition on firefighting, which is far less engaging than the building itself. The **Catedral Nuestra Señora de La Guadalupe** (Mon–Fri 6am–2pm, Sat & Sun 6am–noon & 3–8.30pm) began life as a rustic chapel in 1670, but the current French-inspired Neoclassical structure was rebuilt in the 1920s after the 1918 earthquake destroyed much of its nineteenth-century core. Nuestra Señora de La Guadalupe, the earliest and most sacred incarnation of Mary in the New World, is the patron saint of Ponce, and the annual **Fiesta de La Virgen de Guadalupe** is one of the most important festivals on the island (her feast day is December 12), involving candlelit processions and special concerts. The exterior of the cathedral, with its stately towers and brickwork dome, is more attractive

Carnival of the devil masks

Ponce's *carnaval* starts one week before Ash Wednesday, a tradition that goes back officially to 1858, making it the oldest in Puerto Rico. It's nothing like the crazy celebrations in Rio or New Orleans (this version is more family oriented and a lot more local – you won't see many foreign tourists), but still loads of fun: just make sure you book accommodation well in advance.

The carnival opens with a procession of masked figures known as **vejigantes**. The original purpose of the *vejigante* was to scare people (they traditionally represented demonic Moorish warriors), and these days you'll see them merrily thwacking kids that line the streets with a *vejiga*, a dried, cow's bladder blown up like a balloon. *Vejigantes* wear incredibly ornate **masks** made of papier-mâché and embellished with outlandish colours and devilish horns.

The programme of week-long festivities includes a *danza* competition, the unveiling of Miss Ponce Carnaval (chosen from a local high school), concerts and special exhibitions in Plaza Las Delicias. The merrymaking ends on Shrove Tuesday with the **Entierro de la Sardina** (Burial of the Sardine), a mock funeral procession attended by hyperbolic cries and wails from everyone in sight. A dummy is symbolically burnt at the climax, signifying the purging of sins before the beginning of Lent. For more information call ☎787/841-8044 or check ⓦwww.visitponce.com.

than the interior, though the stained-glass windows depicting saints are beautifully crafted and an ornate alabaster *retablo* graces the altar.

Designed by celebrated architect Manuel Domenech for local banker Carlos Armstrong Toro in 1899, the **Museo Casa Armstrong-Poventud** (Wed–Sun 8am–4.30pm; $3; ☎787/840-7667) on the northwest side of the plaza (c/Unión 9) has one of the most elaborate facades in the city, with sensuous caryatids flanking the main entrance; inside the richly decorated interior has been artfully renovated and enhanced with period antiques.

Casa Wiechers Villaronga

It's also worth a quick peek inside **Casa Wiechers Villaronga** (Wed–Sun 8.30am–4.30pm; free; ☎787/843-3363) on Calle Reina Isabel at the corner of Calle Méndez Vigo, a short stroll west of the plaza. This was the home of local architect **Alfredo Wiechers**, who designed the house in 1911 in his signature Art Nouveau-inspired style, with pink rounded porticos, stylish Ionic columns and undulating iron railings. The interior has been restored, replete with period furniture and mosaic tiled floors, though alas, no air conditioning. Wiechers, the Ponce-born son of the German consul to Puerto Rico, studied in Paris and Barcelona, where he was influenced by Gaudí's *modernisme*. Life became difficult for Germans living in Puerto Rico during World War I, and he sold his house to the Villaronga-Mercado family in 1918, before leaving the island forever the following year.

Museo de la Historia and Museo de la Música

Two blocks east of the plaza along Calle Isabel, the **Museo de la Historia** (Tues–Sun 8.30am–5pm; free; ☎787/844-7042) chronicles the rich history of the city from the Taíno period to the modern day. Free English-speaking guides are on offer here – it's best to wait for one, as the information given in the ten small galleries inside is solely in Spanish. The first series of exhibits tells the story of the city chronologically, while the next group tackles diverse themes such as health, the economy and education, as related to Ponce. The museum occupies a grand Neoclassical mansion designed by Blas Silva Boucher in 1911.

Further down Isabel, at the junction with Calle Salud, the **Museo de la Música** (Wed–Sun 8.30am–4.30pm; free; ☎787/848-7016) was the former townhouse of the **Serrallés family** (see p.218), and another winning design by Alfredo Wiechers, with stained-glass windows, hand-painted floor tiles, carved mahogany louvres and soaring 3.5m ceilings. Built in 1912, it was home to the family until they moved to the *castillo* (which was a summer house at first) and they eventually sold this house to the city in 1992 after a long period of abandonment. The interior decor is more interesting than the displays inside, essentially a collection of **musical instruments** (Spanish labels only), from the Puerto Rican folk, *bomba*, classical and particularly *plena* traditions, the latter a genre developed in Ponce in the early twentieth century. Look out for the florid mural by **Miguel Pou** depicting eminent musicians of the island, covering a whole wall.

Panteón Nacional Román Baldorioty de Castro

Ponce's tranquil old cemetery, the **Panteón Nacional Román Baldorioty de Castro** (Tues–Sun 8.30am–5pm; free), is the resting place of some of the city's most important citizens, fifteen minutes' walk northwest of the plaza at the top of Calle Torres. The cemetery opened in 1843, and Ponce's elite were buried here during the boom years of the nineteenth century. The cemetery closed in 1918, and was gradually forgotten: vandals took their toll on the grandiose tombs, a period the site guardian calls "the poor's revenge on the rich". Marble was stripped and graves robbed. In 1980 the city started to restore the devastated site, and today it is a preserved historic monument, its neatly manicured gardens interspersed with ruinous brick tombs and the remains of grand monuments, hinting at its former glory.

The first plot on the main avenue is the tomb of **Antonio Paolí** (1871–1946), the accomplished Ponce-born tenor reburied here in 2005 under a circular white colonnade. Next is **Rafael "Churumba" Cordero Santiago** (1942–2004), the much-loved former mayor of Ponce, with a lion at the foot of his stately black tomb. You'll also see the resting place of **Roberto Sánchez Vilella** (1913–1997), who was governor of Puerto Rico 1965–69 and grew up in Ponce; the tomb and statue of **Román Baldorioty de Castro**, the energetic abolitionist who died in Ponce and was buried here in 1889; and **Manuel Tavarez** (1843–1883), father of Puerto Rican *danza*, in a flat marble tomb. Beyond lie the ruins of other wealthy family vaults (mostly unmarked), the largest belonging to the **Serrallés** family

El Cantante

One of the most talented yet tragic figures in the world of **salsa**, **Héctor Lavoe** was born in Ponce in 1946. He moved to New York in 1963, beginning a sparkling musical career that began with traditional *bolero* songs. Making his big break with band leader **Willie Colón** in 1967, he went solo in 1973, and had a string of catchy hits such as *Bandolera*, *Sóngoro Cosongo* and *Joven contra Viejo*, but *El Cantante* ("the singer") became his signature tune, his eventual nickname, and title of the biopic movie released in 2007. Lavoe helped solidify the growing New York Latin sound of the era, soon to be known as **salsa** (see p.275), but despite his apparent success, he struggled with a largely unsupportive music industry, drug addiction and depression for most of his career – after a suicide attempt in 1988, a penniless Lavoe died of AIDS-related complications in 1993. Initially buried in the Bronx, he was re-interred at the **Cementerio Municipal de Ponce** in 2002, along with his son Héctor Junior and wife Nilda Rosado. In addition to laying flowers at the white marble headstone, fans commemorate his birthday here on September 30. The annual "**Lavoe Weekend**" of concerts takes place on La Guancha boardwalk (see p.219) around this time.

(see p.218) with room for twelve people – only one body survived the pillaging. While the rich and famous took up the main plots, victims of the 1856 cholera epidemic were buried near the left-hand wall, and the poor were collected in mass graves at the back.

Casa de la Masacre de Ponce

Though the primary purpose of the small but thought-provoking **Casa de la Masacre de Ponce** (Wed–Sun 8.30am–4.30pm; free; ☎787/844-9722) is to commemorate the Ponce Massacre of 1937 (see below), it's really a spirited presentation of the whole history of the **Puerto Rican independence movement**. Beginning with Puerto Rico's struggles against foreign invaders in the early Spanish period, it traces the progress of the nationalist cause in the early nineteenth century, building up to the massacre itself. Pedro Albizu Campos and his Nationalist Party and the events of the 1950s, are given special focus. The exhibition ends, somewhat optimistically, with the successful ousting of the US Navy from Vieques in 2003.

The museum is especially poignant because this is the former headquarters of the Nationalist Party, and the massacre took place just outside. If you ask, you'll usually find enthusiastic guides, many of whom are still politically active, willing to translate the predominantly Spanish information on display – this is a rare chance for most visitors to meet some genuine independence supporters. The museum is on Calle Marina south of the plaza, at Calle Aurora.

Museo de Arte

With an impressive collection of over 4500 paintings and sculptures, the **Museo de Arte** (Wed–Mon 10am–6pm; $6; ☎787/848-0505, ⓦwww .museoarteponce.org) is a real surprise, a treasure-trove of fine European art in the heart of the Caribbean. Founded by former governor Luis A. Ferré in 1959, the museum completed a stunning **renovation** in 2010. The museum is south of the Casa de la Masacre at Avda Las Américas 2325 (PR-163), a twenty-minute walk from the plaza.

The Ponce Massacre

The **Ponce Massacre** of seventeen civilians has assumed mythical status on the island, not just within the independence movement, but for many ordinary Puerto Ricans too, despite taking place over seventy years ago. The killings occurred amid growing tension: in the 1930s, the increasingly frustrated **Nationalist Party**, led by Ponce lawyer **Pedro Albizu Campos** and advocating full independence for Puerto Rico, became more militant, and relations with the police deteriorated rapidly. On Palm Sunday, 1937, the party organized a march in Ponce to commemorate the anniversary of the abolition of slavery, but at the last minute Governor Winship revoked their permit – he had surmised, correctly, that the march would also be an indirect protest against the recent incarceration of Albizu. Indignant, the marchers decided to continue as planned: in trying to break up the protest, police fired on the crowd with machine guns, killing seventeen civilians – men, women and one twelve-year-old girl. Two policemen also died. Over one hundred people were wounded, many while trying to run away, and in the aftermath hundreds more were arrested. The massacre led to widespread anger across the island, especially when an official inquiry proved inconclusive and an investigation by the American Civil Liberties Union held the governor responsible. The massacre has only been taught in schools since 1990, and was largely covered up by the US government. Now there are subdued ceremonies honouring the dead held every year at the Casa de la Masacre.

The first-floor galleries

What makes this museum so intriguing is that the traditional chronological approach has been replaced by a thematic scheme that makes it much easier to absorb the range of work on display. The **first-floor galleries** focus on subjects ranging from "Stories of Love and Loss" to "Sacred Places" and "My Puerto Rico". Genres and styles are mixed up, though inevitably, given the way themes occur in the history of art, certain periods tend to cluster together. It's worth giving in to the approach and just wandering around without a specific target in mind, but there are some obvious highlights.

Some of the galleries oldest and rarest works are displayed in gallery 2, fourteenth-century Italian altarpieces and murals from the early Renaissance. Gallery 4 houses **Konstantin Makovsky**'s vast canvas of *The Choosing of the Bride* (1886), his romantic imagining of medieval Russia, while gallery 5 contains **El Greco**'s typically unsettling *St Francis & Brother Leo Meditating* (1605). Expressive paintings of *St Andrew* and the *Greek Magus* (both around 1620) by **Anthony Van Dyck** and **Peter Paul Rubens** respectively hold court in gallery 7.

Puerto Rican master **Francisco Oller** painted *La Ceiba de Ponce* in 1888, on show in gallery 13 with Ponce artist **Miguel Pou**'s romantic *Los Coches de Ponce* (1926). Here also is the strangely hypnotic *Mangrove* by Myrna Báez, the Modernist Puerto Rican painter. You'll find more Puerto Rican work in gallery 18, including Rafael Tufiño's subtle *La Botella* (1963).

Ponce is probably the last place you'd expect to find British nineteenth-century art, yet gallery 15 is dedicated to an extraordinary collection of work from the **Pre-Raphaelite** school (1848–52) and its successor, the **Aesthetic Movement** (1870–80). The monumental *Sleep of King Arthur in Avalon* (1898) by **Edward Coley Burne-Jones** perfectly captures the movement's idealized view of the medieval period. Also here is **Dante Gabriel Rossetti**'s *Roman Widow* (1874), a moving example of his later work: a widow of ancient Rome sits beside the urn containing her husband's ashes, playing two instruments in an expression of grief.

The second-floor galleries

The thematic approach continues upstairs, though the paintings are also grouped in roughly chronological order. Look out for the portrait of *Martín Zapater* by **Goya** (though this is a little drab, the jet-black background only hinting at Goya's formidable talents) and *Portrait of a Young Lady* from **Thomas Gainsborough** in gallery 25. **Francisco de Zurbarán**'s intense *Crucifixion* (1630) dominates the Baroque work in gallery 29. The crowning glory of the museum, however, is in gallery 30. *Flaming June* (1895) was **Frederic Leighton**'s masterpiece, a sensuous depiction of a sleeping girl wrapped in a brilliant orange robe, an allusion to classic depictions of the goddess Venus, and simply unforgettable. The Pre-Raphaelite painting was famously acquired by Ferré in 1963 for a bargain price, thanks to the painter's low standing at the time.

Museo Castillo Serrallés and Cruceta del Vigía

Crowning the hills just to the north of Ponce Centro, the **Museo Castillo Serrallés** (Thurs–Sun 9.30am–6.30pm, last entry 5.30pm; $8.50, $5 gardens only, $12.80 with Cruceta del Vigía; ☎787/259-1774, ⊛www.castilloserralles.org) was once the luxurious base of the powerful Serrallés family, the sugar barons who established the **Don Q** rum empire. Plush mansion rather than fortress, it presides over the city like a medieval castle nonetheless, its delicate Moorish arches, ornamental tower and terracotta tiling evoking Granada's majestic Alhambra palace. Built in Spanish Revival style in 1930, the house served as the family's summer home until 1935, when it became their primary residence.

Don Q

The best-loved and most fiercely guzzled rum in Puerto Rico is **Don Q** (Ⓦ www.donq .com), still proudly produced in Ponce by the **Destilería Serrallés** near the airport (which was once its private airstrip). Like the Barcardís, the Serrallés family hail from Catalunya in northern Spain, and it was patriarch **Juan Serrallés Colón** (1834–1897) who emigrated to Puerto Rico and established Hacienda Mercedita in 1861 as a sugar-cane plantation, still the location of the current distillery. In 1865 he began to produce quality **rum**, using a French still you can see in the Castillo Serrallés, but it wasn't until 1932 that the Don Q brand was launched, named after the much-loved Cervantes character, Don Quixote. Don Q Gold and especially Don Q Cristal are now staples in almost every home and bar on the island, and if you order a *piña colada*, it will almost certainly contain the latter. Don Q is still owned by Destilería Serrallés, which also produces the Ron Llave, Palo Viejo and Granado brands, as well as Ronrico and Captain Morgan for distribution in the Caribbean (Seagrams has US distribution rights). Sadly, tours of the distillery are not available.

Though a small exhibition room is dedicated to sugar and rum-making inside, the mansion is primarily a window into the life of Puerto Rico's upper classes in the early twentieth century, the rooms perfectly maintained with all the lavish accoutrements. Tours lead you through *salons* crammed with period furniture and extravagant decor in pristine condition.

The house can only be visited on guided tours that usually run every 30 to 45 minutes and take around one hour, beginning with a short **video** about the family and Don Q. Times are not set and the language of the tour (Spanish or English) depends on who turns up, so call in advance to avoid a wait. You can also enjoy fabulous views of Ponce from the flower-filled gardens. Taxis charge around $10 to drive up the hill from the plaza – you can walk back down in around forty minutes, but take lots of water. Looming above the house is the **Cruceta del Vigía** (Tues–Sun 9.30am–6.30pm; $5.50; ☏787/259-3816), a 30m-high concrete cross offering another lofty view over the city and Caribbean beyond (via elevator). An original wooden cross was built as part of a pirate warning station in 1801, and destroyed by Hurricane Georges in 1989. The concrete cross that replaced it was completed in 1984, in part to honour the security guard, Don Luis, who manned the station until his death in 1916.

Isla Caja de Muertos

If you visit Ponce on a weekend, take the ferry to **Isla Caja de Muertos** (Coffin Island), a sun-swept reserve of spotless beaches and dolphin-rich waters, 8km offshore. The island covers an area of just 1.5 square kilometres, and other than a few barbecue grills, gazebos and a DRNA ranger station, is bereft of facilities. The main draw is the chance to lounge on the narrow but inviting stretches of white sand near the jetty (Balneario Pelicano), but you can also **snorkel** off the reef-encrusted shore and hike along a surprisingly steep trail to the limestone outcrop in the centre (almost 70m straight up – take lots of water). At the top you'll find a **Spanish lighthouse** built in 1887 (automated but still working), and sweeping views of the main island.

Island Venture Water Excursions ($17; ☏787/842-8541, Ⓦwww.island venturepr.com) runs a **ferry** to the island from **La Guancha** (see p.213) on Saturdays, Sundays and most holidays. The boat usually departs at around 8.30am and returns at around 4.30pm (45min one-way), but call in advance, as during the busy summer months there are multiple departures. Take all the food and water you need, and a bag for garbage – leave nothing on the island.

Eating and drinking

Eating options in **Ponce Centro** are surprisingly poor, limited to local cafeterias, a handful of smart restaurants and fast food on the plaza. The best cheap eats can be found inside the **Mercado** (Mon–Fri 6am–5pm, Sat till 4pm, Sun till noon) two blocks north of the plaza (see map, p.212).

Ponceños spend more time zipping around the outskirts in search of good meals, particularly along the section of PR-2 known as **Las Cucharas**, 6.5km west of the city. Restaurants here face the Caribbean on the southern (east bound) side of the highway, and though the quality of the seafood makes a trip worthwhile, you need to watch the manic traffic when getting back onto the road. **Playa de Ponce**, the slightly shabby former port area at the end of PR-123, 3.2km south of the centre, also contains a handful of good-quality restaurants, while **La Guancha** is packed with families on weekends – parking (free) is easy, and the boardwalk (*tablado*) is lined with bars and *kioscos* selling all the usual Puerto Rican favourites.

Ponce Centro

Archipiélago c/Cristina 76 ☎787/812-8822, ⊛www.archipielagopr.com. Ponce's best restaurant also boasts the most scintillating night view of the city from its sixth-floor roof terrace. It's not cheap, but the innovative creations of local chef Alejandro Vélez Blasini are worth a splurge. Mains include stuffed chicken filled with mushrooms and sun-dried tomato, served with chorizo cream and baked pasta ($24.95), and cornmeal-breaded *mahi-mahi* served with dill hollandaise sauce and sweet plantain gnocchi with spinach ($18.95). There's also plenty for vegetarians and a stunning wine list. Wed–Sat 5pm–midnight, Sun noon–5pm.

Café Café c/Mayor 2638, on the corner of c/Aurora ☎787/841-7185, ⊛www .cafecafeponce.com. Also known as *Café Mayor*, this charming colonial house serves fresh juices indoors or in the leafy garden, as well as the best Puerto Rican coffee on the island (from $2). The secret: they expertly roast their potent, aromatic beans on the premises. You can also buy the raw product ($4/bag), order sandwiches ($2–6) and

local dishes like *mofongo* (from $12), and admire the coffee-inspired murals on the walls. Mon–Fri 8am–3pm, Sat 11am–3pm.

Chef's Creation c/Reina 100 ☎787/848-8384. This crowd-pulling cafeteria is the best place to gorge on cheap plates of no-frills local food ($6–7): pick up a tray, select what you want and grab a table indoors or on the patio at the back. It's standard stuff: fried chicken, rice and beans, stews and roast pork, but everything is fresh and perfectly cooked. Mon–Sat lunch only.

Isabel 46 (aka *La Casa de las Tías*) c/Isabel 46 ☎787/840-4149. The home-cooked Puerto Rican food in this "house of aunts" (aka the two owners Titi Graciela and Titi Wilda), has a cult following, despite the long waits and small space; the setting in a classic *criollo* home is wonderfully atmospheric and the food is superb, featuring creations such as glazed rib eye in guava and wine sauce and yellow rice with crab, *tostones* and beans. Wash it down with the house *sangría*. Mains $20–30. Wed–Sat 11am–10pm, Sun noon–6pm.

King's Cream c/Marina 9223, on Plaza Las Delicias. This venerable ice cream parlour sells

Snacking at La Guancha

La Guancha's harbourside boardwalk at the end of PR-12 is crammed with locals on weekends, eagerly trawling the long line of Puerto Rican snack stalls. Stand-out *kioscos* include *La Mexicana* (no. 8) for its *pinchos*, *emapanadillas* and *piña coladas* in plastic cups; *Miramar* (no. 2) for fried chops and *mofongo*; and *El Pilón Borincano* (no. 15; ☎787/449-4707) for roast chicken, and *pulpo* salad. You won't pay more than $6 for anything. For a sit-down meal indoors (with a/c), head to *El Paladar* (daily 11am–11pm; ☎787/842-1401) in the centre, which serves sumptuous *churrasco*, though service is sometimes poor. The upstairs bar is the best place for a cold beer or cocktail with a view. You'll also see giant **tarpon** and scores of brown **pelicans** being fed by the crowds (it's $1 for a bag of sardines) at the southern end, near the Asociación de Pescadores. You can also take a **boat** equipped with a bar around the bay in the evening (Fri & Sat 8pm–1am, Sun 5–9pm; $6; ☎797/842-8541).

around twelve refreshing home-made flavours, from tangy tropical fruits such as passion fruit and coconut, to deliciously smooth chocolate, vanilla, and local favourites *tamarindo* and *guanabana* (soursop). Cups and cones range $1.40–1.75. Take-away only. Daily 9am–midnight.

Restaurante Rincón Argentine c/Salud 69, at c/ Isabel ☎787/284-1762. For a welcome break from Puerto Rican food, try this Argentine steak house, set in a gorgeous colonial villa with shady patio, palm trees and wrought-iron railings. The service and sometimes the food can be hit and miss, though the grilled meats are usually safe bets (mains $15–30).

Tompy Cafeteria c/Isabel 56 ☎787/840-1965. Compact, no-nonsense canteen with plastic tables and a solid choice for cheap, filling breakfasts of ham and eggs ($3.25) and sandwiches (from $1.50). The *comida criolla* lunches are equally good value: *mofongo* for $3.50 and *chuletas* from $6. Closed Sun. *Café Tomas* next door is a smarter, sit-down affair. Mon 11am–4pm, Tues till 9pm, Wed–Sat till 11pm, Sun noon–7pm.

Greater Ponce

La Monserrate PR-2 km 218, Las Cucharas ☎787/841-2740. Worthy alternative to *Pito's* with similar sea views and seafood menu, without the hype (mains $9–30). The attractive, wood-lined interior is reminiscent of a ship's galley, and you can dine on the open-air terrace at the back.

Pito's Seafood Café & Restaurant PR-2 km 218.7, Las Cucharas ☎787/841-4977, ⓦwww.pitosseafoodpr.com. If you come to Las Cucharas just once, try this justifiably lauded seafood restaurant, a pretty pink wooden building right on the water. Locals grumble that it's become too touristy (and it is somewhat overpriced), but the food is consistently good quality, and the clean, open deck offers bewitching views across the Caribbean. Fri & Sat nights kick off with live music and plenty of cocktails, and the vast menu includes offers fresh lobster, shellfish, red snapper and delectable house specialities such as trunkfish and shrimp wrapped in bacon (mains $9.50–30).

Restaurant El Ancla Avda Hostos 805, Playa de Ponce ☎787/840-2450. This award-winning but low-key restaurant is the best in the old port district. Ideal for lunch, the graceful, aging interior retains a loyal local following, with superb seafood (mains from $9.50), great pitchers of *sangría*, and punchy *piña coladas*. It faces the harbour, right on the water, but parking is limited. Closed Mon.

Bars and clubs

The streets of central Ponce might seem dead after 6pm, especially early in the week, but there are a few bars and clubs around, especially near the main plaza, and it gets much livelier at the weekends. **La Guancha** can also be fun, with dancing and drinking spilling out onto the boardwalk Thursday to Sunday nights. Other options are more spread out and not that practical unless you're used to driving around the city at night. Note also that local **resort hotels** *Holiday Inn* and the *Hilton* have casinos, popular bars and discos (see p.213), and *Tompy Cafeteria* (see above) is a good place for a cheap beer at night.

Akua Lounge Plaza Nuevo Mundo Suite D-1, Blvd Miguel Pou ☎787/433-2209. Fashionable restaurant and lounge bar best known for its outstanding tapas and *mojitos*. Contemporary decor, beadwork and a parachute ceiling complement the resident DJs spinning hip-hop, r'n'b house and Latino sounds. Tues–Wed 11.30am–midnight, Thurs–Sat till 3am.

Hollywood Café PR-1 km 125.5, Blvd Miguel Pou ☎787/843-6703, ⓦwww.hollywoodcafeponce.com. Consistently packed out with younger *Ponceños*, offering pub fare, pool tables, booming music and live salsa at the weekends. On Wed college students pile in for *el noche del pela'o*, roughly "night of the broke ass", when drinks are dirt cheap ($1 rum shots and Coronas). Tues–Sun 5pm–2am.

Kenepa's Café Bar Edificio Café Plaza, C/Unión 3, Plaza Las Delicias ☎787/363-6674, ⓦwww .kenepascafebar.co.nr. Most popular bar on the plaza, with a congenial crowd spilling onto the street later in the evening. Also does menu of local food ($9–18). Wed–Sat 4.30pm–2.30am, Sun 4pm–1am.

Lupita's c/Isabel 60 ☎787/848-8808. This Mexican restaurant also operates as a popular bar, with live music, expertly mixed margaritas and genial staff. Closed Mon.

South City Dance Club Los Caobos Industrial Park, Marginal Villa Flores (next to Edif. Froilan Alfrombras and Banco Popular) ☎787/645-2897. Top club in Ponce, the latest of a long line of ever-changing joints in this space. Expect techno to hip-hop, decent sound system and crowds of hyper-cool *Ponceños*. Thurs–Sat 9pm–3am.

Spot's Lounge Bar c/Mayor 33 ☎787/901-6078 . In a very cool old *criollo* building, this "house of the open bar" offers all-you-can-drink Coors beer for just $1, after $7 entry on Thursdays and $10 on Fridays; on Saturdays drinks are $3 each.

Moving on from Ponce

Cape Air operates four to five daily **flights** to San Juan (25min) from **Aeropuerto Mercedita** – take a taxi from the city ($13). Parking is free at the airport, and you can grab basic food and drinks at the *B52 Café and Sports Bar*.

The **Terminal de Carros Públicos Carlos Garay** (or just *"la terminal"*) is on Calles Vives and Victoria, three blocks north of Plaza Las Delicias. Most of the *públicos* serve the surrounding area, and although signs suggest routes to Coamo, San Germán, Mayagüez, Guayama and Jayuya, it's hard to find cars to these places in practice – turn up before 7am to be sure. The most useful and frequently used route is operated by Choferes Unidos de Ponce (☎787/842-1222) to Río Piedras in **San Juan** ($15 per person, or $45–60 for the whole car). Drivers will usually take you all the way to the beaches or Old San Juan for $25–30 per person.

Driving out of the city is easy, especially heading to San Juan (1hr 30min) or points east on the smooth PR-52 *autopista* (toll road). Unfortunately the *autopista* ends just west of the city, and PR-2 is much slower and often bristling with traffic – it's still a four-lane highway, however, and you should reach virtually anywhere in the southwest, beyond Mayagüez, within an hour or so.

Listings

Airlines Cape Air ☎787/844-2020 or 1-800/227-3247; Jet Blue Airways ☎1800/538-2583.
Banks Plaza Las Delicias has plenty of banks with ATMs.
Car rental All the major firms are located at the airport: Avis ☎787/842-6154; Budget ☎787/848-0907; Hertz ☎787/843-1685; Thrifty ☎787/290-2525.
Emergencies General ☎911
Hospitals and clinics Hospital Damas, 2213 Ponce bypass, PR-2 (☎787/840-8686); Hospital Manuel Comunitaro Dr Pila, Avda Las Américas, east of Avda Hostos (☎787/848-5600).
Internet access Internet cafés are lacking in the centre of Ponce, though most hotels have internet access and you can pick up free wi-fi anywhere

near Plaza Las Delicias. The Historic Archive office (Mon–Fri 8am–noon & 1–4.30pm) at c/Marina 9215, on the east side of the plaza, offers free use of computers and internet,.
Laundry Caribbean Cleaners, Avda Las Américas 13; Express Laundromat, Avda Pámpanos 1; Zayas Laundry, c/Victoria 425.
Pharmacies Try Farmacia San Jorge at c/Atocha and c/Victoria (Mon–Sat 8am–6pm; ☎787/840-5979) or Walgreens at c/Estrella 65 (Mon–Fri 8am–7pm, Sat 8am–6pm).
Post office The most convenient is at c/Atocha 93, four blocks north of the plaza (Mon–Fri 7.30am–4.30pm).
Taxis Ponce Taxi ☎787/842-3370; Borinquen Taxi ☎787/843-6100; Unión Taxi ☎787/840-9127.

Around Ponce

Just north of Ponce are two of the most memorable sights on the island, both associated with the region's long and eventful history. The **Centro Ceremonial Indígena de Tibes** is one of the most significant **Pre-Taíno** archeological sites ever found, and a tantalizing window into the culture of this now lost civilization, while **Hacienda Buena Vista** is a captivating nineteenth-century plantation.

Centro Ceremonial Indígena de Tibes

Evidence of pre-Columbian civilization has been rare in the Caribbean until relatively recently, but the **CENTRO CEREMONIAL INDÍGENA DE TIBES** (Tues–Sun 9am–noon & 1–4pm; $3; ☎787/840-2255) remains one of the region's greatest discoveries, proof of highly complex societies long before the Spanish conquest. The site was inhabited for 1500 years by a series of migrating peoples and primarily used as a burial ground and ceremonial centre, littered with ball-courts and standing stones. Like Caguana (see p.163), this has none of the grandiose ruins of Central America, but the guides do their best to bring the site alive with illuminating facts and anecdotes, and if you visit early, you'll almost certainly have it to yourself. Tibes is clearly signposted off PR-503 at km 2.2, due north of central Ponce. Note that you can only visit the site with a **guide** (free; tours last up to 1hr): weekdays you should be able to pick up an English-speaking one at the entrance, though if the park is busy (unusual), you may have to wait. Note that the site cannot be reached by public transport.

Some history

In 1975, a local farmer stumbled across ancient ruins uncovered by flooding in the wake of Hurricane Eloise, and archeologists finally got working on the site a year later. They found nine ball-courts, three plazas and the largest indigenous **cemetery** ever discovered on the island, comprising 187 human skeletons (one of which is displayed in the museum) from the **Igneri** and **Pre-Taíno** periods (see p.261). The Igneri people established Tibes and used the site from around 300 to 600 AD as a sacred burial ground, but it was later re-inhabited by Pre-Taíno peoples, who constructed the ball-courts and seem to have used it primarily as a ceremonial and burial centre (the remains of which survive today). The Igneri may have played an early form of the ball-game (see below), but just for sport, while it started to assume a more spiritual and symbolic meaning under the Pre-Taínos.

Our understanding of *el batey* or the **ball-game** (*pelota* in modern Spanish), is almost completely based on a few early Spanish accounts. Played with two teams, passing a rubber ball between them (with anything but the hands), it had many similarities to the game played in Mesoamerica, and had a serious ceremonial function.

In around 1100 the site was abandoned after extensive **flooding** of the Río Portugués, and it remained lost for almost nine hundred years. The academic impact of Tibes was seismic: previously, little was known about Pre-Taíno cultures, and the ball-game was considered a relatively recent phenomenon, while the construction of so many stone structures implied a highly organized society able to plan, mobilize, control and sustain many workers. Some experts go further, claiming that the plazas were positioned to reflect the seasonal solar equinox and solstice, making Tibes the oldest astronomical observatory in the Caribbean.

The museum

To get the best overview of the island's Pre-Columbian indigenous cultures, start at the enlightening **museum** at the entrance. Exhibits are arranged chronologically, beginning with the **Archaic** culture 4500 years ago (see p.261) and ending with the Taínos, embellished with displays of pottery, stone tools and other artefacts. You'll also learn about the history of the site, and the **Cohoba ritual**, where Taínos would inhale powdered (and hallucinogenic) *cohoba* seeds in order to communicate with the gods. Don't miss the intricate Igneri shell amulets shaped like frogs, haunting Taíno idols and the curious giant stone in the corner, carved over two thousand years ago – some of the guides think it was a musical instrument. Everything is labelled in English and the informative **video** has English subtitles.

The site

The site itself covers 32 acres along the banks of the Río Baramaya (officially the Río Portugués), a tranquil clearing in the forest that includes a small **botanical garden** containing native plants and trees. Beyond here are the ruins themselves, clearly defined ball-courts and plazas lined with stones. The **Plaza Principal** is the largest structure and where most of the burials were found: the monolith in the centre marks the spot where a baby was interred in a vase, obviously a location of great spiritual or ritual significance. Next door is the Sun or **Star Plaza**, comprising six triangular stone platforms and most likely used as a sort of astronomical calendar. Surrounding these core plazas are the main ball-courts, many very long and lined with standing stones, while paving stones denote where seating areas once stood. The most unusual is the **Batey de Herradura** (Horseshoe Ball Court, named because of its shape), measuring 35m long by 9m wide and constructed by the Pre-Taínos. The largest is the **Batey de Cemí**, lining the Río Baramaya for 76m, also constructed by the Pre-Taínos. **El Batey del Cacique** is the oldest court, measuring 15m by 10m and located on the north side of the site, with two parallel rows of stones.

Hacienda Buena Vista

Coffee and sugar once dominated the Puerto Rican economy, a legacy beautifully preserved at the **HACIENDA BUENA VISTA** (Wed–Sun tours at 8.30am, 10.30am, 1.30pm & 3.30pm; $8; ☎787/722-5834 ext 240 Mon–Fri, 787/284-7020 weekends and holidays), offering a rare opportunity to tour one of the island's historic plantations. Note that you must **reserve a tour in advance** – don't just turn up. English tours normally run at 1.30pm and last around two hours, but call to check. You can take additional tours of the especially fertile grounds and Río Canas gorge – these last two hours (Wed–Sun 8.30–10.30am; $7) or four hours (Fri & Sat 8am–noon; $10), and are usually in Spanish only.

Some history

The hacienda was established as a small farm for cacao, corn, plantains and coffee in 1833 by **Salvador de Vives**, a Spanish émigré from Venezuela, who had moved to the island in 1821 after the South American nation became independent. Between 1845 and 1847, his son Carlos Vives built the mill-course, most of the buildings you see today and a corn mill, expanding production of coffee and corn-meal so that the plantation was booming by the early 1870s. Technology and investment were important, but as in the rest of Puerto Rico, the real foundation of plantation wealth was the back-breaking labour of African **slaves**. The **abolition of slavery** in 1873 proved the first of many blows to the Vives empire, including **Hurricane San Ciriaco** in 1899, which devastated the plantation. In 1904 the hacienda started to produce oranges for the US market, a much smaller trade which nevertheless kept it going until the 1930s. By the 1950s the virtually abandoned estate was appropriated by the government, which distributed four hundred acres to landless *Ponceños*, while the Conservation Trust acquired the remaining 86 acres preserved today.

The plantation

The core of the plantation retains the attractive, European style of the main house. Running through the yard is a narrow but fast-flowing mill-course built in 1845, which leads back towards the river and an extremely lush gorge – the plantation was once powered by water. The tour starts inside the old coffee storage room and **main house** above, all painstakingly restored in 1890s style. From here you'll be led around the main outhouses (including the **slave house** that once quartered 57 slaves), before following the mill-course above the Río Canas to the gorge at the **Salto Vives** – the vista through the bushes to the falls and pool below is the "beautiful view" ("*buena vista*") that the hacienda was named after. On the way back you'll visit the creaky wooden **roasting house** and the whirling millstones of the original **corn mill** built by Carlos Vives.

The hacienda is around 17km from Ponce Centro, at PR-123 km 16.8. It's clearly signposted with a small car park on site.

Yauco and around

Many Puerto Rican towns claim to be the capital of coffee, but only **YAUCO** owns the franchise. For over one hundred years, the town has been synonymous with the island's most respected and eagerly sought brands – **Café Yaucono** remains the best-selling Puerto Rican coffee by a long margin. Yet the coffee-growing highlands of Yauco municipality lie far to the north of the actual town, which is part of the arid southwest and better suited to sugar cane. What really makes Yauco so appealing is its vastly underrated ensemble of dazzling *criollo* buildings, early colonial ruins and culinary specialities, largely ignored by foreign tourists.

Arrival, information and accommodation

Driving into Yauco, make for the free **car park** that covers the hill above the Plaza del Mercado on Calle Comercio (follow PR-368 to Sabana Grande). You can also use the parking meters ($0.25/30min) nearer the main plazas. The **Oficina de Turismo** (Mon–Fri 8am–4pm; ☏787/267-0350) acts as the tourist centre and has some enthusiastic English-speaking members: visit their office next to the Centro de Arte Alejandro Franceschi on Parque Arturo Lluberas. You can access **free wi-fi** in the centre of town.

Yauco is best seen by car as a day-trip from the coast or Ponce, but a convenient hotel option nearby is *Best Western Pichi's Hotel* (☏787/835-3335, ⓦwww .bestwestern.com; ❺), a swish place just outside Guayanilla, at PR-127 km 8.6 (just off PR-2).

The Town

Yauco grew up around **Plaza Fernando Pacheco de Matos**, the central square surrounded by a plethora of graceful buildings. The **Iglesia Parroquial Nuestra Señora del Santísimo Rosario** (Thurs 8am–5pm; other days call ☏787/856-1222 or the *turismo*), the town's imposing church, was completed in 1934 in grand Spanish Revival style, on the site of the original established in 1754. Stroll one block south along Calle Betances and you'll hit the town's second plaza, **Parque Arturo Lluberas**.

Centro de Arte Alejandro Franceschi

One of the most opulent *criollo* homes in Puerto Rico, the Casa Franceschi stands on the southeast side of Parque Arturo Lluberas, open to the public as the **Centro de Arte Alejandro Franceschi** (Mon–Fri 8am–3pm; free) since 1988. Gifted French architect André Troublard built the house in 1907 for Alejandro Franceschi, a local businessman and philanthropist. On the outside it looks like a pretty, pale blue *criollo*-style house, trimmed with Ionic columns, but what makes it truly unique are the florid French Beaux-Arts interiors, enhanced with fine stucco work, vivid frescoes and bright oil paintings on the ceilings and walls – each room is different, giving the impression of a European palace in miniature (though the house has almost no furniture).

The first hall on the right contains a portrait of Franceschi and his wife, while the room on the left with bright pink walls was their daughter's bedroom. The **bathroom** (the one at the back, on the right) is the most impressive space in the house, ringed with exuberant frescoes painted by Polish artist H. Shoutka. Images of the Madonna and various angels grace the ceiling, while the walls boast three playful ocean-themed murals and a more unusual depiction of Dr Faust, the legendary fictional German figure who sold his soul to the devil. Ponce-born artist

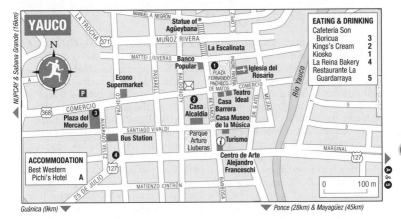

Guánica (9km) ▼

▼ Ponce (28km) & Mayagüez (45km)

Roberto Ríos worked on the warm landscapes adorning the **dining room** (at the back to the left) inspired by Franceschi's rustic plantations.

Casa Museo de la Música

The **Casa Museo de la Música** (Mon–Fri 1–3pm, Sat & Sun 8am–noon; free), a much simpler wooden affair, is far more typical of the humble but appealing *criollo* style of the time. Constructed in 1919, in 1922 it was the birthplace of local celebrity **Amaury Veray Torregrosa**, famous in Puerto Rico as the composer of the much-loved Christmas carol *Villancico Yaucano* (1951). In it, a poor boy from Yauco offers the baby Jesus a rooster, as it's the most valuable thing he has. Exhibits are basic – a few old photos, sheets of music and other memorabilia, but it makes a cosy, more intimate contrast to the Franceschi residence. You'll find the house at Calle Santiago Vivaldi Pacheco 15, around the corner from Casa Franceschi.

Eating and drinking

Yauco has a modest array of **eating** options. For cheap eats, try the cheerful food stalls in the **Plaza del Mercado** (Mon–Sat 5am–5pm, Sun 6am–noon; closed most holidays) on Calle Comercio (opposite the car park), a fine example of Art Deco architecture built in 1924. *Cafeteria Son Boricua* usually has plenty of customers, offering hearty plates of beans, tuna, *pollo asado* and *frituras* for around $5. For a cup of local **coffee**, try the *kiosco* on Plaza Fernando Pacheco de Matos, or grab hot bread and cheap pastries at *La Reina Bakery*, Pacheco and 5 de Julio (☎787/856-2065). For something cooler, *King's Cream* (daily 9am–9pm) on Calle Comercio is an outpost of the popular Puerto Rican **ice cream** chain, with all the usual fresh fruit and chocolate flavours (cones $1.50–1.98).

Puerto Ricans drive from as far as Fajardo to eat at ⚘ *Restaurante La Guardarraya* (Tues–Sun 11am–7.30pm, ☎787/856-4222, ⊛www.laguardarraya.com), at PR-127 km 6, halfway to Guayanilla from Yauco. The chief attraction is the house speciality, *chuletas can-can*, fried pork chop with thick rinds that resemble the can-can underskirts of the 1950s ($12.25). The dish was created here in 1959 by Don Juan Vera-Martínez and the restaurant is still owned by his family.

Guánica and around

Blessed with one of the south coast's most flawless natural harbours, **GUÁNICA** is a once-prosperous sugar town with a typically torpid plaza and a couple of low-key sights. The real reason so many people flock here is the adjacent **Bosque Estatal de Guánica**, a unique dry forest of twisted trees and stumpy cacti, with well-maintained hiking trails winding down to a glorious coastline of sparkling **beaches** and sprawling mangroves. The coast is also accessible by road, its highlight the coral- and mangrove-smothered **Guilligan's Island** just offshore, where you can float in crystalline waters rich with fish and crabs. With the Central Cordillera draining moisture from the trade winds, this area has the lowest annual rainfall on the island, meaning you are virtually guaranteed hot, sunny days.

Guánica is 9km southwest of Yauco on PR-116: you'll pass the turning to the forest first (PR-334), before reaching the road to the beaches (PR-333), which effectively bypasses the town. The main road to the centre is PR-332, at the next junction. Needless to say, you need a **car** to get the most out of the area, as things are extremely spread out.

Accommodation

The best places **to stay** lie along the coast, on the southern edge of the forest in the Punta San Jacinto area, where you have access to all the main attractions right on the doorstep.

Copamarina Beach Resort PR-333 km 6.5 ⊤787/821-0505, ⊛www.copamarina.com. Guánica's only resort hotel, with tasteful, low-rise wooden villas lining a narrow strip of beach and set within leafy gardens. Spacious rooms are decked out with rattan, tropical-inspired furnishings, cable TV and fridge, and all the extras are on site: tennis courts, watersports, spa, fitness centre and dive shop, as well as the posh *Alexandra* restaurant. You'll pay an extra 10 percent "resort fee". ❼

Guilligan View Apartments San Jacinto 27 ⊤787/821-4901, ⊛www.guilliganview.com. Next to *Mary Lee's*, this large house right on the water contains two basic apartments managed by the affable Rafael Rodríguez, both with kitchen and sea views. ❹

Mary Lee's by the Sea San Jacinto 25, PR-333 km 6.7 ⊤787/821-3600, ⊛www.maryleesbythesea.com. Fabulous ensemble of ten apartments and houses furnished in a whimsically florid style by sprightly octogenarian Mary Lee Alvarez, a US expat who settled here after fleeing Cuba in the 1960s. Spacious rooms and cosy bedrooms are lined with rattan floor tiles and bedecked with cheery multicoloured hand-sewn towels, duvet covers and cushions. Even the bathrooms feature installations of sand, plastic plants, fairy lights and shells. The apartments below Mary's house overlook the cay-studded bay: all of them have kitchens and a/c, but only some can be rigged up for satellite TV ($10/day). Use of the washing machine is free. Take the turning off PR-333, just beyond *Copamarina*, and follow the signs. ❹

Bosque Estatal de Guánica

Much of Guánica's seductive coastline falls within the **Bosque Estatal de Guánica** (daily 8am–5pm; free), a 37 square kilometre forest reserve that incorporates some of the driest and most unusual flora on the island. Its heart lies high above the coast, accessible via PR-334, which ends 3km from PR-116 at a car park and small information booth (Mon–Fri 6.30am–3.30pm; ⊤787/724-3724) supplying basic maps (if closed, check at the ranger station nearby). The reserve is crisscrossed by twelve well-kept and mostly signposted trails, with literally hundreds of species of **bird** flittering around the gnarled trees and bushes, in a withered landscape often reminiscent of outback Australia. Noting that Guánica is now the largest remaining tract of tropical dry coastal forest in the world, UNESCO made it a Biosphere Reserve in 1981.

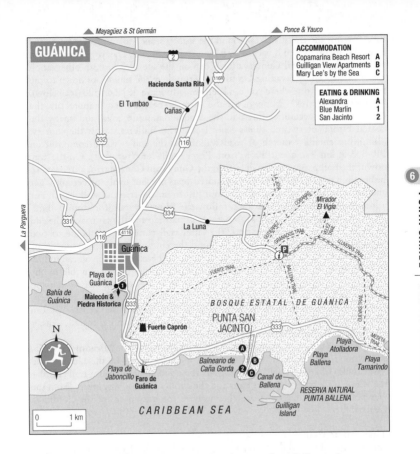

It's important to remember, however, that there are **four different forest types** here, with only one being truly exceptional: the **dry scrub forest** that lines the southern slopes, studded with the imaginatively named Spanish dildo cactus, squat melon cactus and *gumbo-limbo* trees with peeling red bark. Two-thirds of the reserve is covered in **deciduous forest** (most of the area around the information booth, which contains the majority of the bird life), while one-fifth (mostly in the sinkholes and ravines of the east side) is **evergreen forest**. **Coastal forest** lines the shore, characterized by bonsai-like shrubs and mangroves.

Impressive as all this sounds, you might find the forest a little underwhelming: unless you have a keen interest in botany, the dry landscape can get monotonous and you'll have to be here at dawn to catch most of the birds. The best strategy is to take a whole day and tackle one of the longer trails in order to appreciate the bizarre diversity of the area, combining the hike with a few hours on the beach. You'll need to bring plenty of water and preferably start early. December to April is the driest period, and you'll find the most colour, flowers and odd bouts of rain, between September and January.

The trails

One of the best hikes is the **Fuerte** trail (5.5km), which follows the ridges west from the information booth, providing stupendous views of the sea and Guánica bay. Towards the end it snakes around the stubby stone lookout tower known as **Fuerte Caprón**, which is backed by a long stone staircase. The tower was built in the 1930s by the Civil Conservation Corp on the site of a Spanish observation tower (destroyed by invading US troops). From here the trail drops down to the road (PR-333), from where you can keep going to Playa de Jaboncillo (see below).

Alternatively, trekking down to the easterly beaches you'll appreciate the transition from deciduous forest to the unique dry scrub zone, and finally the coastal littoral of twisted *gumbo-limbo* trees. The **Ballena** trail is the shortest (2km), but entails a stretch of road-walking at the end – you'll come out on PR-333 at km 8.6, about 500m from Playa Atolladora (turn left). On the way down, the trail passes a 200m detour to the **Guayacán Centenario**, a tree said to be between five hundred and seven hundred years old, but small and certainly not ancient-looking (it will take you an hour just to see the tree and walk back). For a longer and more energetic walk, follow the **Llúveras** trail (for around 4km), then the **Cuevas** dirt trail (1.5km) to Playa Tamarindo and the car park at the end of PR-333. As you might expect, the latter trail passes a cave, home to two species of bat (though you can't go beyond the entrance), as well as a grove of 3m-tall prickly-pear cacti near the coast. From the beach car park you can follow the shoreline via the **Meseta** trail (3.5km), one of the most enjoyable in the reserve – it climbs slowly from the beach along low-lying cliffs of *sebucán* and prickly-pear cactus, past rugged headlands of sea grape and purple milkweed, ending in a forest of dwarf white mangroves, buttonwood and cedar. You can also **drive** to the beach car park at the end of PR-333 to walk this trail – either way, you must retrace your steps to get back.

To just get a taste of the forest, make a shorter loop up to the **Mirador El Vigía**, a viewpoint on Criollo II, the highest hill in the reserve. Use the Llúveras and Velez trails (1.5km in total), returning via the undulating Granados trail (1km) – the whole walk takes about an hour and the climb up is not very steep. From the viewpoint on top, the forest stretches away to the hazy peaks of the Cordillera Central.

The beaches

While hiking down to the **beaches** from the hills of the dry forest is an enticing (if sweaty) option, most visitors explore the coastline by car on PR-333. Heading south from Guánica, you'll see the turning to **Playa de Jaboncillo** at km 3.1, a steep, potholed gravel road, just about manageable with a normal car. The road leads down to a secluded cove with grills, toilets and gazebos, and usually fewer people than the other beaches.

Guánica's wildly popular public beach, the **Balneario de Caña Gorda** (mid-May to mid-Aug daily 8.30am–6pm; mid-Aug to mid-May Wed–Sun till 5pm; parking $3) is at km 5.8 and officially outside the reserve. Perfect for families, it has all the facilities (including toilets), a compact tree-lined stretch of fine sand, and clear, calm water. Be warned, however, the beach can get overwhelmingly busy at weekends and holidays, especially in the summer – the car park may look big, but at these times it fills up quickly and the road outside gets jammed with traffic.

Continue along PR-333 and you'll slip back into the forest reserve, a wilder, undeveloped coastline where you can simply pull off wherever you see an inviting strip of sand. At around km 9.1 you'll reach **Playa Atolladora**, which has several sections of choppy water set around a headland, and a short drive further on, **Playa Tamarindo**, where PR-333 ends in a dusty car park. This attractive arc of sand is perfect for swimming or lounging away the afternoon – when it cools down, tackle the **Meseta** trail, which continues along the coast for another 3.5km (see above).

Guilligan's Island

Officially Cayo Aurora, **Guilligan's Island** (daily 9am–5pm) is an idyllic outcrop of thick mangroves bordered by white coral sand, just off the Guánica coast. The sobriquet recalling the US television series *Gilligan's Island* was added in the late 1960s as a marketing gimmick (but retaining a Spanish twist), and today it falls under the same DRNA management as the forest reserve.

A ferry plies back and forth from the main island, where you'll find a few barbecue huts and plenty of shade, but this isn't really a beach – being completely hemmed in by mangroves is what makes the lagoon so magical. Swim or just drift around in the incredibly clear (and shallow) water, where shoals of parrot fish and crabs huddle beneath the roots, or snorkel over the reef just beyond the jetty.

The **ferry** (Tues–Fri 9am & 11am only, Sat–Sun & holidays 9am–5pm; last boat back 5pm; $7.32 return; ☏787/821-4941) sails from the pier in front of the *San Jacinto* restaurant, on the narrow road that splits off PR-333 towards *Mary Lee's by the Sea* (taking just 10 to 15 minutes). Note that at weekends and holidays, especially in the summer, cars begin to line up at the ferry car park at around 6am, and the island can get swamped (the ferry takes 45 people per trip, with a maximum 350 allowed on the island). Taking the **private launches** from *Copamarina* or *Mary Lee's* (both charge around the same price) is a good idea, as you can set your own pick-up time and combine the trip with a visit to Ballena (see below) – you'll have to be a guest to organize this, however.

Reserva Natural Punta Ballena

Reserva Natural Punta Ballena is the flat, palm-covered headland beyond the residential area containing *Mary Lee's*. Confusingly, "Ballena" is used to describe the bay on the reserve's east side, the magnificent beach to the west and east, and sometimes the Canal de Ballena that splits the mainland from a small mangrove island offshore – Cayo Ballena. When most locals talk about Ballena, they mean the **beach**, a treeless strip of soft, fine sand with a steep drop-off – the current between the beach and the mangrove cay is quite swift, though the water isn't deep, and it's a fun place to swim, especially with shoals of trumpet fish flashing past, and pelicans nesting in the mangroves nearby.

When Guilligan's Island is full, the public ferry sometimes dumps passengers on Ballena beach ($6.42) – at other times it should be deserted, and it is most easily reached by private boat from *Copamarina* or *Mary Lee's*. Otherwise it's a long walk from Playa Atolladora.

Eating and drinking

Other than the usual fast-food chains on PR-116 at the edge of town, eating options in Guánica are disappointingly sparse. The best place for a posh meal is the *Copamarina* resort, while Puerto Rican tourists grab snacks at the cluster of *kioscos* at PR-333 km 1.4, as the road bypasses Guánica on the way to the beaches – stick with simple things here, like the *frituras* or corned-beef *empanadillas*.

Alexandra *Copamarina Beach Resort*, PR-333 km 6.5 ☏787/821-0505. The only fine-dining option in the area, an elegant indoor restaurant facing the ocean, with floor-to-ceiling windows and billowing white curtains. The menu is a blend of Puerto Rican and Italian influences, with a special focus on seafood, but you can also order sizzling meats such as pork chops, with tropically inspired pineapple sauce (mains $20–45). For lunch or something a little less formal, try the resort's *Las Palmas Café*.

Blue Marlin Avda Esperanza Idrach 59, Guánica Malecón ☏787/821-5858. Old-fashioned cantina-style restaurant, right on the *malecón* (seafront) facing the bay, offering a reasonable seafood menu ($13–14) and cold Medalla ($2–3); in between meal times, the bar caters to a steady stream of loyal regulars and the odd tourist, though things get more animated on weekends when it hosts live music and salsa. Closed Mon & Tues.

San Jacinto km 0.5, San Jacinto ☎787/821-4941. Restaurant that sees a steady trade from the Guilligan's Island ferry. The baked or fried fish, prawns ($18) and lobster ($25) are always fresh, while kids get a special menu of pizza and burgers.

If you want to save money, opt for the rice and meat dishes ($3–4) sold from the self-service window outside, and eat at the tables nearby. The *chapín empanadillas* are the best choice, bursting with fish, and they also pour a mean *piña colada* ($3) and coffee ($0.75). Daily 9am–late.

The old sugar country

The now empty plains between the southeast coast and the mountains, once the heart of **sugar country**, show few signs of their former glory. Yet the inviting hot springs at **Coamo** and the graceful old sugar towns of **Arroyo** and **Guayama** are steeped in history, legacies of the great wealth created in the colonial and early American periods. The last in particular is a smaller, less pretentious version of Ponce, well stocked with ramshackle but striking architecture, and a smattering of galleries and museums. The lack of beaches means you'll see few tourists here, and for once the coast is not the main attraction. **Salinas** is the modest exception, with a yacht-filled marina, seafood specialities and a spread of tempting offshore cays to explore. Access to the region is easy via PR-52 and PR-53, slicing through vast swathes of abandoned, overgrown plots of land that testify to the drastic collapse of not just the domestic sugar industry, but all of Puerto Rico's traditional agriculture since World War II.

Coamo and around

Founded in 1579, **COAMO** is one of the oldest towns in Puerto Rico, best known today for its rustic outdoor **hot springs**. The town itself is 34km from Ponce and a short drive from *autopista* PR-52, the oddly appealing cluster of ageing buildings in the centre evidence of its long history. There are no options for lodging here – your best bet is to stay near the hot springs themselves (see opposite), or visit for the day from Ponce or the coast.

The Town

Downtown Coamo is worth a detour to soak up the bustling, no-nonsense atmosphere and pretty buildings around the central **Plaza Luis Muñoz Rivera**, dominated by the main church, the **Iglesia Católica San Blás de Illesca**. The current building dates from 1784. The interior is unusually ornate, with a fine Neoclassical *retablo*, and you'll also see a rare painting by **José Campeche**, *El Bautisterio* – the artist originally had three paintings inside the church, but one was lost and the other, *Las Animas*, deteriorated so badly it had to be copied and replaced by Francisco Oller in 1888. The latter is near the main entrance (on the right as you come in) – the blonde woman at the base is said to have been Oller's mistress at the time.

On the plaza's southwest corner, the **Museo Histórico** (free; ☎787/825-1150) occupies an eye-catching, reddish townhouse with a tranquil *patio interior* that virtually drips with a sense of colonial Spain; the odd collection of bits and pieces inside reflects Coamo's chequered history. It's normally only open on weekdays (8am–4.30pm) or by appointment – check at the Instituto de Cultura next door (Mon–Fri 8am–4pm). The house was built in the nineteenth century by **Don Clotilde Santiago**, a wealthy landowner, and much of his original mahogany and cedar furniture is on display inside.

Eating and drinking

Your choices in Coamo are restricted to the usual range of Puerto Rican diners, stalls and rustic restaurants outside the town. On the southwest corner of the plaza, *El Faro Deportivo* is a cheap dive bar, propped up by a colourful assortment of beer-nursing locals and open from early afternoon daily. The best local food can be found at the **kioscos** lining PR-14 south of town: *Don Pablo's* van specializes in roast chicken ($3 for half, $6 for whole chicken), and is usually parked just outside the downtown area (on the right driving into town). If you're looking for a sit-down meal, *La Guitarra* at PR-153 km 12.4 (☎787/803-2881) is the best of several restaurants between Coamo and the highway, a creaky wooden house serving *lechón* and other rural Puerto Rican favourites from $8.50.

Baños de Coamo

Local legend has it that Juan Ponce de León's biggest (and fatal) mistake was to seek the fountain of youth in Florida, when the true source of eternal life was in Puerto Rico all along, at the **Baños de Coamo** (Coamo hot springs). The elderly locals hobbling down to the baths for a daily dip may appear to throw doubt on this claim, but even if you've been to hot springs elsewhere, the sheer novelty of scalding hot mineral pools in the Caribbean makes them all the more enticing. The water shoots out of the ground at 43°C, but cools quickly in the baths: its therapeutic qualities stem from healthy doses of carbonic and sulphuric acid combined with magnesium carbonate.

You have two choices here: the slightly smarter and larger pools within the *Hotel Baños de Coamo* (daily 9.30am–5.30pm; non-guests $5), lined with some of the brickwork from the original nineteenth-century Spanish hotel and spa, or the **public pools** (daily 6am–7pm; $3) at the end of the lane that continues to the right of the hotel (park along the road). These were spruced up in 2010 and feature small but clean landscaped baths surrounded by flowers. If you visit during weekdays in "winter", you'll usually have them to yourself.

Hotels have been welcoming visitors to the hot springs since 1847, and though the current accommodation is basic, the *Hotel Baños de Coamo* (☎787/825-2239; ❸) offers a bucolic setting on the Río Coamo. Rooms are set in slightly worn two-storey wooden chalets in flowery, overgrown gardens above the river, with balconies, air conditioning and basic cable TV. Some rooms are in dire need of renovation – check yours on arrival. The hot springs are at the end of PR-546 and signposted off PR-153, which runs between Coamo and the PR-52 *autopista*.

Playa de Salinas

Facing a bay of tiny, mangrove-swamped islands, the small village of **PLAYA DE SALINAS** makes a convenient pit stop on the drive along the south coast. It's been a favourite of yacht owners for years, with the marina and most of the restaurants clustered at the end of PR-701, a few kilometres south of the largely uninteresting agricultural town of **Salinas**.

Accommodation

The ageing *Posada El Náutico* (☎787/824-3185, ✉jarce@coqui.net; ❸), Marina de Salinas, at the end of PR-701, is a bit frayed around the edges, but is still the best place **to stay** if you end up in Salinas. The basic motel-like rooms come with air conditioning, fridge and local TV, and the coin **laundry** serving the marina is open to guests (daily 8am–9pm).

The beach and cays

Despite the name, Playa de Salinas is essentially a cluster of low-rise homes and restaurants lining a bay thick with groping mangroves, and there is no actual beach as such. **Polita's Beach** (Sat, Sun & holidays 9am–11pm; $3 parking; ☎787/824-4184) is just off PR-701 in the middle of the village, little more than a break in the dense wall of knotted mangrove roots, which nevertheless becomes inundated with salsa-dancing locals on weekends and holidays, enjoying the music, snacks and drinks at the **kioscos** here.

Some of the cays offshore do have beaches, and make far more enticing targets: **Cayo Mata** is the largest, but the closest is **Cayo Matita**, around 200m from the jetty and surrounded by a narrow strip of sand. With more time and energy you can explore the **Cayos de Ratones** further out, but make sure you know exactly where you're going before setting off. The most enjoyable (and eco-friendly) way to explore the cays is to rent **kayaks** from the *Posada El Náutico* ($15 first hour; $10/hr thereafter), but you can also take 35-minute boat rides around the bay on *La Paseodora* (Sat, Sun & holidays 1–6pm, longer hours July–Aug; $5). This small ferry sails from the Terminal de la Paseodora (☎787/824-2649), a little jetty next door to *El Balcón del Capitán*. The captain will normally drop you off on one of the cays if you ask, and pick you up later.

Eating and drinking

PR-701 takes you past several **restaurants** that hug the shore, most featuring **mojo isleño**, a piquant sauce made with tomatoes and garlic, usually added to fish or various *frituras*.

El Balcón del Capitán, c/Principal A-54, PR-701 (Mon–Sat 10.30am–10.30pm, Sun till 9.30pm; ☎787/824-6210) specializes in grand lobster dishes and fresh fish, with an outdoor terrace on the water (mains $7–30), while nearby *El Roble* at c/ Principal A-79 is open similar hours (☎787/824-2377) and is known for its *siete potencias* "seven power stew", crammed with seafood. You can also eat at *Restaurante Costa Marina* (☎787/752-8484) inside the *Posada El Náutico*, on the second floor of a wooden boathouse, providing bird's-eye views of the marina and islet-studded bay. It features an expansive but fairly standard menu of Puerto Rican roast meats and seafood (mains $9.95–24) but is also the best place for a coffee or cocktail.

Aguirre and around

Much of the fragile coastline between Salinas and Guayama is protected within DRNA reserves, centred on the **Reserva Nacional de Investigación Estuarina de Bahía de Jobos**. The reserve covers around 11.5 square kilometres of mangrove forest and freshwater wetland, including habitats for the endangered brown pelican, peregrine falcon, hawksbill sea turtle and West Indian manatee. The best place to get oriented is the **visitor centre** in Aguirre, where you can also learn about the various hiking and kayaking trails in the reserve.

Aguirre

The sprawling **Central Aguirre Sugar Company** complex at the end of PR-705, just south of PR-3, was constructed between 1899 and 1902 by a US syndicate, becoming one of the largest sugar plants in the Caribbean and precipitating the development of **AGUIRRE** town, a self-contained community entirely dependent on the sugar factory. The company ceased operations in 1980, and the government maintained a small sugar operation here until everything closed in 1990. Today Aguirre is remarkably vibrant, with many former employees still living in the houses nearby, though all the chief buildings are abandoned and the plant itself is locked up, a slowly decaying monument to the island's now moribund sugar industry.

PR-705 makes a loop through the town and past its only real attraction, the Jobos reserve's **Centro de Visitantes** (Mon–Fri 7.30–11.45am & 1–3.45pm; ☎787/853-4617) at PR-705 2.3km, occupying what was once the social club or "Casa Club" of the *Hotel Aguirre*. When it comes to ecology and the environment, this is the most illuminating information centre on the island, with a large exhibition area covering every aspect of the conservation work in the Jobos estuary, as well as the rich array of marine and bird life in the area. Displays also cover the various habitats in the reserve, including coral reefs, and the history of Aguirre itself.

Guayama

In the nineteenth century **GUAYAMA** was one of the grandest towns on the island, overflowing with money garnered from nearby sugar-cane plantations. Though it remains a large, lively place, it's the legacies of that period, chiefly its fine **architecture**, that make a visit worthwhile today. The local **Oficina de Turismo** (Mon–Fri 8am–4pm) is housed in the attractively renovated birthplace of **Luis Palés Matos** (1898–1959), acclaimed poet and creator of the genre known as Afro-Antillano, a blend of Afro-Caribbean words and Spanish. You'll find the "Casa del Poeta" at Calle Ashford and Baldorioty, just off the plaza.

Accommodation

If you get stuck in Guayama, aim for the tatty but bearable *Molino Inn Hotel* (☎787/866-1515, ⓦwww.molinoinn.net; ❸) at PR-54 km 2.1, just outside the centre. Its twenty motel-style rooms are a little faded, but adequate for a one-night stay, with rattan furnishings, air conditioning and basic cable TV.

The Town

Driving into town on PR-3, stop first at the **Centro de Bellas Artes** (Tues–Sun 9am–4.30pm; free), an imposing Neoclassical structure built in 1927 and formerly the Supreme Court. Today it houses an odd assortment of fine art, archeology and sculpture, much of the latter created by local artist Gladys Nieves. The building itself is the real attraction, though the **Sala Taína** contains a couple of ghoulish Taíno petroglyphs and a small collection of Taíno tools, ceremonial objects and ceramics. The **Sala de Simón Madera** is dedicated to the composer of the popular **danza** *Mis Amores*, containing his old violin, desk and portrait. Madera supposedly wrote the dance in Casa Cautiño (see below), and died in Guayama in 1957.

Plaza Cristóbal Colón

In town itself, you should be able to park close to the central **Plaza Cristóbal Colón**, a large square dotted with aromatic West Indian bay trees. Built in a neo-Romanesque style in 1874, the **Iglesia San Antiono de Padua** graces the east side of the plaza, its soaring towers incorporating medieval influences such as a *westwerk* (an entrance area with upper chamber) and an elaborate rose window of stained glass, though local comparisons with Notre-Dame are pushing things a bit. It's open for Mass (Mon–Fri 6–7.30am & 4.30–7.30pm, Sat 6.30–8.30am & 6–8pm, and all day Sun), but tends to be locked up at other times.

On the north side of the plaza, the **Museo Casa Cautiño** (Tues–Sat 9am–4.30pm, Sun 10.30am–4pm; free) comes closest to capturing the refined opulence of the sugar era, a frost-white *criollo* villa, immaculately restored as a small period museum. The rooms feature some of the original furniture and European artwork collected by the former owners, but the real star is the house itself. It was completed in 1887 for Don Genaro Cautiño Vázquez, a local celebrity who was at various times the mayor, judge and colonel of the local militia. His descendants lived here until 1981, when the house was donated to the state in lieu of taxes.

Eating and drinking

Guayama's central plaza is lined with plenty of unexceptional **places to eat**, serving Puerto Rican snacks, pizza and sandwiches, but for historic ambience *El Suarito* (☎787/864-1820) at c/Derkes 6 is hard to beat, a Spanish-style canteen lodged in an open-front colonial building dating from 1862. *Suarito* opened in the 1950s and while some of the clientele look like they've been regulars since then, the cheap *comida criolla* (dishes for $5–6) is tasty enough (roast chicken, pork chops), and the bar serves cold Medalla for $1.75 and sandwiches for $2.50.

Alternatively, cool down with one of the freshly made ice creams at 🎋 *Rex Cream* (daily 9.30am–10.30pm), c/Derkes 24, which has all the usual innovative flavours from lime, tamarind and *guanabana* (soursop), to chocolate and pistachio ($1.50–4.25). *Rex* also has a small branch on the northeast corner of the plaza.

Arroyo

Once a thriving port, **ARROYO** is a ghost of its former self, a "Little Paris" lined with fancy mansions, where the local plantation elite would promenade in horse-drawn carriages. Though it attracts plenty of sentimental Puerto Rican tourists at the weekends, attempts to spruce up the town after years of decline have had mixed results. It's this undeveloped, no-frills Puerto Rican quality that makes it appealing, however, with a motley collection of pubs and canteens maintaining the raffish if not quite seedy charm of a small port district, and the main street still boasting some exquisite townhouses from its golden age.

The Town

Calle Morse (PR-178) runs through the heart of Arroyo from PR-3 to the *malecón*, lined with the most florid examples of wooden *criollo* architecture. The best stretch is the final section south of the tiny plaza. The town does have a **tourist office** (Mon–Fri 8am–noon & 1.30–4.30pm; ☎787/839-3500 ext 231), just north of the plaza on Calle Morse (on the right as you head onto town), which has plenty of Spanish information about the town, and the latest updates about sights and events.

The only real "sight" in Arroyo is the **Museo Antigua Aduana** (Wed–Sun 8.30am–4.30pm; free; ☎787/839-8096) just south of the plaza at c/Morse 65, though the most striking thing about it is the incredibly opulent entrance, crowned with a US shield and bald eagle glittering with Mayan-like splendour. The former customs house contains galleries of local contemporary art, and items related to the first telegraph line laid in Latin America, installed by Samuel Morse in 1859.

Calle Morse ends at the **malecón** or seafront, also known as Paseo de Las Américas, a dusty, run-down and usually deserted area, which only comes to life on weekends when the bars nearby fill up with boozing locals.

Eating and drinking

Eating options in Arroyo are not particularly inspiring, and you're better off heading 10km east to the restaurants along the coast (see p.118).

In Arroyo itself the *malecón* sports a couple of unappealing dive bars and diners, while a better option is *Panadería La Arroyana* at the end of Calle Morse, at no. 53 (Sun–Thurs 6am–9pm, Fri & Sat till 11pm; ☎787/271-4884). Grab a toasted sandwich ($1.50–4.50), cake or coffee for just $0.75. *Danny's BBQ* (closed Sun; ☎787/271-2158) at no. 66, in a cul-de-sac just off Calle Morse, knocks up juicy *pollo asado* ($6.50).

For **a drink**, *El Trombon del Mar* nearby is normally open during the day, and is one of the more attractive options along the *malecón*, with a wooden bar, cheap local booze and, worryingly, a well-used karaoke machine.

La Ruta Panorámica

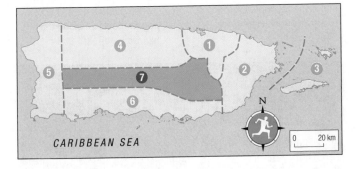

CARIBBEAN SEA

0   20 km

CHAPTER 7 # Highlights

✳ **Lechoneras** Feast on a sumptuous meal of *lechón*, roast suckling pig, served at the rustic mountain shacks in Guavate, north of the Carite forest. See p.240

✳ **Cañón de San Cristóbal** Scale the precipitous, jungle-clad walls of this mesmerizing canyon, a jagged gash through the hills best explored with an experienced guide. See p.243

✳ **Bosque Estatal de Toro Negro** This beguiling forest reserve covers some of the highest peaks in Puerto Rico, with tranquil trails, bubbling falls and cooling freshwater pools. See p.247

✳ **Cerro de Punta** Hike or grind your car up the potholed road to Puerto Rico's highest peak, an isolated, mist-drenched summit towering above the whole island. See p.248

✳ **Jayuya** Get to grips with Puerto Rico's Taíno soul at this sleepy mountain town, with its evocative museum, haunting petroglyphs and the annual Festival Nacional Indígena. See p.251

✳ **Coffee** The unspoiled hill town of Maricao is famed for its exceptional coffee – celebrated at the Festival del Café each year – and family-owned plantations sell rich, potent roasts all along the highway. See p.258

▲ The Salto de Doña Juana

7

La Ruta Panorámica

Slicing across the physical and spiritual heart of Puerto Rico, the **Ruta Panorámica** follows the highest ridges of the Central Cordillera for 266km. This scenic highway cuts through some of the least explored but most rewarding parts of the island, snaking among mist-shrouded peaks, scintillating viewpoints and dense, dimly lit forests. This is rural Puerto Rico at its most traditional, a patchwork of small **coffee** farms shrouded in *palo colorado* forest, where the local *colmado* (shop) doubles as a bar, and smoky roadside barbecues cook up roast pork and thick wedges of banana. It's a landscape inhabited by the descendants of the **jíbaros**, the hard-working peasant farmers who first colonized the jungle-drenched slopes and who embody much of Puerto Rico's romantic ideas about its past: humble but wise, poor but proudly independent.

You can follow the route in either direction, but the further west you drive, the more rural and traditional things become. The **Bosque Estatal de Carite** is one of four **forest reserves** along the way, with basic camping facilities and trails in various states of use, while the **lechoneras** of Guavate roast succulent hunks of pork nearby. Keep heading west and you'll reach workaday **Aibonito**, host to an exuberant **flower festival** and the staging post for the **Cañón de San Cristóbal**, a dizzying gorge en route to **Barranquitas**, one of the region's most absorbing towns. Straddling the centre of the island, the **Bosque Estatal de Toro Negro** is Puerto Rico's most alluring forest park. Nearby **Jayuya** has become the focus of a mini-Taíno revival, and **Adjuntas** remains a conservative, traditional hill town, though it's home to **Casa Pueblo**, a cultural centre and hub of environmental activism. Finally, perched on the western end of the cordillera, sleepy **Maricao** is enveloped by some of the world's finest **coffee** plantations, and is home to the best of the mountain hotels, *Hacienda Juanita*.

Driving the Ruta Panorámica

The route, officially **La Ruta Panorámica Luiz Muñoz Marín** after the first elected governor of Puerto Rico, is really an interlocking network of around forty different rural highways, so you should follow the small brown "Ruta" signs throughout – these can be unreliable, however, so invest in a detailed atlas or map of the island. You'll need two or three days to see everything, and longer if you intend to stop for some hiking along the way.

On the east coast, the road begins as a loop between Yabucoa and Maunabo, incorporating scenic coastal highway PR-901 (see p.116). From Yabucoa, PR-182, a narrow road that rarely sees much traffic, takes you into the mountains, and eventually, via PR-181 and PR-7740, into the **Bosque Estatal de Carite**.

Despite their somewhat hazardous reputation, driving the twisty roads up in the mountains is far less dangerous than the speeding highways of San Juan, assuming

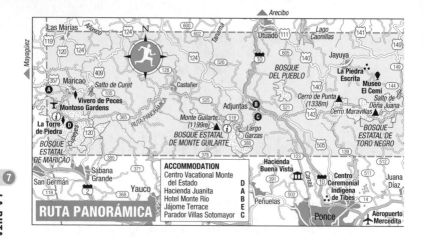

you stay within the fairly slow speed limits (usually 35mph), and take your time. All the roads are paved but heavy rain can cause problems, and there are some traffic black-spots around Aibonito. **Places to stay** are usually off the main route, and it's worth booking ahead as rooms are limited, though you should have no trouble finding **petrol stations**. Note that to **camp** in any of the forests, you'll need to get permits in advance from the DRNA in San Juan (see p.26).

Bosque Estatal de Carite

Rising gently from the east coast, the Ruta Panorámica winds its way past isolated farms for 25km before running into the **BOSQUE ESTATAL DE CARITE**, a lush mountain forest of *pino hondureño*, subtropical *palma de lluvia* and aged *palo colorado* trees. Covering an area of around 27 square kilometres, the land ranges from 240 to 900m above sea level, making it several degrees cooler than the coast, and was once laced with 25 **hiking trails**, though Hurricane Georges washed most of these away in 1998. The most popular of those remaining is the 800m trail leading to **Charco Azul**, an inviting freshwater swimming hole.

The forest **information office** is on the north side of the reserve in **Guavate** (see opposite), which isn't really very convenient unless you're driving from San Juan (coming from the east you'll have driven through the forest by the time you reach it). The more compelling reason to visit this area is to trawl the numerous *lechoneras* nearby, purveyors of magnificent barbecued meat.

Santuario de La Virgen del Carmen

Also known as the Montaña Santa ("Holy Mountain"), the **Santuario de La Virgen del Carmen** (open 24hr; free; ☎787/736-5750, ⓦwww.santuariopr.org) is one of Puerto Rico's most revered **shrines**, clearly signposted off PR-7740.

Little is known about the woman who lived here between 1901 and 1909, but **Elenita de Jesús** was undoubtedly a strong Catholic evangelizing presence in the region at a time when many feared that, under US control, Protestant faiths would swamp the island. Her intense devotion to God and extreme piety convinced local people that she was an incarnation of Mary herself, the **Virgen del Carmen**, and after her death the mountain became a popular place of prayer and pilgrimage.

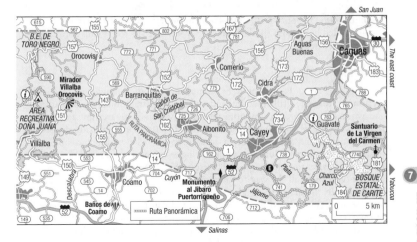

Such practices have always sat uneasily with the Catholic Church, and in 1997 the Bishop of Caguas ruled that Elenita was definitely not Mary, only a woman "of extraordinary spiritual gifts and piety". Nevertheless, many Puerto Ricans continue to believe.

Across from the car park you'll find the Nuestro Templo del Santuario or just **La Capilla**, a simple single-storey chapel constructed in 1985 on the site of three previous shrines dating back to the time of Elenita. Inside you'll find images of Mary and a small chapel dedicated to Charlie Rodríguez (see p.90). Beyond the car park, **El Arco de La Virgen** is a white gate that leads to a grassy trail up the hill, past representations of the fourteen Stations of the Cross to **Las Tres Cruces** (three wooden crosses), depicting the Crucifixion. It's an especially venerated spot, with arresting views across the forest, often shrouded in mist in the early mornings.

Area Recreativa Charco Azul

Beyond the *santuario* the road widens, and when PR-7740 meets PR-184 it's worth leaving the *ruta* for the **Area Recreativa Charco Azul** (daily 9am–5pm), a short 1km detour south at PR-184 km 16.6. The "blue pool" is the most popular attraction in the forest, a freshwater pond at the end of the 800m **Charco Azul Trail**. It's deep enough for paddling and usually swimming, and can get busy on weekends, but at other times you'll probably have it to yourself. The area is clearly signposted, with a car park and picnic area on the right, and the trailhead to the pool, campground and toilets on the left.

Area Recreativa Guavate

From Chaco Azul, PR-184 climbs 5km through the forest to the junction with PR-179, the *ruta*'s highest point in the reserve, before curling around the **Area Recreativa Guavate** (Mon–Fri 9am–4.30pm, Sat & Sun 8am–5pm), a further 1.5km down the slopes at km 27.3. This is technically a spur of the Ruta Panorámica, as the main route follows PR-179 south, but worth a detour nonetheless. Named after the *barrio* of Guavate, the recreation area is a series of shady picnic spots along both sides of the road, with a **campground** off to the left. You'll also find a few muddy hiking **trails** in the area – for the latest on conditions keep driving another 3km north to the tiny DRNA **Oficina Oficial de Manejo**

(Mon–Fri 7am–3.30pm; ☎787/747-4545) on the left. Ask here for basic maps (it's usually staffed by Spanish speakers only). Beyond here the forest ends abruptly in *lechón* paradise (see below).

Eating

No trip to Puerto Rico would be complete without sampling at least one **lechonera**, roadside grills that barbecue whole pigs, traditionally over charcoal and wood fires, to produce mouthwatering roast pork with a crispy, fatty skin. Basted with *jugo de naranjas agria* (sour orange juice), *lechón* is normally devoured with plantains and **aji-li-mojili**, a local dressing. The undisputed home of professional roasters is **Guavate**, with the highest concentration of *lechoneras* on PR-184, just after the entrance to the forest in the Los Montañez sector, but you'll see plenty of them all the way to junction 31 on *autopista* PR-52. On weekends, and especially Sundays, these places double as salsa clubs, with thousands of *sanjuaneros* clogging the roads, drinking beer and dancing till late. Most *lechoneras* operate canteen-style systems where you order from the counter: *lechón* is normally priced by weight (around $8.50 per pound, or 400g), while you can choose a variety of sides such as rice and beans, plantains or bananas.

The best place to aim for is ⌘ *Lechonera El Rancho Original,* PR-184 km 27.5 (☎787/747-7296). Though many places only open on weekends, this lauded shack starts roasting daily for breakfast. You can park at the front (they also have an ATM), though on weekends you may have to use the car park nearby ($3). *Lechonera Los Piños,* PR-184 km 27.7, further down the road from *El Rancho,* is open longer hours and serves special sausages and *arroz con guinea* (rice with guinea hen) as well as the main event (Mon–Thurs 5am–8pm, Fri–Sun till 10pm; ☎787/286-1917).

Cayey

The prosperous town of **CAYEY** is the first major settlement on the *ruta*, a fast-expanding community thanks to the PR-52 *autopista* that sweeps right through it. The town was formally established in 1773 and is said to be named after the Taíno word for "place of many waters", though it's also sometimes known as *La Ciudad de las Brumas* ("the city of the fog") due to its misty location sandwiched between the mountains. It's only worth a brief pit stop to grab some food and to check out the enlightening museum on the outskirts.

Accommodation

Set on a small hilltop just off the *ruta*, 9km from downtown Cayey, *Jájome Terrace*, at PR-15 km 18.6 (☎787/738-4016, ⓦwww.jajometerrace.com; ❹) is a guest-house and restaurant with spectacular views over the Jájome Valley. Rooms are clean and comfy, with bright white walls and a balcony (the best feature), though some are starting to show their age and you won't get TV or phones (mobile reception is also bad); only five of the ten rooms have air conditioning (it's usually cool enough with ceiling fan). You'll see the small parking area just off PR-15, around 500m after the junction with PR-741.

The Town

Cayey is a typical Puerto Rican town, with strip malls on the outskirts and a jumble of low-rise buildings in its cramped centre. It does, however, boast a small University

The archetype of the **jíbaro** has achieved iconic status in Puerto Rico, despite referring to the humble, hard-working and generally poverty-stricken **farmers** who worked the island's rugged interior over the last four hundred years. Originally applied by the Spanish to runaway Taíno slaves, by the end of the nineteenth century the term "jíbaro" had come to represent the agricultural working class, a *criollo* blend of all the early inhabitants of the island. The idealization of the *jíbaro* began in the 1920s, when artists such as Ramón Frade started to paint romantic images of the Puerto Rican countryside and what he considered its noble peasantry, and when the Popular Democratic Party (PDP) was founded in 1938, it adopted the *jíbaro* hat, the *pava*, as a symbol of its commitment to the common man. After World War II things started to change: the terms *jíbaro* and *jíbara* (for women) became more pejorative, equating to something like "bumpkin" or "hillbilly", a connotation vividly described by Esmeralda Santiago in *When I Was Puerto Rican* (see p.279). Today, in rapidly modernizing Puerto Rico, the true *jíbaro* has disappeared, and for many the word has regained its romantic associations, evoking nostalgia for a more traditional, stable and simpler time. Few Puerto Ricans would be happy being called *jíbaro*, but most retain respect for what the term has come to symbolize: Puerto Rico's traditional roots.

of Puerto Rico campus, and here you'll find a real gem, the **Museo de Arte Dr. Pío López Martínez** (Mon–Fri 8am–4.30pm, Sat & Sun 11am–5pm; free; ☎787/738-2161), dedicated primarily to local boy **Ramón Frade** (somewhat confusingly, the museum is named after its founder, a university professor). Frade, who was born in Cayey in 1875 became part of what's sometimes termed the **Costumbrista school** of painters, with his idealized view of rural Puerto Rican life and particularly the *jíbaro* (see above). Inside you'll find temporary exhibits related to his work, as well as La Casa Frade, a faithful reproduction of the artist's childhood home, with clapboard walls, period furniture and replicas of some of his most famous works, including *El Pan Nuestro* ("Our Bread") now displayed in San Juan, (see p.61). The museum also has a collection of *cartels*, the exuberant posters used to promote Puerto Rican festivals and musicals. Everything is presented beautifully, but labels are usually in Spanish only. The museum sits just inside the main entrance of the university on PR-14, heading out of Cayey towards Caguas. Use the free car park on site.

Eating

The best **places to eat** in Cayey tend to lie on the main roads and mountains outside the town centre. Failing that, you'll find all the usual fast-food chains on PR-1 as it skirts the town.

El Cuñao PR-1 km 65.5 ☎787-263-0511. Around 8km west of Cayey, conveniently positioned on twisting PR-1 and the Ruta Panorámica itself, this justly popular local lunch stop has friendly staff and glorious *lechón asado* (less than $10), *morcilla* sausages, rice and beans, *mofongo* and all the other core *criollo* dishes. Try and park on the road outside. Daily 7am–6pm.

El Mesón de Jorge PR-14 km 57 ☎787/263-2800. This modern dining room serves high-quality Puerto Rican cuisine: *asopaos* from $10, six types of *mofongo* from $12 and succulent *chuletas*

($22.50). The restaurant is located at the junction of PR-14 and PR-1, a few kilometres east of the town centre: it's the wooden building off PR-14, behind the car dealership. Wed & Thurs 11am–9pm, Fri–Sun till 10pm.

Sand and the Sea PR-715 km 5.2 ☎787/738-9086. For a stunning location and convivial atmosphere, it's hard to beat this rustic perch overlooking the mountains, with awe-inspiring views of the south coast beyond. The food is fairly standard Puerto Rican fare, though (mains $15–20). Follow the signs to *Siempre Viva – Sand and the Sea* is next door. Open Sat & Sun only.

Aibonito and around

One of the largest towns on the Ruta Panorámica, **AIBONITO** is known as *La Ciudad de las Flores* ("the city of flowers"), a sobriquet marked by a giant **flower festival** every summer. Just to the north, the **Cañón de San Cristóbal** cuts across the hills like a narrow slit, its soaring, fern-smothered walls the ideal stomping ground for hikers and adrenaline junkies, while the **Mirador Piedra Degetau** offers a gentler but equally spectacular panorama of the region. Despite the oft-quoted legend that the town's name stems from its beauty (an early Spanish visitor is said to have exclaimed "*Ay, que bonito*" on seeing the area), you'll see little evidence of this outside festival time, and it's a sprawling, unattractive place often choked with full-size SUVs barely able to pass through the narrow mountain roads.

Accommodation

The *Posada El Coquí*, at PR-722 km 7.3 (⊙787/735-3150; ❸) looks unappealing from the outside, set above the "Happy Plaza" shopping mall and a fried chicken takeaway, but it's surprisingly comfortable, with thirteen large, modern rooms equipped with kitchenette, cable TV and air conditioning. It's not far from the junction with PR-14 – make sure you call in advance.

The Town

The only reason for a trip into Aibonito is the **Festival de las Flores** (held between the last weekend of June and the first weekend of July), a cornucopia of blooming orchids, ginger flowers, rambling bougainvilleas and even miniature *flamboyant* trees. The festival has a permanent site on the outskirts of the town, just off PR-722 km 6.7, where up to sixty booths sell all manner of blossoming plants and workshops are held by local experts. **Live music** is also a big draw, with salsa and *merengue* stars flying in to attend, and there are plenty of arts, crafts and food stalls to complement the flora. Parking is free, and entrance is usually around $7.

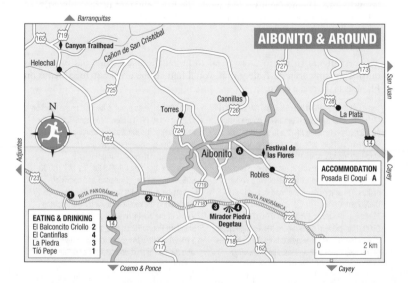

At other times there's little to see in the town centre, and with the Ruta Panorámica running along the ridges south of Aibonito, heading downtown is unnecessary unless you need to visit the bank or stay the night.

Eating

As with many towns in the mountains, the best **restaurants** in Aibonito can be found outside the centre, though there are plenty of US fast-food chains lining PR-14 on the eastern edge of town, should you get desperate.

El Balconcito Criollo PR-7718 km 3.1, just before the junction with PR-14 ☎787/735-2005. This welcoming restaurant is a wooden building with veranda and eating area overlooking a small gulley. It does all the usual *criollo* dishes, as well as delicious roast pork and chicken, and there's plenty of parking. Tues–Sun 9am–11pm.

El Cantinflas PR-722, at the junction with PR-162 ☎787/735-8870. For a more casual experience, pull over at this no-frills place just before the *mirador*, specializing in spicy fajitas and other standard but filling Mexican fare like burritos and tacos for just $1.75–3. You can also get drinks at the bar (live music on weekends), and enjoy views of Aibonito from the back. Sun–Thurs 10am–10pm, Fri & Sat till 1am.

La Piedra PR-7718 km 0.8 ☎787/735-1034. Right on the *ruta* (next to the Mirador Piedra Degetau), this is one of the most popular restaurants in the area thanks to its equally spectacular views, quality Puerto Rican food, and entertaining owner, radio talk-show host Joe Esterás. Try the perfectly grilled baby pork ribs with *tostones*, or the innovative "mountain and sea" blend of *pechuga* (chicken breast), veal, lobster and shrimp in red wine and brandy, the *pollo a la monte*. Don't leave without trying the exquisite home-made *flans*: ginger, vanilla, coconut and cheese custard. Wed–Sun 11am–10pm.

Tió Pepe PR-723 km 0.3 ☎787/735-9615. This is a smarter, more refined place to eat, ideal for dinner after a hard day's driving, and set in lush gardens with its own large parking area. You'll get a posher version of all the *criollo* classics here: substantial *mofongo* stuffed with seafood, and seventeen dishes based on locally reared, plump *pechuga* (chicken breast; mains from $12). Look out for the sign on the left. Wed & Thurs 11.30am–8pm, Fri & Sat till midnight, Sun till 10pm.

Mirador Piedra Degetau

Once the tranquil "thinking place" of writer and politician Federico Degetau (1862–1914), the **Mirador Piedra Degetau** (Wed–Sun 9am–6pm; free) is a 730m-high viewpoint offering jaw-dropping views of the island – on a clear day you can spy Ponce and the Caribbean to the south, and the edges of San Juan along the north coast. The *piedra* in the name refers to the large boulder where Degetau was inspired to write some of his most philosophical prose – easy to imagine, despite the site being spoiled somewhat by the wooden observation tower that looms nearby. You'll find the *mirador* around 16km from Cayey at PR-7718 km 0.7, just beyond the PR-722/162 junction south of Aibonito.

Cañón de San Cristóbal

Just a few kilometres north of Aibonito, the **Cañón de San Cristóbal** is a rugged 9km-long gorge created by the raging waters of the Usabón, Aibonito and Piñonas rivers. Tucked away in the folds of rolling hills and farmland, the canyon is hard to make out from above, its sheer sides smothered in dense subtropical foliage, clinging moss and swaying ferns, but the drop down in places reaches a hair-raising 230m. Exploring the gorge takes some effort, but that's part of the appeal: clamber to the bottom and you'll enter a lost world of plunging waterfalls (some the island's highest), churning pools and a plethora of endemic Puerto Rican flora, freshwater fish, snakes and rare birds such as the red-tailed hawk. In between the rocks it's still possible to see overgrown TVs and abandoned fridges, rusting and half-hidden in the jungle, a reminder that this was used as a municipal garbage dump for over twenty years. In 1974 the **Conservation Trust** stepped in to halt this shocking state of affairs, and today around 5 square kilometres of the gorge are protected.

Exploring the canyon

The canyon can be difficult to reach on your own, and virtually impossible to make out from the road: Puerto Rican tourists sometimes battle their way down steep, overgrown trails from the side roads off PR-725, but these are unmarked and can be hard to find, and treacherous in wet weather. The safest and easiest option is to contact the Conservation Trust in advance, and join one of their regular **tours**, ranging from easy one hour jaunts to the canyon rim (Wed–Sun 9am & 1pm; $10, $8 online; Spanish only; ☎787/722-5882 or 787/722-5844; ⓦwww.fideicomiso.org), to serious four-to five-hour hikes along the canyon floor (from $50).

You can also visit the helpful Trust office at the **Vivero Árboles Más Árboles** (Mon–Fri 1–3.45pm; free; ☎787/857-3511) outside Barranquitas, but it can be a real pain to find: leave Barranquitas on PR-156 towards Comerío, and take a right turn at around km 17.7, after the *McDonalds'* (the road is poorly signposted "Calle B"). Follow this street to the end, turn left along Calle A and keep going a little further to where the road narrows – the office is up a drive on the right.

At other times, contact respected **local guide** Samuel A. Oliveras Ortiz (☎787/857-2094 or mobile 787/647-3402, ⓦbarranquitaspr.net/tours), who can arrange hiking and abseiling in the gorge most weekends. Prices range $90–135 per person, depending on group size and activity.

Barranquitas

Since its foundation in 1804, the humble hill town of **BARRANQUITAS** has produced so many famous Puerto Ricans that it's known as the *Cuna de Próceres*, the "cradle of important persons". Much of the old town was destroyed in the great fire of 1895, hurricanes adding to the damage over the years, and though only a handful of historic homes remain, it can be an absorbing place to spend a few hours, with a compact core of steep, narrow streets and a couple of important sights. The town's chief claim to fame is as the burial place of two political heavyweights, **Luis Muñoz Rivera** (whose home has been turned into a museum) and his son, **Luis Muñoz Marín**, but it also has a reputation for high-quality arts and crafts, best appreciated at the annual **Feria Nacional de Artesanías**. Established in 1961, this takes place around July 17 to commemorate the birthday of Muñoz Rivera, livening up the central plaza with over two hundred stalls.

Arrival and information

Driving into the centre, look for the **free car park** on PR-156, near the garage and junction with PR-719, the road from Aibonito. To get to the central plaza, walk up the road behind the Shell garage (which becomes Calle Barceló), and you'll reach the square in five minutes. On the way, stop by at the **municipal tourist office** (Mon–Fri 8am–4pm; ☎787/857-2065 ext 2300) to make sure everything is open: places can close without warning during festivals or if someone is ill. The office is located inside the **Casa Museo Joaquín de Rojas**, a beautifully restored wooden house on Calle Ubaldino Font (just off Barceló). Completed in 1930, it was named after a nineteenth-century mayor and sports vaulted ceilings, original Spanish tiles and a typically wide *criollo* veranda. You

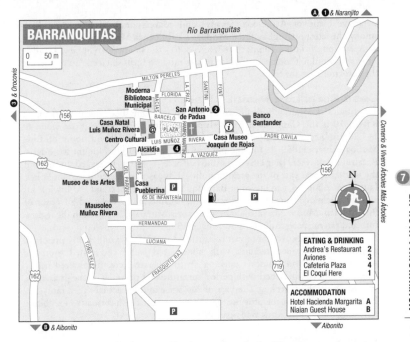

can have a peek inside during office hours, but the building is more engaging than the exhibits, a jumble of old photos, local artwork, farm tools and other bits and pieces.

Banco Santander (Mon–Fri 8.30am–4pm) has a branch at c/Barceló 60, with a 24-hour **ATM** that accepts most cards. You can access the **internet** at the public library (see p.246).

Accommodation

The best place to stay near Barranquitas is the *Hotel Hacienda Margarita* (☎787/857-4949; ❸), just north of town along a narrow lane off PR-152, in the *barrio* of Quebrada Grande. The turn-off is at km 1.7, but the signpost is hard to spot coming from town (it faces north, just before a huge car dealership). The hotel comprises a series of rustic *cabañas* on the hillside and a main building with seventeen standard rooms, with TV and air conditioning in every unit, and terraces and balconies providing stupendous views over the mountains to the east, the hotel's best feature. Rooms are old-fashioned and ageing a bit, but comfy enough.

The *Niaian Guest House* (☎787/857-1240; ❷) is a cheaper, perfectly adequate alternative, with doubles equipped with air conditioning, TV and microwave at PR-143 km 57, in the *barrio* of Helechar, near the junction with PR-162.

The Town

The centre of Barranquitas lies clustered around the main square, the modest but grandly titled **Plaza Bicentenaria Monseñor Miguel A. Mendoza**, adorned with an ornate iron bandstand (or gazebo) and delicate fountain. Locals claim with some justification that it's the prettiest plaza in Puerto Rico, ringed by an attractive blend of Art Deco, Spanish and contemporary architecture; chief among the latest is the glass-faced **Moderna Biblioteca Municipal** (Mon–Thurs 8am–8.30pm, Fri till 4.30pm; ☏787/857-6661), the smart town library, a stylish cube that wouldn't look out of place in any modern Spanish city. You can access the **internet** here for free.

Casa Natal Luis Muñoz Rivera

The town's chief attractions lie west of the plaza. One block away at c/Muñoz Rivera 10 is the **Casa Natal Luis Muñoz Rivera** (Wed–Sun 8.30am–noon & 1–4.20pm; $2; ☏787/857-0230), the birthplace and childhood home of **Luis Muñoz Rivera** (1859–1916), the poet turned politician who fought for Puerto Rican autonomy and later US citizenship (see p.267). Widely respected throughout the island, he was part of the greatest political dynasty in Puerto Rico: his father, Luis Muñoz Barrios, was mayor of Barranquitas between 1856 and 1874, while his equally celebrated son, Luis Muñoz Marín, became the first elected governor of Puerto Rico. Muñoz Marín's daughter, Victoria Muñoz, also served in the legislature and ran unsuccessfully for governor in 1992.

The simple clapboard house was constructed in 1850, a wonderfully preserved example of *criollo* architecture, with honey-gold walls, corrugated roof and shuttered doors, and windows opening up to a narrow, cream-coloured porch. The interior is embellished with period furniture and portraits of the great man, and you can take a peek at a replica of his office and his actual car, a rare 1912 Pierce Arrow kept in the attached garage. Note that the informative exhibition outlining his life and work is in Spanish only.

Mausoleo Muñoz Rivera

Muñoz Rivera was buried at the **Mausoleo Muñoz Rivera** (Wed–Sun 8.30am–noon & 1–4.20pm; free), where the body of Luis Muñoz Marín joined him in 1980. Their stately combined tomb is flanked by the smaller memorials to Amalia Marín Castilla (wife of Muñoz Rivera) and Doña Inés María Mendoza, second wife of Luis Muñoz Marín, who died in 1990. Behind the tomb is a small memorial hall decorated in florid murals depicting the key events in both men's lives. To get here from the *casa natal*, keep walking up Calle Muñoz Rivera and turn left.

Eating

Eating options in central Barranquitas are disappointingly poor, and most locals will direct you to restaurants outside town.

Andrea's Restaurant c/Barceló (near the plaza). This simple restaurant serves similar Puerto Rican food to *Cafeteria Plaza* (see opposite), but it's much newer and a pleasant place for a sit-down lunch or inexpensive sandwich (meals for around $10). Mon–Sat 8.30am–5pm.

Aviones PR-143 km 57 ☏787/857-8955, ⓦrestaurantaviones.com. The region's newest tourist sensation, with seating inside two old aeroplanes (seriously), staff wearing flight attendant uniforms and a "Control Tower" games room. The menu features fairly standard Puerto Rican dishes (mains $15–22), but it's a lot of fun. The planes tend to be open at weekends only – at other times you eat on the surrounding tables. Daily from 9am–10pm.

Cafeteria Plaza c/Muñoz Rivera 21 ☏787/857-4909. This basic diner on the plaza (next to the town hall) offers all the usual Puerto Rican favourites as well as cheap sandwiches (under $5) and coffee. Mon–Sat 6.30am–4pm.

El Coquí Here PR-152 km 3.6 ☏787/857-3828. This shack-like restaurant serves tasty Puerto Rican classics and a few unusual specialities: home-made smoked pork sausages, smoked chicken and goat and rabbit meat platters with *mofongo* (from $12). You'll find it north of Barranquitas; the sign is on the right. Fri–Sun 11am–8pm.

Bosque Estatal de Toro Negro

West of Aibonito the Ruta Panorámica climbs ever higher, eventually skirting the loftiest mountains in the Central Cordillera and slicing through the heart of the **Bosque Estatal de Toro Negro** (also known as the Reserva Forestal Toro Negro; see map p.238), one of the largest forest reserves on the island. This is the longest continuous stretch of the highway and the most rewarding – an emptier road that traverses the roof of the island along a series of misty ridges draped in thick sierra palm and pine forest. The route affords almost endless vistas of the north and south coast, glittering on the horizon.

Accommodation

The only way to **stay the night** within the forest is to **camp**. The *Los Viveros* campground (☎787/724-3724; $4 per person) in the Área Recreativa Doña Juana (see below) has a small car park, barbecue pavilions, showers, washbasins and toilets. It's one of the most tranquil campgrounds on the island, close to the gurgling waters of the Quebrada Doña Juana and several trails, but as usual you'll need to obtain a permit from the DRNA in advance (see p.26).

Exploring the forest

The Ruta Panorámica passes through the Toro Negro on PR-143, and all points of interest are accessible off this road. The forest covers around 27 square kilometres and is divided into seven segments: the most convenient for visitors contains the **Área Recreativa Doña Juana** and peak of the same name, while after a small gap, a larger and higher section incorporates the watershed of the Río Toro Negro, **Cerro Maravillas**, and Puerto Rico's tallest mountain, **Cerro de Punta**. Although the two peaks are easy to climb, it's frustratingly difficult to explore this potentially more dramatic section without a specialist map and preferably a local guide, as trails are unmarked and hardly ever maintained – casual hikers should stick to the Área Recreativa Doña Juana for a taste of the forest.

Mirador Villalba Orocovis

Soaking up the vast panorama unfolding from the **Mirador Villalba Orocovis** (Wed–Sun 9am–6pm; free), it's easy to feel you've reached the very top of Puerto Rico. To the south, Ponce and the Caribbean seem remarkably close, and on the other side of the road you can just make out the north coast. The *mirador* is a series of landscaped platforms atop a 610m ridge in the Montañas de Corozal, just before the Toro Negro proper and around 28km west of Aibonito, at PR-143 km 39.8. Parking spaces are plentiful inside the gates, but even if you pass by when it's locked up on Monday or Tuesday, just pull over on the road to enjoy the views. The *Restaurante Villa Oro* on site is really just a small shack serving up fritters and other snacks when the *mirador* is open.

Área Recreativa Doña Juana

Laced with easy walks through virtually untouched expanses of forest, the **Área Recreativa Doña Juana** is the best place to abandon your car and get **hiking**. Around 6km beyond the *mirador*, this is the first and most enjoyable section of the Toro Negro, set along the banks of the Quebrada Doña Juana, a bubbling tributary of the Río Toro Negro.

The forest **information office** (daily 7am–4pm) is at km 32.4, 600m beyond the small **parking area** for the swimming pool. Pick up basic maps here and ask about the latest conditions of the trails (rangers usually speak Spanish only), though serious hikers should order topographical maps from the US Geological Survey before they arrive (see Basics, p.42). The most rewarding trail starts opposite the office, the 4.4km **Camino El Bolo**, which climbs gradually to the **Torre Observación**, a wooden lookout tower. When you reach the sealed road at the top of the ridge, turn left – the final section to the tower branches off this road to the right, five minutes beyond here. The climb to the top should take 45 minutes to one hour, an enchanting hike through a staggering variety of vivid tropical flowers and *palo colorado* trees, and usually deserted – reach the summit and it really feels like being lost in the wilderness, with little more than the breeze and chirping frogs for company. To get back, return to the sealed road and turn right to continue down to PR-143, or turn left to find the **Vereda La Torre** (tower trail), another path that leads back to the car park. This is a grass and gravel track that makes a slightly faster alternative to the Camino El Bolo. Hiking down this way, the Vereda La Torre ends at the **Piscina de Agua**, an ageing and wholly unattractive concrete swimming pool (free) fed by a stream. From here, take the **Vereda La Piscina** (pool trail), a 500m sealed path that follows the Quebrada Doña Juana down to the car park.

Los Viveros

In between the car park and the information office is the small turning to the campground, **Los Viveros**, a short 200m walk or drive along a steep, narrow road (heading west, it's on the right). You can continue along the road on foot from the campground, turning right at the bridge and following the muddy clay path another 1km down the river to the **Charco La Confesora**, a large pond, and a couple of other trails: the Camino Doña Petra (1.5km) connects with PR-564 to the east, while further downstream the Camino Ortolaza (2km) leads west to PR-143. You can make a loop by returning to the campground on the main roads, as traffic is light, especially during the week, but take extra care on the corners. Some trails are poorly marked so take a map with you.

Cerro Maravillas

Known as *El Cerro de los Mártires* ("The Mountain of the Martyrs"), **Cerro Maravillas** (1207m) is the most infamous peak on the island and accorded shrine-like reverence by Puerto Rico's independence movement. On July 25, 1978, two independence activists were ambushed here while preparing to destroy the communication antennas on top, and the subsequent cover-up of their execution-style murder resulted in a massive public outcry (see p.270).

A few kilometres beyond the Area Recreativa Doña Juana, PR-149 branches north off the Ruta Panorámica to Jayuya (see opposite), but if you continue on PR-143 for another 6.5km you'll reach the junction with PR-577 (the road is marked but easy to miss). This narrow road quickly leads to the summit (the fifth tallest peak in Puerto Rico); about 200m up, in between the towers, you'll see two stone crosses (and sometimes Puerto Rican flags and flowers) marking the spot where **Arnaldo Darío Rosado** and **Carlos Soto Arriví** died. A memorial is held here every July 25, attended by hundreds of people.

Cerro de Punta

The **tallest peak in Puerto Rico** and a relatively straightforward climb, **Cerro de Punta** (1338m) is a few metres shorter than Ben Nevis (the UK's highest point), a lofty mound of cloud forest often draped in bewitching threads of mist. As you'd expect, the views are mind-blowing, and best appreciated in the mornings before the clouds move in. Few tourists make it to the summit, adding to the sense of isolation, though you may see workers tending to the communication towers on top. Don't hesitate; it's perfectly legal to scale the mountain.

From the large gravel car park at its base, just under 5km from the turning to Cerro Maravillas, a weathered road leads 1.5km to the antennas on top: it's only advisable to take your car if you have a four-wheel drive, though plenty of time-pressed travellers manage to grind their rental vehicles to the summit. Note that the car park and road are unmarked: heading west, it's on your right at around km 17 on PR-143. The route up is fairly steep, but shouldn't take more than an hour if you decide to hike it. Beyond the communication towers, the actual grassy peak (the *punta* itself) can be reached via an overgrown stairway – a concrete block marks the summit. On a clear day you can see up to 100km, with a hazy San Juan in the distance.

For more of a **challenge**, tackle the peak from the northern side – the trail starts at *Hacienda Gripiñas* (see p.251) and can be hard to follow, so ask at the hotel for directions first. Assuming you don't get lost, experienced hikers should be able to get up and down in one day.

Eating

You're better off bringing a picnic to the Toro Negro, as **eating** options are scarce, but on weekends you can grab some wood-fire-roasted barbecue at *Las Cabañas Doña Juana* (Sat, Sun & holidays 9am–6pm) on PR-143, 2km beyond the Area Recreativa Doña Juana and just before the junction with PR-149. Buy a whole roast chicken for $8, or half for $4, with other snacks including *yuca* (white manioc), *arroz can Gandules*, *guineos* and *alcapurrias*, all between $0.75–2.

From the Toro Negro to Jayuya

From the Toro Negro and the Ruta Panorámica the best way to **Jayuya** is to head north on PR-149 then PR-144, cutting through the thickly wooded hills and mountains that separate the valleys of the Río Toro Negro and Río Grande de Jayuya. En route are some of the most absorbing sights in the region: poignant museums, ancient Taíno petroglyphs and an elegant waterfall.

Salto de Doña Juana

Just 2.3km north of the Ruta Panorámica, PR-149 passes right in front of the **Salto de Doña Juana**, a graceful 60m waterfall framed by rocky cliffs, where the chilly waters of the Quebrada Doña Juana tumble into the Río Toro Negro. The falls are at around km 41.6, but the road here is very narrow and the only place to stop is a small space just beyond the bridge over the river. Failing that, you can make a brief stop on the bridge itself, as the road is not particularly busy. The junction with PR-144 is another 1.4km from the falls.

Coabey

After twisting through jungle-coated mountains for around 8km, PR-144 drops into the Jayuya valley and the *barrio* of **Coabey** (km 9.3), home to a couple of striking museums. Both are clearly visible from the road, with plenty of parking nearby.

Museo El Cemí

The **Museo El Cemí** (Mon, Thurs–Sun 9.30am–4.30pm; $1) is one of the most distinctive buildings on the island, a dappled white and grey dome set in a grassy park, with a mouth-like entrance that resembles a giant fish. Architect Efrén Badia

Cabrera won the competition to design the museum, which opened in 1989 in the form of a giant *cemí*, a representation of the Taíno gods and one of the most common artefacts dug up on the island. Inside you'll find an upper gallery of vivid Taíno **petroglyphs**, marked in white and depicting various symbols and anthropomorphic images, while the first-floor archeological collection comprises stone tools, axes, necklaces, pottery, stone collars and examples of the *cemí* itself, the "spirit of god", all with English labels. Overall the collection is rather modest, but given the setting, certainly more evocative than city museums. Don't miss the small **Taíno burial site** outside: thanks to pressure from the United Confederation of Taíno People, the remains of a 1500-year-old indigenous woman and other human bones found here are no longer on display inside the museum. Note that the museum usually closes for lunch around noon to 1pm.

Museo Casa Canales

The old wooden house opposite the Museo El Cemí is the **Museo Casa Canales** (same hours as Museo El Cemí; $1), a typical rural *criollo* home of the late nineteenth century, but also an emotive memorial to the failed aspirations of the island's *independentistas*. The original was built by **Don Rosario Canales Quintero** (1854–1924), one of the founders of Jayuya in 1883 and its first mayor in 1911. However, what you see today was meticulously built from scratch as a replica in the 1990s, as the original collapsed in the 1970s. With a backdrop of towering, forest-covered mountains and creaky timbered floors, this is about as evocative of old Puerto Rico as it gets, each room faithfully stocked with period furniture. The house also serves as a simple local history museum: the Sala Jayuya contains documents and other bits and pieces relating to the town, while the Sala Paliques is a study dedicated to the son of Rosario Canales, the writer and humorist **Nemesio Canales Rivera** (1878–1923), who wrote under the pseudonym Paliques. The Sala Revolución commemorates the **1950 uprising**, when the rebels stored weapons and met here before marching on the town. One of the leaders, **Blanca Canales Torresola** (1906–1996), was the daughter of Rosario Canales.

The collection of modern buildings near the museum includes an art and crafts shop (Fri–Sun 10am–4pm), selling local Taíno-inspired carvings, instruments, books on the area (in Spanish), ointments made from the seeds of native trees and elegant, locally carved *santos*.

Hacienda San Pedro and Café Tres Picachos

Coffee aficionados should check out the family-owned plantations in the hills off PR-144, producers of some addictively aromatic gourmet brews. **Hacienda San Pedro** (Mon–Sat 8am–6pm, Sun 10am–5pm; ☎787/823-2083, ⓦwww.cafe haciendasanpedro.com), just off the main road at PR-144 km 8.4, was established in 1894 by Tomás Rivera. It's been operated by three generations of the Atienza family since 1931, producing a rich, spicy coffee with a bitter chocolate aftertaste (it also contributes to the famous Yauco Selecto brand). You can buy coffee in the store on site, try an espresso or a cappuccino, and visit their small museum, which has exhibits about the farm and the coffee-making process.

Meanwhile, the Martínez Rivera family produces the highly rated **Café Tres Picachos** (Mon–Sat 8am–6pm; ☎787/828-2121, ⓦwww.cafetrespicachos.com) at PR-539 km 2.7, off PR-144 in the *barrio* of Saliente. The brand was established in 1960 by the Torres Díaz family and acquired by the current enthusiastic owners in 1999. You can visit the plantation to buy freshly roasted coffee, and if you call in advance, take a peek at their small **Museo de Antiguedades** (Mon–Sat

9am–4pm), a dusty but oddly compelling collection of Taíno artefacts and coffee-related paraphernalia. The coffee is named after **Los Tres Picachos** (1186m), the nearby mountain whose three peaks are said to represent the three camels of the biblical Holy Kings (or Three Wise Men).

La Piedra Escrita

Another 2km along PR-144 from Coabey, just beyond the 7.5km mark, **La Piedra Escrita** (open 24hr; free) is one of the most accessible **Taíno petroglyph** sites on the island. From the car park and *El Tripe G* snack bar, a wooden boardwalk switchbacks down to the Río Saliente and an enormous 9m-high granite boulder that almost blocks the river. The rock forms a natural pool of cool, peat-coloured water that attracts plenty of swimmers, but far more impressive are the 52 curly petroglyphs clearly marked in white on the side of the stone. The abstract carvings date from around 600 to 1200 AD and comprise mystical spiral shapes, simplistic stick figures that seem to represent people, and the heads of unidentified creatures with big round eyes. Research into Taíno petroglyphs is relatively new, and while it's not known what any of these symbols mean, an increasingly vocal Taíno movement is demanding that La Piedra Escrita is better protected and treated with respect (daredevils tend to use the rock as a diving board). From here it's just over 1.5km into central Jayuya.

Jayuya

Nestling on the banks of the Río Grande de Jayuya, deep in the Central Cordillera, the mountain town of **JAYUYA** might seem unremarkable, but it's come to occupy a central role in the mythology of modern Puerto Rican identity. Littered with low-key but enigmatic reminders of the island's past, the town is the closest thing Puerto Rico has to a Taíno spiritual centre, most vividly expressed during the annual **Festival Nacional Indígena**. Traditionally regarded as the stereotype of hicktown by sophisticated *sanjuaneros*, Jayuya's symbolic importance was recognized in 1950, when *independentistas* briefly occupied the town and proclaimed the Republic of Puerto Rico (see p.270). Like Barranquitas, Jayuya also has a reputation as an arts and crafts centre, and more recently, the area has been rebuilding its reputation as one of Puerto Rico's top **coffee-producing** regions.

Accommodation

The best **place to stay** is *Parador Hacienda Gripiñas* (☎787/828-1717, Ⓦwww .haciendagripinas.com; ④), a former coffee plantation established in 1858 and a hotel since 1975. Rooms are fairly compact and nothing special, with air conditioning and cable TV but otherwise a little worn. However, the setting is gorgeous, with white-timbered buildings with rusty red roofs on the hillside, wonderful views across the mountains and an excellent restaurant (see p.253). The hotel sits in an isolated valley at the end of PR-527 at km 2.5, around 4km south of Jayuya.

The Town

Jayuya is a laidback mountain community proud of its indigenous heritage, with Taíno symbols and tribal markings daubed onto fences and kerbsides all over town. Though a farm was established here in 1533, Spanish settlers in the valley did not prosper, and the settlement wasn't officially founded until 1883, when it was named after the last Taíno *cacique* of the area, Hayuya.

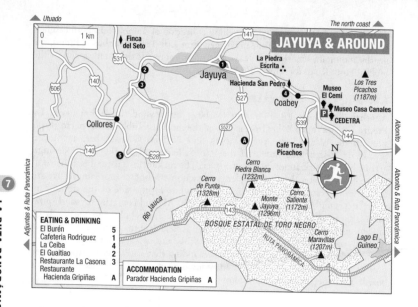

Start at the central **Plaza de Recreo Nemesio R. Canales**, with a large representation of **El Sol de Jayuya** carved into the ground, one of the most vivid of all Taíno petroglyphs found in Puerto Rico. The simple church, **Nuestra Señora de la Monserrate** is usually locked, but features a classic Spanish Colonial facade in pale yellow, crowned with three bells.

The bird's-eye view over the town and mountains beyond are enough to justify the short climb from the plaza up the stone steps to the cultural centre, and just before the top, standing guard over the town, is Tomás Batista's **sculpture of Cacique Hayuya**. The image was created in 1969 to commemorate the Taíno ruler – his village was destroyed by the Spanish in 1513 during the aftermath of the Taíno rebellion (see p.263). Behind the bust is **La Tumba del Indio Puertorriqueño**, a tomb containing a Taíno skeleton that is intended to symbolize the island's native population, interred here in 1974 and framed by reproductions of two petroglyphs, *La mujer de Caguana* and *La Danzante del Otoa*. You'll have to peek through the rails at the actual tomb, as it's usually locked up – as with other indigenous sacred sites, it's attracted its share of criticism in recent years from Taíno activists who believe it's grossly disrespectful to display the remains of their ancestors. The words inscribed on the walls loosely translate to "An Indian of Borinquen, a primitive man of the island, whose blood and culture live on in our race".

Above the tomb, the **Centro Cultural de Jayuya** (Mon–Fri 8am–noon & 1–4pm; free) on Calle San Felipe is a fine Neoclassical building constructed in 1920, which served as the municipal hospital until 1966. The centre has two rooms of permanent exhibitions (a small collection of Taíno artefacts and wooden *santos*), and some space for temporary local art displays.

With no official **car parks** in town, leave your car where you can find a space near the plaza, or aim for the unofficial parking areas near the bridges over the river.

Finca del Seto

To get a taste of the area's rich **coffee-growing** traditions, arrange a visit to **Finca del Seto** (the owners prefer you **email** in advance; Ⓔ Fincadelseto@gmail.com), a small plantation nestling in the shadow of Cerro Morales on PR-531, north of

Jayuya in the *barrio* of Caonillas La Ceiba. Their fresh, open-kettle-roasted coffee, *Finca del Seto Café*, is sold in one-pound (454 grams; $14) or eight-ounce (227 grams; $7.50) bags – try this rich, potent brew and you'll understand why Puerto Rico was once the coffee capital of the world.

Eating and drinking

As usual, many of the best **restaurants** in the area are in the hills surrounding Jayuya town centre, though there are a couple of cheap places near the plaza: to grab a cake, bread or a drink, try the *Panadería Repostería El Rey* (usually open Mon–Sat 7am–9pm) on the southwest corner (c/Figuera). **Nightlife** is virtually nonexistent, but some locals tend to congregate in the shack-like *Colmado El Indio* for a few beers after work, which hangs over the hillside on Calle San Felipe near the cultural centre – the views over the town are magical at night.

El Burén PR-528, km 5.4 ☎787/828-2589. If you're not in a hurry, make time for this rustic country diner, tucked away in the hills southwest of town and offering a vast panorama of mist-drenched mountains. The menu features all the usual Puerto Rican classics, but this is one place you really ought to try them: the ubiquitous *mofongo* is made with freshly mashed plantains here and filled out with fresh seafood, while the home-made *sorrullitos* (corn fritters) make an addictive side dish. Closed Mon–Wed.

Cafetería Rodríguez c/Guillermo Esteves 65 ☎787/453-2697. No-frills place serving up standard *comida criolla* and lip-smacking roast chicken, in the old Jayuya market building on the main street. Inside you'll find a few tables, locals sipping potent cups of coffee and the smell of roast meats wafting out of the door. Closed Tues.

La Ceiba PR-144 km 8.9 ☎787/828-3017. This popular local café, run by the Oliveras González family, is the best place to grab a bite on the Coabey side of Jayuya (it's near the Museo el Cemí). Usually open all day, with a small seating area inside and a shack on the road serving cheap *tostones*, rice and beans, *pechuga* (all under $7), and various cocktails, beer, and rums, especially popular on the weekends.

El Guaitiao PR-144, near the Shell garage and the junction with PR-531 ☎787/415-8933. Anyone craving sumptuous barbecue *lechón* and roast chicken (from $4) should make a stop at this roadside grill on weekends, though it also usually opens for drinks in the evenings. *Guaitiao* is a Taíno word for a peaceful meeting between strangers. Thurs–Sun noon–midnight.

Restaurante La Casona PR-144 km 1.3 ☎787/828-3346. On the main road beyond *Guaitiao*, this restaurant is a wooden house with veranda, timbered interior and lots of parking. It's the most convenient place for a sit-down meal of Puerto Rican food near town, with pool tables and live music livening things up in the evenings. Mains from $7. Sat & Sun 1–10pm.

Restaurante Hacienda Gripiñas PR-527 km 2.5, ☎787/828-1818. Inside the *parador* (see p.251), the best feature of this popular *mesón gastronómico's* is its location: a handsome building on the old coffee plantation. The Puerto Rican dishes are much better than the generic seafood, steaks and soups, with the chicken and shrimp *asopao* one of the standouts. Mains from $8. Open daily for breakfast, lunch and dinner.

Adjuntas and around

Cradled between some of the highest peaks on the island, **ADJUNTAS** is a remarkably traditional rural community, a million miles from urban Puerto Rico. It sits on one of the island's primary north–south arteries, PR-10, 50km south of Arecibo and 30km north of Ponce, but with the highway now bypassing the town, its torpid centre seems frozen in the 1950s, with none of the strip malls and fast-food outlets that grace most Puerto Rican towns – for now. It's also known as *La Ciudad del Gigante Dormido* ("the city of the sleeping giant") after the ridge of mountains on its western side, which vaguely resemble the outline of a giant, lying face up. The town is perhaps best known in Puerto Rico today as the home of one of the island's most successful conservation movements, **Casa Pueblo**. This local organization waged a long but eventually successful campaign against local open-mining of copper and gold deposits, and is today at the forefront of the Puerto Rican environmental movement. Adjuntas lies just off the Ruta Panorámica, around 32km from the heart of the Toro Negro.

Accommodation

The most comfortable place to stay is the *Parador Villas Sotomayor* (☎787/829-1717, ⓦwww.paradorvillassotomayor.com; ❸), a mini-resort around 2km north of town at PR-522 km 0.2 (just off PR-123 at km 36.6), in a quiet valley surrounded by jungle. Its 35 modern bungalow villas have basic doubles with air conditioning and satellite TV, though it also has larger rooms for four to six people with kitchenettes. Extras include a swimming pool, tennis and basketball courts, pool table, bikes for rent and horseriding – the activities, family focus and all-inclusive offers are extremely popular with Puerto Ricans on weekends.

Cheaper and more convenient for the town centre is the *Hotel Monte Río*, c/César González 18 (☎787/829-3705; ❶), a budget option with simple but adequate doubles and friendly staff. All come with rackety air conditioning, clean bathrooms and local TV, but furnishings are a bit frayed around the edges. Get a room on the third floor, where the balconies provide pleasant views of the town, the large pool and surrounding hills (check out the "sleeping giant" from the back). The near-legendary **buffet** in the restaurant began as a stopgap in the aftermath of Hurricane Georges in 1998 and is one of the best deals on the island (see opposite), but it can be a little tricky to find the hotel: coming into Adjuntas, keep following signs for PR-123 past the plaza, and when you turn right onto Calle Barbosa, look immediately for a small lane through the buildings on the left, next to La Suerte Game Room. Hard to spot, but you should see a tiny sign to the hotel here.

The Town

Adjuntas was formally established in 1815 on the banks of the Río Saltillo (which eventually becomes the Río Grande de Arecibo), though a settlement has stood here since the early eighteenth century. Its modern centre lies up from the river around the impressively manicured **Plaza Arístides Moll Boscana**, named after local hero, physician and writer Dr Arístides Moll (1880–1965). The plaza has a small church at each end and the 1927 **Ayuntamiento** (town hall) at the southwest corner, a striking building with a green facade sporting some fancy Mudéjar tiling. Next door is the town's cultural and tourism department (daily 8am–noon & 1–4pm; ☎787/829-5039), located in the historic Casa Bruno Ruíz de Porras, doubling as the **Museo de Cultura**, a mildly interesting collection of documents and artefacts.

Casa Pueblo

The most compelling reason to stop in Adjuntas lies 200m south of the plaza on PR-123, at c/Rodolfo González 30 – an innovative cultural and environmental centre known as **Casa Pueblo** (Mon 8am–1pm, Tues–Sun 8am–3.30pm; suggested donation $2; ☎787/829-4842, ⓦwww.casapueblo.org). The arresting pink *criollo*-style house was purchased in 1985 by a group of environmentalists that had already been protesting the development of local **open-air copper mining** for five years – the mining posed a catastrophic threat to the local ecosystem. It took fifteen years of campaigning, but in 1995 the government passed a bill prohibiting open-air mining in Puerto Rico, and by the following year the land formerly threatened by the mine was turned into a small reserve, the **Bosque del Pueblo**. Founder Alexis Massol-González received the prestigious Goldman Environmental Prize in 2002 on behalf of the group, and today Casa Pueblo supports sustainable development and conservation projects all over the island, also conducting a number of toxicity studies on Vieques.

The main house acts as a performance centre and art space, with a small shop selling local arts and crafts, coffee beans grown by the project (Café Madre Isla), T-shirts and books. Most of the wall space is dedicated to charting the group's history and environmental campaigns through photographs and various media coverage. At the back is a small **Mariposario** (butterfly house) and garden, where caterpillars are reared on lettuce leaves. The whole place is powered by solar energy.

Eating

Adjuntas is an excellent place to try home-style **Puerto Rican food**, and though your choices are fairly limited, everything is superb value. On the north side of the plaza at c/Rodolfo González 56, the *Panadería La Esquina de la Amistad* sells basic cakes, bread and snacks in a grand 1922 building, while the small kiosk across on the plaza, *Coffee Lover's Expresso Bar* serves decent snacks and coffee from 75 cents. The Centro Ahorros supermarket at c/Barbosa 7, holds enough staples to put together a **picnic**.

Restaurants

Monte Río c/César González 18 ⊕787/829-3705. Famed throughout the region for its filling home-cooked and unfeasibly cheap lunch buffet of *criollo* classics: you'll get a choice of two types of rice with beans, four meats, two salads, two desserts, sides such as plantains, and as much juice, coffee and soft drinks as you can manage. Eat as much as you like for just $7 – one of the best bargains on the island. Mon–Fri 11am–3.30pm, Sat & Sun 11am–2pm.

Restaurant Starlight de Güigüi PR-123 km 32.7 ⊕787/829-1823. This restaurant attracts diners from across the island, mainly for its huge plates of *chuletón a la starlight*, luscious pork chops served with a giant pile of plantains ($7). The wooden veranda is packed out on weekends, so get here early. It's right on the *ruta*, a few minutes' drive south of town on PR-123. Don't confuse this restaurant with the far inferior "original" *Restaurant Star Light* up the road: established in 1967, the owner later leased this place to chef Güigüi, but seeing the latter's success, kicked him out, forcing Güigüi to start his own restaurant. Mon–Thurs 11am–10pm, Fri & Sat till midnight, Sun till 11pm.

Drinking and nightlife

Almost everything shuts down in Adjuntas after 6pm, and other than slumping in quiet hotel bars, nights comprise of little more than listening to the cacophony of *coquis* and watching twinkling lights from your hotel balcony – you might also be serenaded by the explicitly unromantic thumping of *reggaetón* tunes from car radios as bored youths cruise up and down the main streets. If you want to mingle with locals on weekends, try the bar at the *Monte Río* or *T&J Sport Bar*, which

Adjuntas coffee

Once the largest exporter of citron in the world, R&A de Jong (Mon–Fri 7am–4pm; ⊕787/829-2610), founded by Dutchman Andries de Jong in the 1960s, is now dedicated solely to the production of **Café Bello**, a high-quality **coffee**. Their plant is just north of town at PR-123 km 36.6 – you can stop to buy coffee and take a tour of the premises, but it's best to call in advance if you can.

You can also buy gourmet coffee at **Hacienda Patricia** (Mon–Fri 8am–5pm; Sat & Sun by reservation only, 10am–5pm; ⊕787/813-1878), home of the Segarra family's sun-dried and wood fire-roasted Arabica beans. The plantation that was established in 1900, right on the Ruta Panorámica (PR-143 km 6.6, about 11km before Adjuntas – on the left just after the junction with PR-140). You can usually try their product in a small café on site.

occupies an old clapboard house on Ríos Rivera near the plaza (Thurs till 11.45pm, Fri & Sat till 1.45am).

Bosque Estatal de Monte Guilarte

Covering around 14 square kilometres of dense sierra palm forest, the **Bosque Estatal de Monte Guilarte** covers the mountains west of Adjuntas, at an altitude of between 800m and 1200m. The most accessible sections lie on the Ruta Panorámica (PR-518), close to **Lago Garzas**, a pretty storage reservoir built for a hydroelectric power station, and around **Monte Guilarte** itself, the reserve's highest peak.

Accommodation

Camping at Guilarte is not allowed, but the DRNA manages five rustic **cabañas** ($20/night) close to the information office (see below). Each cabin has four berths with mattresses, and room for six people (you must provide your own bedding), but as always, you'll need to contact the DRNA in advance to stay here (see p.26).

Monte Guilarte

From Adjuntas, PR-518 rises swiftly into the mountains, passing the placid waters of **Lago Garzas** after around 9km. Just under 5km from Lago Garzas (at km 12.2), PR-518 meets PR-131 in the heart of the forest: turn left here for **Monte Guilarte** (1199m), the sixth highest peak on the island and one of the few that isn't sprinkled with antennas. Here at the junction you'll find the forest **information office** (usually Mon–Fri 7am–3.30pm, Sat & Sun 9am–5.30pm), where you can check current conditions, but little else (there are no maps). The road ends a few metres ahead at a small car park and trail that leads to the peak – the hike to the top normally takes 45 minutes to an hour, and you'll probably have it to yourself, especially on a weekday. The path can be slippery but it's a relatively easy climb, rewarded by stellar views over the whole of western Puerto Rico.

From Monte Guilarte it's another 50km to **Maricao**, one of the longest, most spine-jarring sections of the Ruta Panorámica along narrow, often potholed roads through some of the most rural and isolated districts of Puerto Rico. You won't see much traffic, and the only village en route is **Castañer**, which has a petrol station and basic café. Take your time: this bucolic landscape of close-knit communities and family farms, lush palm plantations and sprawling mango trees, is a window into the lost world of the *jíbaro*, rapidly disappearing in ever-modernizing Puerto Rico.

Bosque Estatal de Maricao

Created in 1919, the **Bosque Estatal de Maricao** covers around 40 square kilometres, making it one of the largest forest reserves on the island, home to 26 bird species (eleven endemic) and hundreds of different trees, plants and flowers. The problem is that only a fraction is easily accessible to visitors and most people end up simply breezing through on the Ruta Panorámica. The forest **headquarters** (usually Mon–Fri 7am–3.30pm, Sat & Sun 8am–3.30pm; ☏787/838-1040) is signposted off the main road (PR-120) at around the 16.2km mark, 2km beyond La Torre de Piedra and around 6km before the town of Maricao. They don't have any maps, but if you can speak Spanish the rangers can tell you about a couple of trails in the area, and the road to the office leads up to a **picnic area** with fine views of the west coast.

Accommodation

The Compañía de Parques Nacionales runs the functional *Centro Vacational Monte del Estado* (☏787/873-5632; cabins ❷, villas ❹) at km 13.2 on PR-120, a rustic holiday camp with 24 large *cabañas* and villas equipped with fireplaces, primarily targeted at local families. It does have a pool, playground and table tennis tables, among the activities on offer, and can be fun for kids. It's $3 to park your car. See p.26 for booking information.

La Torre de Piedra
Coming from Adjuntas, the forest starts around 45km from Monte Guilarte, at the junction of PR-366 with PR-120, but stopping is pointless until you've passed the *centro vacacional* and reach **La Torre de Piedra** (daily 8am–5pm; free) a few metres further on (km 14). This 12m stone observation tower looks a bit like a square medieval castle turret, a whimsical product of the Civil Construction Corp in the 1930s. This is the last major viewpoint on the *ruta*, an 800m perch offering a vast panorama of the entire west coast, from Cabo Rojo to Mayagüez and beyond, and also the bizarre symmetry of karst country to the northeast.

Maricao and around
Justly regarded as **La Ciudad del Café** ("coffee city"), the languid mountain settlement of **MARICAO** is one of the most traditional on the island, the haunt of Taíno rebels, *jíbaros* and some of the world's best **coffee** for over two hundred years. At harvest time the town is bathed in the aroma of roasting coffee beans, blazing red berries plucked from bushes that carpet the slopes nearby. Other than enjoying the pleasures associated with its premier crop, Maricao makes an enchanting last or first stop on the Ruta Panorámica, with its celebrated **coffee festival**, a small but engaging **fish hatchery** and the vast **forest reserve** just out of town.

Accommodation
From Maricao itself it's only 2km to the ⚘ *Hacienda Juanita*, at PR-105 km 23.5 (☎787/838-2550; ❸), one of the island's most enchanting hotels. At an altitude of 488m and surrounded by incredibly tranquil, forest-coated hills and gardens, some of its white-timbered buildings date back to 1834, when the coffee plantation was established by Corsican immigrants (a small amount of coffee is still produced here, though it's been primarily a hotel since 1976). Rooms are tastefully furnished with wooden pillar beds and chairs, antiques and satellite TV; it also has a pool, tennis courts and nature trails. Add around $40 for breakfast and dinner packages.

The Town
Maricao has a small, compact centre of ramshackle wooden *criollo* houses with verandas, and a smattering of cheap cafés and shops, though it's rarely busy – on Sundays the place seems totally abandoned. While sights may be lacking around central **Plaza de Recreo Luis Muñoz Rivera**, the town does have a certain lazy charm, and its narrow streets are perfect for aimless wandering.

Just outside the centre, on PR-410 a few metres from PR-105 (the Ruta Panorámica), a cleft in the hillside hides the **Gruta San Juan Bautista**, a small grotto and waterfall dedicated to San Juan (St John). A short pathway and steps lead up both sides of a statue above the waterfall, an image of Jesus being baptized by the saint. It's a shady, peaceful spot and easy to park nearby.

Eating and drinking
Like Adjuntas, Maricao has only a handful of **places to eat**, but most have heaps of character and fabulous home-cooked Puerto Rican food. **Nightlife**, unsurprisingly, is limited. In town itself, there are several cheap, no-frills canteens knocking out *criollo* staples, but none is especially good.

Coffee to keep the devil awake

"Con café de Maricao, hasta el diablo se desveló"

The words of eminent Puerto Rican poet **Luis Lloréns Torres** (who attended school here) eloquently capture the powerful quality of Maricao's **Arabica coffee beans**: "after drinking coffee from Maricao, even the devil couldn't sleep".

Still regarded by many connoisseurs as the home of the world's best coffee, Puerto Rico is undergoing a remarkable **coffee renaissance** after decades of stagnation. Coffee was introduced to Puerto Rico in around 1736, most likely from the French colonies of Martinique and Haiti, and boomed in the nineteenth century. In 1887, **Don Angel Agostini**, a Yauco resident of Corsican descent, went to Paris to begin a hugely successful marketing campaign that resulted in the Pope becoming a regular customer of Puerto Rican *café*, along with half the salons of Europe.

Maricao's rainforest environment, volcanic soils and proximity to cooling sea breezes make it perfect for coffee growing, while its location on the western side of the island protects it from hurricanes. To fully appreciate its rich coffee legacy, attend the three-day **Festival del Acabe del Café** in February (usually around President's Day), an annual celebration that marks the end of the coffee harvest (Sept–Jan). It's one of the island's most popular festivals, so be prepared for crowds. In addition to special exhibitions and live music concerts, the central plaza is packed with stalls selling arts and crafts, *criollo* food and, of course, locally produced coffee.

Café Hacienda Juanita is still produced at the *La Casona de Juanita* (see below), a direct descendant of the legendary coffees that once graced the tables of the Vatican, and can be purchased at the hotel shop. **Hacienda Adelphia** (☎787/473-9512, ⓦwww.cafedemaricao.com) at PR-105 km 37.5, in Sector Union, produces the much-sought-after **Offeecay** brand. Its gourmet Gold series coffees are for serious connoisseurs. You can buy them at the festival or directly from the plantation, but you must call ahead. **Café Real de Puerto Rico** at PR-105 km 23.6 (☎787/833-1698, ⓦwww.cafedepr.com) is produced by a local collective in the Maricao and Jayuya areas, but is primarily sold via their website. **Hacienda Caracolillo**, at PR-105 km 42.8 (☎787/838-2811) in the *barrio* of Indiera Baja is part of the Grupo Jiménez stable and produces **Café Concierto** ($12.95 for eight ounces), an exquisite roast, as well as contributing to the respected export brand, **Yauco Selecto**. Call in advance to ask about buying fresh from the plantation.

🏃 **La Casa de Los Tostones Gigantes**
PR-120 km 22.7 ☎787/458-3005. This inviting outdoor restaurant is just off the *ruta* on the edge of town, set under a lush grove of giant bamboo. But the food is the real star: try the *palitos de plátano* ($3), bananas cut and fried like chips; *rellenas con bacalao guisado* ($4.50), bananas with stewed codfish; and the shrimp *mofongo* (mains $8–12; all served with giant house *tostones* and rounded off with mouthwatering home-made vanilla *flan*. Fri–Sun 11am–8pm.

🏃 **La Casona de Juanita** *Hacienda Juanita* (see above) ☎787/838-2550. A charming restaurant, set in a timbered plantation building with a terrace overlooking the valley below. Specialities include *Serenata de Viandes con Bacalao* (cod with local vegetables), *salcocho criollo* (creole soup), *arroz con gandules* (rice with pigeon peas) and the sensational *pastelon de guineos niños La Juanita* ($11.75), corned beef and sweet banana pie. Daily 8am–10.30am, noon–9pm (last orders 8pm).

Lee Mary's Pizza c/José de Diego 6. This is another canteen-type place that serves basic pizza ($5), cakes and *frituras*, along with Café Rico and Yaucono brand coffee. It's on PR-105 on the way heading out of town and open most days.

Vivero de Peces de Maricao

Tucked away in a meandering valley at the end of PR-410, 2km from Maricao, the **Vivero de Peces de Maricao** (Thurs–Sun 8.30–11.30am & 1–3.30pm; free) is a sleepy fish hatchery, raising largemouth bass, sunfish and catfish to stock the island's reservoirs. The landscaped ponds and gardens on the banks of the Río Maricao are extremely tranquil, lost deep in the forest.

Contexts

Contexts

History

The fate of Puerto Rico has been tied to foreign powers since Juan Ponce de León waded ashore in 1508. Yet the island also has a strong tradition of struggle and rebellion, beginning with desperate Taíno resistance against the Spanish and ending, most recently, with the successful campaign to eject the US Navy from Vieques.

Prehistory

Little is known of the history of Puerto Rico before the arrival of the Spanish – its flourishing civilizations used no form of writing and were comprehensively wiped out in the early years of colonization. The **oldest human remains** have been found on Vieques and date from four thousand years ago, evidence of the **Archaic** (*Arcaico*) or Ortoiroid culture of simple hunter-gatherers that migrated across the Caribbean between 2500 and 200 BC. After 200 BC, communities on Puerto Rico became more sophisticated, developing farming and ornate pottery. Traditionally divided into three separate peoples, anthropologists now believe that cultures developed through a more complex blend of migration and integration. The first phase is known as the **Igneri** (or Saladoid), when yucca, corn, sweet potato and tobacco were introduced from the mainland. Between 600 and 1200 AD the Igneri evolved into autonomous groups or tribes and life became increasingly ritualistic, religious and more organized (*bateyes* or ball-courts became important) – this period is known as the Ostionoid or **Pre-Taíno**. By the thirteenth century Puerto Rico was dominated by the **Taíno**, the people encountered by the early Spanish explorers.

The Taíno

When Christopher Columbus sailed into the Caribbean in 1492, the people he met described themselves as *taíno*, but rather than the name of a tribe, the word simply meant "good" or "noble". On Puerto Rico, the tribes actually called themselves **Boriken**, their name for the island. The Taíno label has stuck, however, applied as an umbrella term for various peoples sharing similar culture from Cuba to the Bahamas.

The Taíno lived in small communities scattered across the island, their cultivation of cassava, corn and tobacco supplemented by hunting and fishing. By 1508 the

Who are the Puerto Ricans?

Most Puerto Ricans (around 80 percent) are classified as white, predominantly of Spanish origin, with 8 percent black, 0.4 percent Amerindian (Taíno) and 0.2 percent Asian (mostly Chinese). However, so many Taíno women were taken as wives by the early Spanish colonists, it's likely that the real genetic picture is far more complex: some DNA tests suggest that up to 60 percent of the population has Taíno genes. In Puerto Rico, the word **criollo** has come to refer to the mixing of all these racial and cultural elements, and is applied generally to anything native to the island, while **Boricua** represents the island itself: deriving from the Taíno word **Boriken** (meaning "brave lord"), Puerto Ricans often use the phrase *Yo soy Boricua* ("I am Boricua") to identify themselves.

island was divided into at least twenty major Taíno kingdoms, each ruled by a chief or **cacique** but under the nominal control of an overlord, **Agüeybaná I**. Agüeybaná (meaning "great sun"), held court at Guainía, on the south side of the island. However, it seems more probable that the power of *caciques* was measured in terms of people not territory, and the existence of kingdoms with actual boundaries is unlikely. Of more importance was the **spiritual life** of the Taíno, a pantheist system of animist belief marked by the creation of numerous **cemís**, stone idols, and the worship of **Yukiyú**, their chief deity, and **Atabey**, his mother. **Juracán** was a malevolent god, associated with the vicious storms that batter the Caribbean and from whose name the word "hurricane" derives (the Taíno also gave us the hammock, from *hamaca*).

The Spanish conquest

Without question, the period of **Spanish rule** – which lasted almost four hundred years – has had the most influence on Puerto Rican culture. In addition to the Spanish language, Catholic Church, and the social and culinary traditions that dominate the island today, mangos, coconuts, bananas, yams, goats, pigs, cattle, sugar cane and coffee were all introduced after 1493.

Columbus

We'll never know for certain where **Christopher Columbus** (Cristóbal Colón in Spanish) first landed on Puerto Rico – records indicate that the island was sighted on his second voyage to the New World on November 19, 1493, and that his seventeen ships took on fresh water somewhere on the west coast. Though Aguada celebrates the event every year, new research suggests the fleet anchored closer to the modern towns of Añasco or Rincón. Portentous as this first contact was, it had little immediate impact: **Hispaniola** (modern Haiti and the Dominican Republic) remained Spain's primary base in the region, and it was another fifteen years before colonization was attempted in an organized way. Columbus is credited with naming the island, however: **Isla de San Juan Bautista**, after St John the Baptist.

Juan Ponce de León

Sailing with Columbus on that second voyage was **Juan Ponce de León** (1460–1521) a steely conquistador who had earned his military stripes fighting the Moors in Granada. After arriving in Hispaniola he quickly defeated any Taíno resistance on the island, and was rewarded with the governorship of Higüey province. Ever restless, he landed on the south coast of Puerto Rico on **August 12, 1508**, intent on fresh conquest.

After a friendly exchange with *cacique* Agüeybaná I, he sailed along the north coast of the island and ended up at today's San Juan Bay, which he named "**Puerto Rico**" (see opposite). Ponce de León was appointed **the first governor** of the island by the king of Spain, his initial settlement established inland and named **Caparra** (see p.86), but thanks to an ongoing dispute between the Spanish Crown and Diego Columbus (heir to Christopher's rights in the New World), was replaced by Juan Cerón twice in subsequent years.

Almost immediately, the Spanish began to strip the island of its modest **gold** reserves. The Taíno were set to work digging in open-cast mines and panning for gold in rivers, a system of effective enslavement dubbed the *encomienda*. Caparra proved wholly unsuitable as a base, and settlers began to move to today's **Old San Juan** in 1516; the new city was formally recognized in 1521. Ponce de León sailed for Florida the same year on his quixotic quest for the **Fountain of Youth**, and after being injured by a poison arrow in a skirmish with Native Americans in Florida, died in Havana, Cuba.

Taíno rebellion

The harshness of the *encomienda* system soon alienated the Taíno. **Cristóbal de Sotomayor**, who had established **Villa Sotomayor** in 1510, Spain's second colony on the island, was particularly hated. In November 1510, a *cacique* known as Urayoán had a Spanish captain drowned in the Río Añasco, proving that the Spanish were not immortal beings as the Taíno had feared. In January 1511 a war council brought several *caciques* together under the leadership of "*El Bravo*", **Agüeybaná II** (Agüeybaná I, his uncle, had died in 1510), and the **Taíno Rebellion** began soon after, Villa Sotomayor duly razed to the ground and its leader slain. The Spanish recovered quickly, dispatching forces from Caparra and killing Agüeybaná II in the Battle of Yagüecas. The rebellion rapidly disintegrated thereafter, with thousands of Taíno scattered, killed or sold into slavery: though small groups fought on in the mountains until the 1580s, the Taíno were annihilated – by 1530 fewer than two thousand lived on the island.

The Spanish colony: early challenges

By the 1530s Puerto Rico had become a relative backwater, a bulwark protecting Spain's burgeoning South American empire rather than an economic asset in its own right. With the exhaustion of the gold mines, modest trades in sugar, ginger and cattle-raising kept some cash flowing in, and **smuggling** flourished well into the eighteenth century. Spanish settlers totalled just over four hundred in 1530, outnumbered by the ever-dwindling Taíno and over two thousand **African slaves**, increasingly crucial as a labour force. For much of the subsequent two hundred years the island remained sparsely populated and generally neglected by its colonial master; by 1699 the population of Puerto Rico was barely six thousand.

English and French attacks

It wasn't long before Spain's gold-drenched American empire attracted the attention of other European powers. A motley fleet of **French privateers** (known as "corsairs") sacked San Germán for the first time in 1528, attacking subsequent incarnations of the town into the 1570s, and San Juan became increasingly fortified, with **El Morro** the focus of defensive efforts (see p.59). The first **English**

Rich harbour

The name "Puerto Rico" means "rich harbour", originally applied by Ponce de León to today's San Juan Bay (San Juan was the name of the whole island), and though they're often attributed to a map-reading error, no one really knows how the current conventions arose. In the sixteenth century it seems likely that officials did not distinguish between the new capital city and the sparsely populated island: the colony was simply known as **San Juan Bautista de Puerto Rico**. In 1514 the island was divided into two *partidos* (regions), Puerto Rico and San Germán, and by the 1600s the former had become applied to the whole island, while the city name was shortened to San Juan.

attacks on Puerto Rico took place in 1585, when **Sir Richard Grenville**'s fleet, bound for the nascent colony of Roanoke, Virginia, holed up for a month in Guayanilla Bay on the south coast. In 1595 it was the turn of **Sir Francis Drake**, the feared sea captain the Spanish called "El Draque" (the dragon). Warned in advance, the Spanish were waiting for him: Drake's 27 ships were bombarded as they entered San Juan Bay, and he was forced to retreat. In 1598, George Clifford, **Earl of Cumberland**, was far more successful, remaining the only invader to ever capture El Morro in battle. Learning from Drake's mistakes, he landed his troops on Escambrón Beach, east of Old San Juan, occupied the by-then deserted city and forced the surrender of El Morro fifteen days later. Holding the city proved far more challenging, however, and with his troops virtually wiped out by dysentery, he was forced to abandon Puerto Rico in less than two months.

The Dutch

In 1625, Puerto Rico was sucked into Spain's long struggle with **the Dutch**. Eager to establish a base in the Caribbean, General **Boudewijn Hendricksz** surprised Governor Juan de Haro with a frontal assault on San Juan Bay, taking the city and laying siege to El Morro. After a bitter campaign which saw savage battles, looting and the burning of much of San Juan, the Dutch were forced to retreat within five weeks. The devastation of the city prompted the construction of massive stone walls in the 1630s, but though San Juan was spared further attacks for another one hundred and fifty years, the rest of Puerto Rico continued to be raided by privateers and pirates.

The eighteenth century: growth and reform

In the eighteenth century Puerto Rico's **population** increased dramatically, rising to nearly 130,000 by 1795, in part bolstered by immigrants from the Canary Islands and Ireland, and French settlers fleeing the wars in Haiti. **Smuggling** remained the foundation of the economy throughout the period, despite Spanish attempts to reform trade, reduce tariffs and allow concessions to foreign importers. **Military restructuring** instituted by Alejandro O'Reilly in the 1760s proved crucial, as the island remained a target for foreign powers: without a strong fleet, the imposing fortifications of San Juan, though impressive, emphasized Puerto Rico's continued vulnerability.

The English mounted several minor assaults on the island in the eighteenth century, but the most serious challenge took place in 1797, when Admiral Henry Harvey and seven thousand troops under **Lieutenant-General Sir Ralph Abercromby** attacked San Juan. Having just seized the island of Trinidad the English were confident of success, but after landing his troops safely east of the city, Abercromby failed to dent San Juan's formidable defences or the spirit of the rapidly swelling local militias, reinforced from all over the island. Calculating that a prolonged siege was pointless, he abandoned the attack after a few weeks – the withdrawal has since been portrayed as an epic Puerto Rican victory.

The birth of nationalism

By the early **nineteenth century** Spain's vast American empire was beginning to crack, and **Simón Bolívar** led one South American province after another to independence. Despite a growing sense of **nationalism**, Puerto Rico's ultra-conservative landowners ensured that by 1826, the island, along with Cuba, remained the last of the Spanish colonies in the region.

The Cádiz Cortes

In 1810 the Spanish government called for a parliament that included the colonies for the first time, the **Cádiz Cortes**. Puerto Rico's delegate was **Ramón Power y Giralt**, sometimes regarded as "the first Puerto Rican" in his role as explicitly representing the island and its people. The Cortes duly delivered **Spain's first constitution**, guaranteeing limited representation in local government, which was enthusiastically adopted in Puerto Rico in 1812. However, fearing a loss of power, the Spanish king abolished the constitution two years later, and instead offered the **Cédula de Gracias**, a royal charter pledging free trade and tax breaks, and perks for foreigners emigrating to Puerto Rico. Exiles from Haiti, South America and Europe (including thousands of Corsicans) flooded to the island and the **economy**, largely on the back of the slave-driven **coffee and sugar industries**, boomed for the next sixty years.

Rebellion and repression

The repressive regime of **Governor Miguel de la Torre** (1823–1837) subsequently cracked down on all forms of dissent with a network of spies, heavily enforced laws and swift punishment. Liberals kept a low profile and political progress remained stymied well into the 1860s. De la Torre's regime was successful in convincing most Puerto Ricans that independence would lead to social and economic disaster, but it was the threat of **slave rebellion** that really insured loyalty to Spain. Alleged conspiracies in Bayamón in 1821 and Naguabo in 1823 (both crushed before anything happened) led to the imposition of a harsh **slave code** in 1826, but despite this, a further fourteen plots were exposed by 1843. In that year slaves briefly captured the town of **Toa Baja**, before being brutally suppressed.

The Grito de Lares

By the 1860s, reformers such as **Eugenio María de Hostos** and **Ramón Emeterio Betances** were becoming increasingly disillusioned with the lack of political progress in Puerto Rico. Often considered the **"father of the nation"**, Betances (1827–1898) was the son of a wealthy landowner, and had been educated in France. Returning to Puerto Rico in 1856 to practise medicine, he immediately became involved in underground **abolitionist societies**. Along with his friend **Segundo Ruíz Belvis** (1829–1867), a landowner from Hormigueros, he gradually came to believe that independence from Spain was the only way to solve the island's problems. Both men were exiled by the authorities in 1867: written that year, Betances' **"Ten Commandments of Free Man"** included the abolition of slavery, the right to elect leaders and freedom of speech.

Betances and his co-conspirators planned to strike in 1868. The rebellion began on September 23 in **Lares**, when six hundred rebels led by Manuel Rojas captured the mountain town, arrested local officials and set up a provisional government. The next day they marched on San Sebastián, but their attack was repulsed by local militia, and in the days that followed the insurrection fell apart: by December over five hundred rebels had been arrested. Betances, on the run himself in St Thomas, was unable to help. Though a total failure, the **Grito de Lares** ("Cry of Lares")

C

Puerto Rico's own pirate

Travel anywhere along the coast of Puerto Rico and you'll eventually hear about **Roberto Cofresí**, the home-grown pirate with Robin Hood-like status and a seemingly inexhaustible supply of buried treasure – his birthplace of Cabo Rojo proudly sponsors the "only statue to a pirate" in the Caribbean. Born in 1791 to a wealthy family, Cofresí started out as a legitimate trader, becoming a pirate around 1818: no one knows why, though legend blames ill-treatment at the hands of a foreign sea captain. Ranging from the Dominican Republic to Vieques and St Thomas in the west, his colourful exploits involved plundering and capturing foreign ships (generally from Spain or the US), but also protecting helpless children, and aiding the poor, cementing his patriotic reputation. Following a bruising encounter with a US Navy ship, Cofresí was captured, tried and executed in Old San Juan in 1825. Numerous biographies, ballads, short stories and articles have idolized him ever since.

was the first serious attempt to overthrow the colonial government and declare independence, a symbolic watershed that led to the formation of real political parties and a government that was far more sensitive to the mood of the people.

The abolition of slavery

With the conclusion of the US Civil War in 1865, Brazil, Cuba and Puerto Rico were the only remaining slave societies in the Americas. However, pressure from the US and Great Britain, combined with grassroots sympathy for the slaves among the population, meant that abolition seemed finally possible. Puerto Rican delegations were now regular participants in the Spanish Cortes, and with the Liberal faction in power in Spain in 1873, abolitionists led by **Baldorioty de Castro** (1822–1889) were able to achieve the **emancipation of all slaves** on the island on March 22. The freed slaves still had to work for their former masters for a further three years (on paid contract), and the latter were also to be compensated for their loss of "property". The **abolition of slavery** was one of the main factors in the decline of the sugar industry in subsequent decades, and **coffee** became the premier export crop.

The fight for autonomy

Baldorioty de Castro started fighting for **autonomy** – self-government within the Spanish Empire – in the 1870s, and in 1887 he joined with like-minded activists such as poet **José de Diego** (1866–1918) to create an **autonomist party**. The authorities reacted with the usual wave of repression, jailing the leaders and employing brutal tactics and torture known as *compotes* – Baldorioty de Castro died in 1889 after a period in prison. Things changed when the Liberals again took power in Spain, finally granting **Puerto Rico full autonomy** in 1897. Now led by **Luis Muñoz Rivera** (1859–1916), the autonomist party **won the first elections** in March 1898, just in time for the Spanish–American War.

The Spanish-American War

Puerto Rico became American because of Cuba. When the **Cuban War of Independence** resumed in 1895, José Martí and other Cuban leaders were openly fighting not just for Cuban but for Puerto Rican independence from Spain, and Betances kept in contact with all parties from his exile in Paris. In the 1890s the two groups worked closely together, and at first even courted US help in dislodging the Spanish.

Spurred on by a jingoistic press and businesses with sugar investments in Cuba, pressure for US involvement grew intense – the final pretext for war was the mysterious sinking of the battleship *USS Maine* in Havana harbour in February 1898, blamed on Spanish forces. The **Spanish–American War** began in April, and although Cuba remained the main theatre of operations, Puerto Rico was affected almost immediately by a crippling navy blockade. After San Juan was bombarded by the US Navy in May, **General Nelson Miles** landed 3400 troops virtually unopposed in Guánica on the south coast on July 25. After a small skirmish outside Yauco, he marched into **Ponce** on July 28 without a fight and was greeted by with cheering crowds. From here the US army was able to spread out across the island, though by the time an **armistice** was declared on August 13, Spanish resistance was starting to become far more effective. Betances was horrified that the island seemed to have replaced one colonial ruler with another, writing "what's wrong with Puerto Ricans that they haven't yet rebelled?".

Eugenio María de Hostos tried to rally the *independentista* cause, but while the Treaty of Paris signed in December 1898 granted Cuban independence, Puerto Rico (along with Guam and the Philippines) was simply handed over to the US. General John Brooke was sworn in as the first US governor, and after 390 years, the Spanish were gone.

US rule

After a short period of harsh **US military rule**, the **Foraker Act** of 1900 granted Puerto Rico an elected House of Delegates, chosen every two years, to act as the island's legislature in tandem with an Executive Council. The members of the council, along with the island's governor, were all nominated by the US President. De Diego was appointed to the council, but soon resigned after becoming disillusioned with US rule, which remained decidedly colonial until 1917.

José Celso Barbosa (1857–1921) established the **Partido Republicano** (Republican Party) in 1899 to fight for **US statehood**, and won the first two elections, but in 1904 De Diego and Luis Muñoz Rivera created the **Unión de Puerto Rico** (UPR) to fight for greater self-government: the Union Party won every election from 1904 to 1928.

The Jones Act and US citizenship

In 1910 Luis Muñoz Rivera was elected Resident Commissioner of Puerto Rico to the US Congress, lobbying tirelessly until his death in 1916 for **US citizenship** but also greater **autonomy**, "on the sly" as Rosario Ferré put it. With President Wilson eager to consolidate US ties in the Caribbean as a bulwark against German expansion, the **Jones Act** was finally signed in March 1917, granting US citizenship to all Puerto Ricans and replacing the Executive Council with an elected senate. The governor was still appointed by the US President.

The 1920s to World War II

Puerto Rico experienced a cataclysmic **earthquake** and **tsunami** in 1918, killing 116 people and virtually levelling Mayagüez, yet the island's greatest natural catastrophe of the twentieth century was still to come, striking on St Philip's Day, September 1928. Known as **Hurricane San Felipe**, it killed over three hundred people and destroyed thousands of acres of property, effectively wiping out the island's burgeoning **sugar** and **tobacco** industries. With the **Great Depression** that began in 1929 and **Hurricane San Ciprián** in 1932 adding to the island's woes, the economy was crippled in the 1930s.

Around 65,000 Puerto Ricans fought in **World War II**, and though returning veterans had a modernizing influence on the nation, the island was otherwise unaffected by the conflict.

The independence movement

From the 1920s Puerto Rico's political parties became increasingly fragmented. Despite **women achieving the vote** in 1929, progress towards greater autonomy remained snail-paced and calls for independence became increasingly violent.

When the Union Party dropped the independence of Puerto Rico from its platform in 1922, disgruntled supporters created the **Partido Nacionalista** (the Nationalist Party) to continue the fight for self-determination. **Pedro Albizu Campos** (1893–1965) a Ponce lawyer, became leader of the party in 1930, and the Nationalists vigorously contested the 1932 elections. Failure convinced Albizu that increased **militancy**, not electoral campaigns, was the only way to advance his agenda, and relations with the police rapidly deteriorated in the 1930s.

After a confrontation between students and police in 1935, four Nationalists were killed in what became known as the **Massacre de Río Piedras**, and in 1936 activists Hiram Rosado and Elías Beauchamp **assassinated** Police Chief Francis Riggs – they were both executed by police on capture. Albizu was imprisoned in the US for the next ten years, while his followers were targeted in the **Ponce Massacre** of 1937, a shameful episode that resulted in the deaths of five Nationalists, twelve civilians and two policemen (see p.216). Despite widespread outrage at these events, the Nationalists failed to win lasting political support. Campos didn't help by portraying Puerto Rican culture as entirely Hispanic: in 1936 he made the dubious claims that Spain "had every intention of giving Puerto Rico its liberty" and that Spain was the "founder of North and South American culture".

Frustrated by the lack of progress, Luis Muñoz Marín (1898–1980), respected lawyer and charismatic son of Luis Muñoz Rivera, established the **Partido Popular Democrático** (Popular Democratic Party or PPD) in 1938 to fight for the immediate freedom of the island through democratic means – the party won elections in 1940 and 1944.

Los Borinqueneers

The **65th Infantry Regiment** (@www.valerosos.com) was a segregated unit of the US Army, established in 1899 and composed solely of **Puerto Ricans**, eventually becoming known as *Los Borinqueneers*. Puerto Rican soldiers made important contributions to both **world wars**, but the 65th is most celebrated for its heroism during the **Korean War** (1950–1953), particularly its covering action during the retreat from the Yalu River, as commemorated in *The Borinqueneer* (2007), a documentary by Noemi Figueroa Soulet. Puerto Ricans were also drafted during the Vietnam War and have continued to serve in Iraq and Afghanistan.

The Commonwealth of Puerto Rico

After World War II, the administration of US President Harry Truman moved quickly to dismantle the last vestiges of colonial rule in Puerto Rico. In 1946 **Jesús Piñero** was the first Puerto Rican to be appointed governor, and in 1947 the Jones Act was amended to allow Puerto Ricans to **vote** for the position of governor for the first time. By now Muñoz Marín had come to believe that the **economic development** of Puerto Rico was more important than political independence. Dissenters formed yet another political party in 1946, the **Partido Independentista Puertorriqueño** (Puerto Rican Independence Party, PIP) led by Gilberto Concepción de Gracia. The PIP differed from Albizu's Nationalists in one crucial aspect: they were committed to achieving the independence of Puerto Rico by peaceful, electoral means. In 1948 Luis Muñoz Marín became the **first elected governor** of Puerto Rico, with his *populares* (PPD members) sweeping the legislative elections and the PIP coming in second – Muñoz Marín remained governor of a largely unified nation until 1964.

On July 25, 1952, the **Constitution of Puerto Rico** was approved by voters in a referendum, and the island became the **Estado Libre Asociado** (Commonwealth), the system that remains in place today. This allows self-government in internal affairs as well as fiscal independence, although islanders cannot vote in US presidential elections. Furthermore, the US Congress retains full authority to determine the status of the territory and apply federal law as appropriate. The US also handles defence and foreign relations.

Operation Bootstrap

In the 1940s Muñoz Marín and **Teodoro Moscoso** (who became head of the Puerto Rico Industrial Development Company or **Fomento** in 1950) helped conceive a programme of radical industrialization known as **Operation Bootstrap**. The aim was to boost Puerto Rico's economy by attracting external investment through a system of tax breaks and capital loans, a policy that resulted in hundreds of US factories being established on the island between 1948 and 1968. By the

---

Nuyorican soul

Puerto Ricans started **emigrating to the US** in the 1920s, but the real surge came in the 1950s and 1960s, when thousands arrived in **New York**, flooding the enclave known as **El Barrio**, or Spanish Harlem, in uptown Manhattan, and expanding into the Bronx and Brooklyn. Thanks to a thriving **cultural movement** (p.273), these migrants gradually became known as **Nuyoricans**. The community is celebrated by the **Puerto Rican Day Parade** (🌐 www.nationalpuertoricandayparade.org), which first took place in 1958 and now regularly attracts 100,000 participants and an audience of three million. Depending on how you count them, at least four million Puerto Ricans live in the mainland US today, with around half in New York, though in reality movement back and forth makes this number hard to quantify. You'll rarely hear the redundant term **"Puerto Rican American"**: unlike most immigrants, who must make a symbolic break with their mother country by becoming US citizens, Puerto Ricans are born Americans and face no such dilemma. Nevertheless, although the US community retains passionate cultural links with the island, and has made a huge impact on Puerto Rican culture, art and literature as a whole, there are obvious differences, and many "Nuyoricans" have received a frosty reception on returning to their ancestral home.

1960s textile factories had given way to larger petrochemical plants, and from the 1970s US pharmaceutical companies made Puerto Rico their base. The economy boomed, vehicle ownership exploded and living standards rose. Since the gradual unravelling of Bootstrap in the 1980s, Puerto Rico has remained relatively wealthy compared to other parts of the Caribbean, but unemployment remains high, and poverty is far more widespread than in any state on the mainland – the island remains heavily dependent on financial assistance from the US government.

The postwar Nationalist movement

Not everyone was happy with the PPD and Muñoz Marín. Albizu was released in 1947, but was **jailed again** four years later and had little further impact on the island's politics. His arrest was prompted by the events of 1950, when Nationalists attempted uprisings all over the island: armed attacks were made on La Fortaleza (the Governor's mansion), the police headquarters in San Juan and in fourteen other towns, resulting in 28 deaths. The most serious was the **Jayuya Uprising**, when Nationalists led by Blanca Canales effectively captured the town of Jayuya, and the military took three days to restore order – much of the town was destroyed by fire. Albizu was also blamed for the failed attempt of Griselio Torresola and Oscar Collazo to **assassinate President Truman** in Washington DC, a few days later. Torresola and a policeman were killed, and in the aftermath over three thousand *independentistas* were arrested. Muñoz Marín called them an "insignificant" group of "mad, grotesque, and futile violence-makers … inspired by communism" – and most Puerto Ricans seemed to agree with him.

Finally, in 1954 four Nationalists led by Lolita Lebrón opened fire from the gallery of the Capitol Building in Washington, injuring six Congressmen, hardening opinion in the US still further and effectively silencing the independence movement for two decades. Albizu was pardoned by Muñoz Marín in 1964 and died the following year, claiming to have been the subject of human radiation experiments in prison.

Terrorism

In the **1970s** a new generation of radicals became committed to Albizu's aim of independence through revolution. In 1978, activists Carlos Soto Arriví and Arnaldo Darío Rosado were killed, execution-style, by police while attempting to blow up communication towers on **Cerro Maravillas**. The subsequent cover-up became a major scandal and decisively impacted elections for the governor in the 1980s. In the late 1980s it also emerged that the FBI had been keeping secret files, known as **Las Carpetas**, on anyone suspected of harbouring independence sympathies, an issue that remains controversial today.

The **Fuerzas Armadas de Liberación Nacional** (FALN), set up to further the cause of Puerto Rican independence, was responsible for more than 120 bomb attacks in the US between 1974 and 1983, mainly in New York City. Leader **Filiberto Ojeda Ríos** also helped create the Ejército Popular Boricua (Boricua Popular Army) or **Los Macheteros** in 1976, responsible for numerous attacks since 1978. In 2005, Ojeda Ríos was finally located by the FBI (he had been a fugitive for almost fifteen years), and was killed after an exchange of gunfire.

Culebra and Vieques

Though the majority of Puerto Ricans rejected violence as a means for achieving greater autonomy, opposition to the numerous **US military bases** scattered across the island was far more widespread. The US Navy had occupied parts of

Culebra in 1903, but in the early 1970s a diverse coalition of local organizations began to protest against the navy presence there, resulting in the departure of the military in 1975. Vast swathes of **Vieques** had also been occupied and used as target practice by the US Navy since 1941. The accidental death of civilian **David Sanes** in 1999, killed by bombs dropped during target practice, re-energized the **Navy–Vieques protests** and initiated popular civil disobedience that united the country. Protestors camped on Navy land, supported by Independence Party leader **Rubén Berríos** and a host of Puerto Rican and American celebrities – many were jailed. Protests continued until the US military agreed to leave the island in 2003, and in 2004 the **Roosevelt Roads Naval Station** on mainland Puerto Rico was also closed.

Stalemate

The first **plebiscite** on the political status of Puerto Rico was held in 1967, with 60.4 percent of voters **supporting the Commonwealth**, 39 percent opting for statehood and only 0.6 percent voting for independence (though with the PIP refusing to participate, their supporters tended to abstain). In the aftermath **Luis Ferré** created the pro-statehood **Partido Nuevo Progresista** (New Progressive Party, PNP), going on to win the governorship in 1968 and setting the pattern that continues today, of power switching alternately between the PNP and PPD.

The 1980s and 1990s

By the 1980s it was becoming clear that Puerto Rico was **bitterly polarized** about its political future. PPD governor Hernández Colón's second term (1985–1993) focused efforts on boosting the economy after the recession of the early 1980s and the devastation wreaked by **Hurricane Hugo** in 1989, which destroyed farms and left 28,000 people homeless. The election of PNP candidate **Pedro Rosselló González** in 1993 raised the hopes of statehood supporters, but another **referendum** that year showed support for the Commonwealth at 48.9 percent versus 46.6 percent for statehood, and the following plebiscite, held in 1998, was boycotted by the PPD: 50.5 percent of voters opted for **"none of the above"**, and only 46.7 percent for statehood. Embroiled with scandal, the PNP were defeated in 2001 by **Sila Calderón** of the PDP, Puerto Rico's first female governor, best known for presiding over the closure of US military bases on the island.

Puerto Rico today

Rosselló returned in 2004 to challenge PPD candidate **Aníbal Acevedo Vilá** in a bitterly contested election: Vilá won by just 3000 votes (48.4 percent), sparking a lengthy legal challenge by Rosselló, who never really accepted the result. Vilá's administration proved disastrous for the PPD; in the 2008 elections, the PNP won supermajorities in the House of Representatives and Senate, and PNP candidate **Luis Fortuño** won the governorship. Since then the PNP has sponsored the **Puerto Rico Democracy Act** – which would provide for a federally sanctioned self-determination process for Puerto Rico – through the US Congress. The bill was approved by the US House of Representatives in 2010, but died in the US Senate.

Many Puerto Ricans fear that US statehood would result in a dilution of Hispanic culture and the eventual replacement of the Spanish language (not to mention imposition of Federal income taxes), while most seem to believe that independence would lead to economic catastrophe and political chaos (Rubén Berríos' Independence Party received just 2.74 percent of the vote in 2004).

Conventional wisdom suggests that the current situation, though not ideal, delivers the most economic benefit to the island while retaining a degree of healthy separation from what is perceived as the Anglocentric mainland.

Religion in Puerto Rico

Puerto Rico has been a **Roman Catholic** country since the Spanish Conquest, with 85 percent of the current population members of the Catholic Church. Puerto Rican Catholicism is in theory identical to that practised by the Pope, but a folk religion known as **Santería** developed in parallel with the official church, a syncretism of African (particularly Yoruba) and Catholic beliefs that also flourished in Cuba. Slaves forced to adopt Christianity on arrival in Puerto Rico began to identify their traditional African gods or *orishas* with Christian saints, often to avoid persecution: the Yoruba deity of thunder, Chango, became the equivalent of St Barbara, while Ogun (god of fire, iron and war) was linked with St Peter and St James. Today thousands of Puerto Ricans happily practise elements of Santería while remaining devout Catholics, buying candles, potions and charms in **botánicas**, herbal medicine stores catering specifically to the former – many are owned by a priest or priestess of Santería (*santero* or *santera*), who can provide consultations and advice on everyday problems.

In Puerto Rico, every church you visit will be dedicated to a Catholic saint. The following describes five of the principal figures, though there are hundreds of others.
The Virgin Mary is the most important saint in the Catholic Church, the "mother of God", chosen for the Immaculate Conception of Jesus at the heart of the New Testament. In practice, churches and shrines tend to honour specific **incarnations** of Mary that have appeared over the years, each with their own special name and set of accompanying miracles and powers.

Nuestra Señora de Guadalupe: The most revered apparition of Mary in the New World appeared on Tepeyac hill near Mexico City in December 1531. She spoke Nahuatl, the language of the Aztecs, and a life-size image of Mary as a dark-skinned Aztec woman was miraculously impressed onto the cloth carried by an Amerindian convert named Juan Diego. Her feast day is December 12.

La Virgen del Carmen: Her origins lie within the Carmelite Order, originally a community of monks based on Mount Carmel in Israel, established in the twelfth century – their dedication to Mary gradually led to the association of the name, though it became popularized thanks to the cult of English saint Simon Stock who died in the thirteenth century. Her feast day is July 16.

San Juan Bautista (St John the Baptist): Seminal figure in the New Testament, a mystical prophet who predicts the rise of Jesus and later baptizes him – was later infamously beheaded by Herod Antipas on the behest of Salome. Christopher Columbus was particularly fond of St John, and San Juan Bautista became the first name of Puerto Rico. His feast day is June 24.

Santiago Apóstol (St James the Apostle): One of the original twelve disciples of Jesus and the first to be martyred. Despite being buried in Jerusalem, a tradition emerged that he had either visited or was reburied in Spain, at the town of Compostela. As his cult grew, James became the patron saint of Spain – invoking his name in battle was so efficacious he became known as Matamoros ("Moor-slayer") in the Middle Ages for his supposed help in defeating the Moors. The most exuberant celebration of his feast day (July 25) takes place in Loíza (see p.88).

San Antonio de Padua (St Anthony of Padua): Born in Lisbon in 1195, he became a Franciscan friar and later preached all over northern Italy. Buried in Padua, he became patron saint of Brazil, Portugal, travellers and the poor, but is best known for being the finder of lost articles. In Puerto Rico, Anthony is a popular *santos* (usually depicted with the infant Jesus seated on a book). His feast day is June 13.

Art and culture

Puerto Rican culture is remarkably dynamic, though outside the US it has a surprisingly low profile, and in Europe tends to be completely overshadowed by that of Cuba, especially when it comes to music. Like Cuba and the Dominican Republic, Puerto Rican art has deep roots in the Spanish colonial period, as well as taking inspiration from the island's diverse cultural elements. But what really sets Puerto Rican popular culture apart from its neighbours is the **US connection**, which since World War II has dramatically influenced the path of numerous artists, singers and writers from the island. Indeed, since the 1920s much of what is considered Puerto Rican art or literature has been created by Puerto Ricans born or living in the US, particularly **New York** (see box, p.269). US-based Puerto Rican artists are included here because although their central focus tends to be (quite naturally), the experience of Puerto Ricans living in the US, this reflects the greater debate over the cultural and political future of the island itself. While New York has been important, the domestic art and music scene has also remained vibrant, a proudly independent, Spanish-speaking community that sees itself as more *Latino* than *Americano*.

Fine art

Puerto Rican art in the early Spanish colonial period was generally restricted to **religious** works, usually commissioned for churches, and so-called **caste paintings** made for rich Spanish officials, formal portraits depicting the various races on the island. The first major Puerto Rican painter was **José Campeche** (1752–1809), a masterful exponent of what tends to be called **viceregal art**, the application of European techniques and styles to the colonies of Latin America. Campeche created over four hundred works, most of them for churches and executed in a formal Baroque style that was becoming outmoded in Europe. In the 1700s, Rococo was in vogue, and learning from an exiled Spanish court painter, Campeche mastered this more florid style, exhibited in his numerous **portrait paintings**: his studies of governors, military men and the upper crust of San Juan society offer a comprehensive snapshot of colonial society at the time. Little is known about his private life, other than that he was the son of a freed slave and an immigrant from the Canary Islands.

The second Puerto Rican master was **Francisco Oller** (1833–1917). He received his first major commission at the age of fifteen (a church painting), but unlike Campeche, Oller left the island for Europe in the 1850s, studying in Madrid and ending up in Paris in 1858. Here Oller joined the **Impressionists** and hung out with Paul Cézanne in the 1860s. Though he spent many years in Europe, Oller tended to paint scenes from Puerto Rico, utilizing not just Impressionist techniques on landscapes, but also a bold Realism to portray slavery, poverty and other social injustices. His most celebrated painting in Puerto Rico, *El Velorio* ("The Wake"), is on display at the University of Puerto Rico's history museum (p.70).

The most acclaimed Puerto Rican artists to follow Oller were **Ramón Fradé** (1875–1954) and **Miguel Pou** (1880–1968). Often considered part of the romantic **Costumbrismo** school, with its idealized view of rural Puerto Rico, Frade's *El Pan Nuestro* ("Our Bread") pays homage to the *jíbaro* (Puerto Rican peasant farmer) and is on display in San Juan's national gallery (p.61). Pou had a similar focus, painting Puerto Rico landscapes and earthy *jíbaro* types from his base in Ponce, still home to many of his works.

Modern art has blossomed in Puerto Rico since the 1950s, though many artists have chosen to live in the US. New York-born **Rafael Tufiño** is known for his sombre paintings of the island, while Francisco Rodón and sculptor Tomás Batista came to prominence in the 1960s – much of the latter's statuary is on display in plazas around the island. Carlos Irizarry and Myrna Báez are best known for their abstract paintings, often with a socio-political theme, while San Juan-based Jorge Zeno dabbles in surrealism. The **contemporary art scene** is particularly dynamic, with galleries all over the island showing the latest work.

Dance and music

Puerto Rico has an incredibly rich musical legacy, ranging from folk music inspired by Spanish and African traditions to salsa, modern Latino pop and *reggaetón*.

Folk music

Throughout the Spanish colonial period, **folk music** flourished in rural Puerto Rico, a rich tradition that started with *décimas* (ten-stanza couplets), *coplas* (ballads), *villancicos* and *aguinaldos* (Christmas carols), all of which derived from Andalucían music that came to Puerto Rico in the late seventeenth century. The **seis** is a fast-paced music and line dance that evolved from the *décimas*, becoming emblematic of the Puerto Rican countryside. Ballads would often be accompanied by simple maracas (*güiro*), or a more refined ten-string instrument known as the **cuatro**, and sung by usually male *trovadores* (troubadours).

One of the most popular folk singers today is **Andrés Jiménez**, known as "El Jíbaro" for his proudly Puerto Rican themes. An enthusiastic activist, Jiménez produced an album of protest songs entitled *Son de Vieques* in 2001 at the height of the US Navy–Vieques protests. He is also considered part of the **Nueva Trova** movement, the "New Ballad" style that originated in Cuba and is characterized by folk songs with a political protest theme. In fact **Cuban styles** have continuously blended with Puerto Rican folk traditions over the years. **Bolero** spread quickly to Puerto Rico in the early twentieth century, with **Rafael Hernández** and **Pedro Flores** becoming two of the most successful band leaders: Hernández's *Lamento Borincano* is still loved not just in Puerto Rico but also in Mexico. **Trío Vegabajeño**, led by Fernandito Alvarez and one of the most beloved Puerto Rican *bolero* groups, was formed in 1943 and dominated Puerto Rican music into the 1960s.

Danza

Considered Puerto Rico's national dance and the most formal of its musical traditions, the **danza** was introduced to the island's fad-conscious high society in 1842. The genre is thought to have derived from the *habanera*, brought to the island by Cuban immigrants and resembling a less rigid version of the waltz and classical music of Europe. Puerto Ricans soon made it their own, and the first *danza* composer was **Manuel Gregorio Tavarez** (1843–1883), followed by his student, **Juan Morel Campos** (1857–1896), whose melodies continue to be played across the island. The most famous *danza* is "La Borinqueña", its lyrics transformed into a nationalist anthem by Lola Rodríguez de Tió.

Bomba and plena

The African communities in Puerto Rico developed their own styles of dance and music based on traditions carried across the Atlantic. The **bomba** involves singers accompanied by drums, maracas and *palillos* (castanets). Usually in pairs (but without touching), dancers move in ever more complicated or vigorous ways, challenging the drummer to respond with similarly more intense rhythms. **Rafael Cepeda** (1910–1996) was by far the most celebrated exponent of *bomba*, and his family maintain the tradition with their dance troupe, the Ballet Folklórico de la familia Cepeda.

Since the 1960s *bomba* has been promoted as a national dance, usually paired with **la plena**. *Plena* is a type of rural narrative song, a sort of Puerto Rican country music, developing along the south coast of the island in the late nineteenth century from similar drum-driven African traditions, and also using improvised call-and-response vocals. In the 1930s the style was popularized by **Manuel Jiménez**, or El Canario, and further expanded by artists such as **César Concepción**, but by the late 1960s the genre had almost disappeared. Like *la bomba*, *plena* has been revamped since the 1980s, in part thanks to increased tourism and the efforts of artists like Willie Colón and **Plena Libre**.

Salsa

Perhaps the best known of all Latin sounds, the origins of **salsa** are extremely complex and much debated, with Puerto Rico, Cuba, New York and even Colombia all claiming to be the "home" of the genre. The truth is that salsa is a fusion of several different styles – cha-cha-cha, mambo, *guaguancó*, *son montuno* – all predominantly Cuban, but brought together with the jazz of Harlem and cooked up in **New York** by primarily Puerto Rican musicians. The roots of salsa lie with Cuban band leader **Arsenio Rodríguez** (1911–1970), who expanded Cuban *son* to create *son montuno* in the 1930s, a style which formed the basis of the **mambo** craze of the 1940s. Latin big bands blossomed in New York after World War II, the three most popular led by Cuban trumpeter Mario Bauza, and Puerto Ricans **Tito Puente** (1923–2000) and **Tito Rodríguez** (1923–1973), all incorporating various up-tempo styles ranging from mambo to early salsa – the term, however, was popularized in the late 1960s by **Fania Records**, the New York label that essentially created the modern sound with its stable of predominantly Puerto Rican musicians, the **Fania All-Stars**: Johnny Pacheco (who started Fania in 1963), Willie Colón, Pete "El Conde" Rodríguez and **Héctor Lavoe** (see p.215) among them. In the 1970s salsa became a harder, edgier sound than its predecessors, increasingly urban and political than light and tropical, taking its inspiration from the impoverished *barrios* of the US as much as the Caribbean. Lavoe in particular often performed deeply melancholic songs, with his signature *El Cantante* describing the pain that often lies behind the apparently easy life of the entertainer. He went on to have a successful solo career, his tragic life and premature death in 1993 only serving to confirm his superstar status.

Meanwhile, **El Gran Combo** formed in 1962, soon becoming Puerto Rico's most popular salsa band and now regarded as a national treasure – they still perform on the island and are well worth checking out. Since the 1980s **Gilberto Santa Rosa** and **Marc Anthony** have also been popular, with protégé **Víctor Manuelle** rising to prominence in the last few years as a crooning proponent of *salsa romantica*.

Latino pop

Some of the world's biggest Latino pop stars are Puerto Rican, chief among them **Ricky Martin**. It's been a while now since he made a splash in the English-speaking pop world (his hit "Livin' la Vida Loca" was in 1999), but in Latin

Pop may get all the attention, but Puerto Rico also has a small but thriving **rock scene**, despite losing ground since the 1990s. **La Secta Allstar** released their debut album in 1997, going on to become the most successful Puerto Rican rock band (the band was formed in Florida, but its members were all born in Puerto Rico), and the first to be nominated for a Grammy in 2005. Other bands from the 1990s retain faithful audiences: **Fiel a la Vega** continues to tour and make records, while **Black Guayaba** won the Grammy in 2008 for best Latin Rock album.

America he remains one of the greatest superstars of all time, idolized by fans from Miami to Argentina. Born in San Juan in 1971, Martin started his career with the band **Menudo** in 1984, and continues to perform, make records, and act on stage and TV. He still owns a home in the city, and in 2000 founded the **Ricky Martin Foundation** (Ⓦ www.rickymartinfoundation.org) to fight child trafficking. In 2010 he publicly acknowledged his homosexuality, ending years of speculation.

Puerto Rico has produced numerous other pop stars, from Chucho Avellanet in the 1960s and 1970s to Carlos Ponce in the late 1990s, but one of the most consistently successful, selling over ten million records worldwide, is **Chayanne**, currently based in Miami. Of the US-born Puerto Rican stars, **Jennifer Lopez** has regularly topped the Billboard charts since her first hit in 1999.

Reggaetón and hip-hop

The bass-thumping, car-rattling rhythms of **reggaetón** have became the defining sounds of Puerto Rican youth in the late 1990s, with a global appeal that has long since outgrown the island. Though rapping is a crucial element, *reggaetón* is more than just Spanish hip-hop, with a distinctive back-beat known as "dem bow" that is part Jamaican dance-hall, part salsa: the "reggae" part of the name is a bit deceptive, and the genre owes more to Shabba Ranks than Bob Marley. The roots of Puerto Rican *reggaetón* are often attributed to Panama, where Spanish rappers collaborated with Jamaican ragamuffin DJs in the early 1990s, but Puerto Rican hip-hop was also well established at that time, with rappers such as **Vito C** and producer **DJ Playero** laying the ground work for later *reggaetón* artists.

Today, the top *reggaetón* artists all hail from Puerto Rico: **Daddy Yankee** was one of the first to make it big, his 2004 mega-hit "Gasolina" still one of the best-selling *reggaetón* tracks; Grammy-winner **Don Omar**; **Tego Calderón**; top-selling **Wisin & Yandel**; and Grammy-winning duo **Calle 13**.

Film

M ovies arrived in Puerto Rico with the Americans in 1898, but it wasn't until the 1950s that a small-scale **domestic film industry** really took off, and Puerto Rican actors made an impact in **Hollywood**. The first locally made Puerto Rican film was *Un Drama en Puerto Rico*, shot in 1912 by Rafael Colorado D'Assoy, but subsequent efforts to establish local production companies were short-lived.

The Golden Age

Everything changed in 1953 with the release of **Los Peloteros** ("The Baseball Players"), the story of a penniless children's baseball team inspired to victory by an enigmatic coach, played by Ramón Ortiz del Rivero. Directed by US photographer Jack Delano and still regarded as a classic, the film was part of a government initiative to use movies as a way to boost education and modernize the island. The División de Educación de la Comunidad went on to produce or fund around 117 short and feature-length films with some of Puerto Rico's most gifted actors and directors, a process accelerated by the introduction of television in 1954. Films of note include the musical *El Otro Camino* ("The Other Road"; 1955) and romantic drama *Maruja* (1958), both starring Axel Anderson, a German expat, as well as a host of local actors who became big stars on local TV.

This golden age of *cine Puertorriqueño* didn't last, however: in the 1960s Mexican films dominated the Spanish-language market and by the 1970s Puerto Rican film production had virtually collapsed.

West Side Story

Just as the domestic movie industry was beginning to take off, Puerto Ricans were finally making their mark in **Hollywood**. **José Ferrer** (1909–1992) made his debut with Ingrid Bergman in *Joan of Arc* in 1948, receiving an Academy nomination for best supporting actor. Ferrer won the **Oscar for best actor** for the 1950 film version of *Cyrano de Bergerac*, becoming the first Puerto Rican to win the award. A long and successful career in Broadway and movies followed, including a memorable performance in *Lawrence of Arabia* (1962).

Despite the success of Ferrer and a thriving domestic film industry, perceptions of Puerto Rican culture were ultimately shaped by the movie adaptation of the Broadway hit, **West Side Story** (1961) much to the frustration of Puerto Ricans ever since. Loosely adapted from *Romeo and Juliet*, the story of love amid the rivalry between white and Puerto Rican gangs in New York's Upper West Side has been criticized for its stereotypes of machismo violence and gossipy, subservient women. It nevertheless garnered a best supporting actress award for **Rita Moreno**, the first Puerto Rican woman to win an Oscar.

The 1980s and beyond

Since the late 1980s Puerto Rico has experienced a mini-boom in locally produced movies, and though many have been highly acclaimed, audiences tend to view them as strictly art-house material. Output and revenues remain light years behind the Hollywood blockbusters.

In the 1980s the revival was led by the work of **Jacobo Morales**, whose *Dios los Cría* ("And God Created Them"; 1979), a critical examination of Puerto Rican society through a series of five stories, led to several other lauded movies including

Lo que le Pasó a Santiago ("What Happened to Santiago"; 1989), the first Puerto Rican film to be nominated for an Oscar (for foreign film), and most recently *Ángel* (2007). Marcos Zurinaga's *La Gran Fiesta* (1986) is an accurate portrayal of life in San Juan in the 1940s, while Luis Molina Casanova's comedy *La Guagua Aérea* ("The Airbus"; 1993), set in 1960 and following a group of Puerto Ricans as they prepare to fly to New York, was the most financially successful Puerto Rican film of the decade.

Hits since 2000 have included *Cayo* (2005), a poignant story of a cancer-ridden Vietnam War vet who returns to Culebra to make peace with his past; *Casi Casi* ("Almost, Almost"; 2006), a high school comedy; and *Maldeamores* ("Lovesickness"; 2007) starring Luis Guzmán, comprising three separate love stories. *Talento de barrio* (2008), starring Daddy Yankee, was a major success, despite being panned by critics. Today, the **Comisión de Cine de Puerto Rico** (Ⓦ www.puertoricofilm.com) is responsible for the local film industry, though much of its efforts have been spent attracting US film-makers to shoot on the island.

Puerto Ricans in Hollywood

Puerto Ricans have continued to excel in Hollywood, with **Raúl Juliá** (1940–1994) best known in the US for his role in the *Addams Family* movies. **Benicio del Toro** won an Oscar for his work in *Traffic* (2000), alongside **Luis Guzmán**, who has appeared in numerous movies. **Roselyn Sánchez** came to international prominence in kitschy *Rush Hour 2* (2001), despite remaining committed to the domestic film industry – she starred in *Cayo* (see above) and *Yellow* (2007), about a Puerto Rican dancer who moves to New York.

The now well-established Puerto Rican community in the US has also produced several major stars, notably **Jennifer Lopez**, born in the Bronx to Puerto Rican parents from Ponce. In 2007 she starred in *El Cantante* with husband **Marc Anthony**, about the life of salsa superstar Héctor Lavoe. Though the film upset some Lavoe fans with its focus on Puchi (Lavoe's forceful wife and Lopez's character) and the tragic star's drug addiction, both key performances are excellent and the live salsa sets are fabulous. Brooklyn native **Rosie Perez** has been the star of several movies (*White Men Can't Jump*, *Fight the Power*) and remains a strong campaigner for Puerto Rican rights in the US, highlighted by her thought-provoking movie *Yo Soy Boricua! Pa' Que Tu Lo Sepas!* (I am a Boricua, just so you know!) in 2006. The film primarily explores the identity of New York-based Puerto Ricans, and offers a rather romanticized version of Puerto Rican history, eulogizing Albizu Campos; the Spanish colonization is unequivocally described as "genocide".

Books

Despite its rich literary history you'll find translations of many of the most famous Puerto Rican books in short supply – New York-based authors are the easiest to get hold of. In contrast, there are plenty of books on the history, music and cuisine of Puerto Rico, though outside of North America you'll rarely find these in bookstores; order online or visit shops like Borders in San Juan.

Fiction

Julia de Burgos *Song of the Simple Truth: The Complete Poems of Julia De Burgos* (Curbstone Press). The poems of Puerto Rico's greatest poet are brought together in this bilingual edition for the first time, including her powerful eulogy to the island, *Río Grande de Loíza* – the translation retains much of the original magic.

Rosario Ferré *The House on the Lagoon* (Plume). Beautifully crafted historical saga in the mould of Gabriel García Márquez, following the fortunes of the wealthy Mendizabal family and their house on the shores of Condado lagoon. Sprinkled with references to Ponce, San Juan, actual events and *criollo* culture, this makes for ideal holiday reading.

Manuel Zeno Gandia *The Pond* (Markus Wiener). Gandia's 1890s classic gets a decent airing in this 1999 translation, though be prepared: his "pond" is a dark, grim world of doomed love, incest, rape, starving kids and soul-destroying poverty. Gandia's descriptions of the lush rural landscapes of nineteenth-century Puerto Rico are just as vivid, however, and the story has plenty of twists and turns before the inevitable denouement.

Enrique A. Laguerre *La Llamarada* ("The Flare-up"). Published in 1935, this heartbreaking tale of a young plantation owner torn between ambition and sympathy for the very labourers he exploited, vividly represented rural Puerto Rican life at the time. Much admired in Puerto Rico, Laguerre kept writing well into the 1990s, produced over thirty books and was nominated for the Nobel Prize for Literature in 1999.

Piri Thomas *Down These Mean Streets* (Vintage). Published in 1967, this is a raw evocation of life in Spanish Harlem and the racist suburbs of Long Island for a Puerto Rican migrant in the 1940s and 1950s. Thomas spits out his autobiographical prose, a snappy and sometimes bitter invective against the prejudice of the time.

Luis Rafael Sánchez *Macho Camacho's Beat* (Dalkey Archive Press). This comic novel follows the lives of several *sanjuaneros* in a poetic, sometimes whimsical second-person style, littered with advertising slogans, jokes and pop culture references. The story explores the effects of Americanization on the island, a powerful theme that has lost none of its relevance.

Esmeralda Santiago *When I Was Puerto Rican* (Da Capo Press). Santiago's simple but moving prose tells the story of her early years in rural Puerto Rico, the struggles of her parents and her eventual migration to New York – she paints an unforgettable portrait of the island, and beautifully describes the contrast with the US culture she encounters. Part of an absorbing trilogy that includes *Almost a Woman* and *The Turkish Lover*.

Roberto Santiago (editor) *Boricuas: Influential Puerto Rican Writings – An Anthology* (One World). Collection of essays, poems and short stories from a wide range of Puerto Rican authors, many of whom are hard to find in translation elsewhere, notably José de Diego and René Marqués.

Pedro Juan Soto *Usmaíl* (Sombrero Publishing Company). The author of *Spiks* wrote this classic about the US Navy occupation of Vieques in 1959, when there seemed little hope of anything changing. Following the life of *Usmaíl*, a *Viequense* boy abandoned by his parents, it vividly depicts island life, with a palpably pro-independence bias.

Hunter S. Thompson *The Rum Diary* (Bloomsbury). Written in 1959 before Thompson had perfected his crazy, hallucinatory style, and not published until 1998, this story centres on a journalist who moves from New York to work on a small newspaper in San Juan in the late 1950s: a world of drunken, sex-starved US expats, laced with hefty doses of jealousy, treachery and violence.

Luisita López Torregrosa *The Noise of Infinite Longing: A Memoir of a Family – and an Island* (Rayo). Another autobiographical work, about growing up in Puerto Rico in the 1950s. Each chapter begins in 1994, at the funeral of the author's mother – the resulting reminiscences create a complex portrait of Puerto Rican rural life, cultural roots and the pain of exile.

History and politics

Cesar J. Ayala and Rafael Bernabe *Puerto Rico in the American Century: A History since 1898*. Powerful new history that takes a detailed look at Puerto Rico in the twentieth century, covering both the island and the US diaspora. Especially good, it includes rarely covered topics such as literary and cultural debates, and social and labour struggles.

Eliza Dooley *Old San Juan* (Puerto Rico Almanacs). This little gem, first published in 1955, is packed with all sorts of engaging facts and stories about Puerto Rico's oldest settlement. You can pick it up in El Morro and some San Juan bookshops. Dooley also wrote the *Puerto Rican Cook Book* (1950); the one-time resident of the island later disappeared and is "presumed deceased".

Ronald Fernández *The Disenchanted Island* (Praeger). Crisp modern history of Puerto Rico from a Nationalist perspective, focusing on the island's struggle for independence and its relationship with the US since 1898. Fernández also wrote *Los Macheteros*, an eye-opening account of the home-grown terrorist organization.

Luis A. Figueroa *Sugar, Slavery, and Freedom in Nineteenth-Century Puerto Rico* (University of North Carolina Press). Academic but absorbing account of the black contribution to the history of Puerto Rico. The book traces the progress of freed slaves after abolition in 1873.

Robert H. Fuson *Juan Ponce de León and the Spanish Discovery of Puerto Rico and Florida* (McDonald and Woodward). Other than easy-to-read books for kids, little has been written on conquistador Ponce de León, but this is a great read for history buffs, providing a balanced portrait of Puerto Rico's first governor.

Elizabeth Langhorne *Vieques, History of a Small Island* (Vieques Conservation

& Historical Trust). This slim locally produced book is the only real history of Vieques, though it concludes in the mid-1980s, just before things got interesting. Can usually be purchased in Esperanza for $1–2.

A.W. Maldonado *Luis Muñoz Marín, Puerto Rico's Democratic Revolution* (Universidad de Puerto Rico). This relatively new biography of Luis Muñoz Marín is also a fascinating political history of the island, beginning with Luis Muñoz Rivera and ending with Marín's death in 1980.

G.J.A. O'Toole *The Spanish War: An American Epic 1898* (W. W. Norton & Co). This detailed, colourful tome remains the standard work on the war that proved so fateful for Puerto Rico. O'Toole covers the Puerto Rican campaign in detail, and it's his treatment of events in the

US and Cuba that provide a fascinating context.

Fernando Picó *History of Puerto Rico* (Markus Wiener). The standard history of the island, written by one of Puerto Rico's pre-eminent scholars. The English translation is a bit dry in places, though to be fair this is aimed primarily at an academic audience – Picó concentrates on themes and tendencies, rather than dates and personalities.

Irving Rouse *The Taínos: Rise and Decline of the People Who Greeted Columbus* (Yale University Press). Using Spanish accounts, archeological evidence, linguistic and biological clues, the author has pieced together a remarkable history of the Taínos, beginning with their initial colonization of the Antilles five thousand years ago.

Music

Juan Flores *From Bomba to Hip-Hop* (Columbia University Press). Follows the development of Puerto Rican music in the US since World War II, covering *bomba* to Latin *boogaloo* and hip-hop. The chapter entitled "Lite Colonial" is a blunt discussion about the island's status.

Ricky Martin *Me*. The Latin pop sensation's eagerly awaited autobiography chronicles his early childhood, experiences in boy band Menudo, and reflections on coming to terms with his sexuality and becoming a father.

Josephine Powell *Tito Puente: When the Drums Are Dreaming* (Author-House). This revealing biography of one of the greatest Latin musicians was written by Puente's former dance partner, and is littered with evocative accounts of clubs, concerts and jam

sessions, as well as crucial details about Puente's early life in Spanish Harlem.

César Miguel Rondón *The Book of Salsa: A Chronicle of Urban Music from the Caribbean to New York City* (University of North Carolina Press). Books on salsa are surprisingly thin on the ground, but this is one of the best, thanks to a sparkling translation of Rondón's original Spanish volume.

Marc Shapiro *Passion and Pain: The Life of Héctor Lavoe* (St Martin's Griffin). Fans of El Cantante should enjoy this book, though it's not a typical biography, more a series of intriguing anecdotes and stories about the legendary salsa singer. Some might find the book concentrates too much on Héctor's drug problems and not enough on his struggles with Fania Records.

Food and drink

Charles Coulombe *Rum: The Epic Story of the Drink That Conquered the World* (Citadel). Serious connoisseurs of Puerto Rico's national drink should grab a copy of this comprehensive history, tracing the development of the "kill devil" of Barbados to the rum empire of Bacardi.

Yvonne Ortiz *A Taste of Puerto Rico: Traditional and New Dishes from the Puerto Rican Community* (Plume). This sophisticated take on Puerto Rican cuisine was written by a French-trained former chef, and includes personal recipes as well as traditional dishes. Purists will prefer Valldejuli (below), but this is a solid choice for those looking for a modern, well-presented Puerto Rican cookbook.

Carmen Aboy Valldejuli *Puerto Rican Cookery* (Pelican). This is the acknowledged bible of Puerto Rican cooking, translated from the original Spanish volume (*Cocina Criolla*), which has remained a bestseller since the 1960s. Written by the matriarch of a wealthy Puerto Rican family (with a chapter on rums from her husband), the instructions for hundreds of dishes are simple and easy to follow, including all the classics.

Miscellaneous

David Maraniss *Clemente: The Passion and Grace of Baseball's Last Hero* (Simon & Schuster). Baseball fans should check out this enjoyable biography of Puerto Rico's greatest player, covering Clemente's impoverished early life, his sporting success and experiences of racism over his long career.

Herbert Raffaele *A Guide to the Birds of Puerto Rico and the Virgin Islands* (Princeton University Press). Comprehensive guide describing and illustrating all bird species on the island – serious birdwatchers consistently praise this as the best field guide, with detailed colour plates included along with useful background on the ecology of the region.

Language

Language

Spanish

nglish and Spanish are the official languages in Puerto Rico, but the vast majority of Puerto Ricans only speak **Spanish** fluently. In the major tourist areas, particularly San Juan, most of the people you're likely to deal with will speak or understand English, but learning a few phrases in Spanish will prove invaluable for travelling around the island. Puerto Ricans learn modern Spanish in school, based on Castilian (*castellano*), but the language on the streets is likely to be quite different. **Puerto Rican Spanish** (*Español Puertorriqueño*) evolved from the Spanish spoken by immigrants from Andalucía and the Canary Islands, but incorporates Taíno words, pronunciation habits from African dialects and even English words or phrases in a blend known as "Spanglish".

Pronunciation

Though the rules of **pronunciation** for all forms of Spanish are straightforward and basically the same, there are some noticeable differences between Puerto Rican and Castilian Spanish. For example, the word endings -ado, -ido or -edo are frequently replaced with -ao, -ío and -eo respectively. Pronouncing "r" as "l" is also a trait of Puerto Rican Spanish that has its origin in southern Spain, and like the rest of Latin America, Puerto Ricans follow the Andalucían convention (known as *seseo*) of pronouncing "c" before e and i as an "s" instead of the lisped "th" common in Castilian Spanish (*cerca* is "sairca" instead of "thairka"). Finally, there is a tendency to drop the s and d from the end of words, so you'll often hear "*muchas gracias*" (thank you) spoken "*mucha gracia*". Normally you stress any vowel with an **accent**, otherwise all words ending in a vowel, n or s are stressed on the second to last syllable, while all words ending in other consonants (usually d, l, r and z) are stressed on the last syllable. All vowels and most consonants tend to follow the same rules as their English counterparts, and combinations have predictable results.

a as in "f**a**ther".

e as in "g**e**t".

i as in "pol**i**ce".

o as in "h**o**t".

u as in "r**u**le".

c soft as in "**c**elery" before e and i; hard otherwise, as in "**c**atch".

g like the ch in "lo**ch**" before e or i; hard otherwise, as in "**g**o".

h is always silent.

j also like the ch in "lo**ch**".

ll as the y in "yes".

n as in English, unless it has a tilde (accent) over it, when it become ny: *mañana* sounds like "manyana".

qu pronounced like the English k.

r as in "right", but usually rolled.

rr very strongly rolled.

v sounds like b: *vino* becomes "beano".

z is the same as a soft c: *cerveza* is thus "servesa".

Spanish language basics

Essentials

yes, no, OK	sí, no, vale	good, bad	buen(o)/a, mal(o)/a
please, thank you	por favor, gracias	big, small	gran(de), pequeño/a or chico/a
sorry	disculpe		
excuse me	permiso/perdón	hot, cold	caliente, frío
where, when	dónde, cuando	more, less	más, menos
what, how much	qué, cuánto	today, tomorrow	hoy, mañana
here, there	aquí/acá, allí	yesterday	ayer
this, that	esto, eso	toilets	los servicios/ baños
now, later	ahora, más tarde		
open, closed	abierto/a, cerrado/a	I don't understand	No entiendo
with, without	con, sin	I want..., I'd like...	Quiero..., Quisiera...

Greetings and responses

hello	hola	My name is...	Me llamo...
goodbye	hasta luego/adiós	I am English	Soy inglés(a)
good morning	buenos días	...American	...Americano(a)
good afternoon/night	buenos tardes/noches	...Australian	...Australiano(a)
How are you?	¿Cómo está?/ ¿Qué tal?	...Canadian	...Canadiense(a)
		...Irish	...Irlandés(a)
Pleased to meet you	Mucho gusto	...a New Zealander	...Neozelandés(a)
You're welcome	De nada	...Scottish	...Escosés(a)
What's your name?	¿Cómo se llama usted?	...Welsh	...Galés(a)

Numbers

1	un/uno/una	20	veinte
2	dos	21	veintiuno
3	tres	30	treinta
4	cuatro	40	cuarenta
5	cinco	50	cincuenta
6	seis	60	sesenta
7	siete	70	setenta
8	ocho	80	ochenta
9	nueve	90	noventa
10	diez	100	cien
11	once	101	ciento uno
12	doce	200	doscientos
13	trece	201	doscientos uno
14	catorce	500	quinientos
15	quince	1000	mil
16	dieciséis		

Time and days

What time is it?	¿Qué hora es?	a day	un día
It's one o'clock	Es la una	a week	una semana
It's two o'clock/ two thirty	Son las dos/ dos y media	a month	un mes
noon	mediodía	Monday	Lunes
midnight	medianoche	Tuesday	Martes
the morning	la mañana	Wednesday	Miércoles
the afternoon	la tarde	Thursday	Jueves
the night	la noche	Friday	Viernes
tonight	está noche	Saturday	Sábado
		Domingo	Sunday

Asking directions and getting around

How do I get to...?	¿Cómo puedo llegar a...?	...the supermarket	...el supermercado
		...the tourist office	...la oficina de turismo
Is this the right road to?	¿Es está la carretera para...?	What time does it close/open?	¿A qué hora abre/ cierra?
Is it near/far?	¿Está cerca/lejos?	Where does the bus to...leave from?	¿De dónde sale la guagua/público para...?
Turn left/right	Voltée a la izquierda/ derecha		
Go straight ahead	Siga derecho	What is the fare to...?	¿Cuánto cuesta hasta...?
opposite	frente		
next to	al lado de	Is this the stop for...?	¿Es está la parada para...?
Where is...?	Dónde está...?		
...the bus station	...el terminal de guaguas/públicos	Where can I get a taxi?	¿Dónde puedo coger un taxi?
...bus stop	...la parada de guaguas	Take us to this address	Llévenos a está dirección
...the airport	...el aeropuerto	Fill it up please	Llénelo por favor
...the nearest petrol/ gas station	...la gasolinera más cercana	petrol/gas	gasolina
		motorway/highway	autopista
...the bank	...el banco	road/route	carretera
...the ATM	...el cajero automático	map	mapa
...the bookstore	...la librería	street	calle
...the laundry	...la lavandería	avenue	avenida
...the market	...el mercado	bicycle	la bicicleta
...the pharmacy	...la farmacia	motorbike	la moto
...the post office	...los correos		

Road signs

Adelante	Means "ahead" or "advance": it's your right of way at the upcoming junction	Autos con cambio exacto	Cars with exact change only
		Bosque Nacional	National forest
		Carretera en construcción	Road under construction
Alto	Stop	Cruce	Crossroads

Derecho	Straight ahead	Peligroso	Danger
Entrada	Entrance	Peso maximo	Maximum weight
Entrada y salida de camiones	Entrance and exit for trucks	Salida	Exit
		Sur	South
Esquina	Corner	Termina autopista	End of highway/motorway
Estacionamiento	Parking		
Este	East	Termina Zona 60	End of the 60mph zone
Hacia	To (towards/in the direction of, usually accompanied by road number)	Transito	Indicates direction of traffic, usually on arrow sign
INT/Interseccion	intersection	Vehiculos lentos o pesados usen carril derecho	Heavy or slow vehicles use right lane
Lomo	Speed bump		
Luz/luces	Traffic light/s	Vehiculos Pesados 50	Heavy vehicles 50mph
Norte	North		
Oeste	West	Velocidad maxima 60	Maximum speed 60mph
Pare	Stop		
Paseo solo para parados de emergencia	Lane for emergencies only		

Accommodation

hotel	hotel	...for one night	para una noche
Do you have a room?	¿Tiene una habitación?	Does it include breakfast?	¿Incluye el desayuno?
...with two beds	...con dos camas	May I see the room?	¿Puedo ver la habitación?
...facing the sea	...con vista al mar		
...on the first floor	...en el primer piso	I don't like it	No me gusta
double bed	doble/cama matrimonial	key	llave
		swimming pool	piscina
single bed	cama individual	toilet/bathroom	baño
It's for one person/ two people	Es para una persona/ dos personas	balcony	balcón

Puerto Rican menu reader

Basics

aceite	oil	carta	menu
ají	chilli	cena	dinner
ajo	garlic	cuchara	spoon
almuerzo	lunch	cuchillo	knife
antojito	snacks	cuenta	bill
arroz	rice	desayuno	breakfast
azúcar	sugar	ensalada	salad
botella	bottle	frituras	fried snacks, fritters

huevos	eggs	salsa de Tomate	tomato sauce
huevos fritos	fried eggs	servieta	napkin
huevos revoltillos	scrambled eggs	sopa	soup
mesa	table	tenedor	fork
miel	honey	tostada	toast
pan	bread	vaso	glass
queso	cheese	vinagre	vinegar
sal	salt		

Cooking styles

a la brasa	braised	frito/a	fried
a la parrilla	barbecued	guisado/a	stewed
a la plancha	grilled	lonjas	slices/strips
ahumado/a	smoked	revoltillo	scrambled
al horno	baked	tostado/a	toasted
asado/a	roast		

Puerto Rican dishes

alcapurria	taro fritter stuffed with meat	mofongo	fried and mashed green plantain, usually stuffed with meat
amarillo	baked plantain		
arroz con gandules	yellow rice with green pigeon peas	mondongo	thick beef and vegetable soup
arroz con pollo	yellow rice with chicken	pasteles	shredded root vegetable dumplings
arroz y habichuelas	rice and beans	pastelón de carne	meat pie
asopao (sopon)	thick soup/broth	pastelón de platano	plantain pie
bacalaíto	codfish fritter	patas de Cerdo	pigs' trotters
carne guisada Puertorriqueña	Puerto Rican beef stew	pionono	plantain fritter
chicharrón	pork crackling	queso blanco, queso de hoja, queso del país	Puerto Rican white cheese
chillo entero	fried whole red snapper		
croquetas de pescados	fish croquettes	relleno	ground beef and mashed potato fritters
cuchifrito	deep-fried pork pieces	serenata de Bacalao	codfish salad
		sorullo de maíz, sorullito	cornmeal fritter shaped like a cigar and stuffed with cheese
empanada	turnover/puff pastry, usually fried		
empanadilla	small turnover	tacos	deep-fried rolls
galleta por soda	cracker	tostones	fried green plantains

Fish (*pescados*) and seafood (*mariscos*)

albacora	swordfish	jueyes	crabs
anchoas	anchovies	langosta	lobster
atún	tuna	lobina	largemouth bass
bacalao	cod	merluza	hake
barbudo	catfish	mero	red grouper
calamares	squid	pulpo	octopus
camarones	prawns, shrimp	robalo	snook
carrucho	conch	salmón	salmon
chapín	trunkfish	sardinas	sardines
chillo	red snapper	trucha	trout
chopa	sunfish	tucunaré	peacock bass
dorado	mahi-mahi/dolphin fish		

Meat (*carne*) and poultry (*aves*)

albóndigas	meatballs	gandinza	pork liver
bacon	bacon	guinea	guinea hen
bistec	steak	jamón	ham
buey	beef	lechón asado	roast suckling pig
butifarra	pork sausage	pato	duck
cabrito	baby goat	pavo	turkey
carne Vieja	dry salted beef	pechuga	breast (usually chicken)
cerdo	pork		
chorizo	spicy sausage	pernil de Cerdo	pork shoulder
chuleta	pork chop	picadillo	minced beef
chuletón	T-bone steak	pinchos	kebab (skewered meat)
churrasco	skirt steak		
conejo	rabbit	pollo	chicken
cordero	lamb	ropa vieja	shredded beef
domplin	dumpling	salchichón	salami
filete	beef tenderloin	solomillo	sirloin
gallina	hen	ternera	veal

Fruits (*frutas*)

aguacate	avocado	lechosa	papaya
caimito	starfruit	lima	lime
cereza	cherry	limón	lemon
china	orange	limón Verde	key lime
coco	coconut	mamey	mamey (thick red fruit, mostly eaten in preserves)
fresa	strawberry		
granada	pomegranate		
guanábana	soursop	melón	melon
guayaba	guava	pana, panapen	breadfruit
guineo	sweet banana	parcha	passion fruit

piña	pineapple	tamarindo	tamarind
plátano	plantain	toronja	grapefruit
quenepa	Spanish lime	uvas	grapes

Vegetables (*verduras*)

apio	celery	maíz	corn
berenjena	eggplant/aubergine	malanga	starchy, tubular root vegetable
calabaza	pumpkin		
cebolla	onion	name	yam
chayote	squash family (vegetable pear/ christophine)	papa	potato
		papas fritas	french fries
		pimiento	bell pepper
cilantro	coriander	repollo	cabbage
gandul	green pigeon pea	tomate	tomato
garbanzo	chickpea	yautía	taro root
habichuela	bean	yuca	cassava

Sweets (*dulces*) and desserts (*postres*)

arroz con dulce	rice pudding	galleta	biscuit/cookie
boudin de pasas con coco	coconut bread pudding	helado	ice cream
		hojaldre	puff pastry
dulce de papaya	candied papaya	limber	frozen fruit juice
dulce de plátano	ripe yellow plantains cooked in red wine, sugar and spices	nisperos de batata	sweet-potato balls with coconut
		tembleque	custard made from coconut milk and sugar
flan	custard/crème caramel		

Drinks (*bebidas*)

agua	water	horchata de ajonjolí	drink made of ground sesame seeds, water and sugar
agua de coco	coconut juice		
agua mineral	mineral water		
...con gas	...sparkling	jugo	juice
...sin gas	...still	leche	milk
batidas	fruit shakes	leche de coco	coconut milk
café	coffee	maví	fermented drink made from the bark of the *maví* tree
café con leche	strong black coffee with steamed milk		
café negro	black coffee	piragua	shaved ice drizzled with syrup
café puya	unsweetened black coffee		
		refrescos	sodas/fizzy drinks
café tinta	espresso	ron	rum
cerveza	beer	té	tea
coquito	rum eggnog (Christmas drink)	vino blanco	white wine
		vino tinto	red wine
guarapo de caña	sugar cane juice	vino rosado	rosé wine

Glossary

Bahía Bay.

Balneario Beach with facilities such as showers and toilets, often translated as "public beach", though all beaches on the island are technically public.

Barrio Neighbourhood or city district.

Biblioteca Library.

Bohío Thatched Taíno hut, also applied to simple *jíbaro* dwellings.

Bosque Estatal State forest.

Cañón Canyon.

Capilla Chapel.

Casa House.

Cascada Waterfall.

Cayo Cay, small island.

Cementerio Cemetery.

Embalse Reservoir.

Ermita Chapel.

Estadio Stadium.

Faro Lighthouse.

Finca Farm.

Fuerte Fort.

Iglesia Church.

Malecón Waterfront promenade.

Mirador Viewpoint.

Parque Park.

Playa Beach.

Plazuela Small plaza.

Puerta Gate, door.

Puerto Port.

Punta Headland, point.

Quebrada Stream, small river.

Retablo Altarpiece.

Río River.

Salto Waterfall (from "to jump" or "leap").

Santos Figurines of popular saints, carved from wood.

Small print and
Index

A Rough Guide to Rough Guides

Published in 1982, the first Rough Guide – to Greece – was a student scheme that became a publishing phenomenon. Mark Ellingham, a recent graduate in English from Bristol University, had been travelling in Greece the previous summer and couldn't find the right guidebook. With a small group of friends he wrote his own guide, combining a highly contemporary, journalistic style with a thoroughly practical approach to travellers' needs.

The immediate success of the book spawned a series that rapidly covered dozens of destinations. And, in addition to impecunious backpackers, Rough Guides soon acquired a much broader and older readership that relished the guides' wit and inquisitiveness as much as their enthusiastic, critical approach and value-for-money ethos.

These days, Rough Guides include recommendations from shoestring to luxury and cover more than 200 destinations around the globe, including almost every country in the Americas and Europe, more than half of Africa and most of Asia and Australasia. Our ever-growing team of authors and photographers is spread all over the world, particularly in Europe, the US and Australia.

In the early 1990s, Rough Guides branched out of travel, with the publication of Rough Guides to World Music, Classical Music and the Internet. All three have become benchmark titles in their fields, spearheading the publication of a wide range of books under the Rough Guide name.

Including the travel series, Rough Guides now number more than 350 titles, covering: phrasebooks, waterproof maps, music guides from Opera to Heavy Metal, reference works as diverse as Conspiracy Theories and Shakespeare, and popular culture books from iPods to Poker. Rough Guides also produce a series of more than 120 World Music CDs in partnership with World Music Network.

Visit www.roughguides.com to see our latest publications.

ROUGH GUIDES

Rough Guide credits

Text editor: Alison Roberts
Additional editor: Lucy Cowie
Layout: Anita Singh
Cartography: Ashutosh Bharti
Picture editor: Rhiannon Furbear
Production: Rebecca Short
Proofreader: Karen Parker
Cover design: Nicole Newman, Dan May
Photographer: Tim Draper
Editorial: London Andy Turner, Keith Drew, Edward Aves, Alice Park, Lucy White, James Smart, Natasha Foges, James Rice, Emma Beatson, Emma Gibbs, Kathryn Lane, Monica Woods, Mani Ramaswamy, Harry Wilson, Lara Kavanagh, Eleanor Aldridge, Ian Blenkinsop, Charlotte Melville, Joe Staines, Matthew Milton, Tracy Hopkins, Lorna North; **Delhi** Madhavi Singh, Jalpreen Kaur Chhatwal, Dipika Dasgupta, Perma Dutta
Design & Pictures: London Dan May, Diana Jarvis, Mark Thomas, Nicole Newman;

Delhi Umesh Aggarwal, Ajay Verma, Jessica Subramanian, Ankur Guha, Pradeep Thapliyal, Sachin Tanwar, Nikhil Agarwal, Sachin Gupta
Production: Liz Cherry, Louise Minihane, Erika Pepe
Cartography: London Ed Wright, Katie Lloyd-Jones; **Delhi** Rajesh Chhibber, Rajesh Mishra, Animesh Pathak, Jasbir Sandhu, Swati Handoo, Deshpal Dabas, Lokamata Sahu
Marketing, Publicity & roughguides.com: Liz Statham
Design Director: Scott Stickland
Rough Guides Publisher: Jo Kirby
Digital Travel Publisher: Peter Buckley
Reference Director: Andrew Lockett
Operations Coordinator: Becky Doyle
Operations Assistant: Johanna Wurm
Publishing Director (Travel): Clare Currie
Commercial Manager: Gino Magnotta
Managing Director: John Duhigg

Publishing information

This second edition published November 2011 by
Rough Guides Ltd,
80 Strand, London WC2R 0RL
11, Community Centre, Panchsheel Park, New Delhi 110017, India
Distributed by the Penguin Group

Penguin Books Ltd,
80 Strand, London WC2R 0RL

Penguin Group (USA)
375 Hudson Street, NY 10014, USA

Penguin Group (Australia)
250 Camberwell Road, Camberwell, Victoria 3124, Australia

Penguin Group (NZ)
67 Apollo Drive, Mairangi Bay, Auckland 1310, New Zealand

Rough Guides is represented in Canada by Tourmaline Editions Inc. 662 King Street West, Suite 304, Toronto, Ontario M5V 1M7

Cover concept by Peter Dyer.

Typeset in Bembo and Helvetica to an original design by Henry Iles.

Printed in Singapore
© Stephen Keeling 2011
Maps © Rough Guides
No part of this book may be reproduced in any form without permission from the publisher except for the quotation of brief passages in reviews.
304pp includes index
A catalogue record for this book is available from the British Library
ISBN: 978-1-40538-261-8

The publishers and authors have done their best to ensure the accuracy and currency of all the information in **The Rough Guide to Puerto Rico**, however, they can accept no responsibility for any loss, injury, or inconvenience sustained by any traveller as a result of information or advice contained in the guide.

11 12 13 14 8   7   6   5   4   3   2   1

MIX
Paper from responsible sources
FSC™ C018179

Help us update

We've gone to a lot of effort to ensure that the second edition of **The Rough Guide to Puerto Rico** is accurate and up-to-date. However, things change – places get "discovered", opening hours are notoriously fickle, restaurants and rooms raise prices or lower standards. If you feel we've got it wrong or left something out, we'd like to know, and if you can remember the address, the price, the hours, the phone number, so much the better.

Please send your comments with the subject line "**Rough Guide Puerto Rico Update**" to ℮mail@uk.roughguides.com. We'll credit all contributions and send a copy of the next edition (or any other Rough Guide if you prefer) for the very best emails.

Find more travel information, connect with fellow travellers and book your trip on ⓦwww.roughguides.com

Acknowledgements

Stephen Keeling: Thanks to Bethzaida García at the Puerto Rico Tourism Company, Gary and Jeanette Pollard at Lucia Beach Villas, Jen Gold in Vieques, Elias Robinson in Culebra, Elizabeth Padilla Rodríguez at the Fideicomiso de Conservación and all the kind Puerto Ricans that made researching this guide such a pleasure; thanks also to editor Alison Roberts, who did a fabulous job in London, Lucy Cowie for the additional edits and as always, Tiffany Wu, without whose love and support none of this would have been possible.

Readers' letters

Thanks to all the readers who have taken the time to write in with comments and suggestions (and apologies if we've inadvertently omitted or misspelt anyone's name):

Tanya Altagracia, Cookie Avrin, Annett Franke, Robert Villacres.

Photo credits

All photos © Rough Guides except the following:

Introduction
Guánica, house with Puerto Rican flag mural © Walter Bibikow/AWL
Tres Palmas © Robert Harding/Superstock
Coquí frog, El Verde © Ray Pfortner/Photolibrary

Things not to miss
01 Coral reef off Guánica, Puerto Rico © Stephen Frink/Corbis
02 Old San Juan, buildings on Comercio Street © Walter Bibikow/AWL
04 Playa Flamenco, Culebra, © Kim Karpeles/Alamy
05 Arecibo Observatory © Michele Falzone/Corbis
06 Green Beach, Vieques, © Donald Nausbaum/Getty

07 Bio bay © Frank Llosa
10 Street vendor © Danita Delimont Stock/AWL
12 Kelly Slater, Surfing World Champion, Puerto Rico © Sylvain Cazenave/Corbis
15 Ball-court, Centro Ceremonial Indígena de Tibes © Robert Fried/Alamy
17 Castillo San Felipe del Morro © Miva Stock/Superstock

Black and whites
p.92 El Yunque National Forest © Miva Stock/Superstock
p.120 Sun Bay, Vieques © Michele Falzone/JAI/Corbis
p.168. Facade of lighthouse, Cabo Rojo © F1 Online/Superstock

SMALL PRINT

Index

Map entries are in colour.

INDEX

INDEX

W

Y

I

INDEX

Map symbols

maps are listed in the full index using coloured text

Highway		Museum
Major paved road		Cave
Minor paved road		Country house
Pedestrianized road		Lighthouse
Ruta Panorámica		Viewpoint
Unpaved road		Ruins
Steps		Tower
Footpath/trail		Observatory
Minor trail		Church (regional maps)
San Juan Tren Urbano & station		Golf course
Ferry route		Gardens
Waterway		Gateway
Wall		Fuel station
Chapter boundary		Information office
Place of interest		Post office
International airport		Internet access
Domestic airport/airfield		Hospital
Mountain range		Transport stop
Peak		Parking
Waterfall		Building
Spring		Church (town maps)
Recreation area		Market
Campsite		Stadium
Ranger station		Cemetery
Tree		Park/National park
Bunker		Beach

So now we've told you about the things not to miss, the best places to stay, the top restaurants, the liveliest bars and the most spectacular sights, it only seems fair to tell you about the best travel insurance around

WorldNomads.com

keep travelling safely

Recommended by Rough Guides

www.roughguides.com
MAKE THE MOST OF YOUR TIME ON EARTH

ROUGH GUIDES